Introduction to

ABAP/4®

Programming for SAP™

Revised and Expanded Edition

Send Us Your Comments:
To comment on this book or any other Prima Tech title, visit Prima's Reader Response page on the Web at **www.primapublishing.com/comments.**

How to Order:
For information on quantity discounts, contact the publisher: Prima Publishing, P.O. Box 1260BK, Rocklin, CA 95677-1260; (916) 632-4400. On your letterhead, include information concerning the intended use of the books and the number of books you wish to purchase. For individual orders, turn to the back of this book for more information, or visit Prima's Web site at **www.primapublishing.com.**

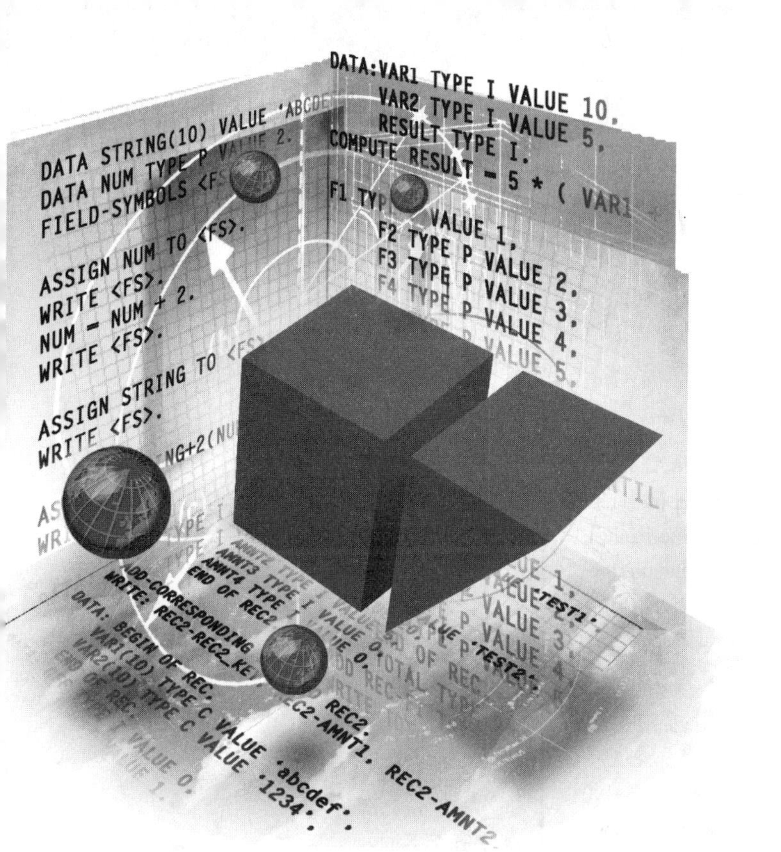

Introduction to ABAP/4® Programming for SAP™

Revised and Expanded Edition

Gareth M. de Bruyn
Robert Lyfareff

PRIMA TECH
A Division of Prima Publishing

Prima Publishing and colophon are registered trademarks of Prima Communications, Inc., Rocklin, California 95677.

ISBN: 0-7615-1392-2

Library of Congress Catalog Card Number: 98-65822

Printed in the United States of America

98 99 00 01 HH 10 9 8 7 6 5 4 3 2 1

Publisher:
Matthew H. Carleson

Managing Editor:
Dan J. Foster

Acquisitions Editor:
Deborah F. Abshier

Senior Editor:
Kelli R. Crump

Project Editor:
Kevin Harreld

Assistant Project Editor:
Kim V. Benbow

Copy Editor:
Judy Ohm

Technical Reviewer:
Ken Kroes

Interior Layout:
Jimmie Young

Cover Design:
Prima Design Team

Indexer:
Sherry Massey

About the Authors

Gareth de Bruyn's background includes chemical engineering, UNIX site administration, and network installations. His experience with SAP began shortly after the technology became available, and he currently works as an independent SAP consultant with a Fortune 50 company. De Bruyn believes SAP technology is revolutionizing international business. He plans to earn a law degree to unite his technical and international business skills to capitalize on this global opportunity.

Robert Lyfareff is a veteran of several successful SAP installation teams over the past four years. Coupled with his formal training in computer science and electrical engineering, this unique SAP experience enables him to write about real-world business situations and issues. What excites and challenges him about his work is the integration and modification of business practices with the new technology. Currently, he works as an independent SAP consultant and author.

Contents at a Glance

APPENDIXES

Dedications

To Mom and Dad, I love you both very much.

—GMD

To Mom and Dad, thanks for all your help.

—RL

Acknowledgments

We want to thank Debbie Abshier and the staff of Prima Publishing for all their technical assistance and for putting up with all of our questions and inquiries.

The authors wish to graciously thank the entire Hewlett Packard Release B Team for their support and valuable feedback. Specifically we wish to thank Ken Kroes, Vivek Talghatti, Scott Trimber, and Alberto Vargas for answering specific questions regarding the technical content of this book.

Finally, the authors want to thank SAP America.

Contents

Introduction

SAP is a German software company that produces the R/3 system. R/3 is an example of an ERP (Enterprise Resource Planning) system. ERP systems are used by corporations to track all information related to the business, including financials, sales, and materials data.

R/3 is based on a client-server architecture and uses a relational database to track all information related to a corporation. It's made up of thousands of small programs called *transactions*. A transaction is a program and set of screens that can be used to enter, change, or display data; monitor events within the R/3 system; and change functionality in the R/3 system. R/3 gathers related transactions into groups known as *modules*. A module is a set of transactions that deal with the same area of business functionality. There are modules for Materials, Financials, Human Resources, Sales, and other common business functions.

Throughout this book, we refer to the R/3 system simply as *SAP* because that's how it's known in the industry. SAP runs on several operating systems, including UNIX, Windows NT, and AS/300, and can use several different databases, including Oracle, Informix, and SQL Server. Within the SAP application, the operating system and database are normally invisible to both users and programmers.

Introducing the SAP Software Program

In the past, other vendors have offered applications that manage a single area of business functionality—such as inventory control, general ledger accounting, or customer lists. Rather than simply package several such applications together into a single box, SAP has instead produced a suite of major business applications that are tightly integrated. One of the reasons for the immense success of SAP is this integration between its modules. Thus, when a vendor fulfills a purchase order by sending the requested materials, inventory levels are adjusted, invoices are verified, checks are issued, and so on. An event in one module, such as Materials, can initiate automatic responses in others, such as Sales or Plant Maintenance. All of this processing takes place within the normal SAP functionality—without any custom programming.

The Role of Configuration in Implementing SAP

What makes this integration work is the configuration of SAP to work with an individual corporation's business practices. In the context of SAP, the term *configuration* refers to the act of assigning values to thousands of possible settings within the modules. These settings give users of SAP tremendous control over how SAP functions.

As you can imagine, corporations are much like individuals—they have very different personalities. SAP must be flexible enough to adapt to many different ways of doing business. For example, a purchase order may be configured to require that a person's name be entered as the requester of the purchase. In this setup, when a user creates a purchase order in the system, he or she must enter the name of the requester in order to save the information. On the other hand, if the purchase order form is set up without this requirement, the system allows a purchase order to be created without the name of the requester.

This configuration is done by analysts experienced in *Business Process Reengineering*, the art of identifying business processes and changing them to achieve greater efficiency. After SAP is installed, these configuration experts customize the modules to meet the corporation's needs, or help the corporation change its business practices to achieve the most efficiency out of SAP. This configuration doesn't usually involve programmers, but is instead done by business analysts. When the configuration process is nearing completion, the programmers are brought in to extend any part of SAP that can't be configured to meet the needs of the corporation.

Although business analysts are responsible for configuration, the impact of this customization process on programmers can't be overstated. A program can't be designed adequately until the configuration is stable. Unfortunately, because of time constraints, the configuration is seldom completely finished before the programmers must begin their design work. This is one of the unique challenges that face SAP programmers.

Programming ABAP/4

ABAP/4 is the programming language used by SAP's developers to build the transactions that make up the R/3 application. It's also used by corporations to customize the R/3 application. In general, ABAP/4 isn't used by customers of SAP to develop complex applications from scratch, but is used instead to provide additional business functionality. For example, it's not necessary for a customer to write a program in ABAP/4 to manage inventory levels because SAP has already written transactions to accomplish this objective.

The two most common uses for ABAP/4 are producing custom reports and developing custom interfaces for SAP. In this context, a report is an ABAP/4 program that reads specific data from SAP's database and then displays the data via a computer screen or a printed page. An *interface*, on the other hand, is an ABAP/4 program that moves data into SAP, or reads data from SAP and writes it out to a system file to be transferred to an external computer system, such as a legacy mainframe. Other uses for ABAP/4 include conversion programs that change data into a format usable by SAP, and custom transactions similar to the SAP transactions that make up the R/3 application, but are written by users to fulfill some business function not provided by SAP. This new version of the book covers programming in ABAP/4 up to the 3.1h release of SAP R/3.

How ABAP/4 and Data Interact in SAP

Almost all ABAP/4 programs manipulate data from the SAP database to some extent. Data managed by SAP is often broken into two categories: *master data* and *transactional data* (called *documents* in SAP):

- Master data is information that usually corresponds to physical objects, such as materials, vendors, customers, or plants.
- A document is information that usually corresponds to an event such as a purchase order, an invoice, a change in inventory, or a sales order. Documents can be identified in the system by a document number, which can be externally assigned or assigned by SAP, depending on the configuration.

Master data is needed in order to create any document; for example, an invoice can't be created without a vendor to issue it. A change in inventory, referred to in SAP as a *material movement*, must refer to a material and a plant. Each SAP module has master data that it manages and documents that are created in the course of normal business operations. For example, the FI module, which manages finances and accounting, manages master data such as general ledger accounts and documents such as journal entries and check payments.

How to Use This Book

ABAP/4 is a fourth-generation programming language with many of the features of other modern programming languages such as the familiar C, Visual Basic, and PowerBuilder. It allows variables and arrays to be defined, modulation of programs via subroutines and function calls, access to the database via SQL, and some event-oriented programming. Because this book covers all these major topics, you can use the information contained here to learn how to write ABAP/4 programs that meet the most demanding business requirements.

SAP is an extremely complicated system; no one individual can understand all of it. This book focuses on ABAP/4 programming but includes background information on the SAP environment, within which all ABAP/4 programs run.

Each chapter discusses an area of ABAP/4 programming such as displaying data, accessing the SAP database, and using conditional operators. The chapters build on each other, with examples taken from real-world business problems.

The first half of the book is a reference, detailing the specific ABAP/4 commands to accomplish typical programming objectives. The second half of the book looks at specific business requirements such as writing reports, developing data interfaces, and performance tuning of SAP.

Part I—ABAP/4 Basics

The first seven chapters of this book introduce you to important basics of ABAP/4 programming such as data types, conditional operators, and how to display or print data within SAP. These chapters assume that you have some familiarity with basic programming techniques but you don't need to be an expert by any means. The chapters are broken down into functional groups such as looping and using the data dictionary:

- **Chapter 1**, "Data Types and Definitions," is an introduction to ABAP/4 syntax, variables, and data types.
- **Chapter 2**, "Displaying and Printing Data," shows you how to display text to the screen and printer. It includes detailed information on formatting text and variables for display.
- **Chapter 3**, "Manipulating Data," covers the commands for arithmetic calculations and manipulation of character strings.

- **Chapter 4**, "Using Conditional Operators," explains how to use commands to evaluate conditions and control the execution of a program.
- **Chapter 5**, "Using the Looping Commands," discusses the types of looping commands available in ABAP/4.
- **Chapter 6**, "Working with Internal Tables," introduces the ABAP/4 concept of the *internal table*—a temporary database table used in programming.
- **Chapter 7**, "Working with the Data Dictionary," is an introduction to the SAP data dictionary. A *data dictionary* contains information about what's in a database (often called "Meta-Data" because it's data about data). This chapter shows you how to get information about the SAP database.

Part II—Accessing the Database

The whole point of creating programs for SAP is to work with data. This part of the book provides detailed information on how to write programs that read, modify, delete, and use records from the database:

- **Chapter 8**, "Using SAP SQL to Access Database Tables," describes the ABAP/4 implemention of SQL, which is a set of industry standard commands that you can use to read or change information in a database.
- **Chapter 9**, "Working with External Files," covers commands used to manipulate text files outside the SAP system. Text files are often used by SAP to exchange information with external information systems.
- **Chapter 10**, "Advanced Data Output," continues the discussion of displaying and printing the data that began in Chapter 2. The chapter gives details on how to do more advanced output work, including hiding information from specified users and using ABAP events to control output.
- **Chapter 11**, "Adding Subroutines to Your Program," explores how to use subroutines to break up a large program into small self-contained objects. This chapter presents a number of examples of using sub-routines in SAP.
- **Chapter 12**, "Using Function Modules," describes how to use *function calls*—subroutines that exist independently of any single ABAP/4 program. This chapter shows you how to make function calls in a pro-

gram and how to write your own customized function calls.

- Chapter 13, "Working with Logical Databases," explains how you can use logical databases to retrieve information from the SAP database.
- Chapter 14, "Writing a Report," presents some common reports that produce information for users of SAP. Using ABAP/4 to produce custom reports is the most common of all activities.

Part III—Advanced Technical Issues

There are a number of common problems that all SAP installations must solve. Part III of this book presents common business problems and ABAP/4 programs that solve them. The examples are taken from several years' experience at several major installations:

- **Chapter 15**, "Writing a Data Extract," discusses the process of developing programs to extract data from SAP and write it to an external file. Data extracts are a form of outbound interface—a program that sends information to a system external to SAP.
- **Chapter 16**, "Writing a BDC Session," covers inbound interfaces. Inbound interfaces are usually implemented in the form of a BDC session in SAP. This chapter shows how to write a BDC session to load external data into SAP.
- **Chapter 17**, "Working with SAP Security and Authorizations," covers how your programs are tied in to SAP security. Adding security and authority checks are covered in this chapter.
- **Chapter 18**, "The ABAP/4 Debugger,"covers the ins and outs of using SAP's debugging tool. Techniques and technical guides are presented in this chapter.
- **Chapter 19**, "ABAP/4 Runtime Analysis / SQL Trace" deals with the performance tools that come with SAP R/3. These two tools give the programmer a powerful tool to review the performance of his programs.
- **Chapter 20**, "Performance Tuning" doesn't cover a specific business problem. Instead, it's a central resource on techniques used to solve an always important technical problem: execution speed.
- **Chapter 21**, "Integrating ABAP/4 Reports with the Web" introduces the new Web integration tools that come with the new 3.1 version of SAP. The chapter covers using the new Web development tool, SAP@WEB Studio, as well as some introductory information on getting your reports published on your Web server.

Part IV—Appendixes

- **Appendix A**, "Using the ABAP/4 Editor," is a brief tutorial or review of how to use the editor interface to work with the programming commands. Read this appendix if you're not yet familiar with how to work with the editor or if you need a refresher.
- **Appendix B**, "System Fields," is a listing of important SAP system fields that contain information on the state of the system.

Available on the Web Site

All source code from the book's examples, as well as sample versions of the programs in the text and executable code for all types of SAP applications are available at **www.primapublishing.com/abap4.**

Conventions Used in This Book

This book uses a number of typographical conventions to make it easier for the reader to understand how to use the commands, syntax, menus, and so on:

- Commands, options, parameters, and so on are presented in a special `monospaced computer typeface`—for example, the `LOOP AT` command. Command syntax shows variables in *`italic monospace`*. Syntax lines and code lines are separated from the regular text with blank lines for readability. A typical syntax line, for example, might look like this:

```
EXTRACT field group.
```

In this example, you would substitute the appropriate field group name for *`field group`* when typing the command.

- Table names (`MSEG`), field names (`BKPF-GJAHR`), and other parts of the database are also printed in the computer typeface.
- Terms being defined or emphasized appear in *italics* within regular text.
- Text that the reader is instructed to type appears in **`bold monospace`**.
- Menu commands and options are indicated with a vertical bar to divide menu levels: Tools |Case | Development.

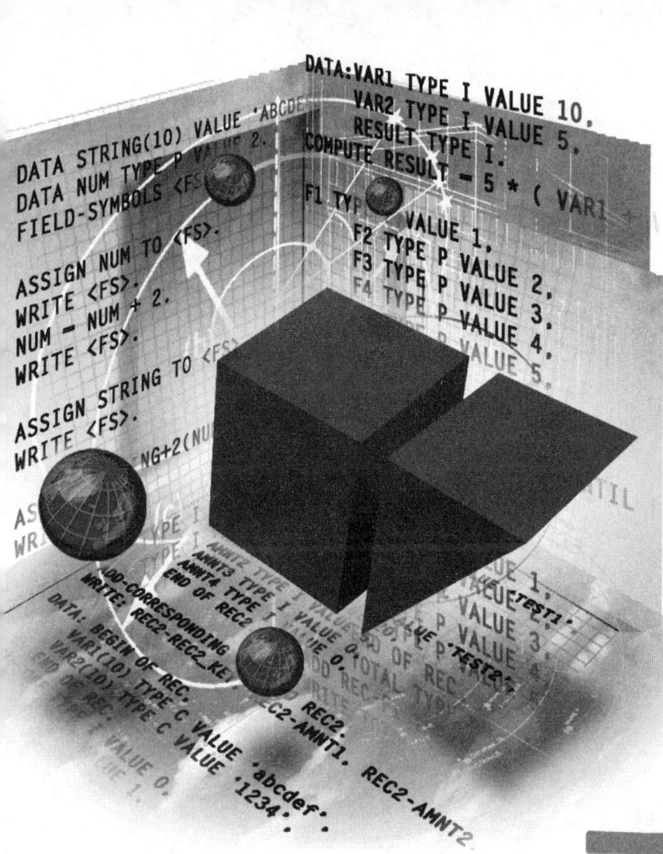

PART I

ABAP/4 Basics

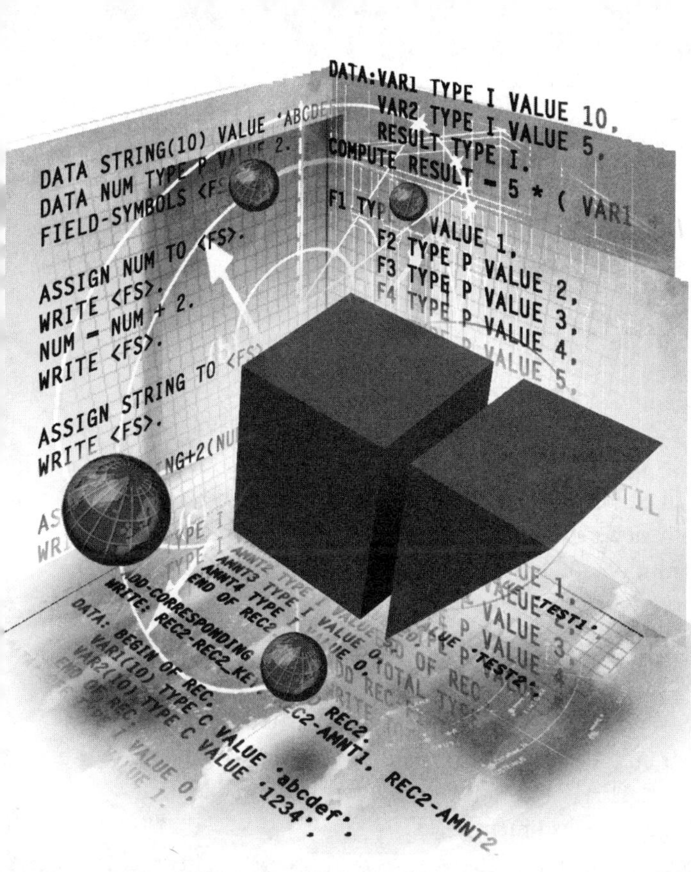

Chapter 1

Data Types and Definitions

In This Chapter

- Building ABAP/4 Statements
- Using Variables
- Assigning Values to Variables

This chapter introduces some of the basics of ABAP/4 programming. ABAP/4 is an event-driven language that consists of *multiple statements*. The general rules for programming in ABAP/4 are much like those for other languages; this chapter describes some of the differences and also reviews some of the similarities. The chapter proceeds fairly rapidly through descriptions of features (statements, procedures, comments, and so on) that are common to programming languages, with the assumption that these parts of basic programming are already familiar to you, from C++, Visual Basic, and so on.

The second part of this chapter covers the data types supported by ABAP/4 and how to define variables for use in programs. The data types should be familiar to anyone with prior programming experience. ABAP/4 supports several types of variables that can be used by the programmer to accomplish many tasks.

This chapter doesn't cover how to write a complete program; instead, it draws contrasts between the requirements and syntax of ABAP/4 and the familiar strategies of languages that are commonly in use throughout the programming community. Specific areas where new ABAP/4 programmers trip up are pointed out in detail; but in general, showing examples of correctly written code is more helpful than long descriptions in getting the point across.

Building ABAP/4 Statements

In ABAP/4, statements consist of a command and any variables and options, ending with a period. Keep in mind the following points when considering how to write statements:

- The ABAP/4 editor converts all text to uppercase except text strings, which are surrounded by single quotation marks ('), or comments (described shortly). This doesn't mean that case is unimportant in ABAP/4. Data stored in the SAP database can be stored in mixed case, and both data and commands that interact with the operating system are affected by case.
- Unlike some older programming languages, ABAP/4 doesn't care where a statement begins on a line. You should take advantage of this

fact to improve the readability of your programs by using indentation to indicate blocks of code.

- ABAP/4 has no restrictions on the layout of statements; multiple statements can be placed on a single line, or a single statement may stretch across multiple lines.
- Blank lines can be placed anywhere in a program and should be used to help separate blocks of related code from unrelated code.

The following example demonstrates the freedom ABAP/4 allows in the formatting of program statements:

```
WRITE 'Hello World'.  WRITE 'You can use multiple statements on a line'.
WRITE 'Or a single command can
stretch across many
lines.  It is all the same to SAP'.
          WRITE 'Statements can begin anywhere on a line.'.
```

Commenting Your Code

Like most languages, ABAP/4 allows for the use of *comment statements* inside programs or inline. A comment is a statement that isn't processed by the system; it's used by a programmer to document the purpose of various statements in a program. The use of comments is critical in developing programs within SAP. Because of the extensive use of contractors, high turnover in ABAP/4 programmers, and rapidly changing business processes, comments can save time and money when code needs to be modified.

Programmers have a responsibility to leave behind well documented code. Most companies don't consider a programming job complete until it's fully documented both offline and online. The comments within a program can be used as a starting point for the offline documentation that many companies now demand.

Inline comments may be declared anywhere in a program by one of two methods:

- Full-line comments are indicated by placing an asterisk (*) in the first position of the line, in which case the entire line is considered by the system to be a comment. Comments don't need to be terminated by a period because they may not extend across more than one line:

```
* Echo the current user to the screen
WRITE W_USER.
```

```
*Now prepare to compute balance
*This is a monthly balance only
```

- Partial-line comments are indicated by entering a double quote (") after a statement. All text following the double quote is considered by the system to be a comment. Partial-line comments also don't need to be terminated by a period because they may not extend across more than one line:

```
WRITE W_USER.  "Echo the current user to the screen
```

Unlike ABAP/4 statements, commented code isn't capitalized by the ABAP/4 editor.

Improving Statement Readability with the Colon Notation

To reduce the amount of typing needed in a program, ABAP/4 allows a simple form of inline code expansion called *colon notation*. Inline code expansion is the ability of the system to fill in certain pieces of code for a programmer, saving repetitive typing. Consecutive statements can be chained together if the beginning of each statement is identical. This is done with the colon (:) operator and commas, which are used to terminate the individual statements—much as periods end normal statements. The final identical statement is terminated with a period, as a normal ABAP/4 statement would be.

Here's an example of a program that could save some keystroking:

```
WRITE 'Hello '.
WRITE 'World '.
WRITE  W_SYSTIME.
```

Using the colon notation, it could be rewritten this way:

```
WRITE: 'Hello ',
       'World ',
       W_SYSTIME.
```

Like any other ABAP/4 statement, the layout doesn't matter; here's an equally correct statement:

```
WRITE: 'Hello ', 'World ', W_SYSTIME.
```

Because the system simply duplicates all code found before the colon, even more complicated statements are possible.

For example, the following lines:

```
MOVE SY-SUBRC TO W_ONE.
MOVE SY-SUBRC TO W_TWO.
MOVE SY-SUBRC TO W_THREE.
```

become this version:

```
MOVE SY-SUBRC TO:  W_ONE,
                   W_TWO,
                   W_THREE.
```

And then this example:

```
PERFORM DEBIT_GL USING W_ACCOUNT1 W_AMOUNT1.
PERFORM DEBIT_GL USING W_ACCOUNT2 W_AMOUNT2.
```

becomes this:

```
PERFORM DEBIT_GL USING: W_ACCOUNT1 W_AMOUNT1,
                        W_ACCOUNT2 W_AMOUNT2.
```

As you can see, there's no subtle logic behind the colon notation. The system duplicates the code found to the left of the colon. This feature can be a big help as you create longer programs. The colon notation reduces the amount of keystroking and increases the readability of the code.

Defining Programs (REPORT)

The first non-comment line in a program must be the REPORT statement. This command names the program and may affect the way in which output is formatted by the system. This is the syntax:

```
REPORT program name  [NO STANDARD PAGE HEADING]
     [LINE-SIZE number of columns]
     [LINE-COUNT number of lines[(number of lines reserved for footer)]]
     [MESSAGE-ID message id].
```

The REPORT statement is automatically generated by SAP whenever a new program creates, although it has no options.

The following list describes the options:

- `[NO STANDARD PAGE HEADING]` disables the default page header generated by SAP and allows the programmer to define a custom page header.
- `[LINE-SIZE` *number of columns*`]` defines the number of columns appearing in the output of the program. The number may range up to 255. If the output of the program is to be printed, the number of columns must not exceed the maximum for the paper size being used, normally 132 characters for North American printers. Because ABAP/4 supports very limited typesetting and no scalable fonts, all printing is done in monospaced fonts up to the column limit.
- `[LINE-COUNT` *number of lines[(number of lines reserved for footer)]]* defines the number of lines on each page of output. The second option reserves a specific number of lines for the page footer. SAP doesn't provide a default page footer; if you want a page footer, you must reserve the space with this option.

  If the output of the program is to be printed, the total number of lines must not exceed the maximum for the paper size being used, normally 65 lines for North American printers.
- `[MESSAGE-ID` *message id*`]` determines which set of messages is used by the program when the MESSAGE command is used. This command is discussed in Chapter 2, "Displaying and Printing Data."

Some examples:

```
REPORT ZTEST1
      LINE-SIZE 132
      NO STANDARD PAGE HEADING
      LINE-COUNT 56(1).

REPORT ZGLOUT
      LINE-SIZE 80
      LINE-COUNT 65.
```

Using Variables

One of the most basic operations of a programming language is providing temporary storage of data. Once upon a time, programmers had to track these storage locations manually. Modern programming languages allow for the assignment of *variables*, a symbolic reference to a memory location that stores information temporarily. These variables persist only during the execution of the program, and the data they contain is lost when the execution is complete—unless it's transferred to a database table or system file.

Variables must be declared in the program. This declaration process consists of telling the system what type of data (integer, character, and so on) will be stored in the temporary location associated with the variable.

Variable Data Types

All variables must be declared *before* they're used in the program. The following list describes some of the rules regarding use of variables in ABAP/4:

- Variables can be declared at any point in a program, but for the sake of consistency, should be defined at the beginning of a program or subroutine.
- Variables can be up to 30 characters in length and should be long enough to allow for easy reading of their functions.
- Begin each variable with a letter and then any mixture of letters and numbers. The hyphen or dash (–) is allowed but should never be used because it has a specialized function (described shortly). Instead use the underscore character (_) to separate distinct words.
- No variable can have the same name as an ABAP/4 command.
- ABAP/4 follows traditional rules about the scope of variables. All variables defined at the program level are considered global and are visible to all subroutines. Variables defined within subroutines are visible only to that subroutine. Variable scope is discussed further in Chapter 11, "Adding Subroutines to Your Programs."

Table 1-1 describes the data types used in ABAP/4.

Defining Variables (DATA)

Variables are defined using the DATA statement, which has two possible forms:

```
DATA var[(length)]  [TYPE type] [DECIMALS number] [VALUE initial value]

DATA var LIKE table-field [VALUE initial value]
```

The following sections describe the two forms.

Table 1-1 ABAP/4 Data Types

Type	Description	Example
C	Character	"Example Char"
D	Date	"19961101"
F	Floating point number	5e7
I	Integer	600
N	Numeric text	00600
P	Packed decimal	100.50
T	Time	"223010"
X	Hexadecimal	23A

DATA Statement Form One

Form one explicitly defines the type and length for the variable. This form is appropriate for variables that aren't dependent on values in the SAP database, such as counters or flags. If no length is specified, the variable uses the default for that data type. If no data type is specified, the variable defaults to character.

For example:

```
DATA REP_PRICE(8) TYPE P DECIMALS 2 VALUE '1.00'.
```

This statement creates a variable named `rep_price`, which is a packed decimal of length 8, with two of the spaces reserved for decimals, and a default value of 1.00.

> **NOTE**
>
> When working with decimals in ABAP/4, the number must be surrounded by single quotes ('') in much the same way a string is placed in quotes. Numbers without a decimal can be written without the single quotes. The decimal point doesn't figure into the length of the field.

The following statement creates a variable named gl_flag, which is a character string of length 1 and initially blank:

```
DATA GL_FLAG.
```

DATA Statement Form Two

Form two allows the type and length of the field to be determined dynamically at runtime. This notation tells the system to look up the data type and length of the specified field and use that information to define the variable. Thus, if a data element such as a Company Code or Business Area changes, the program code won't need to be altered to reflect those changes. Any active field found in the SAP data dictionary can be used with LIKE in a DATA statement, as in this example:

```
DATA ERROR_FLAG LIKE SY-SUBRC.
```

This statement creates a variable that has the same data type and length as the field SUBRC found in the table SY. If a change is made in the data dictionary to SY-SUBRC, that change is used by the program with no recoding.

The following example creates a variable that has the same data type and length as the field werks (used to store plant codes), found in the table T001W, with a default value of PDR1 (on the following page):

```
DATA CO_CODE LIKE T001W-WERKS VALUE 'PDR1'.
```

Remember to surround character strings with single quotes.

When declaring multiple variables using the colon notation, the two forms can be mixed, as in this example:

```
DATA: REP_COUNT(8) TYPE I VALUE 1,
      GL_FLAG,
      ERROR_FLAG LIKE SY-SUBRC,
      CO_CODE LIKE T001W-WERKS VALUE 'PDR1'.
```

Grouping Variables into Records

In addition to single-value variables, ABAP/4 allows the grouping of several variables into a single *record*. Records are used when you have a group of related data that needs to be kept together.

For example, a mechanical part could be described by a name, a part number, cost, and weight. It's possible to declare four separate variables to hold that information, but a variable called name could mean many different things. Suppose you are writing a program to track parts used by engineers in the field. You would have a name for the engineer, a name for the part, and, perhaps, a name for the customer site. How do you keep all these name variables straight? What you could do is declare a record called part that consists of four fields: name, number, cost, and weight. Additional records could be declared for engineer and customer.

Record Syntax

Records are referenced as *record name-field*. They are defined by using a group of DATA statements with the following syntax:

```
DATA BEGIN OF record name.
DATA field 1.
DATA field 2.
.
.
DATA field N.
DATA END OF record name.
```

The individual fields within the record may be defined using either of the `DATA` statement forms and any of the options, as in the following example:

```
DATA BEGIN OF MATERIAL_DUMP.
DATA MATL# LIKE MARAV-MATNR.
DATA MATL_PRICE(12) TYPE P DECIMALS 2.
DATA MATL_QTY(6) TYPE P DECIMALS 1.
DATA CHANGE_FLG VALUE 'N'.
DATA END OF MATERIAL_DUMP.
```

To access the `matl_price` field with this example, the programmer would have to use the notation `material_dump-matl_price`. When defining records, the colon notation greatly improves the readability of the statement. This statement is functionally equivalent to the previous one, but much easier to read:

```
DATA: BEGIN OF MATERIAL_DUMP,
        MATL# LIKE MARAV-MATNR,
        MATL_PRICE(12) TYPE P DECIMALS 2,
        MATL_QTY(6) TYPE P DECIMALS 1,
        CHANGE_FLG VALUE 'N',
      END OF MATERIAL_DUMP.
```

Defining Records (INCLUDE STRUCTURE)

Much as you can use the `LIKE` command to dynamically assign a data type to a variable, you can use the `INCLUDE STRUCTURE` command to dynamically declare a record. For example, if you want to re-create the `material_dump` record from the preceding section, but instead of the custom record created in the last example use the SAP materials table (`MARAV`) as the record layout, here's how you'd do it:

```
DATA BEGIN OF MATERIAL_DUMP.
     INCLUDE STRUCTURE MARAV.
DATA END OF MATERIAL_DUMP.
```

With this statement, if any changes are made to the SAP materials table, those changes are automatically made to the `material_dump` record—with no changes needed to the programming code. The structure included must be either an active table or a structure from the SAP data dictionary. It's also possible to combine the `INCLUDE` statement with explicit fields in one record:

```
DATA BEGIN OF MATERIAL_DUMP.
     INCLUDE STRUCTURE MARAV.
DATA: CHANGE_FLG VALUE 'N',
     END OF MATERIAL_DUMP.
```

In this case, the record contains all fields found in the `MARAV` table plus the `change_flg` field.

Defining New Data Types (TYPES)

In addition to the eight data types built into ABAP/4, it's possible to define new data types within a program. These new data types are often referred to as *user-defined types*. Typically, new data types are used to define variables which map to business concepts. For example, a financial program might make reference to a bank account number, so several variables might be needed to track different bank account numbers. They could be defined directly as:

```
DATA: CUST_ACCT(28) TYPES C,
     MER_ACCT(28) TYPES C,
     TMP_ACCT(28) TYPES C.
```

In this case, three variables are created to hold account numbers. Instead of defining each variable in terms of the standard ABAP/4 character data type, you could declare your own new type called `BANK_ACCT`.

```
TYPES BANK_ACCT(28) TYPES C.
DATA: CUST_ACCT TYPES BANK_ACCT,
     MER_ACCT TYPES BANK_ACCT,
     TMP_ACCT TYPES BANK_ACCT.
```

This approach has a number of benefits. One, it allows you to define the exact data type only once in the `TYPES` statement and then use it multiple times in your program. If the length of a bank account changes from 28 to 35 at a later time, you can simply change the TYPES statement instead of having to change every variable throughout the program. Two, this approach is much easier to read and understand. Finally, it is immediately clear that all three of the variables in the example hold the same type of information.

New types are defined using the TYPES statement, which has three possible forms:

```
TYPES name[(length)]  [TYPE type] [DECIMALS number]

TYPES name LIKE table-field

TYPES BEGIN OF rectyp.
Ö
TYPES END   OF rectyp.
```

TYPES Statement Form One

The syntax of the TYPES statement is identical to the DATA statement. You must remember that TYPES does not actually create a variable; you must still define the variable with a DATA statement. The first form of the TYPES statement defines the data type explicitly. For example:

```
TYPES:  PRICE_TYPE(8) TYPE P DECIMALS 2,
    NAME_TYPE(24),
    PART_TYPE(28),
   COUNT_TYPE TYPE I.
```

TYPES Statement Form Two

Form two allows the type and length to be determined dynamically at runtime. This notation tells the system to look up the data type and length of the specified field and use that information to define the type. Any active field found in the SAP data dictionary can be used with LIKE in a TYPES statement, as in this example:

```
TYPES: FLAG_TYPE LIKE SY-SUBRC.
```

This form is not very common since the LIKE option and the TYPES command both have very similar functionality. Typically, only LIKE is used, for example, when defining a record as in the next section.

TYPES Statement Form Three

The third form of the TYPES statement allows for user-defined record types. Like variable records, a user-defined record type consists of grouping several types into a single-record type. The syntax is:

```
TYPES BEGIN OF record name.
TYPES field 1.
TYPES field 2.
.
.
TYPES field N.
TYPES END OF record name.
```

Using the colon notation can improve the readability of these statements as seen in these examples:

```
TYPES: BEGIN OF PART_LIST,
         MATERIAL(18) TYPE C,
         DESC(36) TYPE C,
         PRICE TYPE P DECIMALS 2,
  END OF PART_LIST.

DATA: NEW_PART TYPE PART_LIST,
        OLD_PART TYPE PART_LIST.
```

Defining Constant Data Elements (CONSTANTS)

In addition to variable data elements, it is valuable to have data elements which do not change their value. These elements are referred to as *constants*. A constant is declared like a variable but it must be assigned an initial value and this initial value never changes. If you try to change the value of a constant, a syntax error occurs. Using a constant can make your code clearer and easier to maintain. Often values must be coded directly into a program such as the total number of manufacturing plants a company has. If you simply code the number '7' directly in the code, it may be difficult to update the code later when the number changes to '8'.

Constants are defined using the CONSTANTS statement, the syntax is identical to that of the DATA statement with the exception that the VALUE addition is always required and the OCCURS option is never allowed:

```
CONSTANTS var[(length)]  [TYPE type] [DECIMALS number] VALUE initial value [IS
INITIAL]

CONSTANTS var LIKE table-field VALUE initial value [IS INITIAL]

CONSTANTS: BEGIN OF rec,
           ...
           END   OF rec.
```

Some examples:

```
CONSTANTS C_PLANTS TYPES I VALUE 7.
CONSTANTS CHARX VALUE 'X'.
CONSTANTS C_CLIENT LIKE VBAK-MANDT VALUE '100'.
CONSTANTS: BEGIN OF C_PART,
    MATNR LIKE MARA-MATNR VALUE IS INITIAL,
    DESC(24) VALUE 'Default Part',
    CHGNUM TYPE I VALUE 1,
  END OF C_PART.
```

Using Runtime Parameters

Another type of variable is the *runtime parameter*. Parameters enable a user to pass data to an ABAP/4 program at the time it's executed. For example, a report may be written to use a parameter to narrow the range of the report to a particular month or a range of products.

There are two types of parameters in ABAP/4: The first allows a user to enter a single value, and the second allows the user to enter multiple values. The following sections provide details on the two parameter types.

Using PARAMETERS to Define Variables

The first type of parameter is defined with the `PARAMETERS` statement, which has the following syntax:

```
PARAMETERS parm[(length)] [TYPE type] [LIKE field] [DEFAULT val]
  [LOWER CASE] [AS CHECKBOX] [RADIOBUTTON GROUP num ] [OBLIGATORY].
```

Much like using the `DATA` command, the data type of a parameter can be defined by using the `LIKE` option or the `TYPE` option (which explicitly defines the data type). Unlike variables, parameters must have a name made up of fewer then eight characters or numbers. Another difference is that parameters can't use the DECIMALS option. Also, parameters can't be part of a record.

The PARAMETER command has several options that you can use:

- DEFAULT *val* assigns a default value to a parameter, much like the VALUE option of the DATA command. This default value is seen by the user at runtime and can be overwritten by the user.
- LOWER CASE allows entry of lowercase data. By default, SAP converts all data entered to uppercase, unless this option is specified.
- AS CHECKBOX is only used with a parameter one character in length. Instead of appearing as a text box, it creates a push button which the user can click to be on or off. If the user sets the push button to on, the variable will contain an 'X'. This can be used when the user is presented with a yes/no option.
- RADIOBUTTON GROUP *num* is only used with a parameter one character in length. Like the CHECKBOX option, it creates a push button which the user can click on or off. The difference is that several push buttons can be grouped together and the user may only select one of them. The others are deselected automatically when the user checks one.
- OBLIGATORY forces the user to enter some value before the program will execute.

Following are some examples of how to use PARAMETERS.

This statement creates a parameter p_minqty of type integer, with a default value of 1; a value must be filled in before the program will execute:

```
PARAMETERS P_MINQTY TYPE I DEFAULT 1 OBLIGATORY.
```

In the following statement, a parameter of length 30, type character, is defined with a default value of matl_dump.txt. This parameter allows lowercase characters and must be filled in before the program will execute:

```
PARAMETERS P_FILENM(30) DEFAULT 'matl_dump.txt' OBLIGATORY LOWER CASE.
```

This example creates a list of three check boxes. The user can choose one or more of these check boxes:

```
PARAMETERS: P_SHOW1 AS CHECKBOX DEFAULT 'X',
    P_SHOW2 AS CHECKBOX,
    P_SALL AS CHECKBOX.
```

This example creates a list of three option buttons, from which the user can choose only one:

```
PARAMETERS: R_ALL RADIOBUTTON GROUP 001,
     R_NONE RADIOBUTTON GROUP 001 DEFAULT 'X',
     R_EVEN RADIOBUTTON GROUP 001.
```

Using SELECT-OPTIONS to Define Variables

The second type of parameter is defined with the SELECT-OPTIONS command. Unlike a parameter, a select-option allows the user to enter a set of multiple values and/or ranges of values. When the user enters one or more ranges of values, they are stored in an internal table that the system uses to evaluate comparisons against the select-option. The internal table has the same name as the select-option. See Chapter 6, "Working with Internal Tables," for an explanation of internal tables. Also, a select-option must be declared FOR a database field or a previously defined variable, but usually a database field is used.

The programmer doesn't have to anticipate when the user will enter multiple values or ranges. The processing is handled entirely by the system and requires no additional programming. This set of values can then be used in comparisons, such as IF, SELECT, and CHECK with the operator IN. For examples of the use of SELECT-OPTIONS, see Chapter 8, "Using SAP SQL to Access Database Tables," and Chapter 13, "Working with Logical Databases."

The syntax is as follows:

```
SELECT-OPTIONS var FOR field [DEFAULT val] [DEFAULT val option]
  [DEFAULT [NOT] val TO val] [MEMORY ID id] [MATCHCODE OBJECT object]
  [LOWER CASE] [NO INTERVALS] [NO EXTENSION] [OBLIGATORY].
```

Most of the options are identical to those of the PARAMETERS command. Some of the differences are the additional default options and the lack of a check box option:

- DEFAULT *val* sets the select-option equal to a single value.
- DEFAULT *val option* sets a default value and an optional operator such as equal, greater than, or not equal to. Table 1-2 describes the available operators.
- NO INTERVALS forces users to enter an exact value by not allowing them to enter ranges of values.
- NO EXTENSION forces users to enter a single value or range by not allowing them to enter multiple ranges and values.

Table 1-2 Optional Operators

Operator	Description
EQ	Equal
NE	Not equal
CP	Contains part of a string
NP	Doesn't contain part of a string
GE	Greater than or equal to
LT	Less than
LE	Less than or equal to
GT	Greater than

- `DEFAULT [NOT]` *val* TO *val* sets a default range of values to be included by the select-option. Using the `NOT` option allows a range of values to be excluded.

The following statement creates a variable `s_date` for the field `BLDAT` (Document Date) from the table `BKPF` (Financial Documents) with a default range from January 1, 1998 to December 31, 1998:

> **NOTE**
>
> Dates appear in quotes. See Chapter 3, "Manipulating Data," for more information on assigning values to date fields..

```
SELECT-OPTIONS S_DATE FOR BKPF-BLDAT DEFAULT '19980101' TO '19981231'.
```

This statement creates a variable `s_doc#` for the field `BELNR` (Document Number) from the table `BKPF` (Financial Documents), with a default value greater than or equal to 0050000000:

```
SELECT-OPTIONS S_DOC# FOR BKPF-BELNR DEFAULT '0050000000' OPTION GE.
```

Using RANGES to Define Variables

The `RANGES` command creates a variable which behaves identical to one declared with the `SELECT-OPTIONS` command. Unlike a select-option, variables defined with the `RANGES` command do not appear to the user as a runtime parameter. They must be filled using the default option or directly by the programmer. The syntax of the `RANGES` command is similar to `SELECT-OPTIONS`:

```
RANGES var FOR field [DEFAULT val] [DEFAULT val option]
  [DEFAULT [NOT] val TO val].
```

Some examples:

```
RANGES: R_PLANT FOR VBAP-WERKS,
     R_DATE FOR BKPF-BLDAT DEFAULT '19980101' TO '19981231'.
```

Like variables declared with `SELECT-OPTIONS`, variables declared with `RANGES` are stored in an internal table. The structure of the table for both types of variables is the following:

```
DATA: BEGIN OF var OCCURS 10,
                          SIGN(1),
                          OPTION(2),
                          LOW  LIKE f,
                          HIGH LIKE f,
                       END   OF var.
```

The `OCCURS` option is explained in Chapter 6, but for now it is only important to understand what values are placed in each field. The `Low` field holds the low value of the range. The `High` field holds the highest value in the range. The `Option` field holds the operator for this range (see Table 1-2 for valid operators). Finally, the `Sign` field holds the value `I` or `E`. When the sign is `I`, it indicates the range is inclusive, meaning that comparisons with any value which falls inside of the range is true. When the sign is `E`, it indicates the range is exclusive, meaning that comparisons with any value which falls inside of the range is false.

Table 1-3 Field Values

Field	Value
Sign	I
Option	BT
Low	12/1/1998
High	1/1/1999

For example, if you entered an inclusive range of 12/1/98 to 1/1/1999 into the `R_DATE` range just declared, the values stored are shown in Table 1-3.

In another example, if the range was all dates not greater than or equal to 1/1/1998, the field values would be as shown in Table 1-4.

Table 1-4 Field Values

Field	Value
Sign	E
Option	GE
Low	1/1/1998
High	

As you can see from this example, when you are using operators such as "not greater than" or "not equal," there is no high value to the range only low. Ranges and Select-Options are used extensively in ABAP/4 and more examples of their usage are presented in later chapters. For now it's only important to know how they are declared.

Using Field Symbols

The final type of variable is called a *field symbol*. A field symbol is different from all the previous types of variables discussed because it doesn't actually hold values. Instead, it maintains a reference to another variable that has been defined by a `DATA` or `PARAMETERS` statement. This is similar to the concept of a *pointer* in a language such as C. Instead of holding a value such as `5`, a field symbol references a variable such as `counter`, which has previously been defined as an integer variable with the value `5`. Thus, if the command `COUNTER = COUNTER + 1` is issued, the field symbol would automatically refer to the value `6` without any additional programming. This is because the field symbol doesn't hold a particular value, but instead refers to another variable.

Field symbols have a particularly annoying syntax—the name of the field symbol must always be enclosed by angle brackets. So the field symbol `POINTER1` would appear in the program as `<POINTER1>`. When referring to a generic field symbol, this book uses `<fs>` as a placeholder.

Here's the syntax:

```
FIELD-SYMBOLS <fs>.
```

Notice that there's no data type specified. Because field symbols don't hold any value—they simply point to the contents of other variables—the field symbol doesn't care what type of variable it points to. In fact, this is what makes field symbols so powerful. A single field symbol may refer to numbers, dates, and character strings—all in the same program.

The ASSIGN command is used to assign a variable to a field symbol. This command is explained in detail in Chapter 3. For now, simply examine this example of how different variables can be assigned to a single field symbol.

```
DATA: STRING(4) VALUE 'Test',
     NUM TYPE P VALUE 100,
     TODAY TYPE D VALUE '19960124'.
FIELD-SYMBOLS <TEMP>.
ASSIGN STRING TO <TEMP>.
WRITE <TEMP>.
ASSIGN NUM TO <TEMP>.
WRITE <TEMP>.
ASSIGN  TODAY TO <TEMP>.
WRITE <TEMP>.
```

Here's the output:

```
TEST 100 19960124
```

Assigning Values to Variables

An initial value may be assigned to a variable by using the VALUE option of the DATA command. But variables are useless if they can't be changed within the execution of a program. ABAP/4 provides several ways to make changes to the value of a variable, as described in the following sections.

Using MOVE to Assign Variables

The most basic way to change the value of a variable is to use the MOVE command. The MOVE command has two forms, which are functionally equivalent:

```
MOVE value TO var.

var = value.
```

The first version should be familiar to COBOL programmers, while the second is commonly found in languages such as C or Pascal. Either version is acceptable, but for the sake of consistency, you should choose one version and stick with it throughout a program.

When using the second form, multiple assignments are allowed, occurring right to left. For example, this code assigns the value 10 to QTY3, QTY2, and QTY1:

```
DATA: QTY1 TYPE I,
      QTY2 TYPE I,
      QTY3 TYPE I.
QTY1 = QTY2 = QTY3 = 10.
```

Following is an example of using the colon notation in conjunction with the MOVE command to do multiple assignments:

```
DATA: QTY1 TYPE I,
      QTY2 TYPE I,
      QTY3 TYPE I.
MOVE: 10 TO QTY1,
       QTY1 TO QTY2,
       50 TO QTY3.
```

In the next example, two records are declared and values are assigned to the doc# and doc_date fields of the finance_rec record. Then temp_rec is assigned the values of finance_rec:

```
DATA:  BEGIN OF FINANCE_REC,
         DOC# LIKE BKPF-BELNR,
         DOC_DATE LIKE BKPF-BLDAT,
        END OF FINANCE_REC.

DATA:  BEGIN OF TEMP_REC,
         INCLUDE STRUCTURE FINANCE_REC.
DATA   END OF TEMP_REC.
FINANCE_REC-DOC# = '0004000000'.
FINANCE_REC-DOC_DATE = '19990101'.
TEMP_REC = FINANCE_REC.
```

This type of assignment is possible because temp_rec and finance_rec have the same structure. If two records with dissimilar structures are assigned, the results are uncertain.

Data Type Conversion During Assignments

ABAP/4 allows an assignment to be made using variables of two different data types. When this occurs, ABAP/4 automatically converts the data from the source type to the target type. This type of conversion is usually referred to as an *implicit conversion* by the system. Normally the programmer doesn't need to worry about this type of conversion, as long as the values being converted make sense logically.

For example, assigning a character field containing the value `-256` to a packed field is no problem. But if the character field holds the value `DOG`, an error results when ABAP/4 makes the conversion attempt.

Chapter 3 includes more information about implicit conversion.

Summary

Here ends the discussion on the declaration and assignment of variables. Of course, variables in and of themselves are of little use without commands to display and manipulate them. Those commands are the focus of the next two chapters.

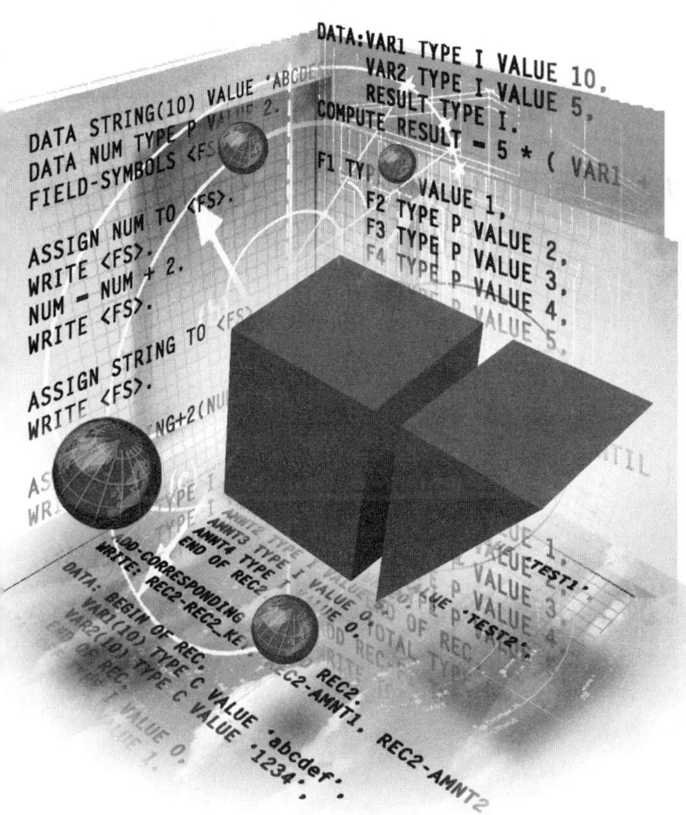

Chapter 2

Displaying and Printing Data

In This Chapter

- Setting Up the Page (`REPORT`)
- General Features of the `WRITE` Statement
- Formatting the Output
- Using Text Elements
- Advanced Features of the `WRITE` Statement
- Displaying Messages
- Using the `FORMAT` Command

One of the most basic tasks of the ABAP programmer is writing code to generate reports for end users. To code reports, you need the commands to output the data and general text to the screen and subsequently to paper. The beginning of this chapter covers how to output and format data and text to the screen. The rest of the chapter deals with data and page formatting. The commands discussed include `WRITE`, `SKIP`, `ULINE`, `POSITION`, `MESSAGE`, and `FORMAT`.

Figure 2-1 shows the difference between what a program would output as text (column headings) and data (the numbers under the column headings). This chapter discusses both text and data; the figure illustrates the difference between the two.

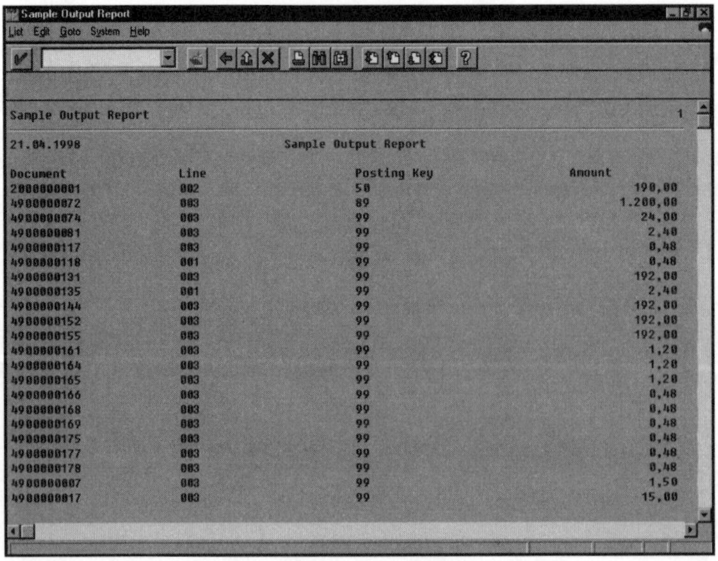

FIGURE 2-1

A report with differences shown between text and output data

NOTE

One point to realize early on is that whatever is sent to the screen can very easily be sent to the printer to produce a hard copy. Because we are working more and more in a paperless society, this chapter presents options other than printing the data, but sometimes hard copies are essential. Alternatives to printing include instant download capability to the user's PC (covered in Chapter 12, "Using Function Modules"), and spool display (covered in Chapter 10, "Advanced Data Output").

Setting Up the Page (REPORT)

The first item you must consider is the page definition of your output. You must define in the `REPORT` statement on the first line of code how many lines you want per page and how many columns per page. *Columns* are the number of characters that can be printed on a single row of type across the page, from one side to the other; *lines* are the number of rows that can appear on a page from top to bottom.

For SAP, certain formats are defined for each type of printer (for instance, for the Hewlett-Packard LaserJet III). The system comes with default formats, but custom formats can be defined as well. Each format includes column and line spacing. The lines and columns of the report should match one of the print formats of the printer that is to be used for the output.

NOTE

The values of the lines and columns are fixed and can't be set by a data field to make the values variable.

The `REPORT` command was covered briefly in Chapter 1, as you use it to start a program, but let's review the syntax:

```
REPORT program name  [NO STANDARD PAGE HEADING]
     [LINE-SIZE number of columns]
     [LINE-COUNT number of lines[(number of lines reserved for footer)]].
MESSAGE-ID message id.
```

If the *`number of lines`* and *`number of columns`* values aren't specified, the default values are specified by the default print format defined by the user profile. Under the

System menu, a user default can be defined to specify the default printer. If you don't use the `LINE-COUNT` and `LINE-SIZE` options, the syntax for `REPORT` is pretty simple:

```
REPORT program name.
```

With this version of the command, the system would use the user default printer. You can display the *user defaults* (system settings defined for each user) by navigating along the menu path illustrated in Figure 2-2 (System | User Profile | User Defaults), and then specify a printer at the resulting user default screen.

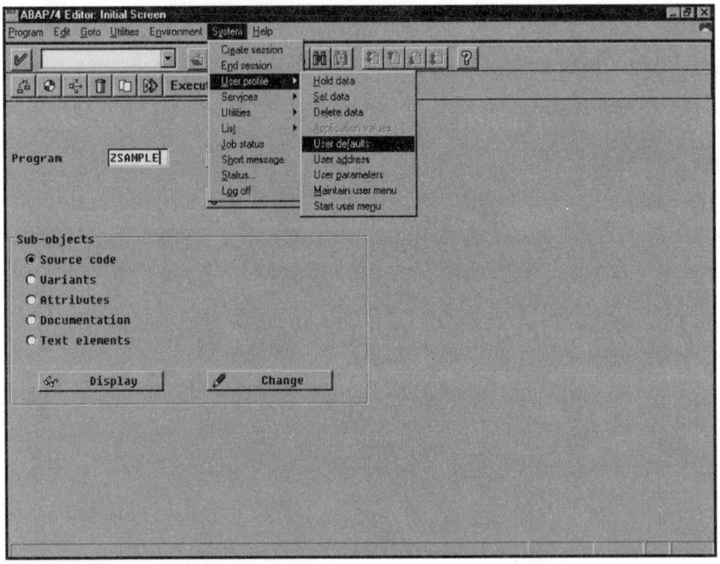

FIGURE 2-2

The menu path to the user default screen

The `MESSAGE-ID` command is related to the `MESSAGE` command (explained later in this chapter in the section, "Formatting the Output"). The SAP system keeps a library of messages defined by a two-character definition. For each definition, the ABAP program can call 1,000 possible messages, numbered from `000` to `999`. Often, programs in the same module (for example, `SD`, `FI`, `MM`, or `PP`) or with the same purpose (such as `Report`, `Extract`, or `Interface`) use similar messages. The `MESSAGE-ID` command defines which message-ID library is used. Many different ABAP programs can then reference the same library of messages, rather than defining a unique library for each program. The message libraries keep the system messaging lean and efficient. (See the later section on the `MESSAGE` command "Displaying Messages (`MESSAGE`)" for a more detailed discussion.)

General Features of the WRITE Statement

The first and most basic command of ABAP is the `WRITE` statement. The general syntax is as follows:

```
WRITE data.
```

data can be pure text, a field name, or a previously defined variable.

> **NOTE**
>
> One important point to realize early on when working in ABAP/4 is that every line of code must end with a period. When you generate (SAP's terminology for *compile*) the program, if the periods are missing, the compiler won't be able to determine where one line ends and another begins. Make sure that every line of code ends with a period. If a period is forgotten, the code generally won't compile. When you first begin programming in ABAP/4, don't be discouraged if you forget periods. To find that a missing period is your only problem is a much better scenario than finding a large flaw in programming logic!

Outputting Plain Text

To output text to the screen or to a printer, enclose the text in single apostrophes (' '). The syntax to write text within the `WRITE` command is as follows:

```
WRITE 'text'.
```

Here's an example of a command with text:

```
WRITE 'This is TEXT output'.
```

The output from this line would be as follows:

```
This is TEXT output
```

Text can also be output using text elements. Text elements are discussed later, in the section "Advanced Features of the `WRITE` Statement."

Outputting Field Names (Variables)

The syntax to output a field name or a variable is generally the same as outputting plain text to the screen, except that the quotes are replaced by a variable name:

```
WRITE field name.
```

The field name can either be a field defined in the data declaration portion of the program, or a field that's part of an internal or database table, also defined in the data declaration portion of the program. Here's an example:

```
*DATA DECLARATION PORTION OF PROGRAM
DATA:      W_FIELD(12) TYPE C.
*OUTPUT PORTION OF PROGRAM
MOVE 'ABAPER' TO W_FIELD.
WRITE W_FIELD.
```

In this example, the output field will be called `W_FIELD`, is a character field, and has a length of 12. In the data manipulation portion of the program, the word ABAPER is placed inside this field. The output from these lines of code would be as follows:

```
ABAPER
```

Outputting Groups of Text and Data Fields

To output multiple pieces of data, just separate them with commas and add a colon at the end of the `WRITE` statement:

```
WRITE: 'I am a soon to be', W_FIELD.
```

The output would be as follows:

```
I am a soon to be ABAPER.
```

> **NOTE**
>
> Notice that the value `ABAPER` falls directly one space after the text. `W_FIELD` is defined as a type `C` field, which by default makes it left-aligned. Other data types might differ. Positioning the items horizontally on a line is covered in the following section.

Formatting the Output

The general format for the `WRITE` statement is as follows:

```
WRITE /column position(length) data.
```

The *`column position`* setting defines at what position the *`data`* is output. The slash (/) denotes a new line. The number inside the parentheses (*`length`*) defines the maximum number of characters output from that data. Look at this example:

```
WRITE: /15(10) 'ABCDEFGHIJKLMNOP'.
```

The output to the screen would be

```
               ABCDEFGHIJ
```

The data is displayed after 15 spaces, and only 10 characters of the data are displayed.

Column Positioning

To place the data in the desired position in the output, you specify the number of the column on which the first letter of the data field or text must start:

```
WRITE 20 W_FIELD.
```

The output in this case would be the word ABAPER printed 20 characters to the right of the left edge of the page or screen.

Dynamic Positioning and Output

Column positioning as well as output length can be determined dynamically. However, the syntax of the WRITE command changes to WRITE AT rather than just WRITE. The synax is demonstrated as follows:

```
DATA:      W_POSITION TYPE I VALUE 10,

           W_LENGTH TYPE I VALUE 5.

DATA:      W_DATA(30) VALUE 'ABCDEFGHIJKLMNOPQRSTUVWXYZABCD'.

WRITE AT /W_POSITION(W_LENGTH)W_DATA.
```

The output is:

```
          ABCDE
```

The output starts at the 11th position and only displays 5 characters, just as specified by the variables declared. The dynamic positioning can also be used with the ULINE command defined later in this chapter. As with the WRITE command, the new syntax is ULINE AT.

Breaking to a New Line (Inserting Carriage Returns)

When you want to break to a new line of data, add a slash (/), followed by the data that you want to include on the next line:

```
WRITE:/     'First Line',
      /     'Second Line'.
```

Here's the output:

```
First Line
Second Line
```

If you leave out the second slash, like this:

```
WRITE:/     'First Line',
            'Second Line'.
```

the two texts would appear adjacent to each other:

```
First Line Second Line
```

Controlling the Output Length

It's possible to control output length of a field by using this general syntax:

```
WRITE (output length) field name.
```

The output length of the field displayed on the screen or page is determined by the number in the parentheses (*output length*). The field name can also be text enclosed in quotes. Here's a typical example:

```
DATA:     W_FIELD(10) TYPE C.
MOVE: '0123456789' TO W_FIELD.
WRITE:/(5)      W_FIELD.
```

The output from this code would be

```
01234
```

Because the output length is defined as 5 in this example, only five characters are displayed on the screen or page.

When you write a program, a functional analyst talks with the user and finds out from them what they want displayed on the report. The analyst then writes program specifications and passes on those specifications to the programmer (you). At times the amount of data that the user wants in a report exceeds the maximum column length of the report. Some functional analysts know from experience to check if what the user wants can actually be provided in a proper fashion.

TIP

Always begin your first `WRITE` statement with a slash following it, just in case a previous `WRITE` statement was overlooked. An example of when this might happen is when a different part of the program is used to output data to the screen. This other part of the program might be a subroutine, or just a previous section of code. If the forward slash is neglected, the data appears on the screen on the same line as the previous output.

Here's an example:

```
WRITE:/'FIRST SECTION OF CODE'.
code between WRITE statements
WRITE 'SECOND SECTION OF CODE'.
```

The output from this would be

```
FIRST SECTION OF CODE SECOND SECTION OF CODE
```

The desired output in this case would be achieved if the slash is put on the second `WRITE` statement:

```
WRITE:/ 'FIRST SECTION OF CODE'.
WRITE:/ 'SECOND SECTION OF CODE'.
```

The output would be

```
FIRST SECTION OF CODE
SECOND SECTION OF CODE
```

By providing that slash, a carriage return is guaranteed and the data output is

Controlling the output length on some unimportant fields may free some space for more information to be displayed on the report. An example of this situation might involve a report where the company name is displayed. If the company name is `ABC CORPORATION OF THE GREATER MISSISSIPPI AREA`, rather than display the entire name, `ABC CORPORATION` would generally suffice.

As a general rule, check some sample data to see what will be output and try to determine the minimum number of spaces that can be displayed in order to minimize output without confusing end users.

Table 2-1 Field Type Default Alignment

Type	Output	Justification
C	Character	left
D	Date	left
F	Floating point number	right
I	Integer	right
N	Numeric text	left
P	Packed decimal	right
T	Time	left
X	Hexadecimal	left

Default Data Alignment

The rule of thumb for the default alignment of data types is that character fields are left-justified and numeric fields are right-justified. Table 2-1 shows the default alignment for typical field types in SAP.

Using Text Elements

Text elements are fields (maintained by the user) that hold text that's used throughout the program. For a report, for example, all the column headings might be defined as text elements.

Figures 2-3 and 2-4 illustrate where text elements would be used in data output. Figure 2-3 shows the output of the text elements as column headings in a report; Figure 2-4 shows where the text elements are defined.

Text elements are defined with the menu path Goto | Text Elements | Numbered Texts in the ABAP/4 editor screen. You first choose Goto | Text Elements, as shown in Figure 2-5, and then select Text Symbols on the Text Elements screen (see Figure 2-6). Click on Change.

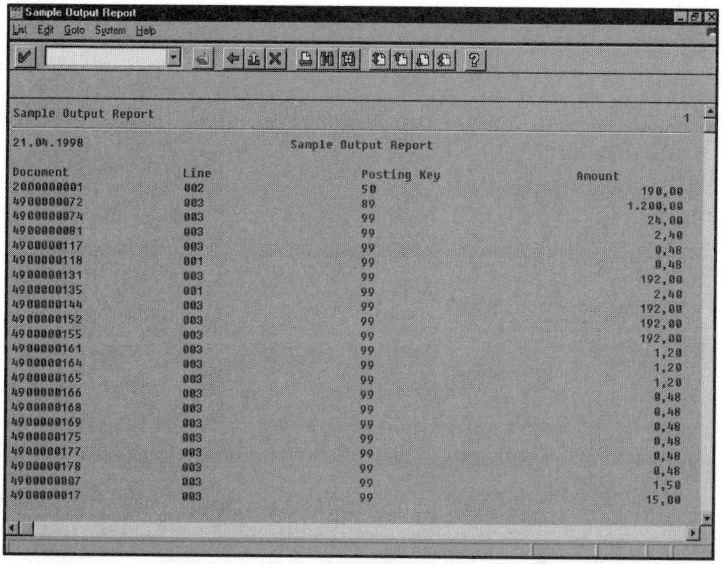

FIGURE 2-3

A report with column headings as text elements

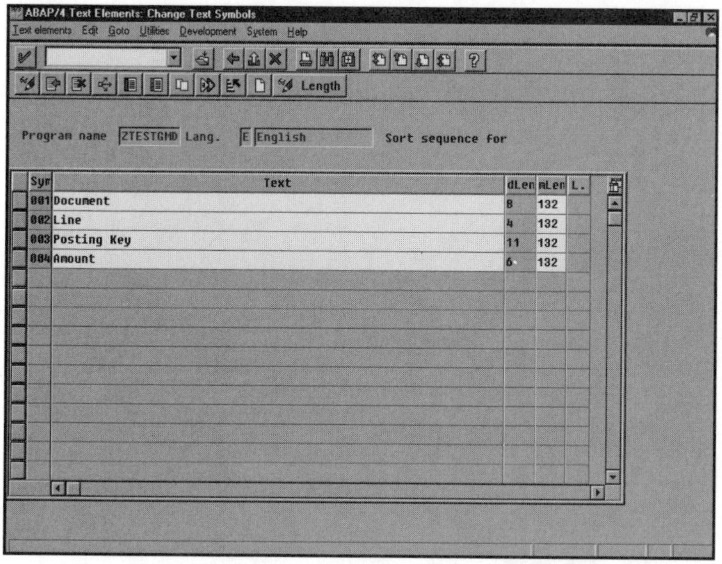

FIGURE 2-4

The Text Elements screen with column headings defined

A screen with several columns appears (see Figure 2-7). The column that holds only three characters is for the number associated with the text. The longer field holds the text associated with that number, as in the following example:

```
001 Document
```

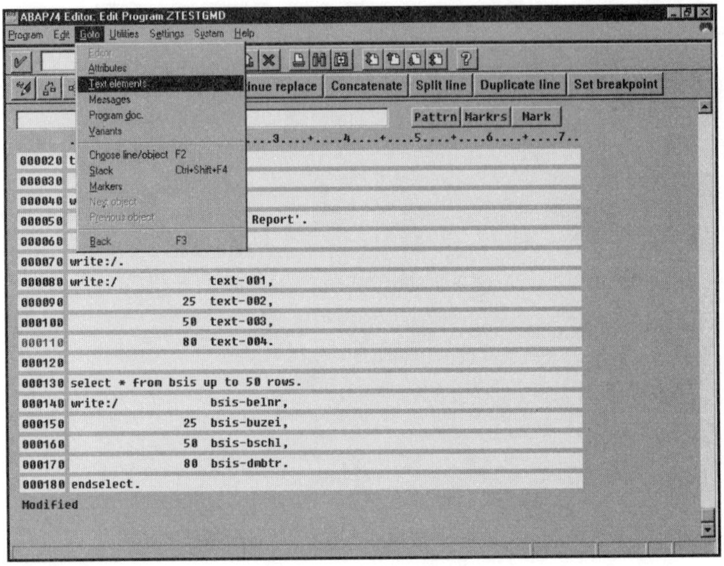

FIGURE 2-5

The menu path to the Text Elements maintenance screen

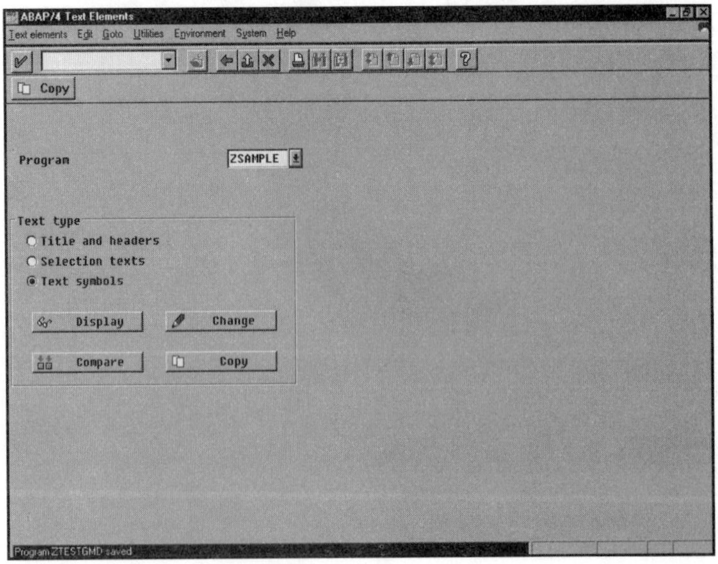

FIGURE 2-6

The Text Elements maintenance screen

To enter or define a text element, follow the menu path Goto | Text Elements | Text Symbols; type a number into the column on the left and its associated text in the column adjacent to it. After entering the text, click the Save button on the menu bar to save your new entry. (Refer to Appendix A for definitions of each menu bar button.)

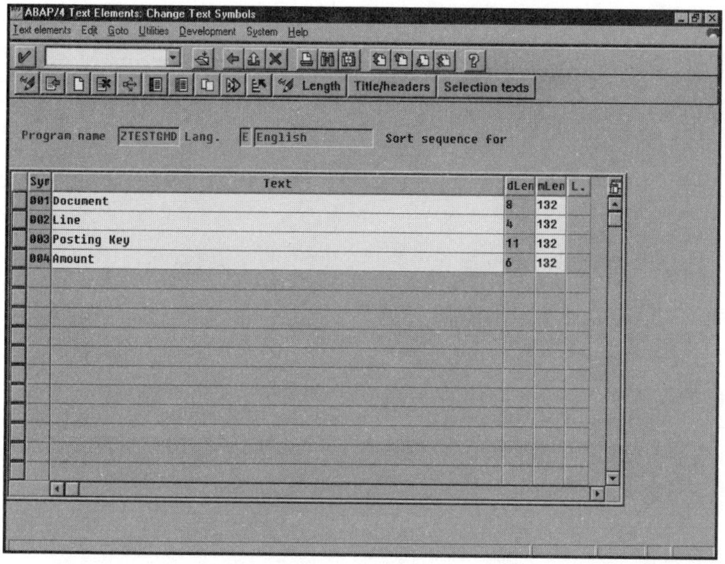

FIGURE 2-7

The Text Symbols maintenance screen

After the text is entered, a number associated with it, and the data saved, you can then return to the ABAP/4 editor. Click the green Back arrow button twice to return to the ABAP/4 editor screen.

To output this text, you use a `WRITE` command with this general syntax:

```
WRITE TEXT-text element number.
```

The *`text element number`* is the number you assigned to the text element (refer to the left-hand column of Figure 2-7). Here's an example of such a command:

```
WRITE     TEXT-001.
```

Using the data from Figure 2-7, the output would look like this:

```
This is text element 001
```

Text elements can be defined for numbers 1 to 999. They can also be defined as *alphanumeric*, meaning that the range also exists from A to ZZZ. (But the examples in this book, along with most code, use just numeric.) There are text elements defined for *input parameters* (selection texts) and for titles and headers (header texts). *Selection texts* are texts associated with `PARAMETER` or `SELECT-OPTION` fields defined in the data declaration portion of the program. To associate a text with a parameter or select-option, follow the same menu path as before (Goto | Text Elements). This time, click the Selection Texts button (see Figure 2-8). A list of parameters and select-options appears on-screen with a column adjacent to the fields for text entry.

If a parameter or select-option is defined in the data declarations portion of the program, it is listed in the left-hand column of this screen. Type the text that you want to be associated with that field in the column adjacent to the field; the text you type appears on-screen on program startup.

For example, suppose that you had in mind the following code:

```
PARAMETERS: P_YEAR LIKE BSEG-GJAHR.
```

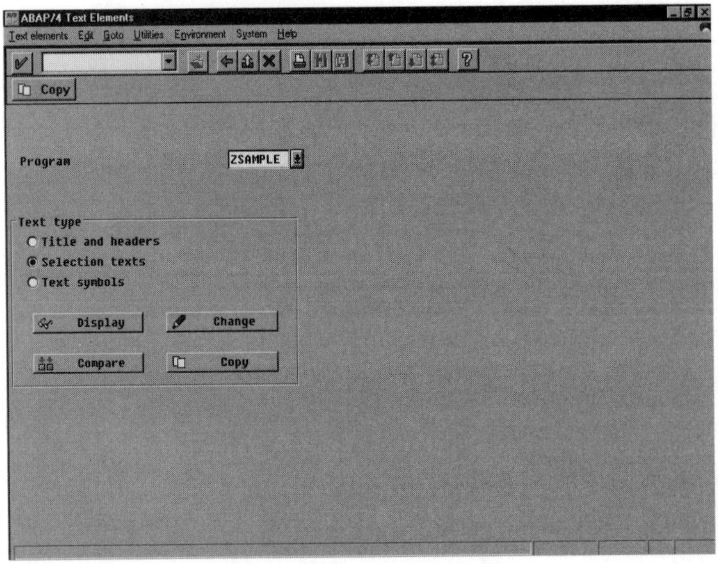

FIGURE 2-8

The Text Elements maintenance screen with the Selection Texts option selected.

This code defines a parameter to enter the fiscal year on-screen upon startup. If you follow the menu path Goto|Text Elements|Selection Texts and associate the text `FISCAL YEAR` with it, as shown in Figure 2-9, the initial startup screen of the program looks something like Figure 2-10.

To access the Titles and Headers Text Elements screen, follow the same menu path to the Text Elements screen (Goto | Text Elements), select the Titles and Headers option button, and then click the Display button or the Edit button to access the screen (refer to Figure 2-8). The Title and Header screen looks like Figure 2-11.

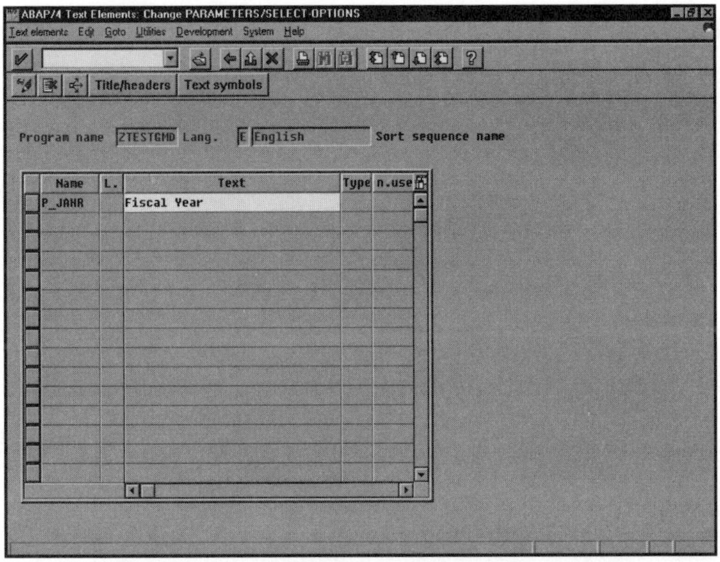

FIGURE 2-9

The Selection Texts maintenance screen

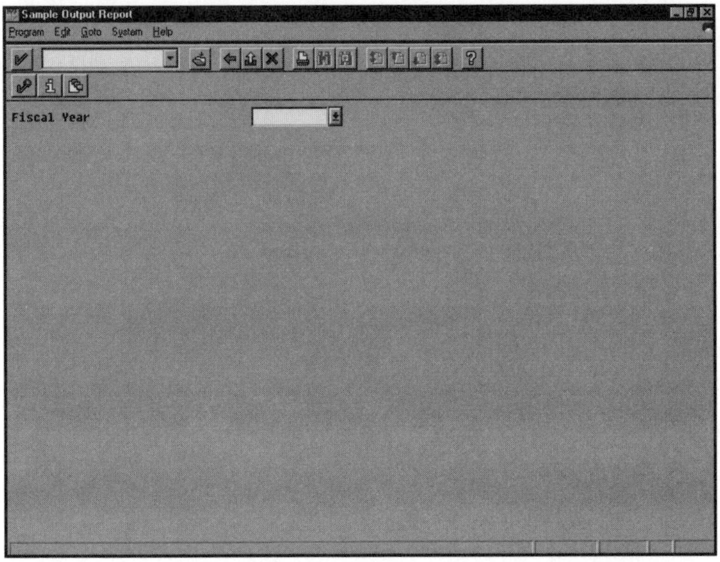

FIGURE 2-10

Sample output using selection texts

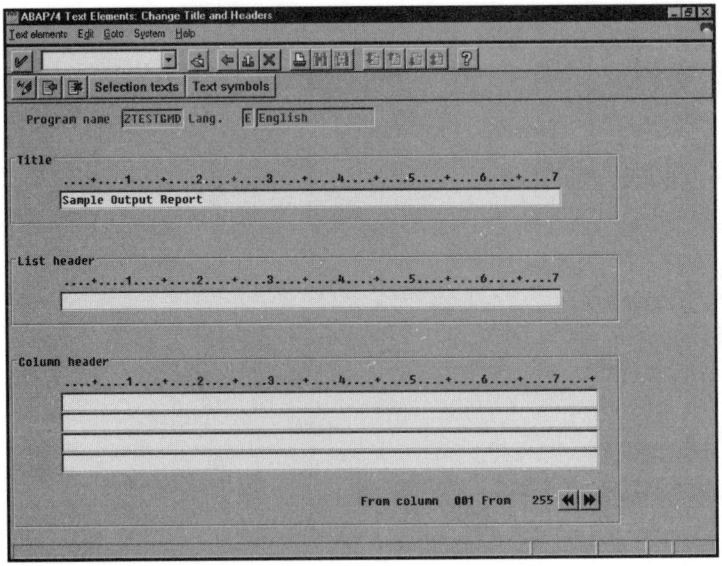

FIGURE 2-11

The Title and Header maintenance screen

These text elements are used in reporting. The title is printed at the top of the page, and the header can be used to output column headings or something below the title. Generally these texts aren't used, however, because reports are usually more complex than the simple lists to which these text elements cater.

Advanced Features of the WRITE Statement

The general syntax of the `WRITE` statement with the advanced options listed is as follows:

```
WRITE field [USING EDIT MASK mask]
            [USING NO EDIT MASK]
            [NO-ZERO]
            [NO-SIGN]
            [DD/MM/YY]
            [MM/DD/YY]          [DD/MM/YYYY]
            [MM/DD/YYYY]
            [CURRENCY currency]
```

```
[UNDER field]
[NO-GAP]
[DECIMALS number of places behind decimal point].
[LEFT-JUSTIFIED, CENTERED, RIGHT-JUSTIFIED]
```

Each variation of the command is explained in the following sections.

Masking the Output (USING EDIT MASK and USING NO EDIT MASK)

The `USING EDIT MASK` command places your data in a specified format of your choice. For example, in the following command:

```
DATA:      W_TIME(8) TYPE C.
MOVE '123456' TO W_TIME.
WRITE W_TIME USING EDIT MASK '__:__:__'.
```

The output would be as follows:

```
12:34:56
```

Each underscore represents one character in the data field. Anything other than an underscore (in this case, the colons) is output as regular text.

Sometimes you have data using a format defined by the Data Dictionary, but you would prefer to use a different format for the output of that data. To output the data using no format, you use the command `USING NO EDIT MASK`:

```
WRITE      SY-UZEIT USING NO EDIT MASK.
```

`SY-UZEIT` is the system field for the current time. At 5:34 a.m., the output would appear in the following format:

```
053400
```

`USING NO EDIT MASK` is generally used for date and time fields.

Suppressing Blanks (NO-ZERO)

The `NO-ZERO` command follows the `DATA` statement. It suppresses all leading zeros of a number field containing blanks. The output is usually easier for the user to read. Here's an example of a number field containing leading zeros that's pretty difficult to read:

```
DATA: W_NUMBER(10) TYPE N.
MOVE 23 TO W_NUMBER.
WRITE W_NUMBER.
```

The output from this code would be:

```
0000000023
```

With the NO-ZERO command, the leading zeros are suppressed:

```
WRITE W_NUMBER NO-ZERO.
```

Here's the output:

```
23
```

Suppressing Number (+/-) Signs (NO-SIGN)

The NO-SIGN command suppresses signs with the integer (I) and packed field (P) data types. The NO-SIGN command is similar to the NO-ZERO command. It suppresses all signs in the output:

```
DATA: W_INTEGER(10) TYPE I.
MOVE 5 to W_INTEGER.
W_INTEGER = W_INTEGER * -1.
WRITE W_INTEGER NO-SIGN.
```

Although the output should be –5, the NO-SIGN suppresses the negative sign. The output would be

```
5
```

You would use this option when you want data in an absolute value format. Also, when sending data to other systems, the format for the data on the other system might have the negative sign formatted differently from SAP, so you would want to suppress the SAP negative sign.

Choosing a Date Format

Depending on user requirements, dates are output in a variety of ways. Date formats are an important item to focus on if you're working for an international company. In the United States, the date format is mm/dd/yyyy; in the European community, the format is dd/mm/yyyy. The formatting commands for dates are as follows:

DD/MM/YY Displays days, months, and then the last two digits of the current year.

MM/DD/YY The same format as DD/MM/YY except that the month and day positions are reversed.

DD/MM/YYYY The same format as DD/MM/YY except that all the digits of the year are displayed.

MM/DD/YYYY The same format as MM/DD/YY except that all the digits of the year are displayed.

The formats discussed previously are used in the following context:

```
WRITE SY-DATUM date format.
```

Suppose today is December 25, 1950. For the following command:

```
WRITE SY-DATUM DD/MM/YY.
```

the output would be:

```
25/12/50
```

With this version:

```
WRITE SY-DATUM MM/DD/YY.
```

you would get this:

```
12/25/50
```

Here's another version:

```
WRITE SY-DATUM DD/MM/YYYY.
```

Here's what you'd see:

```
25/12/1950
```

And, finally:

```
WRITE SY-DATUM MM/DD/YYYY.
```

would produce this:

```
12/25/1950.
```

> **NOTE**
>
> Tables are discussed in detail in Chapters 7, "Working with the Data Dictionary," and 8 "Using SAP SQL to Access Database Tables," but basically, to view the contents of a table, you use the general table display transaction code, SE16, or follow the menu path from the first screen after login (Tools | Application Development | Overview | Data Browser). Enter the table name TCURX, press Enter, mark off the field(s) you want to display, and click the Execute button. The different currency types are displayed in a report format on the screen.

Displaying Currency (CURRENCY)

Due to SAP's international presence, the need to display currency in the appropriate formats brings the CURRENCY command into play. The format for using this command is as follows:

```
WRITE data CURRENCY currency
```

data is a numeric data field that holds the currency value and *currency* is the currency format defined in the SAP table TCURX. The currency formats are generally defined for all countries; however, some smaller or newer countries might need to be added. Examples of different currencies include pounds, dollars, deutchmarks, and rands.

Aligning Fields Vertically (UNDER)

The UNDER command enables you to position your text/field under a previous field. This convenient feature allows for easy maintenance of reports. Instead of changing all the position numbers of all the data, you only have to change the header data. All the subsequent data automatically falls directly under the specified header.

For example, in the following code lines, Field1 is displayed at column position 20. Field2 is displayed on the following line, also at column position 20, right under Field1 (see Figure 2-12). If for some reason a user decides that the report format must be changed (which happens frequently), you only have to change the position number of Field1, and Field2 automatically relocates itself to that new position:

```
WRITE:/20      field1.
WRITE:/              field2 UNDER field1.
```

Figure 2-12 illustrates how the UNDER command works. The first text is written to a line and contains the word OVER. The second text is written UNDER the first text and contains the word UNDER. The code for this example would be as follows:

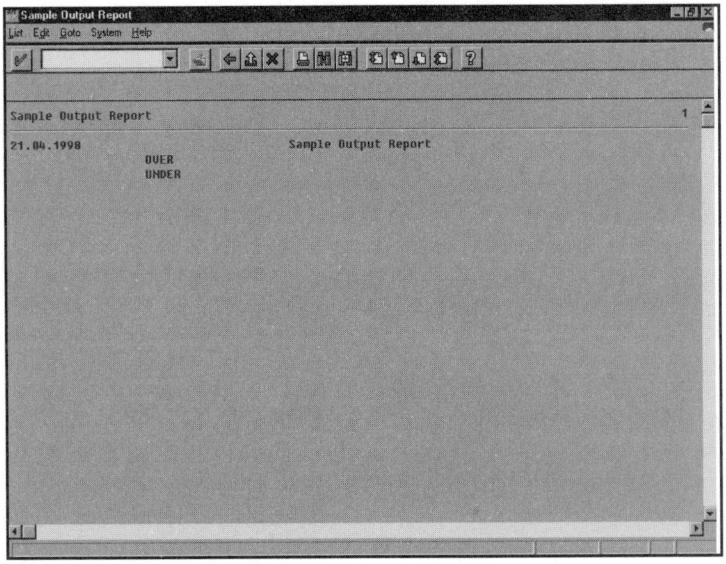

FIGURE 2-12

This figure demonstrates output using the `UNDER` *command.*

```
DATA:      W_DATA1(20) TYPE C,
           W_DATA2(20) TYPE C.
MOVE 'OVER' TO W_DATA1.
MOVE 'UNDER' TO W_DATA2.
WRITE:/20 W_DATA1.
WRITE:     W_DATA2 UNDER W_DATA1.
```

Closing Gaps Between Fields (NO-GAP)

To display several fields one right after another, with no gaps between, you have two choices:

- Move all the fields into one long field and use the `CONDENSE` *`field`* `NO-GAPS` command (discussed in Chapter 3, "Manipulating Data").
- Write out the individual fields and attach the `NO-GAP` command at the end of the code line.

Here's an example of the `NO-GAP` command:

```
DATA:      W_FIELD1(3) TYPE C,
           W_FIELD2(3) TYPE C,
           W_FIELD3(3) TYPE C.
MOVE:      'ABC' TO W_FIELD1,
           'DEF' TO W_FIELD2,
```

```
          'GHI' TO W_FIELD3.
WRITE:    W_FIELD1 NO-GAP, W_FIELD2 NO-GAP, W_FIELD3.
```

The data output is a concatenation of all three fields:

```
ABCDEFGHI
```

When might you want to concatenate fields? Suppose that the user has entered a file name and path separately. Because the entire path must include the file name, you would want to concatenate the two together. This is an example of how you might use the `NO-GAP` command.

Specifying Decimal Places (DECIMALS)

For packed fields, integers, and floating-point numeric fields, it's sometimes necessary to specify the number of places displayed after the decimal point. The `DECIMALS` command specifies the number of places:

```
DATA:     W_NUMBER(10) TYPE P DECIMALS 9.
W_NUMBER = '1.234567890'.
WRITE     W_NUMBER DECIMALS 2.
```

For this example, the output has two decimal places:

```
1.23
```

When prices are figured, many times the decimals are more than two places, but *price* is only two decimals long. The output must then be only two decimal places in length; the `DECIMALS` command allows for this situation.

Specifying Justification (LEFT-JUSTIFIED, CENTERED, RIGHT-JUSTIFIED)

For any field, the justification can now be set using the commands just listed. The syntax is as follows:

```
DATA:     W_NAME(20) TYPE C.

W_NAME = 'BARNES'.

WRITE:/ W_NAME RIGHT-JUSTIFIED.
```

The output is as follows:

```
              BARNES
```

The alignment refers to the output field. When used with the WRITE TO command, the alignment refers to the target field.

Transferring Data with a Specified Format (WRITE ... TO)

You will appreciate the advanced WRITE features when you need to convert data to a certain format for an interface from SAP to another computer system. You might think that to move data from one field to another, you would use the MOVE command. This assumption is correct when working solely inside the SAP environment. However, when data needs to be transferred from one field to another field and then sent to another system in the form of a file, it needs to have a certain format. The MOVE command doesn't modify the format of the data. The WRITE ... TO command has the functionality you need to move the data in a specified format.

Here's the syntax:

```
WRITE field1 TO field2[+offset(length) [advanced options]].
```

This code transfers the contents of *field1* to *field2* in the format defined by the advanced options previously discussed in this chapter. The data in the first field can be placed anywhere in the second field, utilizing the offset and length features, which are both numeric fields. *offset* represents the starting column in *field2* where the data from *field1* will be placed. *length* defines how many characters of *field1* will be placed in *field2*. It's also plausible to use the offset and length with *field1* to specify which characters are placed in *field2*.

Here's an example using the WRITE command in this fashion:

```
DATA:      W_DATE(8) TYPE C VALUE '122550',
           W_DATE2(8) TYPE C.
WRITE W_DATE TO W_DATE2 DATE MM/DD/YYYY.
WRITE W_DATE2.
```

The output of W_DATE2 would be

```
12/25/1950
```

Essentially, the WRITE command, used in this fashion, is similar to the WRITE command with advanced features in combination with the MOVE command.

Inserting Horizontal Lines (ULINE)

The `ULINE` command automatically inserts a horizontal line across the output. It's also possible to control the position and length of the line. The syntax is pretty simple:

```
ULINE.
```

Here's an example:

```
WRITE 'THIS IS UNDERLINED'.
ULINE.
```

This command outputs a solid horizontal line across the page, as shown in Figure 2-13.

If you want to be a bit more specific about how the underline should look, use this syntax:

```
ULINE /position(length)
```

Add the slash (/) if a new line (carriage return) is desired. *position* specifies the column number in which the line will start, and *length* indicates how many spaces the line should extend.

Look at this example:

```
WRITE 'THIS IS UNDERLINED'.
ULINE (18).
```

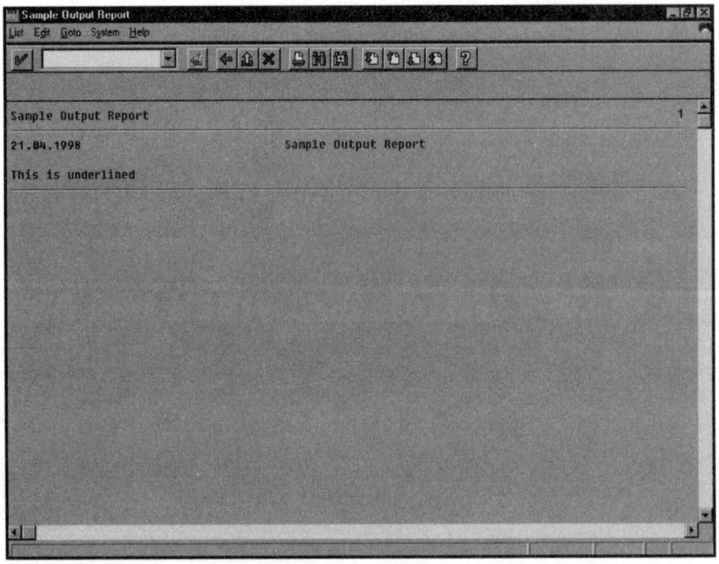

FIGURE 2-13

Underlined output

The output is shown in Figure 2-14.

Just as with the `WRITE` command, *`position`* and *`length`* are fixed values and can't be defined by variables.

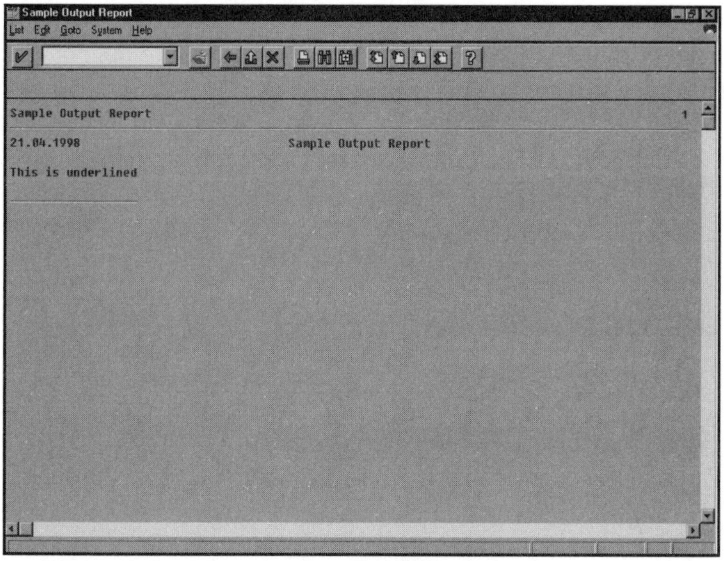

FIGURE 2-14

Underlined data with a specified length on the underline

Inserting Blank Lines (SKIP)

The `SKIP` command inserts blank lines on the page or moves the cursor to a certain line on the page. This command skips one line:

```
SKIP.
```

Here's an example:

```
WRITE 'This is a line of a report'.
SKIP.
WRITE 'This is another line of a report'.
```

And here's how it looks:

```
This is a line of a report

This is another line of a report
```

It's possible to use the `SKIP` command to insert multiple blank lines onto the page:

```
SKIP number of lines.
```

The output from this context of the command would be several blank lines defined by *number of lines*. The SKIP command can also position the cursor on a desired line on the page:

```
SKIP TO LINE line number.
```

This command is used to dynamically move the cursor up and down the page. Usually, a WRITE statement occurs after this command to put output on that desired line. Keep in mind that the number of the line to which you want to skip can't exceed the number of lines defined by the page (the number defined by the LINE-COUNT statement in the REPORT statement at the beginning of your program). For example, if you define the page as having 60 vertical lines and your command says SKIP TO LINE 80, the command won't work and the data won't appear on that page.

Controlling Horizontal Positioning (POSITION)

The POSITION command is like the SKIP TO LINE command except that it controls where the cursor is positioned horizontally:

```
POSITION N.
```

TIP

It's a good idea to maintain as few message IDs as possible. Try to group programs together and have all of them use the same message ID. For example, a group of different reports from the Finance module that focus on the general ledger might all share the same message ID, or a group of interfaces might share common error messages. If a group of programs all use only one message ID (or message library), space in the system is conserved, and the messages are easily maintained.

The *N* is defined as any number from zero to the number of columns defined in the LINE-SIZE command along with the REPORT statement on the top of the page. Just as with the SKIP TO LINE command, the POSITION command can't specify a number greater than the number of columns defined horizontally across the page.

Displaying Messages (MESSAGE)

The MESSAGE command displays messages defined by a message ID specified in the REPORT statement at the beginning of the program. The syntax of the message ID is discussed earlier in this chapter. Essentially, the message ID is a two-character code that defines which set of 1,000 messages the program will access when the MESSAGE command is used. This ID can be either an ID already defined in SAP, or a custom user ID that your company defines.

The messages are numbered from 000 to 999 and are maintained via the menu path Goto | Messages. Associated with each number is message text, up to a maximum of 80 characters in length. When *message number* is called, the corresponding text is displayed.

Here's the syntax of the MESSAGE command:

```
MESSAGE message type message number [WITH text].
```

message type is a single character that defines the type of message displayed and the events associated with that message, as described in Table 2-2.

Table 2-2 Characters for Use with the MESSAGE Command

Message	Type	Consequences
E	Error	The message appears and the application stops halts at the current point it is at. If the program is running in background mode, the job is canceled and the message is recorded in the job log.
W	Warning	The message appears and the user must press Enter for the application to continue. In background mode, the message is recorded in the job log.
I	Information	A pop-up window opens with the message text, and the user must press Enter to continue. In background mode, the message is recorded in the job log.
A	Abend	This message class cancels the transaction that the user is currently using. (Developing online transactions is an advanced ABAP/4 topic, utilizing Screen Painter and Menu Painter. You don't develop any transactions in this text.)
S	Success	This message provides an informational message at the bottom of the screen. The information displayed is positive in nature and is just meant for user feedback. The message does not impede the program in any way.
X	Abort	This message aborts the program and generates an ABAP/4 short dump.

Usually error messages are used to stop users from doing things they aren't supposed to do (for example, running a large system-draining report online rather than in background mode, where the system handles it more efficiently). Warning messages are

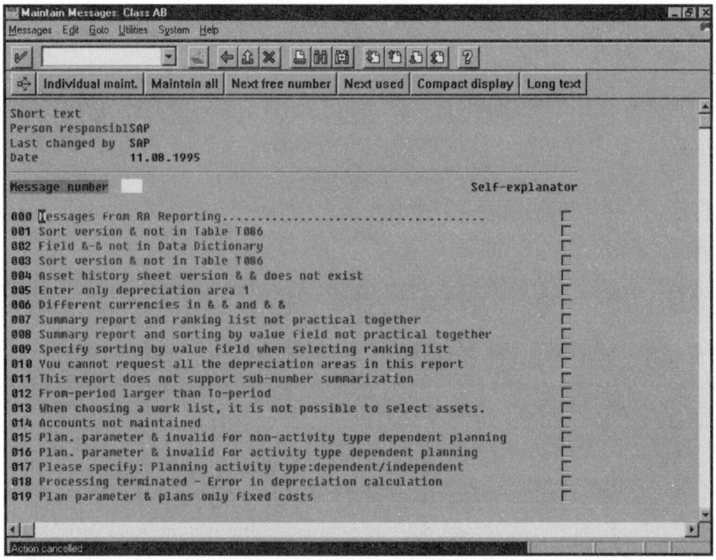

FIGURE 2-15

The message maintenance screen

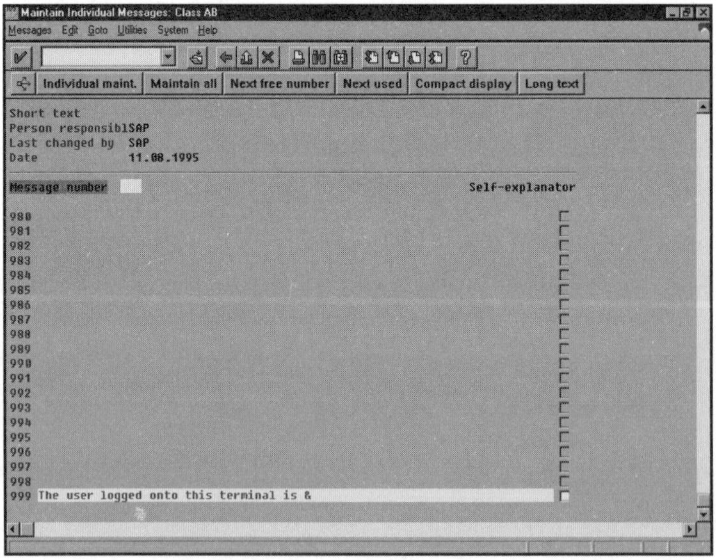

FIGURE 2-16

The new message for **999** *in the message maintenance screen*

generally used to remind the user of the consequences of his/her actions. Information messages give the user useful information (for example, `The purchase order you created was saved`).

For example, if you created the message shown in Figure 2-15 for message ID AB, the `MESSAGE` command:

```
MESSAGE E011.
```

would give you this message:

```
EAB011 This report does not support sub-number summarization.
```

You can use the `MESSAGE` command with variables to make the messages dynamic. In the message text, an ampersand (&) is considered a string. Add a `WITH` statement to the `MESSAGE` command, along with the field name that will replace the ampersand:

```
MESSAGE E999 WITH SY-UNAME.
```

TIP

If your system administrator frowns on the maintenance of message classes and IDs, a way to display a message of your choice is to use a blank message number and associate a text element along with it:

```
MESSAGE E999 WITH TEXT-001
```

Assume that TEXT-001 contains the text `SAMPLE TEXT`. The output would display the following information:

```
EZZ999 SAMPLE TEXT
```

One negative aspect of this method is that the contents of `TEXT-001` aren't incorporated into the job log if the program is run in background mode.

`SY-UNAME` is the system field that holds the user ID of the user currently logged on, or the user ID of the person who scheduled a background job. For a detailed list of all the system fields, see Appendix A, "Using the ABAP/4 Editor." System fields are very useful in programs; you should become familiar with the System table.

Multiple ampersands can be used in the `MESSAGE` definition. It's up to you to define the text of the messages and the requirements of the message IDs.

The `WITH` *`text`* addition overrides the message number stored in the message ID library. Instead of writing the text associated with the message number, *`text`* is output. *`text`* can be a text element or text enclosed in single quotes:

```
MESSAGE E999 WITH 'This system is slow.  Please be patient'.
```

The output would be

```
E999: This system is slow.  Please be patient
```

Using the FORMAT Command

The `FORMAT` command defines screen attributes and some printed attributes. This command controls the format in which the data is displayed. The general syntax for the command is as follows:

```
FORMAT [INTENSIFIED]
       [INTENSIFIED OFF]
       [COLOR color]
       [COLOR OFF]
       [INVERSE]
       [INVERSE OFF]
       [RESET].
```

The `FORMAT` command by itself does nothing. Instead, four additions help define the format of the output:

- INTENSIFIED
- COLOR
- INVERSE
- RESET

These settings are described in the following sections.

Boldfacing (INTENSIFIED)

If you want the text to be **boldfaced**, use the `INTENSIFIED` addition:

```
FORMAT INTENSIFIED.
WRITE 'WORD'.
FORMAT INTENSIFIED OFF.
```

NOTE

Obviously, we can't show a color example in this printed text! However a list of colors can be found if the words 'HELP FORMAT' are typed in the command line in the ABAP/4 editors. While colors are nice, remember that some users can possibly be color blind. Keep all users in mind.

In this case, the word **WORD** appears in bold on the screen. Notice that after the `WRITE` statement another `FORMAT` command turns the `INTENSIFIED` addition off. Turning these formats on and off is helpful, as you want to be selective about what appears on your page.

Changing Colors (COLOR)

The possible colors from which you can choose are from 0 to 7. A little experimentation on the part of the programmer will show what these colors are set to on that user's system. Here's how the `COLOR` variation of the `FORMAT` command works:

```
FORMAT COLOR color.
WRITE 'WORD'.
FORMAT COLOR OFF.
```

Reversing the Text (INVERSE)

Another addition is `INVERSE`. The background color becomes the foreground color and vice versa:

```
FORMAT INVERSE.
WRITE 'WORD'.
FORMAT INVERSE OFF.
```

The output would be:

WORD

Restoring the Default Settings (RESET)

The last addition to the FORMAT command is RESET. This addition resets all the formats to their original system defaults. The syntax for RESET is:

```
RESET.
```

Summary

Data output is one of the simplest but most important features of ABAP/4. The format of a report helps the users get their jobs done and reflects back on the MIS team coordinating the SAP system.

The WRITE command outputs data or text to the page. It's possible to position that data where you want on the page and control how much of the data is visible by using column positioning and output length. The SKIP command inserts one or multiple blank lines on the screen. It also can position the cursor dynamically on any line on the page. The POSITION command also positions the cursor on a particular line on the screen. The ULINE command outputs a solid horizontal line across the page. This line can also be positioned and the output controlled in the same way the WRITE command controls its output. Text elements hold text that the report utilizes throughout the report. Message IDs hold text in the same manner, except that the messages can be used by a variety of programs, whereas text elements are local to that particular program. The FORMAT command simply defines the format of the output text on-screen.

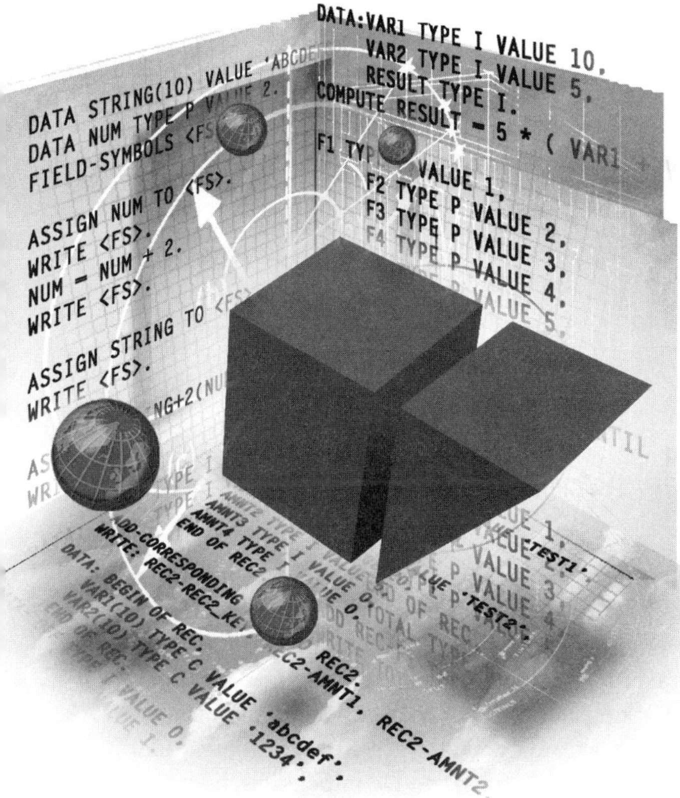

Chapter 3

Manipulating Data

In This Chapter

- Working with Numeric Data
- Manipulating Character Data
- Working with Date Variables
- Using Time Variables
- Manipulating Field Symbols

So far you have seen how to declare a variable, assign a value to a variable, and output the value of a variable using ABAP/4. The next area of interest is manipulating the values of variables.

Variables can be broadly classified into numeric or character data. ABAP/4 has commands to manipulate both types of data. The most common type of manipulation of numeric data is arithmetic computation, such as addition or multiplication of data. For character data, the most common type of manipulation is string manipulation, such as concatenation of strings or taking substrings of character data. This chapter also explores a special form of character data—date and time variables. Finally the use of field symbols (introduced in Chapter 1, "Data Types and Definitions") is discussed in detail.

All the techniques discussed in this chapter for character and numeric data have identical effects whether they're manipulating individual variables or fields within a larger record.

Working with Numeric Data

The first type of data to be manipulated is *numeric*, which includes integer, packed, floating, and hexadecimal data types. Numeric data is altered using arithmetic functions, from addition to cosines.

Performing Math (COMPUTE)

The command to perform arithmetic operations on numeric data is `COMPUTE`. The `COMPUTE` command has the following syntax:

```
[COMPUTE] var = expression.
```

In this case *`expression`* may be any combination of arithmetic operators and ABAP/4 functions. ABAP/4 supports the arithmetic operators shown in Table 3-1.

Table 3-1 ABAP/4 Arithmetic Operators

Operator	Description
+	Addition
–	Subtraction
*	Multiplication
/	Division
**	Exponential
DIV	Integer quotient of division
MOD	Integer remainder of division

In addition to these operators, ABAP/4 also provides common functions which work with all number types, as described in Table 3-2.

Table 3-2 ABAP/4 Arithmetic Functions

Function	Description
SIGN( )	Sign, returns 1,0,–1
ABS( )	Absolute value
TRUNC(X)	Truncate, returns integer portion of X
FRAC(X)	Fraction, returns decimal portion of X
CEIL(X)	Ceiling, smallest whole number value not less than X
FLOOR(X)	Floor, largest whole number value not greater than X
STRLEN( )	Integer length of a character string, excluding trailing spaces

Finally, ABAP/4 also provides several functions, which return floating-point numbers, as described in Table 3-3.

Using these operators and functions, you can assemble expressions.

Expressions are evaluated from left to right; however, when multiple operators or functions are combined into a single expression, the order of evaluation is as follows:

1. ABAP/4 functions
2. **
3. *, /
4. DIV, MOD
5. +, –

For operators with equal precedence, such as multiplication and division, the order is determined left to right. Except for the exponential operator which is evaluated right

Table 3-3 ABAP/4 Floating-Point Functions

Function	Description
EXP( )	Exponential function
LOG( )	Natural logarithm
LOG10( )	Base 10 logarithm
SIN( )	Sine
COS( )	Cosine
TAN( )	Tangent
TANH( )	Hyperbola tangent
SINH( )	Hyperbola sin
COSH( )	Hyperbola cosine
ASIN( )	Arc sine
ACOS( )	Arc cosine
ATAN( )	Arc tangent
SQRT( )	Square root

to left in the case of multiple usage such as 2**3**4. This order of operation can be altered by use of parentheses.

In the following case, the value of RESULT would be 51:

```
DATA: VAR1 TYPE I VALUE 10,
      VAR2 TYPE I VALUE 5,
      RESULT TYPE I.
COMPUTE RESULT = 5 * VAR1 + VAR2 / 5.
```

In this case, the value of RESULT would be 15:

```
DATA:VAR1 TYPE I VALUE 10,
     VAR2 TYPE I VALUE 5,
     RESULT TYPE I.
COMPUTE RESULT = 5 * ( VAR1 + VAR2 ) / 5.
```

Notice the single space separating all operators, including the parentheses, in the COMPUTE statement. An arithmetic operator in ABAP/4 is considered a word and must be preceded and followed by blanks like any other word. The following code would generate a syntax error:

```
COMPUTE RESULT = 5*(VAR1+VAR2)/5.
```

The exception to this rule involves ABAP/4 functions for which the parentheses is considered part of the command:

```
DATA:VAR1 TYPE I VALUE 10,
     VAR2 TYPE I VALUE 5,
     RESULT TYPE F.
COMPUTE RESULT = SIN( VAR1 + VAR2 ) / 5.
```

Notice that no space separates `SIN` and the opening parenthesis, but that spaces are included between the opening parenthesis and `VAR1`.

Controlling Precision in Expressions

When an expression involves decimals, ABAP/4 maintains any intermediate results to the maximum possible precision. Rounding, if necessary, occurs only during the final assignment.

In the following example, the value of `RESULT` is `0.67` because the system evaluated the expression as (`.33333...` + `.33333...`) and then `.66666...` and finally rounded it to `.67` because result has only two decimal places:

```
DATA RESULT TYPE P DECIMALS 2.
RESULT = 1 / 3 + 1 / 3.
```

Alternatives to COMPUTE (ADD, SUBTRACT, MULTIPLY, DIVIDE)

In addition to the `COMPUTE` command, four commands for addition, subtraction, multiplication, and division can perform simple computations. They compute only a single operation and aren't widely used. The syntax for the commands is as follows:

```
ADD value TO var.

SUBTRACT value FROM var.

MULTIPLY value BY var.

DIVIDE value BY var.
```

The equivalent of each command, using `COMPUTE`, would be as follows:

```
ADD value TO var.          var = var + value.

SUBTRACT value FROM var.   var = var - value.

MULTIPLY value BY var.     var = var * value.

DIVIDE value BY var.       var = var / value.
```

The following statements are identical:

```
ADD 1 TO W_COUNTER.

W_COUNTER = W_COUNTER + 1.
```

Adding Sequential Fields (ADD)

Often a single record in SAP contains several numeric fields that need to be summed. For example, a record from the general ledger may contain twelve fields holding the debits or credits for each month of a year. In order to get a year-end balance, all twelve of the fields must be summed. The `ADD` command can sum fields in a record if they're sequential and identical in size. The syntax is as follows:

```
ADD field 1 THEN field 2 UNTIL field N [TO var] [GIVING var].
```

The `TO` option takes the sum of *`field 1`* through *`field N`* and adds it to *`var`*. The `GIVING` option replaces the value in *`var`* with the sum.

In the following example, the output would be `15`:

```
DATA: BEGIN OF REC,
      F1 TYPE P VALUE 1,
      F2 TYPE P VALUE 2,
      F3 TYPE P VALUE 3,
      F4 TYPE P VALUE 4,
      F5 TYPE P VALUE 5,
      END OF REC,
      TOTAL TYPE P VALUE 10.
ADD REC-F1 THEN  REC-F2 UNTIL REC-F5 GIVING TOTAL.
WRITE TOTAL.
```

In this case, SAP takes the values in `REC-F1`, `REC-F2`, `REC-F3`, `REC-F4`, and `REC-F5` (`1`, `2`, `3`, `4`, and `5`, respectively) and adds them to get a result of `15`. Then the program places `15` in the variable `TOTAL`, replacing the old value of `10`.

In the next case, the output would be `25`:

```
DATA: BEGIN OF REC,
      F1 TYPE P VALUE 1,
      F2 TYPE P VALUE 2,
      F3 TYPE P VALUE 3,
```

```
      F4 TYPE P VALUE 4,
      F5 TYPE P VALUE 5,
      END OF REC,
      TOTAL TYPE P VALUE 10.
ADD REC-F1 THEN  REC-F2 UNTIL REC-F5 TO TOTAL.
WRITE TOTAL.
```

Again, the fields in REC are added together to get 15; in this case, however, the GIVING option isn't used, so 15 is added to the value contained in TOTAL (10) to get 25.

Using the CORRESPONDING Commands

Another group of commands for dealing with arithmetic operations on records are the commands ADD-CORRESPONDING, SUBTRACT-CORRESPONDING, MULTIPLY-CORRESPONDING, and DIVIDE-CORRESPONDING, which perform operations on fields of the same name, much as the MOVE-CORRESPONDING command moves all fields of the same name from one record to another. The syntax for these commands is identical to the syntax of MOVE-CORRESPONDING. Also like MOVE-CORRESPONDING, these commands are very inefficient and shouldn't be used in most circumstances.

Example:

```
DATA: BEGIN OF REC1,
      REC1_KEY(5) TYPE C VALUE 'TEST1',
      AMNT1 TYPE I VALUE 5,
      AMNT2 TYPE I VALUE 10,
      END OF REC1.
DATA: BEGIN OF REC2,
      REC2_KEY(5) TYPE C VALUE 'TEST2',
      AMNT1 TYPE I VALUE 20,
      AMNT2 TYPE I VALUE 5,
      AMNT3 TYPE I VALUE 0,
      AMNT4 TYPE I VALUE 0,
      END OF REC2.

ADD-CORRESPONDING REC1 TO REC2.
WRITE: REC2-REC2_KEY, REC2-AMNT1, REC2-AMNT2, REC2-AMNT3, REC2-AMNT4.
```

The output of this code would be:

```
TEST2 25        15        0        0
```

The ADD-CORRESPONDING command adds fields in two records with identical names, if they contain numeric variables, and places the result in the second record. In this case, REC1 and REC2 are added. The fields with common names between the two are AMNT1 and AMNT2, so those are added and the result is placed in REC2. REC1-AMNT1 holds 5 and REC2-AMNT1 holds 20, so the result of 25 is placed in REC2-AMNT1 and displayed by the WRITE command. For the next field, REC1-AMNT2 holds 10 and REC2-AMNT2 holds 5, so the result of 15 is placed in REC2-AMNT2 and displayed by the WRITE command. The other fields in REC2 have no corresponding fields in REC1, so they're left unchanged by the command.

Manipulating Character Data

ABAP/4 provides several commands to manipulate character data. Text processing is one of the most common functions in ABAP/4 programming. It's used in the conversion process, for example, when information formally stored in legacy systems is moved to SAP, or to process information transmitted to SAP during ongoing interfaces. These commands allow a programmer to carry out common operations such as working with substrings, replace characters, or search strings. When working with character data, ABAP/4 provides a system variable called SPACE. As the name implies, this is the equivalent of ' ' and is of use in many operations.

Defining Substrings with Offsets

A *substring* is a portion of a full character string. For example, the string DOG is a substring of THE SMALL DOG IS BROWN. No command exists to extract a substring from a variable; instead, ABAP/4 provides a notation, similar to the notation used in both the WRITE and MOVE commands, to deal with substrings. The notation is referred to as the *offset notation*, and uses this syntax:

```
var+offset(length)
```

In this syntax offset is the number of positions from the leftmost character in the variable at which you want to start, and length is the total number of characters to extract. Assuming that TEMP contains the string abcdefghij, Table 3-3 shows some examples of possible substrings you could create from TEMP with the offset notation.

Table 3-4 Substrings Created with the Offset Notation

Field	Contents
TEMP+3	defghij
TEMP+1(4)	bcde
TEMP+0(10)	abcdefghij

This notation can be used in a statement in which you would typically use a variable. Normally, when the MOVE command is used to assign a value to a variable, it replaces any prior value. But when you use the offset notation, only the individual characters specified by the notation are replaced:

```
DATA VAR1(10) TYPE C VALUE 'abcdef'.
DATA VAR2(10) TYPE C VALUE '123456'.

MOVE 'X' TO VAR1+2.
WRITE: / VAR1.
```

The output would be abX; the offset of +2 moves the value X into the third position of VAR1 and clears the rest of the variable, because no explicit length is given.

```
MOVE 'Z' TO VAR2+3(2).
WRITE: / VAR2.
```

The next output would be 123Z 6 because the offset of +3 moves the value Z into the fourth position, and the length of 2 tells the system to overwrite two characters of VAR2. Because Z has only one character, the second character is overwritten with a space.

```
MOVE VAR1+1(1) TO VAR2+1(1).
WRITE: / VAR2.

WRITE: / VAR2+1(3).
```

The final output would be b3Z. In this case, both variables have offset and length. The MOVE command takes VAR1+1(1) which is b, starts at the second character, and takes a length of 1. This value is placed in VAR2+1(1), starting at the second character and taking a length of 1, so if VAR2 is 123Z 6 this would be the position occupied by 2. To make it more complicated, the WRITE command also specifies offset and length. So after the MOVE command VAR2 holds 1b3Z 6. The WRITE command specifies VAR2+1(3); starting at the second position and taking three characters, this gives you b3Z.

Using Variable Offsets to Define Substrings

In addition to using constants for the *offset* and *length* values, you also can use integer variables to vary the substring being displayed. Variable offsets can be used only with the to portion of the `WRITE ... TO` command. If you wish to use a substring as a source use the `MOVE` command instead. Variable Offsets are especially handy when combined with the ABAP/4 looping commands, as discussed in Chapter 5, "Using the Looping Commands."

Here's an example of integer values used with `WRITE ... TO` to vary a substring:

```
DATA: BEGIN OF REC,
      VAR1(10) TYPE C VALUE 'abcdef',
      VAR2(10) TYPE C VALUE '1234',
      END OF REC.
DATA: OFF TYPE I VALUE 0,
      LEN TYPE I VALUE 1.

WRITE 'X' TO REC-VAR1+OFF(LEN).
WRITE: /, REC-VAR1.

ADD 1 TO OFF.

WRITE 'X' TO REC-VAR2+OFF(LEN).
WRITE: /, REC-VAR2.
```

Output:

```
Xbcdef

1X34
```

In this example, `REC-VAR1` is initialized to `abcdef`. The first `WRITE ... TO` command moves `X` to `REC-VAR1+0(1)`. The offset of `0` means to start at the first character and the length of `1` causes only one character to be replaced. This results in the output of `Xbcdef`. Then the next `WRITE ... TO` command moves `X` to `REC-VAR2+1(1)`. The offset of `1` means to start at the second character and the length of `1` causes only one character to be erased. So `REC-VAR2` starts as `1234` and after the `WRITE ... TO` command becomes `1X34`.

The ability to work with substrings is a powerful tool and forms the basis of all text processing in ABAP/4. It's used extensively in future chapters when programming reports and interfaces.

Other Text-Processing Commands

A number of ABAP/4 commands are designed to manipulate character variables. They are used in many ways: in reports, to control the appearance of data; in interfaces, to format incoming and outgoing data; in interactive transactions, to process user requests.

Shifting Characters Right or Left (SHIFT)

The SHIFT command is another text-processing command. In its most basic form, it shifts the contents of a field one position to the left, erasing the leftmost character and placing a space in the rightmost position.

There are three versions of this command. This is the simplest:

```
SHIFT var [CIRCULAR] [RIGHT] [LEFT].
```

The second version of SHIFT enables the programmer to specify the number of times to shift the contents of the variable:

```
SHIFT var BY N PLACES[CIRCULAR] [RIGHT] [LEFT].
```

The third version causes the command to continue to shift the contents of the variable until a specified character is reached.

```
SHIFT var UP TO character[CIRCULAR] [RIGHT] [LEFT].
```

The following list describes the options you can use with SHIFT:

[CIRCULAR] Causes the leftmost character to be moved to the rightmost position of the variable.

[RIGHT] Causes the shift to move the contents of the string from left to right.

[LEFT] The default for SHIFT, moves the contents of the string from right to left.

Here's an example:

```
DATA: TEMP(5) VALUE '12345',
      NUM TYPE I VALUE 3.
```

```
SHIFT TEMP.
WRITE: /, TEMP.

SHIFT TEMP BY NUM PLACES CIRCULAR.
WRITE: /, TEMP.

SHIFT TEMP UP TO '5' RIGHT.
WRITE: /, TEMP.
```

And the resulting output:

```
2345
5 234
    5
```

The fourth version shifts the contents of the variable to the left only if it begins with the value specified in *val* and continues to shift left as long as the first character is the value specified in *val*. It will pad the end of the string with blanks.

```
SHIFT c LEFT DELETING LEADING val.
```

The final version is the opposite of number four. It shifts the contents of the variable to the right only if it ends with the value specified in *val* and continues to shift right as long as the last character is the value specified in *val*. It will pad the beginning of the string with blanks.

```
SHIFT c RIGHT DELETING TRAILING val.
```

Here's an example (remember SPACE is the same as ' '):

```
DATA: TEMP(14) VALUE '      The Start',
    TEMP2(10) VALUE 'The EndXXX'.

SHIFT TEMP LEFT DELETING LEADING SPACE.
SHIFT TEMP2 RIGHT DELETING TRAILING 'X'.
WRITE: /, TEMP.
WRITE: /, TEMP2.
```

And the resulting output:

```
The Start
   The End
```

Changing the Capitalization (TRANSLATE)

The TRANSLATE command converts a character string to all uppercase or lowercase or replaces a character with another character.

The first two versions of this command translate a string to uppercase and lowercase, respectively:

```
TRANSLATE var TO UPPER CASE.

TRANSLATE var TO LOWER CASE.
```

The third version replaces characters in *var* based on the pattern in the string submitted:

```
TRANSLATE var USING string.
```

string must consist of pairs of characters. The first character in the pair is the character to be replaced and the second is the character to replace with. The pairs aren't separated by spaces, because spaces are valid characters that can be used as replacements.

Examples of the TRANSLATE command:

```
DATA: STRING(10) VALUE '   abcdefg',
          TEMP(6)  VALUE 'a1A2 X'.


TRANSLATE STRING TO UPPER CASE.
WRITE: /, STRING.


TRANSLATE STRING USING TEMP.
WRITE: /, STRING.
```

Output:

```
   ABCDEFG
XXX2BCDEFG
```

In the first case, the TRANSLATE command simply changes the variable to uppercase. In the second, TRANSLATE uses the variable TEMP to translate one character to another. It changes all 'a' to '1', then all 'A' to '2' and finally all ' ' to 'X', thus changing 'ABCDEFG' to 'XXX2BCDEFG'..

Replacing Individual Characters (OVERLAY)

Another command that replaces characters with other characters is OVERLAY. This command compares two strings and replaces any spaces in the first with the corresponding character from the second. If the first string is longer than the second, spaces in positions exceeding those of the second string remain unchanged.

This command isn't widely used but has some applications when working with text masks.

Here's the syntax:

```
OVERLAY var1 WITH var2 [ONLY var3].
```

The ONLY option enables you to provide a list of characters to be replaced in the first string, instead of just spaces. So if *var3* is a period followed by an asterisk ('.*'), any occurrence of a period or asterisk in *var1* is replaced with the corresponding character in *var2*.

Examples:

```
DATA: STRING(25) VALUE 'JONES **** FIELD ENGINEER',
      MASK(25) VALUE '1234567890123456789012345'.
WRITE / STRING.
OVERLAY STRING WITH MASK.
WRITE / STRING.
OVERLAY STRING WITH MASK ONLY '*+-'.
WRITE / STRING.
```

Output:

```
JONES **** FIELD ENGINEER
JONES6****1FIELD7ENGINEER
JONES678901FIELD7ENGINEER
```

Replacing Multiple Characters (REPLACE)

Similar in function to the TRANSLATE command is REPLACE. Where TRANSLATE replaces individual characters, REPLACE replaces several characters:

```
REPLACE string1 WITH string2 INTO var [LENGTH len].
```

The command replaces the first occurrence of *string1*, from left to right, with the contents of *string2* in the variable specified. These strings are case-sensitive. The LENGTH option limits the search to the length specified, searching from left to right.

The return code is set to 0 if a string is replaced or greater than zero if no replacement is made.

Example:

```
DATA TEMP(33) VALUE 'Now was the time for all good men'.
REPLACE 'was' WITH 'is' INTO TEMP.
WRITE TEMP.
```

Output:

```
Now is the time for all good men
```

Searching for Characters (SEARCH)

Another related command is SEARCH. In this case, a variable is searched for a word and the return code informs the program if that word was found. A word is any group of characters delimited by any of the following characters:

(space) + ! ; / , ? . ( ) : =

The use of the asterisk (*) as a wild-card character is allowed. If the asterisk precedes the string to be searched, any word ending in the string is a match. If the asterisk follows the string, any word beginning with the string is a match. To search for words ending in ing, for example, the string would be '*ing'. You can place a string to be searched between two periods to indicate it can be found in the middle of a variable. To look for the following string inside of a variable:

```
mid
```

the string would be

```
'.mid.'
```

The search is conducted from left to right. If any of the characters is found, the search is successful and the return code is set to 0; otherwise, it is set to 4.

Following is the syntax for the SEARCH command:

```
SEARCH var FOR string [ABBREVIATED] [STARTING AT number] [ENDING AT number] [AND
MARK].
```

The following list details the options available for the SEARCH command:

[ABBREVIATED] This option allows other characters to be inserted between the characters of the string, as long as the first character of the string and the first character of the word in the variable match. So a variable containing `Pipe,2in. ceramic` would produce a match with the string `'Pipe2ceramic'`.

`[STARTING AT` *`number`*`]` Starts the search at the specified position and continues from left to right. The first character in the variable is considered position `1`.

`[ENDING AT` *`number`*`]` Stops the search at the specified position.

`[AND MARK]` If the string is found, all the characters of the string and any characters occurring between them (if the `ABBREVIATED` option is used) are converted to uppercase in the variable.

Example:

```
DATA QUOTE(50) VALUE 'SMITH, JOHN ACCOUNTANT II 04/18/91'.

SEARCH QUOTE FOR 'ACC*'.
WRITE / SY-SUBRC.    "0 indicates success, 4 failure
SEARCH QUOTE FOR 'ACCOUNTANT' STARTING AT 15.
WRITE / SY-SUBRC.
SEARCH QUOTE FOR 'ACON' ABBREVIATED.
WRITE / SY-SUBRC.
```

The first search succeeds; the value of `SY-SUBRC` is set to `0`. The second search fails because starting at the fifteenth position, there is no string `ACCOUNTANT` to be found. So `SY-SUBRC` is set to `4`, indicating that the command failed. The third search succeeds because the `ABBREVIATED` option tells it to ignore the space in `AC ON`. So the output is as follows:

```
0
4
0
```

The `SEARCH` command can also be used to search an internal table for a string (See Chapter 6 for a description of internal tables). The string can use any of the forms described in the previous section. Use the following syntax for searching an internal table:

```
SEARCH itab FOR string [ABBREVIATED] [STARTING AT line] [ENDING AT line] [AND
MARK].
```

The value of SY-SUBRC is set to 0, if the search string is found in the table. The value of SY-TABIX will contain the index of the line, which contains the string. Finally the SY-FDPOS field will hold the offset of the string within the line.

Dividing Strings (SPLIT)

The SPLIT command is used to break up a character string into smaller parts. It accepts a string, a delimiter, and a list of variables or an internal table. The delimiter is used to indicate when to end each part of the string. Each part of the string is placed into a separate variable or a separate row of the internal table.

Syntax:

```
SPLIT str AT char INTO var1 ... varN.
SPLIT str AT char INTO TABLE itab.
```

For example, when translating an interface file into a data structured:

```
DATA:  BEGIN OF WS_MATL,
                 MATNR LIKE MARA-MATNR,
                 WERKS LIKE MARC-WERKS,
                DESC(30),
                DIV(2),
             END OF WS_MATL.

DATA INPUT(100) VALUE '  92345-A52,USA1,    Pipe 3 m. L Joint, A1'.

SPLIT INPUT AT ',' INTO WS_MATL-MATNR WS_MATL-WERKS
                                          WS_MATL-DESC WS_MATL-DIV.

WRITE: / WS_MATL-MATNR,
             / WS_MATL-WERKS,
             / WS_MATL-DESC,
             / WS_MATL-DIV.
```

In this case the output would be:

```
  92345-A52
USA1
    Pipe 3 m. L Joint
A1
```

Merging Strings (CONCATENATE)

One of the most important commands used to manipulate character variables is CONCATENATE. This command merges multiple character strings into a single string. Any trailing spaces are ignored by this command.

Syntax:

```
CONCATENATE var1 var2 var3 INTO var4 [SEPERATED BY char].
```

Here is a pretty simple example:

```
DATA: C1(5) VALUE 'ONE',
            C2(5) VALUE 'TWO',
            C3(5) VALUE 'THREE',
            LAST(30) VALUE 'AND SO ON'.

CONCATENATE C1 ',' C2 ',' C3 ',' LAST INTO LAST.

WRITE: / LAST.

CONCATENATE C1 ',' C2 ',' C3 INTO LAST SEPARATED BY SPACE.

WRITE: / LAST.
```

The output of this would be:

```
ONE,TWO,THREE,AND SO ON
ONE , TWO , THREE
```

Removing Spaces (CONDENSE)

The final command used to manipulate character variables is CONDENSE. This command removes spaces from within a character string. It can be used to concatenate multiple strings into a single string. By default, it removes all but one space between words. If the NO-GAPS option is used, it removes all spaces from within a character string.

Syntax:

```
CONDENSE var [NO-GAPS].
```

For example, when accessing an external system file, you need both a path and a file name. If these two pieces of information are received separately and need to be combined, you might find a piece of code like this:

```
PARAMETERS: F_PATH(40) LOWER CASE,
                                F_NAME(20) LOWER CASE.


F_PATH+20(20) = F_NAME.
CONDENSE F_PATH NO-GAPS.
```

If the user enters the following information for F_PATH:

```
/data/incoming/
```

and this line for F_NAME:

```
test01.dat
```

the value of F_PATH after the assignment will be:

```
/data/incoming/     test01.dat
```

The CONDENSE command with NO-GAPS changes that to:

```
/data/incoming/test01.dat
```

Had the NO-GAPS option *not* been used, F_PATH would contain this:

```
/data/incoming/ test01.dat
```

Working with Date Variables

Date manipulation is one of the basics of data processing. Dates can be added or subtracted, and portions of the date can be extracted or altered. Date variables act much like an eight-character field; the data is stored in the format YYYYMMDD. You can control the appearance of the output of a date variable by using an output mask with the WRITE statement.

To extract portions of a date variable, use the substring notation explained earlier in the section, "Defining Substrings with Offsets." For example, to determine the month of a date variable named TODAY, use TODAY+4(2). So if TODAY contains 19960401, TODAY+4(2) is 04 or the fourth month.

The COMPUTE command can also be used to add or subtract dates. For purposes of computation, dates are treated as packed fields containing the total number of days since January 1, 1900. A system field called SY-DATUM contains the current date, much like SY-SUBRC contains the current return code.

Here are some examples:

```
DATA TODAY TYPE D.


TODAY = SY-DATUM.
WRITE: /, TODAY MM/DD/YY,
       /, TODAY+2(2),
       /, TODAY+4(2),
        /, TODAY+6(2).
```

Output:

```
05/31/96
96
05
31
```

This code shows how the offset notation can be used to return part of a date field in order to extract the day, month, or year only.

Now suppose that you want to process invoices and need to know the difference between the ship date and the order date. The billing date will be incremented by that difference. Part of the code would look like this:

```
DATA: BEGIN OF INVOICE,
       DOC#(10),
      ORDER TYPE D,
      SHIP TYPE D,
      BILLING TYPE D,
      END OF INVOICE.
DATA DIFF_DAYS TYPE P.


INVOICE-DOC# = '500001'.
INVOICE-ORDER = '19960401'.
INVOICE-SHIP = '19960418'.
INVOICE-BILLING = SY-DATUM.   "Today is 05/01/1996
```

```
DIFF_DAYS = INVOICE-SHIP - INVOICE-ORDER.
WRITE: 'Shipping Delay', DIFF_DAYS, 'Days'.
WRITE: /, 'Current Billing Date', INVOICE-BILLING MM/DD/YY.

INVOICE-BILLING = INVOICE-BILLING + DIFF_DAYS.
WRITE: /, 'Revised Billing Date', INVOICE-BILLING MM/DD/YY.
```

Output:

```
Shipping Delay 17 Days
Current Billing Date 05/01/96
Revised Billing Date 05/18/96
```

In this example, adding the `DIFF_DAYS` to `INVOICE-BILLING` changes the date fields. When adding and subtracting date fields, the results are always in days.

Using Time Variables

Time `variables` act much like date variables. Like dates, time variables can be added or subtracted, and portions of the time can be extracted or altered. Time variables act like a six-character field; the data is stored in the format `HHMMSS`, where hours are in 24-hour notation.

To extract portions of a time variable, you use the substring notation explained earlier, in the section "Defining Substrings with Offsets." For example, to determine the minutes of a variable named `NOW`, use `NOW+2(2)`.

You can also use the `COMPUTE` command to add or subtract times. For purposes of computation, time variables are treated as packed fields containing the total number of seconds since midnight. The system field called `SY-UZEIT` contains the current time, much like `SY-SUBRC` contains the current return code. ABAP/4 uses military notation; if you want to display time in the more common AM/PM notation, you'll have to do the formatting in your program.

Example:

```
DATA NOW TYPE T.
DATA LATER TYPE T VALUE '171530'.
DATA DIFF TYPE P.
```

```
NOW = SY-UZEIT.        "Assume it 3:15:30 pm
WRITE: /, NOW USING EDIT MASK '__:__:__',
       /, 'It is now', NOW(2), 'Hours and', NOW+2(2), 'Minutes'.

DIFF = LATER - NOW.
WRITE: / 'The difference in seconds between now and later is', DIFF.
```

Output:

```
15:15:30
It is now 15 Hours and 15 Minutes
The difference in seconds between now and later is 7200
```

In this case, time fields are added and subtracted. ABAP/4 converts time fields into seconds for the sake of arithmetic.

Manipulating Field Symbols

The final type of data manipulation to be discussed here is the use of field symbols. As noted in Chapter 1, field symbols don't actually contain data, but instead serve as a pointer to other variables, which in turn contain specific values. Although not widely used, field symbols offer tremendous flexibility. The tradeoff for that flexibility is that it's almost impossible for the compiler to detect errors with field symbols because no type-checking can take place until runtime. So it's critical that you use the field symbols properly. See the example in the next section for possible errors for field symbols.

Assigning a Variable to a Field Symbol (ASSIGN)

The `ASSIGN` command is used to assign a variable to a field symbol. Once assigned, field symbols can be used anywhere that a normal variable can be used (so all previous discussions in this chapter apply to field symbols).

Following is the syntax for `ASSIGN`:

```
ASSIGN var TO <fs>.

ASSIGN (var) TO <fs>.
```

The variable *var* can be any variable or field symbol, regardless of data type. It's acceptable to use an offset and length operator with variables or even field symbols.

In fact, ASSIGN supports variable offsets and lengths just like the WRITE … TO command. Some examples:

```
DATA STRING(10) VALUE 'ABCDEFGHIJ'.
DATA NUM TYPE P VALUE 2.
FIELD-SYMBOLS <FS>.

ASSIGN NUM TO <FS>.
WRITE <FS>.
NUM = NUM + 2.
WRITE <FS>.

ASSIGN STRING TO <FS>.
WRITE <FS>.

ASSIGN STRING+2(NUM) TO <FS>.
WRITE <FS>.
```

Output:

```
2          4          ABCDEFGHIJ CDEF
```

In this example, <FS> is pointed to the field NUM, so when the first WRITE command is issued, 2 is output. Then 2 is added to NUM, so the next WRITE command outputs the new value of NUM (4). Then <FS> is pointed to the field STRING, so the third WRITE command outputs the value ABCDEFGHIJ. Finally, <FS> is pointed at part of the field STRING, showing how the offset notation can be used with field strings. In this case, STRING+2(4) is set to <FS>, so the output of the last WRITE is CDEF.

The following example would generate an error at runtime, but not during the syntax check, because the system doesn't know what the data type of a field string will be until the program runs:

```
DATA STRING(10) VALUE 'ABCDEFGHIJ'.
DATA NUM TYPE P VALUE 2.
FIELD-SYMBOLS <FS>.

ASSIGN STRING TO <FS>.
NUM = NUM + <FS>.    "Adding a string to a number causes an error
                     "But the system does not know until too late
```

In form two of the command, the parentheses surrounding the variable (which must be a character string) indicate that instead of referring to *var* the field string should refer to the variable with the name contained in *var*:

```
DATA: FIELD(8) VALUE 'WS_BUKRS',
      WS_BUKRS LIKE BSEG-BUKRS VALUE 'WRNR'.
FIELD-SYMBOLS <FS>.
ASSIGN (FIELD) TO <FS>.
WRITE <FS>.
```

Output:

```
WRNR
```

The field symbol is set to the field named in the variable FIELD, WS_BUKRS, which has a value of WRNR. So when <FS> is written, the value WRNR is output.

Summary

The ability to work with and change different types of data is central to all programming. As shown in this chapter, ABAP/4 offers a wide variety of commands to manipulate data.

Now that basic data processing is out of the way, you can move on to the procedural elements of the ABAP/4 language. These commands include conditional and looping operators, which are used to take full advantage of the data-manipulation commands just discussed.

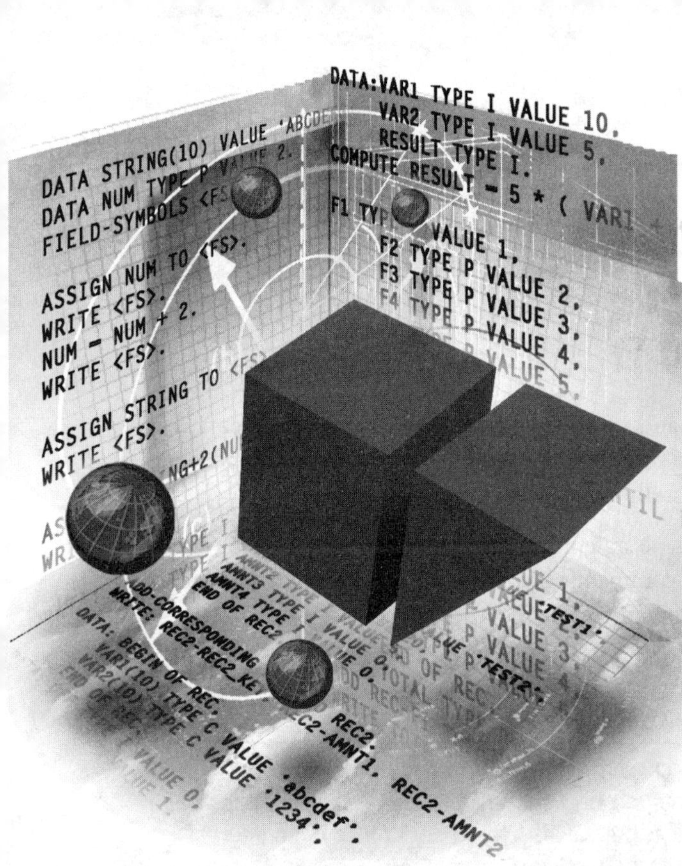

Chapter 4

Using Conditional Operators

In This Chapter

- The CASE Statement
- Using IF with Logical Operators
- Nesting Statements

Logical statements are the heart and soul of programming. These statements sort through all the data and put it into some form of order from which you can generate reports and data extracts that are useful to your company.

ABAP has two pure conditional logic statements: the CASE statement and the traditional IF statement. (The looping commands incorporate logic into their statements as well. See Chapter 5, "Using Looping Commands.")

> **NOTE**
>
> A third conditional statement, ON CHANGE OF, deals with the changing data in a field. Essentially, when the contents of field change, the commands are executed. Single fields generally don't change, but values in the header field of an internal table change as different records of the table are viewed. Here's the syntax:
>
> ```
> ON CHANGE OF field.
>      commands
> ENDON.
> ```
>
> This command is discussed in Chapter 6, "Working with Internal Tables," as an understanding of internal tables is applicable to this command.

The CASE Statement

The CASE statement is used to indicate conditions for data that fall into certain specific categories. For example, you might use the CASE statement with language. If the user logs on with the language set to German, all the output should be in German. If it's in English, the output should be English, and so on. (This is an extreme example, used only to show how the CASE statement works. A more practical example is discussed a bit later.)

The CASE statement can be divided into groups. These groups usually are unique data fields that classify the data in a category. An example of such a group is a country code that defines where the company is located or does business. The CASE statement is used when you have data that falls into certain categories. The general format is as follows:

```
CASE field.
     WHEN value1.
          command lines.
     WHEN value2.
          command lines.
     WHEN OTHERS.
          command lines.
ENDCASE.
```

field is a data field or internal table field holding numeric or character data that defines the group. When those values/characters match one of the values assigned to the WHEN statements, the command lines under that WHEN statement are executed. If the field doesn't match any of the values with the WHEN statements, the WHEN OTHERS statement allows for an exception and the command lines under it are executed.

The WHEN OTHERS statement isn't required; however, it's a good idea to include it so that other programmers who follow you can see that you chose to "do nothing" when none of the data matches:

```
WHEN OTHERS.
*DO NOTHING.
```

Another time to use the WHEN OTHERS statement is when dealing with the system field, SY-SUBRC. As we all know, when something occurs that is not expected (usually an error), the value of SY-SUBRC is set to a value other than zero. You cannot code the statement WHEN <> 0 because it is syntactically incorrect. Instead you use the expression WHEN OTHERS.

```
SELECT SINGLE * FROM MARA WHERE MATNR = 'CDROM'.
CASE SY-SUBRC.
          WHEN 0.
               WRITE: 'THERE IS A CDROM IN THE MATERIAL MASTER'.
          WHEN OTHERS.
               WRITE: 'THERE IS NO CDROM IN THE MATERIAL MASTER'.
ENDCASE.
```

To review the example in plain English, a SQL statement searches the material master table (MARA) for the material 'CDROM'. If there is a CD-ROM, then the program responds to the affirmative. If there is not a CD-ROM, the program responds to the negative.

Here's another example of the CASE statement:

```
DATA:      W_YEAR(4) TYPE C.
W_YEAR = '1997'.
CASE W_YEAR.
     WHEN '1996'.
          WRITE 'The year is 1996!'.
     WHEN '1997'.
          WRITE 'The year is 1997!'.
     WHEN '1998'.
          WRITE 'The year is 1998!'.
     WHEN OTHERS.
          WRITE 'The year is undefined.'.
ENDCASE.
```

This piece of code is hardcoded to respond to year 1997. In a regular program, the year would be a parameter that the user enters, or a field read from a table in the database. In this case, the output would be as follows:

```
The year is 1997!
```

If the year had been earlier than 1996, later than 1998, or anything other than the years mentioned in the WHEN statement, the WHEN OTHERS command line would have written *The year is undefined.*

Note that for character fields, the value associated with the WHEN statement must be in single quotes, but for numeric fields the value associated with the WHEN statement doesn't require quotes. With the WHEN statement, the value is defined. The equivalent statement in English would be, "When *field1* is equal to *value*, do this." No greater than (>), less than (<), or any other logical operators can be used.

TIP

To improve the performance of your program, place the most likely WHEN statement at the top, the next likely after that, and so on. The faster the program makes a logical choice, the fewer lines of code it processes and the faster it runs. In a large integrated system like SAP, performance counts. Obviously, the WHEN OTHERS command always has to be at the end.

The CASE statement is used when the contents of the field are known to exist in a certain set of values. CASE doesn't compare values, check for string contents, or anything complex. It's used simply for this purpose. The simplicity of the statement makes it an efficient tool when making logical decisions and a good command to organize your data if given the opportunity. However, if a more complex comparison is needed, the CASE statement can be replaced by the IF statement, as described in the following section.

NOTE

CASE must end with an ENDCASE statement.

Using IF with Logical Operators

Like the CASE statement, the IF statement is a conditional command that executes command lines after logical expressions have been satisfied. Unlike the CASE statement, however, the IF statement offers the power and flexibility of logical comparisons between fields. The IF statement uses this general format:

```
IF          logical expression #1.
     command lines.
[ELSEIF     logical expression #2.]
     command lines.]
[ELSE.]
     command lines.]
ENDIF.
```

The program checks to see whether *logical expression #1* is true. (*logical expression* and the operators are defined in the following section.) If *logical expression #1* is true, the program executes the command lines under that statement. If not, the program checks the second logical expression. If that expression is true, the command lines under that statement are executed. If that expression is false as well, the program executes the lines under the ELSE statement.

Keep in mind the following points when using ELSE:

- The ELSE statement has an implied logic: If all the other logical expressions are false, the ELSE statement is true. It is comparable to the WHEN OTHERS command in the CASE statement.
- The command lines can consist of any code available in ABAP/4.

- IF must end with an ENDIF statement.
- The logical expressions offer great flexibility in their definition. For example, ELSEIF and ELSE are optional statements. The ELSIF statement lets you specify additional logical expressions if the first logical expression is found to be false, and the ELSE statement specifies commands that are executed if all the logical expressions under IF and ELSEIF are found to be false.

TIP

You can have as many ELSEIF statements as you want; however, for the sake of performance, you should try to limit ELSEIF statements to a maximum of four. As with the CASE statement, put the statement "most likely to be true" first, for better performance. That way, most of the time the program will execute fewer lines of code.

Using Comparison Operators

The logical expression can be defined in several ways. For example, the expression could contain two fields that are compared:

```
DATA:     W_YEAR1(4) TYPE N,
          W_YEAR2(4) TYPE N.

W_YEAR1 = 1996.
W_YEAR2 = 1997.

IF W_YEAR1 > W_YEAR2.
     WRITE 'Year 1 is greater than Year 2.'.
ELSEIF W_YEAR1 < W_YEAR2.
     WRITE 'Year 1 is less than Year 2.'.
ELSE.
     WRITE 'Year1 equals Year2.'.
ENDIF.
```

In this case, the output would be *Year 1 is less than Year 2.* (1996 is not greater than 1997.)

In comparing fields, you can use several operators, with the following syntax:

Table 4-1 Logical Operators

Operator	Definition
>, GT	Greater than
<, LT	Less than
>=, =>, GE	Greater than or equal to
<=, =<, LE	Less than or equal to
=, EQ	Equal to
<>, ><, NE	Not equal to
BETWEEN *value 1* and *value 2*	Inclusively between the two values
IS INITIAL.	The contents of the variable haven't changed
CO	Contains only
CA	Contains any
CS	Contains string
CP	Contains pattern

```
IF FIELD1 operator FIELD2.
     command code.
ENDIF.
```

operator is used to compare FIELD1 and FIELD2. Table 4-1 describes the possible operators.

TIP

As with CASE and ELSEIF, put the most likely logical expression at the top of the IF statement to improve performance.

TIP

In both the WHEN and IF statements, several conditions / logical expressions can be grouped together with 'AND' or 'OR'.

The definition of *inclusive* for the BETWEEN operator means that the two outer range values are included as being part of the TRUE value range. The last four operators in the table are strictly used for string comparison. The first eight comparison operators can be used for either character comparisons or value comparisons.

Comparing Non-Numeric Values

For the greater than/less than operators, two fields are compared; and one is greater than/equal to/less than the other. If the fields being compared are numeric values, it's relatively easy to determine the status (greater than/equal to/less than). For non-numeric values, the way a character is determined to be greater than or less than another character is based on position in the alphabet. A word beginning with *Z* would be "greater than" a word beginning with *A*. And of course two letters that are identical would be equal to each other.

Using Equal/Not Equal Operators

For the equal/not equal comparison operators, the one value is either equal to or not equal to the second value. The logical expression is true or false, depending on which operator is used. The logical expression for the following example is true, as 3 doesn't equal 5; if the not equal sign (<>) is replaced with an equal sign (=), on the other hand, the logical expression is false:

```
IF 3 <> 5.
     WRITE '3 does not equal 5.'.
ENDIF.
```

Table 4-2 `IS INITIAL` **Values**

Data Type	Initial Value
C	...(blank line)
D	00000000
F	0.0
I	0
N	00...0
P	0
T	000000
X	X00

Determining Whether Values Have Changed (IS INITIAL)

For the `IS INITIAL` comparison, the program determines whether the contents of the current variable have changed since the beginning of the program. If the contents are the same, the logical expression is true. It checks whether the contents are equal to the initial value for that type of field, as shown in Table 4-2.

In the following code lines, the program checks whether the contents of a variable have changed. If they haven't, a WRITE statement executes:

```
DATA:      W_DATA(10) TYPE C.

IF SY-DATUM = '122596'.
     W_DATA = 'CHRISTMAS'.
ENDIF.


IF W_DATA IS INITIAL.
     WRITE.'Today is not Christmas'.
ELSE.

WRITE:      'Today is Christmas'.

ENDIF.
```

Determining Whether a Value Is Included in a Range (IS BETWEEN)

The IS BETWEEN comparison operator checks to see whether the mentioned field is equal to or between the two fields mentioned in the logical expression. Because it checks to see whether the field is equal to either of the two limits, this comparison is *inclusive*.

Here, because 3 is in the specified range (3 to 9), the logical expression is true and the WRITE statement is executed:

```
IF 3 BETWEEN 3 AND 9.
     WRITE 'The value is in the number range.'.
ENDIF.
```

Using the NOT Operator

It's possible to set up a logical expression to see whether the logical expression is false by using the NOT command. The format for the NOT command looks like this:

```
IF NOT (logical expression).
     command line.
ENDIF.
```

If the logical expression in the parentheses is true, the entire logical expression is false, and vice versa. It's a little confusing to understand at first, but the NOT statement makes whatever is true false and whatever is false true.

Comparing Character Fields (CO, CA, CS, CP)

The last four comparison operators are used to compare character fields.

CO (Contains Only)

CO is essentially the same as EQ (=), but with a little bit of flexibility. If one field contains only the same data as the other field, the logical expression is true:

```
DATA:     W_FIELD1(4) TYPE C,
          W_FIELD2(4) TYPE C.

MOVE 'ABCD' TO W_FIELD1.
MOVE 'ABCD' TO W_FIELD2.

IF W_FIELD1 CO W_FIELD2.
     WRITE 'The two fields are exactly the same'.
ENDIF.
```

CO is one of the strictest comparison operator. However, if the first field contains only characters that are represented in the second field, the logical expression would evaluate as true.

```
DATA:     W_FIELD1(5),
           W_FIELD2(5).

MOVE 'ABABAB' TO W_FIELD1.
MOVE 'ABC' TO W_FIELD2.

IF W_FIELD1 CO W_FIELD2.
     WRITE 'True'.
ENDIF.
```

The opposite operator of 'CO' is 'NO'. It is equivalent of 'NOT <CO logical expression>'.

CA (Contains Any)

The CA (contains any) operator checks to see whether any letter in W_FIELD1 is in W_FIELD2. In the following example, the logical expression is true because W_FIELD1 and W_FIELD2 share the common letter *D*:

```
MOVE 'ABCD' TO W_FIELD1.
MOVE 'DEFG' TO W_FIELD2.

IF W_FIELD1 CA W_FIELD2.
    WRITE 'At least one letter in field 1 matches at least one letter in field
2.'.
ENDIF.
```

The opposite operator of 'CA' is 'NA'. It is equivalent of 'NOT <CA logical expression>'.

CS (Contains String)

The CS (contains string) comparison operator checks to see whether FIELD2 is contained in FIELD1. The following logical expression is true, as the letters *BC* appear in FIELD1 and FIELD2:

```
DATA:     W_FIELD1(4) TYPE C,
           W_FIELD2(2) TYPE C.

MOVE 'ABCD'        TO W_FIELD1.
MOVE 'BC'          TO W_FIELD2.

IF W_FIELD1 CS W_FIELD2.
    WRITE 'Field 2 is a part of Field 1.'.
ENDIF.
```

If FIELD2 contained the letters *BD* in this example, however, the expression would be false, because FIELD1 contains those letters, but not in that order.

For CS, the system field SY-FDPOS is set to the number of the position of the first character of FIELD1. In this case, SY-FDPOS would contain the value 2. The opposite operator of 'CS' is 'NS'. It is equivalent of 'NOT <CS logical expression>'.

CP (Contains Pattern)

For the last string comparison operator, CP (contains pattern), a few special characters must be defined:

* stands for any string

+ stands for any character

means take the next character literally (i.e. '#*' equals the literal '*' rather than the wildcard.

These special characters allow you to search for strings very loosely inside fields:

```
DATA:     W_FIELD1(4) TYPE C,


MOVE 'ABCD'       TO W_FIELD1.


IF W_FIELD1 CP '*A++D*'.
     WRITE 'Field 1 contains those letters!'.
ENDIF.
```

NOTE

If you're doing lengthy comparisons through a large table, avoid using CP and CS, as they take quite a bit of processing time.

This example searches W_FIELD1 for the letters *A* and *D* with two letters, any two letters, between them, and finds that they do exist two letters apart. Thus, the case is true, and the output is written to the screen.

The opposite operator of 'CP' is 'NP'. It is equivalent of 'NOT <CP logical expression>'.

When you're getting your data from the database, it's preferable to search by string/pattern comparison there, rather than waiting until the data is inside the program. Let the SQL statement and the database do as much work as possible for you. SQL and the SELECT statements for the database are discussed in Chapter 8, "Using SAP SQL to Access Database Tables."

Nesting Statements

CASE statements can be nested inside CASE statements and inside IF statements, and IF statements can be nested in other IF statements and in CASE statements. The nesting offers a powerful tool; however, as nesting grows more complex, so does the difficulty of following what the program is doing. Be careful to map your logic step by step when using either of these statements, or any combination of both of them.

A general rule of thumb is to avoid nesting three or more levels deep. Nesting a CASE statement inside an IF statement inside another IF statement? Try to figure out a better way to sort out your data—your program has become much too precise. On the other hand, here's a good example of nesting:

```
PARAMETERS:     ANSWER(4) TYPE C, "Do you want a gift for Christmas?
                GIFT(10)  TYPE C. "What do you want?


IF ANSWER = 'YES'.
     CASE GIFT.
           WHEN 'TOY'.
                WRITE 'You want a toy'.
           WHEN 'BIKE'.
                WRITE 'You want a bike'.
           WHEN OTHERS.
                WRITE 'I don't know what you want.'.
     ENDCASE.
ELSE.
     WRITE: 'BAH HUMBUG!'.
ENDIF.
```

This example checks to see whether the user wants a gift for Christmas. If he answers yes, the code checks what he wants and outputs it to the screen. If the user says he doesn't want a gift, the program outputs some humor.

Summary

ABAP/4 uses three conditional comparison operators. Use the CASE statement if the value of the field is known. The IF statement can be widely used for any comparisons, but is generally used when comparing two fields. ON CHANGE OF is discussed in Chapter 6.

Remember to put the logical expression or case that's likeliest to be true at the top of your conditional structure so that the program won't waste time checking code that's not useful. By planning ahead, and keeping good habits with your programs, you'll develop good code first, and not fix bad code later. In SAP, the initial emphasis is to get the system up as fast as possible, and then to stabilize it once it's running. If you take a few extra minutes or hours planning now, it could save you days in the future.

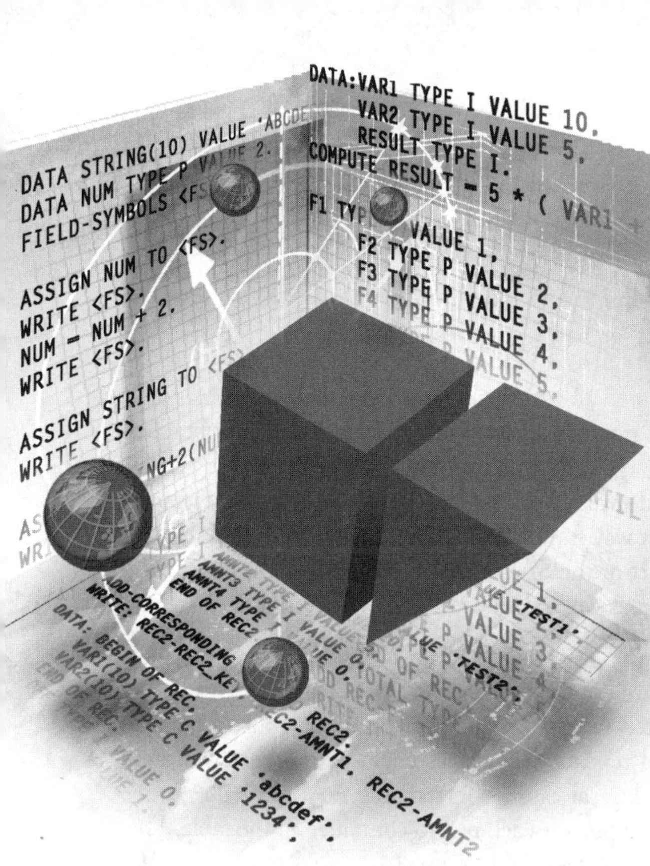

Chapter 5

Using the Looping Commands

In This Chapter

- Using the DO Loop Command
- Using the WHILE Loop
- Using the LOOP Statement

SAP's looping commands play an important role in processing the data obtained from the relational tables. In SAP, large sets of data are processed. The looping commands allow programs to upload, download, or even process data record by record. To upload data in the most efficient way from the database, programs should use the `SELECT *` statement, which is a part of the SAP SQL. This statement is covered in subsequent chapters. At all other times when data needs to be processed, the looping commands will be used.

In ABAP/4, the three main looping commands are `DO`, `WHILE`, and `LOOP`. The `DO` command is used to repeat a process a certain number of times, or until an error is encountered. The `WHILE` command repeats the process enclosed by the `WHILE` and `ENDWHILE` commands, as long as a logical expression remains true. The `LOOP` command loops through internal tables to process each record contained in the table. The `LOOP` command can also be used to process field groups (discussed in Chapter 10, "Advanced Data Output").

Using the DO Loop Command

The `DO` loop is used in ABAP/4 to process a set of commands enclosed by `DO` and `ENDDO`. The general syntax of the command is as follows:

```
DO [ N TIMES].
<commands>
ENDDO.
```

`N` is a numeric value that can also be represented dynamically by a field. If `N TIMES` is added to the `DO` command, `commands` are repeated `N` times, even if an error occurs. `commands` can be any set of ABAP/4 commands that are syntactically correct.

For example, this code will write 66 lines to the page and then terminate:

```
DO 66 TIMES.
     WRITE:/     'This loop pass is number ', SY-INDEX
ENDDO.
```

The output would be as follows:

```
This loop pass is number     1
This loop pass is number     2
This loop pass is number     3
Ö
Ö
This loop pass is number     66
```

The system field, SY-INDEX, automatically stores the number of the current loop pass. When you use the READ and MODIFY commands, you'll rely on the SY-INDEX heavily, along with an index when you process internal tables. The N field can also be a numeric variable.

NOTE

You must be careful to differentiate between the system fields, SY-TABIX and SY-INDEX. SY-INDEX is incremented during specific looping commands such as DO and WHILE, whereas SY-TABIX is incremented when operations are performed on internal tables. SY-TABIX refers to the current record in the internal table. So, while looping through an internal table, SY-TABIX is incremented, not SY-INDEX.

To read through an internal table, one possible way is to read the table line by line until the last line. This code illustrates how you can use a DO loop that has only the number of passes that the table has lines:

```
TABLES: MSEG.

DATA:    BEGIN OF INTTAB OCCURS 50.
      INCLUDE STRUCTURE MSEG.
DATA:    END OF INTTAB.

DATA:    W_LINES(10) TYPE I.

SELECT * FROM MSEG INTO TABLE INTTAB WHERE
                                            MATNR LIKE '4%'.

DESCRIBE TABLE INTTAB LINES W_LINES.
DO W_LINES TIMES.
```

```
        READ TABLE INTTAB INDEX SY-INDEX.
        WRITE INTTAB.
ENDDO.
```

This code reads certain records from the material master table, MSEG, into an internal table with the same structure as MSEG. Once the table is populated from the SQL statement, you use the DESCRIBE TABLE command to put the total number of records from internal table INTTAB into the field W_LINES. Then the DO command loops only that number of times reading exactly each record one by one and printing each of them to the screen. If the number of records inside an internal table is known, it's preferable to use the DO N TIMES command to process the command lines, rather than using the WHILE loop. (However, the LOOP AT command is preferable when dealing with internal tables. See the later section "Using the LOOP Statement" for details.) The previous example is used to demonstrate how the DO loop can be set with a dynamic variable.

Exiting the Loop

If the N TIMES isn't added, an EXIT or STOP command must be incorporated somewhere inside commands. If neither EXIT nor STOP is incorporated, the program enters an endless loop. The program then encounters a runtime error if run online, as the system won't let an application run for more than 15 minutes (depending how the system is configured). If the program is run in the background (as a batch job), the job associated with the program must be terminated by a system operator.

An EXIT command is preferable because the program begins with the subsequent line after the ENDDO statement when EXIT is executed. If a STOP command is called, the END-OF-SELECTION event is triggered. A general way to exit a DO...ENDDO statement is to incorporate an IF...ENDIF statement checking the value of the system error status (SY-SUBRC):

```
DO.
commands
     IF SY-SUBRC <> 0.
          EXIT.
     ENDIF.
ENDDO.
```

If the commands produce a result that changes the system variable, SY-SUBRC, to be a value other than zero, then the EXIT command is executed.

When to Use DO Loops

A good example of when it's preferable to use a DO command is when the program reads in data from an external flat file:

```
PARAMETERS::     P_DATASET(60) default '/users/programmer/dataset.txt' lower case.

DATA:     BEGIN OF INTTAB OCCURS 1000.
DATA:           TEXT(255).
DATA:     END OF INTTAB.



OPEN DATASET P_DATASET FOR INPUT.
DO.
     READ DATASET P_DATASET INTO INTTAB.
     IF SY-SUBRC <> 0.
          EXIT.
     ENDIF.
     APPEND INTTAB.
     CLEAR INTTAB.


ENDDO.
```

Because the program doesn't know how long the data file is, in order to read it into memory, the program continues indefinitely until no more data is found (SY-SUBRC <> 0). The program then exits from the DO loop.

Nesting DO Loops

One important piece of information to note is that DO loops can be nested. Nesting loops means including loops within loops. Although nesting increases the risk of endless loops, it also adds more flexibility to what the program can accomplish.

The following program shows a nested DO loop. The final ENDDO statement is reached when the commands within it are completed 66 times. These commands include a loop of writing text 5 times for every loop pass:

```
DO 66 TIMES.
     DO 5 TIMES.
          WRITE: 'THIS IS A SAMPLE PROGRAM.'.
     ENDDO.
     WRITE 'THIS WILL BE WRITTEN ONLY 66 TIMES'.
ENDDO.
```

The result of running this program is an output of `THIS IS A SAMPLE PROGRAM.` 330 times and 66 lines of `THIS WILL BE WRITTEN ONLY 66 TIMES.`

Using the WHILE Loop

The `WHILE` loop executes the commands enclosed by the `WHILE` and `ENDWHILE` statement until the logical expression associated with the `WHILE` statement becomes false. The general format for the `WHILE` statement is as follows:

```
WHILE logical expression.
     commands
ENDWHILE.
```

The `WHILE` command uses the same comparison operators and logical expressions as the `IF…ENDIF` statement. The `WHILE` command is preferable when considering the performance of the programs. The loop continues until the logical statement is found to be untrue. In a `DO` loop, the loop executes one more time to do the check; a `WHILE` loop terminates exactly as the statement is found to be untrue. The program exits the loop if a false statement is found. Again, `commands` are any set of ABAP/4 commands.

The following code reads through the internal table `INT_TAB` line by line (by the index—that is, the index refers to a specific line number in the table) and transfers one field from the internal table to a working field, `W_FIELD`:

```
DATA: W_INDEX LIKE SY-TABIX


CLEAR W_INDEX.
WHILE SY-SUBRC <> 0.
     W_INDEX = W_INDEX + 1.
     READ TABLE INT_TAB INDEX W_INDEX.
     MOVE INT_TAB-FIELD1 TO W_FIELD.
ENDWHILE.
```

If the internal table contains 100 records, on the 101st loop pass an error occurs (`SY-SUBRC = 4`). The program exits the loop and executes the command after `ENDWHILE`.

NOTE

It's possible to put an EXIT command inside a WHILE loop, but it's preferable to make the EXIT part of the logical expression.

Nesting WHILE Loops

As with `DO`, `WHILE` loops can be nested. Take care that a nested loop doesn't cause the logical expression in the outer loop to change unintentionally. Check all conditions for single-pass loops as well as nested loops, to make sure that the conditions are "air-tight" for the loops to be executing. An example of a problematic nested loop might be one where the first `WHILE` loop is reading an internal table and the logical expression uses the system field `SY-TABIX`. If the second `WHILE` loop also reads another internal table, the `SY-TABIX` value will change back and forth between the two loops and will cause confusion within the program.

Using the LOOP Statement

The `LOOP` command is used to loop through internal tables, and for extracts from field groups (see Chapter 10). The general syntax for the `LOOP` command is:

```
LOOP [AT internal table [WHERE logical expression]]
     commands
ENDLOOP.
```

The `LOOP` command by itself is used to process field groups (covered in Chapter 10).

When the program processes internal tables, it must read a table line into the header line of the table, and then process that line. A good way to read these lines is with the `LOOP AT internal table` command. This command copies the values of the item data into the header data for manipulation by the user, one item at a time. This command is explained in much more detail in Chapter 6, "Working with Internal Tables."

When to Use the LOOP Command

This miniature program loads an internal table `(INT_TAB)` with data, and appends 100 fields into the table. Then, to loop through the table, it utilizes the `LOOP AT INT_TAB` command to read the internal table's fields line by line, and outputs them to the page (code shown on the next page):

```
DATA:     BEGIN OF INT_TAB OCCURS 100,
                 FIELD1(5) TYPE N,
                 FIELD2(5) TYPE C.
DATA:     END OF INT_TAB.


DO 100 TIMES.
     MOVE SY-INDEXIX TO INT_TAB-FIELD1.
     MOVE 'ABCDE' TO INT_TAB-FIELD2.
     APPEND INT_TAB.
     CLEAR INT_TAB.
ENDDO.


LOOP AT INT_TAB.
WRITE:/      INT_TAB-FIELD1, INT_TAB-FIELD2.
ENDLOOP.
```

The comparative latter code using the DO loop is much more complicated:

```
DO.
READ TABLE INT_TAB INDEX SY-INDEX.
IF SY-SUBRC <> 0.
     EXIT
ENDIF.
WRITE:/      INT_TAB-FIELD1, INT_TAB-FIELD2.
ENDDO.
```

If the two codes are compared, the LOOP code is much less complicated, and the DO loop code is processed one more time than the LOOP code. The LOOP code finishes as the last record is read from the table and processed. The DO loop is blind to how many records there are in the table, so the table is read one more time. A error is indicated in SY-SUBRC and then the loop terminates.

Looping Selectively Through Internal Tables

Another great feature of the LOOP command is the LOOP AT internal table WHERE logical expression addition. By defining a logical expression at the end of the LOOP command, the program can specify which lines of the table it reads. For the following example, assume that the internal table that's defined has already been filled with data from the database:

```
DATA:     BEGIN OF INT_TAB OCCURS 1000,
                GSBER LIKE BSEG-GSBER,       "country code
                BELNR LIKE BSEG-BELNR,       "document number
                TEXT1(50) TYPE C.                 "text
DATA:     END OF INT_TAB.

Ö..the table is filled with dataÖ


LOOP AT INT_TAB WHERE GSBER = '01'.
     WRITE INT_TAB-TEXT1.
     WRITE INT_TAB-BELNR.
ENDLOOP.
```

Although there may be 1,000 or more records in this table, only the ones with the country code (GSBER) of 01 will be displayed. This addition is a very efficient way of displaying only information related to certain criteria—a very important capability when processing reports or interfaces.

Another addition to the LOOP command is the LOOP AT <INTERNAL TABLE> FROM <VALUE 1> TO <VALUE2>. <VALUE1> and <VALUE2> can be set dynamically by being defined as variables or statically as predefined numbers. This addition to the LOOP AT command allows the program to loop through only a certain portion of an internal table. This addition is very useful, especially when an internal table contains over thousands of records.

```
DATA:     BEGIN OF INT_TAB OCCURS 1000,
                GSBER LIKE BSEG-GSBER,       "country code
                BELNR LIKE BSEG-BELNR,       "document number
                TEXT1(50) TYPE C.                 "text
DATA:     END OF INT_TAB.
```

```
Ö..the table is filled with dataÖ

LOOP AT INT_TAB FROM 2 TO 10.
     WRITE INT_TAB-TEXT1.
     WRITE INT_TAB-BELNR.
ENDLOOP.
```

Now, if you are really feeling confident in your abilities, combine the last two additions in one statement, which results in the following.

```
DATA:     BEGIN OF INT_TAB OCCURS 1000,
                GSBER LIKE BSEG-GSBER,      "country code
                BELNR LIKE BSEG-BELNR,      "document number
                TEXT1(50) TYPE C.                 "text
DATA:     END OF INT_TAB.

Ö..the table is filled with dataÖ

LOOP AT INT_TAB FROM 2 TO 10 WHERE GSBER = '01'.
     WRITE INT_TAB-TEXT1.
     WRITE INT_TAB-BELNR.
ENDLOOP.
```

By combining both statements, the internal table is selectively read only from records 2 to 10.

Summary

Three commands in ABAP/4 are used to loop through data:

- The `DO` loop is useful when the number of loop passes is known, or when an `EXIT` or `STOP` command is part of the commands in order to prevent an endless loop.
- The `WHILE` loop contains a logical expression along with the `WHILE` command. All commands included between `WHILE` and `ENDWHILE` are executed as long as that logical expression remains true.
- The `LOOP` command is used to loop through internal tables in order to automatically read the data line by line.

It's essential that the programmer understand the subtle differences between these commands and when to use one rather than the other. For example, you need to know that you can put an `EXIT` command inside a `WHILE` loop, but that the preferred method is to make the `EXIT` part of the logical expression. Remember that `SY-INDEX` is incremented for the `DO` and `WHILE` commands and that `SY-TABIX` is incremented for the `LOOP` command.

Quite a bit of looping deals with internal tables, which are discussed in depth in the next chapter.

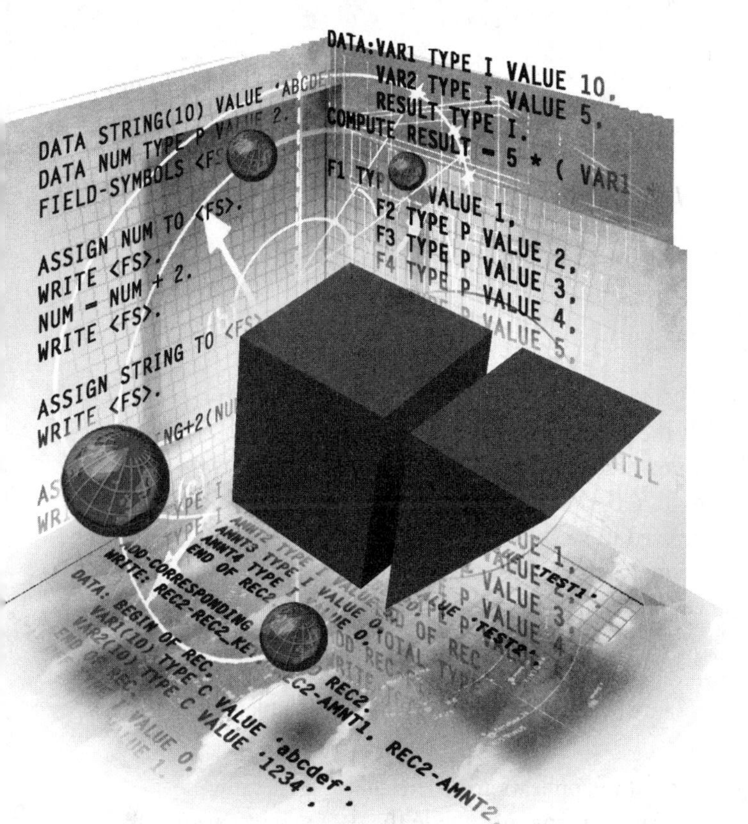

Chapter 6

Working with Internal Tables

In This Chapter

- Understanding the Structure of an Internal Table
- Defining the Table
- Manipulating Data in Tables
- Other Table Commands

In every implementation of SAP, the necessity to process multitudes of records predominates most systems. To store these records, you use internal tables. *Internal tables*—data structures declared in ABAP/4 code—are a very important part of ABAP/4 programming. They are used in 90 percent of every piece of code that's put into production, so you must devote careful attention to learning how to use and—more important—how *not* to use internal tables in your programs.

For example, keep in mind the following points about internal tables:

- Internal tables have the same general structure as a database table, but initially contain no records.
- Internal tables are very useful in applications where they're generally used to keep data in an organized structure, while the data is manipulated in the program. Internal tables store data in the same manner as database tables, except that the data is held in current memory rather than stored on disk somewhere. The data is used by the current program and disappears after the program ends. The data is generally extracted from various database tables and appended or added to the internal table.
- Internal tables don't have primary keys as database tables have, but they can be read with a key in a different manner than database tables are read.
- Because internal tables are held in the current program's memory space, the access time to read and process the data stored inside the internal tables is significantly less than a read of a database table. However, the available memory restricts how much space is allotted to these tables, so there's a tradeoff when dealing with the internal tables. Also, internal table processing uses CPU time. You, as the programmer, must weigh whether it's beneficial for the database or for the CPU to do the work in your data processing.
- There are additional commands to loop through internal tables and process individual records one by one.

This chapter introduces internal tables and explains how to declare them in the data declarations. Reading from, writing to, and modifying the data in the tables are topics covered in later parts of the chapter. The final section deals with looping through internal tables in order to process records and sorting the internal tables.

TIP

If you read any of the chapters in this book twice, make sure that this chapter is one of them. If internal tables are used correctly in your programs, you'll be called a "performance guru." If you don't understand internal tables and use them incorrectly, you'll be known as the programmer who slows down the system.

Understanding the Structure of an Internal Table

An internal table consists of the same structure as a database table. The table has a header record and individual item records. Figure 6-1 shows how an internal table looks in the ABAP/4 debugger. The record with the angle brackets (>>>) is the header record, and the numbered records are the item records. Table 6-1 shows an example of the structure of an internal table.

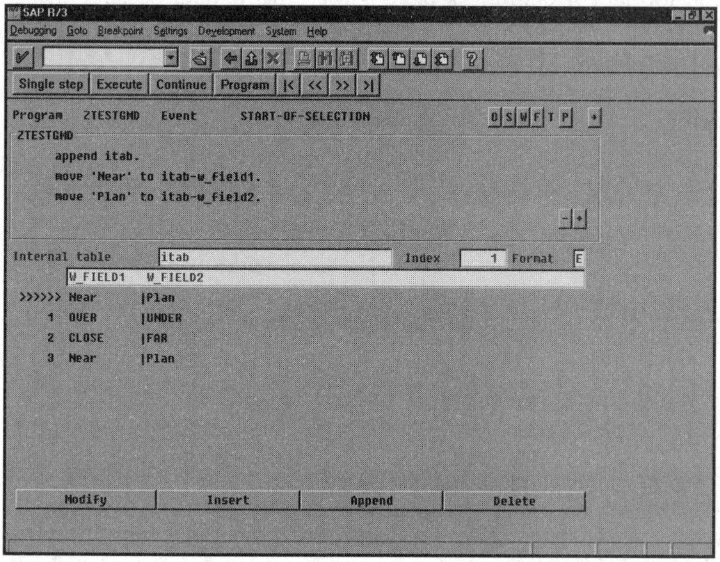

FIGURE 6-1

An internal table containing data in the ABAP/4 debugger

Table 6-1 A Sample Table Structure

	FIELD1	FIELD2	FIELD3	FIELDX
Header				
Item1				
Item2				
Item3				
Item4				

The *header record* is a temporary "holding" record for the internal table. The header record space holds a copy of whichever item record has been read or modified, as well as any new record being added to the table. The header record is where data is stored before it's written to the table or after it's read from the table. When a program loops through the table, the current record is also stored in the header record. The header record is the record that's processed when the table is referenced in the program.

The *item records* are the records already stored in the internal table. When an item record is read—either by a direct read or by looping through the table—a copy of the item record is made to the header record.

Defining the Table

The general format for defining a table is used in the data declaration part of the ABAP/4 code. After the `REPORT` statement and the `TABLES` declaration, the internal table is declared. Here's the general format:

```
REPORT ZSAMPLE1.

TABLES:          VBFA,
                 BSEG.

DATA:      BEGIN OF internal table name OCCURS number of records,
            FIELD1 TYPE C,
            FIELD2 LIKE MSEG-MATNR,
            FIELDX(5) TYPE P.
DATA:      END OF internal table name.
```

The `internal table name` can be any name, but a typical naming convention is to name the internal table `INT_name` where `name` is a general description of the table. The `INT` part of the table name will remind you many lines down in the program that the data structure you're dealing with is an internal table. An example of a bad table name would be naming an internal table `MATERIAL` that listed material numbers along with plant and quantity data. A better name would be `INT_MATERIAL`. Using `MATERIAL` for the name could get confusing when editing the code at a later date.

Another way to declare an internal table is to "include" an existing structure in the Data Dictionary in the internal table. There are two ways to accomplish this task. The first format is:

```
DATA: BEGIN OF INT_STPO OCCURS 100.
INCLUDE STRUCTURE STPO.
DATA: END OF INT_STPO.
```

The benefit of this format is that you can include extra fields in your internal table. An example of extra fields is:

```
DATA: BEGIN OF INT_STPO OCCURS 100.
INCLUDE STRUCTURE STPO.
DATA:       EXTRA_FIELD1(20),
                 EXTRA_FIELD2(20).
DATA: END OF INT_STPO.
```

Usually, the extra fields are one character in length and are used as flags. The second format is:

```
DATA: INT_STPO LIKE STPO OCCURS 100 WITH HEADER LINE.
```

The benefit of this format is that it is only one line.

Determining the Number of Records

`number of records` is a number that at minimum is zero and at maximum is a parameter set by your system administrators. A general rule is that you shouldn't have more than 100,000 records allocated to internal tables in your entire program. This number defines how much memory is allocated from the system to your application.

TIP

A good way to estimate the number of records to be stored in the internal table is to ask the functional analyst who's working with you in developing the specifications for the program. Remember, programming in SAP is a team effort. Use the resources you have at hand, which includes human talent all around you.

CAUTION

Don't just pick a random number out of the air and give that number to your internal table. The consequences of underestimating the number of records is a performance issue with your program. It's better to pick a number that's too small than a number that's too big:

- If the number you choose is too small, each record that's appended to the table after that maximum number is stored in the paging area of memory. This memory area is slower to respond than the allotted memory claimed by your program, and therefore the program runs a little slower.
- If the number is too large, the program fails to initiate and won't run. If the number is very large, it impedes the performance of other applications running on the system. The extra records are stored in the paging area rather than in the memory allocated to the internal table.

Another way to estimate the number of records is to write the program and find out how many records are generally extracted from the database. Then go back into the code and adjust the number of records to reflect an accurate number. This last suggestion is a tough one to do, because most development environments or instances don't have a good data copy of the current production system. Talk to your system administrator to find out the current status of the system.

A typical program with an internal table would follow this structure:

```
REPORT ZSAMPLE.
TABLES:           VBFA,
                 VBAP,
                 BKPF,
                 BSEG.

PARAMETERS:      P_VBELN LIKE VBAP-VBELN,
                 P_GJAHR LIKE BKPF-GJAHR.

DATA:     BEGIN OF INT_TAB OCCURS 1000,
                 VBELN LIKE VBAP-VBELN,          "document number
                 GJAHR LIKE BKPF-GJAHR,          "fiscal year
                 BUKRS LIKE BKPF-BUKRS,          "company code
                 TEXT(50) TYPE C.                  "text
```

```
DATA:     END OF INT_TAB.
DATA:     W_FLAG.                          "flag

START-OF-SELECTION.
DATA SELECTION CODE
```

This code shows what would appear in a typical program. The internal table represents fields that will be copied from the tables listed and then manipulated later in the program. The words at the end of each `LIKE` statement are descriptive remarks. The quotation marks (") denote a comment that begins to the right of the quotation mark.

Using Field Strings

Field strings are useful for a variety of purposes. They can be used as keys to search large internal tables for information. (This application of a field string is discussed in the later section, "Using the WITH KEY addition with READ.")

Field strings consist of multiple fields, just like internal tables. In fact, a field string is best represented in structure by one record of an internal table. However, field strings differ from internal tables in that field strings are only one record in length. Field strings contain no header record; there's only one item record. The manner in which a field string is declared is very similar to how an internal table is declared:

```
DATA:      BEGIN OF F_STRING,
                FIELD1,
                FIELD2,
                FIELD3,
                FIELDX,
DATA:     END OF F_STRING.
```

The structure of a field string is similar to that of a regular data field because there's only room for one piece of data; however, it's also the same as an internal table in that it can contain information about multiple fields.

You can fill a field string and then move it into an internal table where you can append, delete, or modify it. This application of the field string uses it as the data of a single record. The field string, once filled, is then moved to the internal table's header record, where it's processed against the table.

The following program selects data from the user table `ZZUSERS` and places the information in the field string `F_STRING`. Assume that `ZZUSERS` contains all the data needed for this program to work. (It's a fictitious table created for the purpose of this example only.) Once the data is read from the program, the program uses the area code of the telephone number to determine the area in which the user lives, and places the appropriate city in the field. If the area code isn't one of the three cities the program checks, the record isn't added to the internal table:

```
TABLES:     ZZUSERS.

DATA:     BEGIN OF F_STRING,
                NAME(10)            TYPE C,
                ADDRESS(50)      TYPE C,
                PHONE(10)           TYPE C,
                AREA(20)           TYPE C.
DATA:     END OF F_STRING.

DATA:     BEGIN OF INT_TABLE OCCURS 100,
                NAME(10)            TYPE C,
                ADDRESS(50)      TYPE C,
                PHONE(10)           TYPE C,
                AREA(20)           TYPE C.
DATA:     END OF INT_TABLE.

START-OF-SELECTION.

SELECT * FROM ZZUSERS1 WHERE
                    NAME LIKE 'A%'.
MOVE ZZUSERS-NAME              TO F_STRING-NAME.
MOVE ZZUSERS-ADDRESS        TO F_STRING-ADDRESS.
MOVE ZZUSERS-PHONE             TO F_STRING-PHONE,

      CASE ZZUSERS-PHONE+0(3).
           WHEN '202'.
                MOVE 'WASHINGTON DC'        TO F_STRING-AREA.
           WHEN '310'.
                MOVE 'LOS ANGELES'              TO F_STRING-AREA.
           WHEN '916'.
```

```
            MOVE 'SACRAMENTO'          TO F_STRING-AREA.
        WHEN OTHERS.
            MOVE 'UNDETERMINED'          TO F_STRING-AREA.
    ENDCASE.

    IF F_STRING-AREA NE 'UNDETERMINED'.
        MOVE F_STRING TO INT_TABLE.
    ENDIF.

    APPEND INT_TABLE.
    CLEAR F_STRING.
ENDSELECT.
```

The same result is achieved by moving the data to the internal table's header record and, appending or clearing the record, if the area is determined or undetermined respectively. The use of a field string keeps the data transfer uncomplicated. The data is only transferred to the internal table if the condition is finally met.

Field strings are used in the same general manner in field groups (see Chapter 10, "Advanced Data Output").

Including Structures

When internal tables or field strings are declared in the top part of the ABAP/4 program, the structure of each must be defined according to the requirements of the program specifications. Sometimes the structures are very similar to tables already existing in the data dictionary. Rather than type 15–30 lines declaring all the same fields, the table's structure can be defined with the existing structure:

```
TABLES:     TABLE.

DATA:       BEGIN OF INT_TABLE OCCURS 100.
     INCLUDE STRUCTURE TABLE.
DATA:       END OF INT_TABLE.
```

The `INCLUDE STRUCTURE TABLE` command takes the preexisting structure and incorporates it into the structure of the internal table. `TABLE` can be any table (pooled, transparent, cluster, internal) defined already in the data dictionary. To check whether the table that will be included exists, check the data dictionary for that table. The table to be included also must be declared in the `TABLES` statement at the top of the program.

Notice the syntax of the table declaration. A period follows the first `BEGIN OF...` line; in a regular declaration, you use a comma. The `INCLUDE STRUCTURE` line must exist on its own, so the previous line of code must end in a period so that line is executed. (If this syntax is incorrect, a syntax check on the program highlights the problem.)

By including the structure of the preexisting table, you accomplish two tasks:

- If future releases of SAP include changes in the table structure, or if the existing table is modified, the code needs to be changed. When you define fields individually in the program, the code needs to be changed if the new table change affects the program. If the table is included as a structure, however, the program becomes dynamic and uses the current structure defined in the data dictionary.
- The most obvious benefit of typing `INCLUDE STRUCTURE` is the time-savings. Instead of typing multiple lines, you just type one. This benefit is secondary, as the first benefit has more substance—but in the SAP environment, where time is definitely a big factor, this command allows you to save time without sacrificing quality.

Extra fields can be declared in the internal table along with the preexisting structure. They are simply declared before or after the `INCLUDE STRUCTURE` statement:

```
TABLES:     BKPF.


DATA:      BEGIN OF INT_TABLE OCCURS 100,
                F_YEAR1 LIKE BKPF-GJAHR,
                F_YEAR2 LIKE BKPF-GJAHR.
INCLUDE STRUCTURE BKPF.
DATA:          F_YEAR3 LIKE BKPF-GJAHR.
DATA:      END OF INT_TABLE.
```

Manipulating Data in Tables

Once you define an internal table, you should use it to its fullest capacity. SAP provides a strong set of commands for manipulating the data in tables. The commands are discussed in detail in the following sections, but here's a brief overview:

- You can move the data field-by-field to the internal table, or one record at a time—or you can add data to the table by appending it with the `APPEND` command. Using the `COLLECT` command, on the other hand, you can append new data and collect the same data together.

- If the data already exists and you need to change it, that's the time for the MODIFY command.
- Deleting a record? Use DELETE.
- When the data is in the internal table, you use the READ command to read the table. (A later section discloses the differences between reading as a direct or sequential search.)
- You clear an internal table with REFRESH or CLEAR. The differences are discussed shortly. REFRESH purges the entire table and CLEAR clears the header record.

Moving Data into a Table

Initially, an internal table is just a structure consisting only of a blank header record. To fill the table, you must move data into the table. This data transfer is accomplished either by moving individual fields over to the header record, or by moving a complete data record via a field string or from an existing record in another table. After the data is moved into the header record, the record can then be appended to the table and a new item record created. This section explains the differences between moving fields, corresponding data fields, or complete records over to the new internal table.

Moving Data Field-by-Field

The data can be transferred one field at a time until the record is full. If the data is coming from numerous sources, this method is usually the only option and is unavoidable. The positive point to this method is that it provides a good accounting of which data has been moved into the table. If a field is coded to be moved directly into the table, you can count on the fact that the data exists in the correct field in that internal table:

```
DATA:      BEGIN OF INT_TAB OCCURS 100,
                 NAME(10)            TYPE C,
                 AGE            TYPE I,
                 OCCUPATION(15)      TYPE C.
DATA:      END OF INT_TAB.

DATA:      FIELD1(10)      TYPE C VALUE 'ROBERT',
            FIELD2(3)      TYPE N VALUE '36',
            FIELD3(15)      TYPE C VALUE 'ENTERTAINER'.
```

```
MOVE FIELD1 TO INT_TAB-NAME.
MOVE FIELD2 TO INT_TAB-AGE.
MOVE FIELD3 TO INT_TAB-OCCUPATION.
```

The header portion of the internal table now contains the following data:

```
ROBERT      36      ENTERTAINER
```

If you add this record to the internal table, an item-level record is created exactly like the header record. The header record still contains the original values, so essentially the header record is "copied" to the item part of the table.

Moving Data with MOVE-CORRESPONDING

A faster method of moving data is using the command `MOVE-CORRESPONDING`. Use this command if the fields in the internal table are defined as being `LIKE` fields in the database table from which the data is being moved.

CAUTION

Be careful not to define different records as like the same field; otherwise, the application won't move the data in the manner you expected. Instead, the application moves the same field from the database to both fields in the internal table.

In the following example, the fields `BKPF-VBELN`, `BKPF-BUKRS`, and `BKPF-GJAHR` are moved into the fields `INT_TAB-FIELD1`, `INT_TAB-FIELD2`, and `INT_TAB-FIELD3`, respectively:

```
TABLES BKPF.
DATA:     BEGIN OF INT_TAB OCCURS 100,
                FIELD1 BKPF-BELNR,
                FIELD2 LIKE BKPF-BUKRS,
                FIELD3 LIKE BKPF-GJAHR.
DATA:     END OF INT_TAB.

START-OF-SELECTION.

SELECT * FROM BKPF WHERE
                     GJAHR = '1996'.
```

```
MOVE-CORRESPONDING BKPF TO INT_TAB.
APPEND INT_TAB.
CLEAR INT_TAB.
ENDSELECT.
```

The `APPEND INT_TAB` and `CLEAR INT_TAB` commands are used to copy the header record to the item level. These commands are explained in later sections.

`MOVE-CORRESPONDING` takes up more CPU time than moving fields field-by-field or moving an entire record at a time into an internal table. The command is designed to be convenient for the programmer, but the convenience of the programmer over the overall system performance must be weighed when writing applications. All the fields defined inside the internal table also must be properly mapped to their associated fields in the database tables.

NOTE

When using `MOVE-CORRESPONDING`, make sure that no two fields in the internal table are defined as being like the same database field, or you'll get duplicate data. For example, if you defined an internal table with two fields named `W_DOCNO1` and `W_DOCNO2` as being like `BKPF-BELNR`, when `BKPF` is accessed, the field `BKPF-BELNR` would be moved to both of those fields.

TIP

It's important enough to repeat: `MOVE-CORRESPONDING` is much more convenient than moving fields individually or record-by-record, but the command takes up more CPU time. Because system performance is an important issue, every microsecond must be considered when writing your programs.

Transferring Data in Matching Fields

Data can be transferred from one record to another as long as the fields match. A typical application of this method is the transferring of a field string to an internal table:

```
DATA:     BEGIN OF F_STRING,
                NAME(10)            TYPE C,
                AGE(3)          TYPE N,
                OCCUPATION(15)       TYPE C.
DATA:     END OF F_STRING.
```

```
DATA:     BEGIN OF INT_TAB OCCURS 100,
                NAME(10)            TYPE C,
                AGE(3)          TYPE N,
                OCCUPATION(15)      TYPE C.
DATA:     END OF INT_TAB.

MOVE 'JOHN'             TO F_STRING-NAME.
MOVE '100'                  TO F_STRING-AGE.
MOVE 'SALESMAN'     TO F_STRING-OCCUPATION.

MOVE F_STRING TO INT_TAB.
APPEND INT_TAB.
CLEAR INT_TAB.
```

Because the field string in this example contains the same fields as the internal table, the data passes directly from one to the other. If the fields didn't match, the data would be placed as it reads from the field string directly into the internal table (no matter how the field was defined):

```
DATA:     BEGIN OF F_STRING,
                NAME(10)            TYPE C,
                AGE(3)          TYPE N,
                OCCUPATION(15)      TYPE C.
DATA:     END OF F_STRING.

DATA:     BEGIN OF INT_TAB OCCURS 100,
                NAME(10)            TYPE C,
                OCCUPATION(15)      TYPE C,
AGE(3)          TYPE N.
DATA:     END OF INT_TAB.

MOVE 'JOHN'             TO F_STRING-NAME.
MOVE '100'                  TO F_STRING-AGE.
MOVE 'SALESMAN'     TO F_STRING-OCCUPATION.

MOVE F_STRING TO INT_TAB.
APPEND INT_TAB.
CLEAR INT_TAB.
```

A type match error would occur in this example because the processor would see the field string moving a character into an integer field. If both the field string and the internal table contained only fields that contained only characters, the characters of the field string would be moved into the fields of the internal table, regardless of position. For example's sake, suppose that the field string and the internal table from the preceding example contained only fields of type C (all-character fields). The contents of the field string would be as follows:

```
F_STRING-NAME       =         JOHN
F_STRING-AGE =      100
F_STRING-OCCUPATION         =         SALESMAN
```

The contents of the internal table after moving the field string to it would be

```
INT_TAB-NAME =      JOHN
INT_TAB-OCCUPATION=         100         SALES
INT_TAB-AGE  =      MAN
```

The program takes the characters from the field string and fills each field of the internal table individually until each field is filled, and then the next character is put into the next field—until the entire contents of the field string is copied over or the internal table has no more room.

Appending Data to a Table (APPEND)

The APPEND command is used to add a record to an internal table. Once all the fields have been moved to or copied to the header record, the APPEND command copies the contents of the header record to a new item record at the end of the internal table. Here's the syntax:

```
SELECT * FROM database table.
MOVE-CORRESPONDING database table to internal table.
APPEND internal table.
CLEAR internal table.
ENDSELECT.
```

The internal table's header record is filled with the corresponding fields from the database table. Then the APPEND command is issued and the record is copied from the header record to a new item record.

The CLEAR command after the APPEND command is a good programming habit. CLEAR clears the header record of any values, thus ensuring that no old data is transferred to new records. Get used to typing this command along with the APPEND, MODIFY, COLLECT, and DELETE commands.

The following tables illustrate what happens to values when you use these commands. Table 6-2 shows the original values; Table 6-3 shows the changed values after using APPEND; Table 6-4 shows the changes after using CLEAR.

Table 6-2 Internal Table Values Before Using the APPEND and CLEAR Commands

	Field1	Field2	Field3	Field4
Header	ABC	DEF	GHI	JKL
Item1	AAA	AAA	AAA	AAA
Item2	BBB	CCC	DDD	EEE

Table 6-3 Internal Table Values After Using APPEND

	Field1	Field2	Field3	Field4
Header	ABC	DEF	GHI	JKL
Item1	AAA	AAA	AAA	AAA
Item2	BBB	CCC	DDD	EEE
Item3	ABC	DEF	GHI	JKL

Table 6-4 Internal Table Values After Using CLEAR

	Field1	Field2	Field3	Field4
Header	(blank)	(blank)	(blank)	(blank)
Item1	AAA	AAA	AAA	AAA
Item2	BBB	CCC	DDD	EEE
Item3	ABC	DEF	GHI	JKL

The APPEND command copies the contents of the header and places it in a new item-level record. The CLEAR command clears the contents of the header field. APPEND is used to add additional fields to the end of the internal table.

CAUTION

You can copy duplicate records to the internal table, but that's strongly discouraged. If the internal table is copied to the database, a database error occurs. Duplicate records can't exist at the database level.

Modifying Records (READ and MODIFY)

To change the value of a record or a field inside a record, the contents of that record must be copied to the header-level record, altered, and then copied back to the same record number from which the original values were copied. These steps must be followed because otherwise it is impossible to change an existing record; no other method is available.

The first step is copying the contents of the record up to the header level. A READ statement is generally issued for this purpose. The READ statement copies a specified record up to the header record where it can be altered. This is the syntax:

```
READ internal table WITH KEY f_string INDEX idx
```

Table 6-4 shows the contents of an example table before READ statement.

After the READ statement is issued, one of the item records is copied to the header level:

```
READ TABLE INT_TAB WITH KEY 'AAA'.
```

Table 6-5 shows how the table values have changed from those in Table 6-4, after using the READ command.

Table 6-5 Contents of the Table Values After Using READ

	Field1	Field2	Field3
Header	AAA	AAA	AAA
Item1	AAA	AAA	AAA
Item2	BBB	BBB	BBB
Item3	CCC	CCC	CCC

The same results would have been achieved had you issued this command:

```
READ TABLE INT_TAB INDEX 1.
```

The INDEX addition specifies which record at the item level is copied into the header. The number specified can be a variable. Now that the record you want to manipulate is in the header level, you can change the contents of one of the fields to fit your specifications:

```
MOVE 'EEE' TO INT_TAB-FIELD1.
```

NOTE

After the read statement, if no record is found, SY-SUBRC will be set to a value other than 0. Please check Chapter 18 for more information on debugging.

With the record changed, you can issue a command to copy the new record over the old record at the item level:

```
MODIFY INT_TAB INDEX SY-TABIX.
CLEAR INT_TAB.
```

Table 6-6 shows what happens to the table values from Table 6-5 after applying the `MODIFY` statement. The results of the `CLEAR` command are shown in Table 6-7.

Table 6-6 Contents of the Table Values After Using MODIFY

	Field1	Field2	Field3
Header	EEE	AAA	AAA
Item1	EEE	AAA	AAA
Item2	BBB	BBB	BBB
Item3	CCC	CCC	CCC

Table 6-7 Contents of the Table Values After Using CLEAR

	Field1	Field2	Field3
Header	(blank)	(blank)	(blank)
Item1	EEE	AAA	AAA
Item2	BBB	BBB	BBB
Item3	CCC	CCC	CCC

The `MODIFY` command copies the contents of the header record back to the item level with modifications. Even if the record is unaltered, the contents replace the old contents of the item record. As with the `APPEND` command, good programming practice is to use the `CLEAR` command directly after `MODIFY`. Using the `CLEAR` command ensures that the contents of the header record are fresh for the next new record.

It's also possible to modify records using the `INDEX` addition that was introduced along with the `READ` command:

```
MODIFY internal table INDEX index.
```

The addition of the INDEX feature copies the contents of the header record to the item record specified by *index*. *index* is the number of the record at the item level that's copied to the header record.

Deleting Records (DELETE)

Deleting a record from an internal table is essentially like using the MODIFY command, except for the fact that the record isn't changed, but deleted. Here's the syntax:

```
DELETE internal table [INDEX index].
```

The DELETE command compares the contents of the header record with the contents of the item records and deletes the record if it matches exactly. If the INDEX addition is used, the record number at the item level specified by *index* is deleted.

New additions to the DELETE command allow you to delete duplicate records in internal tables as well as deleting certain records. To delete duplicate records use the following syntax:

```
DELETE ADJACENT DUPLICATES FROM internal table COMPARING <fields>.
```

You must specify the internal table as well as the fields that will be compared to determine if records are "duplicate". If no fields are specified, the entire record is compared (all fields).

To delete specific records, there are two different new commands. The first one is:

```
DELETE internal table WHERE <logical expression>.
```

Simply, if the logical expression is satisfied by the record, the record is deleted. The other way to delete specific records is to specify a range of records to delete. The syntax is:

```
DELETE internal table FROM <index1> TO <index2>.
```

The indexes are the beginning and ending record numbers of the block of records to be deleted.

Collecting Records (COLLECT)

Sometimes users want a report or extract that summarizes certain data. If your program is gathering data at the item level from a database table, it would be useful for the application to add the same data together rather than having a long list of data that must be processed later. The COLLECT command is used for this task. COLLECT compares non-numeric fields in the header record against the non-numeric fields in the item-level record. If an exact match is found, the numeric fields are added to the field. Basically, if all the fields that are non-numeric (for example, characters) match another record, the numeric fields are added together and the result is one record in the table, rather than two.

Here's the syntax for the `COLLECT` command:

```
COLLECT internal table.
CLEAR internal table.
```

Table 6-8 shows an example internal table. Table 6-9 shows the same table after running the `COLLECT` command.

Table 6-8 An Internal Table Before Running the COLLECT Command

	Field1	Field2
Header	100	CARS
Item1	250	TRAINS
Item2	50	CARS
Item3	450	PLANES
Item4	33	BIKES

Table 6-9 The Data from Table 6-8 After Using COLLECT

	Field1	Field2
Header	(blank)	(blank)
Item1	250	TRAINS
Item2	150	CARS
Item3	450	PLANES
Item4	33	BIKES

The `COLLECT` command consolidates data. In this example, the number for `CARS` was changed so that the value field increased by 100. Essentially, the header record was added to the item record.

CAUTION

Be careful when choosing `COLLECT` versus `MODIFY`; the two commands produce very different results.

Clearing the Header Record (CLEAR)

The `CLEAR` command completely clears the header record of the internal table. A good programming rule is to clear the header after a record has been appended, deleted, modified, or collected. The syntax is very simple:

```
CLEAR internal table.
```

internal table is the name of the internal table declared in the data section of the program. The `CLEAR` command sets all the fields defined in the data section to blanks or zeros, depending on the data type. The `CLEAR` command can also clear individual fields in the header portion of the internal table, or clear the individual fields themselves:

```
CLEAR internal table-field name.
```

This use of the `CLEAR` command clears only the specified field, rather than the entire contents of the header record.

Earlier it was mentioned that good programming practice is to clear the header portion of the internal table after appending, modifying, deleting, or collecting. If, in the next loop through the process, the program doesn't pick up a certain field from some location, using `CLEAR` guarantees that the previous record's data isn't left inside the header record that is processed against the table. Rather than process incorrect data, it's better to process blank data. You can always enter data in blank fields later. Incorrect data has to be found, analyzed, and then changed. If the header record is cleared after every `APPEND`, `MODIFY`, `DELETE`, or `COLLECT`, no data from the previous record is processed against the table again.

Refreshing the Table (REFRESH)

To remove all the item records of an internal table—thus resetting it to its initial value—use the `REFRESH` command:

```
REFRESH internal table.
```

Essentially, the `REFRESH` command completely purges the internal table of any data. One warning though, make sure you CLEAR the table as well, because refresh does not purge the header line. In a BDC session (covered in Chapter 16, "Writing a BDC Program") there are many times when an internal table is submitted to the database, refreshed, and then filled again.

Reading Internal Tables

Once a table is filled with data by a read from the database tables, a function call, or from an external data file, the program can read the internal table one record at a time. Internal tables are managed more efficiently by the system and read faster than database tables.

CAUTION

Don't depend on internal tables for everything, of course, or the application will take up too much of your server resources.

To read an internal table, you use the `READ` command. `READ` can be used to read a table to find certain records or to read a certain record number. The search on the internal table can be sequential or direct. *Sequential searches* check individual records one by one until the desired record is found. *Direct searches* use a keyed index to read a particular record specified by the application. The generic syntax for the `READ` statement is as follows:

```
READ internal table [INDEX index] [WITH KEY key [BINARY SEARCH]].
```

`internal table` is the name of the internal table defined in the data declaration section of the program. The `INDEX` addition allows the program to read the exact record number specified by the field index, which is a numeric data field. The `WITH KEY` addition lets the application search through the internal table to find a record where the *`key`* field or field string matches the first fields in the internal table. If the `WITH KEY` addition is used, the search time can be decreased if the `BINARY SEARCH` command is also used. The internal table must be sorted using the `SORT` command by the *`key`* fields. A binary search is equivalent to a direct read on a table at the database level. However, one of the stipulations for a binary search to be possible is that the internal table must be sorted by the key fields by which you're reading the table.

If the `READ` command is used without any of the additions, the records in the internal table are read one by one.

NOTE

The `SY-TABIX` system field contains the value of the record number currently being read or processed.

This sample program reads an external file into an internal table. Once all the records have been transferred from the external file, the internal table is read one record at a time and written to the screen, along with the record number (in SY-TABIX):

```
PARAMETERS:     P_DATA(50) TYPE C.

DATA:      BEGIN OF INT_TAB OCCURS 10000,
                 FIELD1(10)      TYPE C,
                 FIELD2(20)      TYPE C,
                 FIELD3(10)      TYPE C,
                 FIELD4(4)      TYPE N.
DATA:      END OF INT_TAB.

START-OF-SELECTION.
* DATA TRANSFER FROM EXTERNAL FILE
OPEN DATASET P_DATA FOR INPUT.
DO.
READ DATASET P_DATA INTO INT_TAB.
APPEND      INT_TAB.
CLEAR      INT_TAB.
IF SY-SUBRC <> 0.
EXIT.
ENDIF.
ENDDO.
CLOSE DATASET P_DATA.

*TABLE READ
WHILE SY-SUBRC = 0.
READ TABLE INT_TAB.
WRITE:      SY-TABIX,
INT_TAB.
ENDWHILE.
```

SY-SUBRC has a value other than zero when all of the records have been read.

This example illustrates that the READ command, if used by itself, reads one record at a time in order. Rather than using READ by itself, however, you could use LOOP AT to process one record at a time. The READ command is powerful and very useful, but it should be used with its two additions. The `INDEX` addition allows the application to read a certain record number and the `WITH KEY` addition lets you search the table for records that match a certain criteria and then processes them.

Using INDEX with READ

The `INDEX` addition to the `READ` command enables the application to read a certain record from the internal table. The internal table name must be specified and the index must be specified:

```
READ internal table INDEX index.
```

`internal table` is the name of the internal table specified in the data declaration part of the application. *`index`* is a numeric data field, also specified in the data section, that has a value ranging from 1 to the last record number of the table. If *`index`* is specified and the number is greater than the number of records in the table, `SY-SUBRC` is set to 4 (or not to zero) which indicates that no record was retrieved.

How does the application know which record it wants to read? The answer is that the index is usually determined from on-screen interactive reporting, in which a list is displayed and the user double-clicks an item to get a more detailed description of that item. The commands you use to get the value of the index are the `AT` events (described in Chapter 14, "Writing a Report").

Using the WITH KEY Addition with READ

If the table is read via a key, specific records can be pulled rather than reading each individual record one at a time. The syntax of the command changes to add the key at the end of the read statement.

```
READ internal table WITH KEY key.
```

The first part of the `READ` statement is the same. The `WITH KEY` addition specifies certain records with the *`key`*, which is a data field or a field string that the application compares against the record to find specific records in the internal table. If *`key`* is a data field, it's the first field in the table. If *`key`* is a field string, the number of fields specified in the field string are the first fields of the internal table. A field string can be used to specify the first few fields as the key in the table:

```
DATA:     W_KEY(10)      TYPE C.
DATA:     BEGIN OF INT_KEY,
                CITY(10)       TYPE C,
                STATE(2)       TYPE C,
                ZIP(5)         TYPE C.
```

```
DATA:      END OF INT_KEY.

DATA:      BEGIN OF INT_TAB OCCURS 10000,
                  CITY(10)            TYPE C,
                  STATE(2)            TYPE C,
                  ZIP(5)              TYPE C,
                  NAME(15)            TYPE C,
                  ADDRESS(20)         TYPE C,
                  PHONE(10)           TYPE C.
DATA:      END OF INT_TAB.

**CODE TO FILL INTERNAL TABLE**
*-----------------------------------------.*
*LOOP #1
*-----------------------------------------.*
MOVE 'NEW YORK' TO W_KEY.
WHILE SY-SUBRC = 0.
READ TABLE INT_TAB WITH KEY W_KEY.
IF SY-SUBRC = 0.
WRITE: INT_TAB.
     ENDIF.
ENDWHILE.

*-----------------------------------------.*
*LOOP #2
*-----------------------------------------.*
MOVE 'NEW YORK'       TO INT_KEY-CITY.
MOVE 'NY'             TO INT_KEY-STATE.
MOVE '99999'          TO INT_KEY-ZIP.
WHILE SY-SUBRC = 0.
READ TABLE INT_TAB WITH KEY INT_KEY.
     IF SY-SUBRC = 0.
          WRITE INT_TAB.
     ENDIF.
ENDWHILE.
```

In the first loop, the internal table is searched only by the first field, which is the city (NEW YORK). The records with the city NEW YORK are written to the screen. In the second loop, the same internal table is read with a different key. The key in the second loop is a field string with several fields specified: Only the records with the city NEW YORK, the state NY, and the zip code 99999 are read from the table and written to the screen.

By using a field string as a key, you can make the search criteria more specific, rather than just searching by one field at a time and then checking to see whether the other fields contain the required data. An alternative to reading the table via a key is looping through the table where certain criteria are met. This feature of the LOOP command is discussed in a later section of the chapter.

Conducting Binary Searches

A read through a table with thousands of records in a sequential search is very time-consuming, especially on large systems. If the table contains more than a thousand records, the search must be changed from a sequential search to a direct search. To make the search direct, the table must be sorted by the key and the search must be binary. To make this change, you use the BINARY SEARCH feature:

```
READ TABLE internal table WITH KEY key BINARY SEARCH.
```

The key must be specified as described in earlier sections. A binary search must have certain criteria specified to the internal table. A binary search on an *internal table* must be specified with a *key*, either by an individual data field or the data fields that make up the field string:

```
SORT internal table BY field1 field2 field3 fieldN.
```

Once the table is sorted, the records can be searched using the binary search. To illustrate the performance benefit of using the binary search over the regular sequential search, a search with three key fields through an internal table with 30,000 records would take 6 *hours* with a regular sequential search and 5 *minutes* with a binary search.

Other Table Commands

There are a few "utility" commands that don't fit any specific categories of commands. These are very useful commands, and we can't leave the topic of table commands without reviewing them briefly.

Determining Table Properties (DESCRIBE)

The DESCRIBE command allows the application to find out specific information about the internal table. DESCRIBE can determine how many lines are in the table as well as the parameter that was defined for the OCCURS statement in the data definition section:

```
DESCRIBE internal table [LINES lines] [OCCURS occurs].
```

DESCRIBE must be used with one of the additions LINES or OCCURS. *internal table* is the name of the internal table as defined in the data declaration portion of the program. If the LINES statement is used, the numeric field *lines* is filled with a number representing the total number of item records in the internal table. If the OCCURS addition is used, the numeric field *occurs* is filled with the defined value, along with the internal table in the data declaration part of the program:

```
DATA:     BEGIN OF INT_TAB OCCURS 10,
                FIELD1(10) TYPE C,
                FIELD2(10) TYPE C.
DATA:     END OF INT_TAB.

DATA:     W_OCCURS      TYPE I,
           W_LINES           TYPE I.

START-OF-SELECTION.

DO 100 TIMES.
MOVE 'abcdefg'      TO      INT_TAB-FIELD1.
MOVE '12345'      TO      INT_TAB-FIELD2.
APPEND INT_TAB.
CLEAR INT_TAB.
ENDDO.

DESCRIBE TABLE INT_TAB        OCCURS        W_OCCURS
LINES           W_LINES.
```

The value of W_OCCURS in the end is 10 as defined in the data declaration portion of the program. However, the value of W_LINES is 100 because the DO loop ran 100 times and put 100 records in the table. These values are useful to make sure that an index value is not too large, or that the available memory of the internal table isn't exceeded.

Sorting Records with the SORT Command

The `SORT` command was mentioned earlier in several examples. Essentially, the internal table can be sorted by its fields in ascending or descending order:

```
SORT internal table     [ASCENDING/DESCENDING]  by field1 field2 field3.
```

`internal table` can be sorted by its fields. The fields specified after *`internal table`* indicate which is the primary sort key, secondary sort key, and so on. You can specify up to 50 keys, using either ascending or descending order. `ASCENDING` specifies that the lowest value is at the top and the highest value is at the bottom. `DESCENDING` uses the opposite order. If no order is specified, ascending order is the default.

Looping with LOOP AT and LOOP AT WHERE

Looping commands are explained in other chapters, but the `LOOP AT` command applies directly to internal tables. `LOOP AT` moves the contents of the item-level records into the header level, where it can be processed. This is the syntax:

```
LOOP AT internal table.
processing commands
ENDLOOP.
```

The `LOOP AT WHERE` statement is essentially the same as the `LOOP AT` statement, except that the `WHERE` clause specifies which records are to be moved up to the header level. The `WHERE` clause is used in the same context as with the `SELECT` statement:

```
LOOP AT internal table WHERE      field1 conditional operator value
                          AND     field2 conditional operator value.


processing commands


ENDLOOP.
```

Using ON CHANGE OF Inside a Loop

When looping through an internal table, to process a command once for each set of records would be very useful. `ON CHANGE OF` allows your programs to accomplish this task.

```
ON CHANGE OF <field> [or <field n>]
<commands>
ENDON.
```

Let's say you have 30 records, 10 of which are for US companies, 10 from Brazil, and 10 for Germany. You wish to add up the total revenue for each country and display it in a report.

```
DATA: BEGIN OF INT_TAB OCCURS 20.
DATA:       REVENUE TYPE I,
             COUNTRY(10).
DATA: END OF INT_TAB.

DATA: W_REVSUM TYPE I,
       W_COUNTRY(10).

SORT INT_TAB BY COUNTRY.

LOOP AT INT_TAB.
ON CHANGE OF INT_TAB-COUNTRY.
     WRITE:/10 W_COUNTRY,  30 W_REVSUM.

     W_COUNTRY = INT_TAB-COUNTRY.
     W_REVSUM = 0.
ENDON.

W_REVSUM = W_REVSUM + INT_TAB-REVENUE.
ENDLOOP.

WRITE:/10 W_COUNTRY, 30 W_REVSUM.
```

The program first sorts all the records of the internal table so that each country's records are grouped together. The program next loops through the internal table and adds up the revenue in the variable, `W_REVSUM`. When a new country is encountered in the loop, the previous country's data is output to the screen and the variables for the country and revenue are initialized. Notice after the loop, that one more `WRITE` statement is included. The purpose of this statement is to print out the last portion of the data.

The output of this small program would look as follows:

```
BRAZIL          12540
GERMANY        345789
USA             24345
```

In summary of this command, the ON...ENDON statement allows applications to process a command once for a certain set of records inside an internal table.

Summary

This chapter has discussed how internal tables are declared, used, and manipulated in ABAP/4 programs. After reading this chapter, you should know how to declare the internal table—field-by-field, or by including database structures in the declaration. You should also now be familiar with reading, modifying, and appending to an internal table.

Internal tables are very important in programming for SAP. Because data in SAP is stored in large database tables, the data must be handled in a table format in the programs. Internal tables enable programmers to do this task.

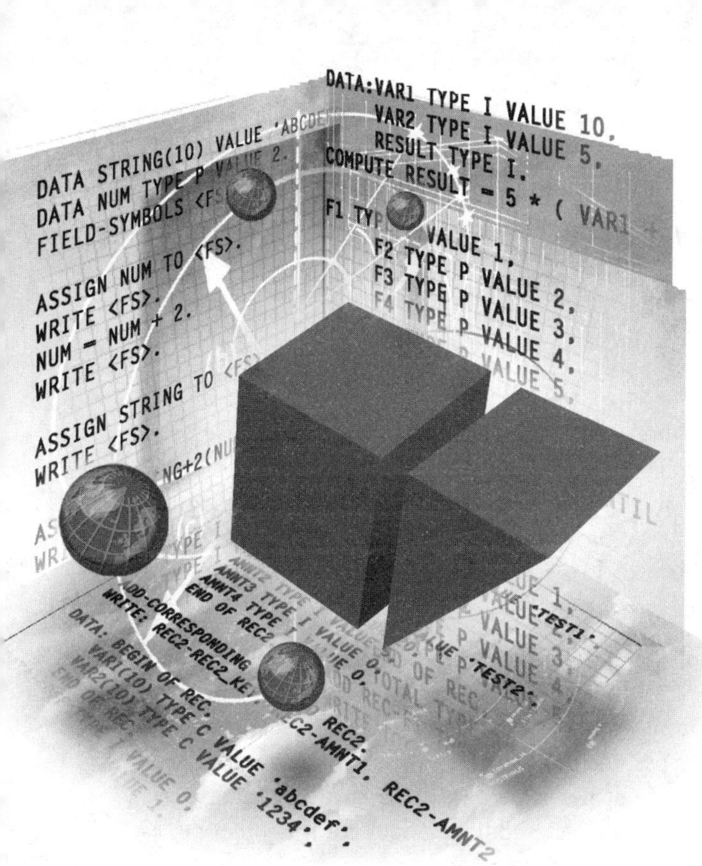

Chapter 7

Working with the Data Dictionary

In This Chapter

- Data and Structure Definitions
- Organizing Your Data
- Data Dictionary Tools

The ABAP/4 developer must acquire several talents to become proficient. The most important is learning how to code in ABAP/4. The second most important is learning how to navigate through all of SAP's tables and data structures. Learning the Data dictionary is very important. A programmer might be able to program an extract, report, or interface, but if the code is accessing data from the wrong place or table type, performance can suffer severely.

Something to realize early on in your ABAP/4 learning experience is that the data from one table is available in several other tables as well. In a typical mainframe environment, the data is available from one place only. In SAP, by accessing smaller tables, or one of the better table types, the programmer can accommodate the needs of the users and create efficient code at the same time. This chapter demonstrates how to find the data you need from the tables and how to look for it in other places besides the very large tables.

The Data dictionary is a very large and important topic. This chapter describes how the Data dictionary is related to coding in ABAP/4. It provides a general overview, with enough technical information to make the reader comfortable and knowledgeable in how to navigate through the millions of records contained in SAP's tables and views. An entire book could be written on how to use the data dictionary. This chapter covers the data dictionary from a programmer's perspective, showing you how to use it effectively only in programming ABAP/4.

Data and Structure Definitions

The importance of knowing SAP terms must be emphasized here because the complexity of the system forces people to work together. In order to work together, everyone needs to be able to speak the same language. Because a team of SAP implementation experts consists of BASIS (system administrators), ABAP/4 programmers, functional analysts, and end users, the importance of communication can't be over emphasized. SAP is a fully integrated system, and in order to implement this system, the teams working together must be fully integrated as well.

Tables

The term *table* usually refers to one of the database tables or relational tables. There are four table types in SAP: *cluster*, *transparent*, and *pool* tables are all *relational tables*. *Internal tables* are defined on two levels. On one level they're local to programs that ABAPers create, and on the second level they represent empty structures used by the system for data manipulation.

A table is a structure that holds data. It consists of one header line and multiple item lines. Table 7-1 shows a blank table that contains no data. (It's shown here just as an example of table structure.)

Table 7-1 A Sample Table Structure

	FIELD1	FIELD2	FIELD3	FIELDX
Header				
Item1				
Item2				
Item3				
Itemx				

The *header line* holds the data that has been currently read by the program. The item lines hold each individual line of data in that data. The data is broken down into fields, which hold data for each related item. Table 7-2 shows an example.

Table 7-2 A Sample Table (INFO) Containing Data

	NAME	CITY	PHONE
Header	BOB	LAS VEGAS	(411) 555-1212
Item1	BOB	LAS VEGAS	(411) 555-1212
Item2	GARETH	NEW YORK	(555) 123-4567

The table called `INFO` contains two records, each with three fields. The fields, `INFO-NAME`, `INFO-CITY`, and `INFO-PHONE`, each contain information for each individual record. In this example, two records exist, one for `BOB`, and another for `GARETH`. Any number of records can exist, but you can't have duplicate records. If you try to add another record with the same data in *`Item1`*, you'll get an error message saying that you're trying to add a duplicate record to the table, which isn't allowed in SAP. This duplicate-records error is applicable to both database and internal tables.

Certain fields are defined as *key fields*. When all these fields are specified, they define a unique record for that table. No two records can have the same key fields. When all the key fields are specified in a SQL call, the read on the table becomes much faster and database access time decreases. All the fields together make up the primary key. When someone refers to reading a table using the primary key, they mean reading the table specifying all of the key fields.

Transparent Tables

A *transparent table* is simply an SAP table that's a real table at the database level.

Pool Tables

Pool tables look like separate tables in SAP, but they're really all one huge table at the database level. So you might have rows from `T001`, `T001W`, and `T023` all mixed together. Part of the key is the table name, so when you want a row from `T001`, it's added to your `where` clause by the system.

Cluster Tables

Cluster tables are no longer used, but a few are left over from previous versions of SAP (Versions 2.2 and earlier). They look like two or more tables in SAP, but at the database level they're really only one. They differ from pool tables in that they're part of a parent-child relationship, like PO Header and PO lines (no longer in 2.1). But there's no real parent table: Every child row duplicates all the parent information, so you don't need to do a join to get parent and child info. It wastes space and is slow to insert data, but very fast for `SELECT`s because no join is done.

In Version 3.1 or 4.0, all tables are transparent tables.

Internal Tables

An *internal table* is a structure defined in the data dictionary that contains no records, or a structure defined inside an ABAP/4 application that initially contains no records. The structure has fields defined, but no data is stored in the table. The programs that use the internal tables populate those tables. Usually, the internal tables are used with function modules or as structures to hold data for input or output to external files. The internal tables defined in the data dictionary are usually predefined to be used with a function module, or as a structure to be filled for a *Batch Data Session* (BDC).

The internal tables defined inside ABAP/4 programs are specified by the programmer and are usually used for data manipulation, sorting, or collecting. Internal tables as a whole don't have primary keys. Searches can be done through these tables (once they are filled) with the `READ` command, which can specify a key. A read on an internal table is generally a sequential search, unless the table is presorted, read by a key, and the search is defined as a binary search. The read then becomes a direct read. All these commands are covered in Chapter 6, "Working with Internal Tables."

Views

Views are transparent tables that have been joined. They have the same properties as transparent tables, but contain much more data, and their primary keys are shared.

Organizing Your Data

The information in the data dictionary is organized in a structured manner. On the top of the structure is the table. Next is the domain, then the data element, and finally the field.

Let's use document numbers as an example to explain how the information is organized. The document numbers themselves would be the domain. A data element might be a sales order number. A particular field might specify the exact sales order for a specific table. By attributing a domain, data element, and field name to each piece of data, SAP has created a very clear picture of where data can be found. Unlike mainframe systems where the data is found in only one place, the data in SAP usually resides in several different tables. By searching the tables by domain or by data element, you can find common fields across multiple tables.

Domains

A *domain* is an object used to describe the type of field in which the data is stored. Examples of domains could be document numbers, short texts, dates, or markers. An analogous example in the real world might be the domains `cars`, `boats`, or `trains`. As you progress down the structure, the descriptions of the data and the fields become more and more specific.

Data Elements

A *data element* is a more specific description of what resides inside the domain. The example of document numbers, short texts, dates, and markers would focus down to invoice numbers, shipping text, billing dates, and timing data, respectively. In regard to the real world example, the data elements associated with cars would break down to Ford, Jeep, Toyota, and Porsche and so on. Again, as you progress down the tree, the descriptions become more and more specific.

Data elements are very important in that they're specific enough to search tables for certain fields, but general enough to still find the data across all the tables. If you searched by domain, you would find that your search results would be much too general to mean anything, and if you searched by field, they would be too specific and the data wouldn't be constant across tables. Fields will have different field names across different tables; however, data elements and domain names will be the same if the same data is contained in that space.

Fields

Fields are the base description of where data resides. The notation for a field is usually preceded by the table to which it belongs. An example would be the billing document header table, `BKPF`. If you were to look at one of the key fields, you would find that invoice numbers, or `VBELN`, would be one of the primary fields in this table. The notation for this field would be `BKPF-VBELN`. The name `VBELN` is specific to this table. In another table, a field with the same data might be called `VBELN_VAUF`. However, the data element for both fields would be the same, as would the domain name. Using the car example, the field name would be the models of cars for that manufacturer. An example for Ford would be *`trucks`* and *`sedans`*.

Data Dictionary Tools

This section describes several of the transactions that you can use to search for data and check the integrity of data.

General Table Display (SE16 and SE17)

General Table Display is one of the main utilities that helps you find actual data in the database. The purpose of this transaction is to display the data from a selected table. By using this utility, the programmer is able to compare the data that the program has read from the tables with the actual data in the tables to see whether his selection criteria are correct.

To access the General Table Display utility, enter **/nse17** in the command box in the top left corner of the screen. The menu path is Tools | Application | Development | Overview | Data Browser. The screen that appears has an input field for the name of a table or view (see Figure 7-1).

Type the table name in the box and then press Enter or click the green check mark next to the command line to display the specified table (see Figure 7-2).

A list of fields appears down the left column of the screen. The boxes enclose the descriptions of each field. Next to each field is a blank input box for data selection. Next to that column is a one-character entry box. This box marks fields that will be displayed when the transaction is executed. The keyed fields have an `X` already in that box. Next to that is another box for input, which is also blank. This box is the *sorting*

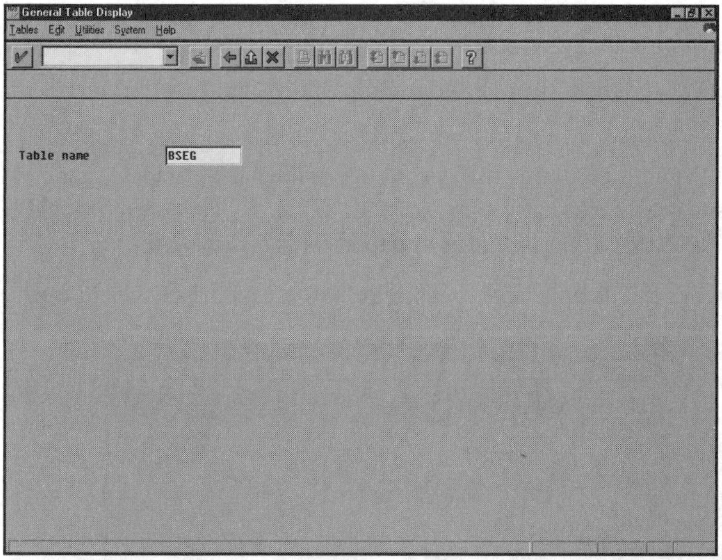

FIGURE 7-1

The initial screen of the General Table Display

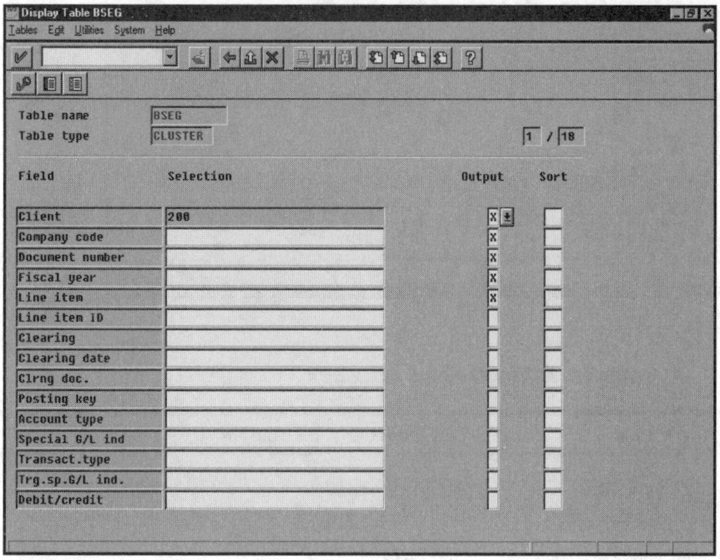

FIGURE 7-2

In this screen, you specify the table or view you want to see.

book. Three buttons appear at the top of the screen, marked Execute, Choose All, and Delete Selection.

The fields containing an `X` are the fields that will be displayed once the Execute button is clicked.

The second box, used to specify criteria for data selection, is probably the most important box on the screen. If the Execute button is clicked with nothing in any of the data selection boxes, the database will get the first 100 records from that table and print the fields on-screen that were already marked with an `X` (see Figure 7-3). If one field is specified, then all the records will be returned that match that field's specification.

Not only would a search of this magnitude hinder the database, but it would be worthless in regard to what you would want to see. A better search would limit one of the fields so that a small number of data records is displayed.

Use Table 7-3 as a sample table to illustrate how a data display would work.

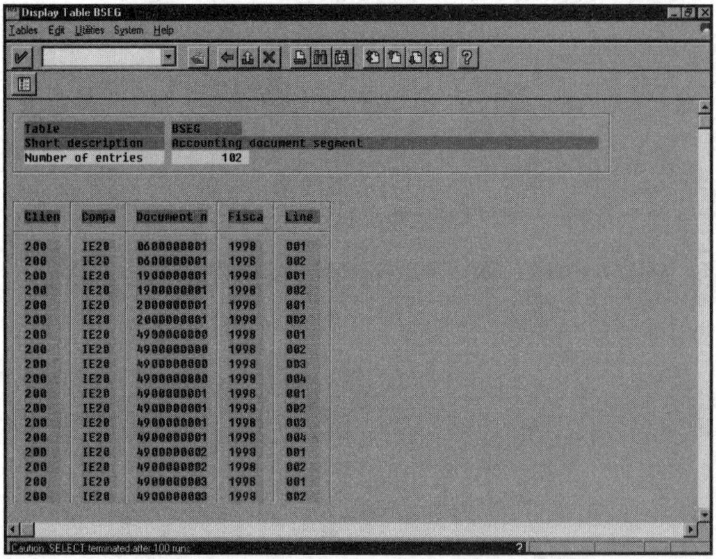

FIGURE 7-3

The output of table BSEG

Table 7-3 A Sample Table Called ROLODEX

NAME	CITY	TELEPHONE NUMBER
Bob	New York	(303) 555-1212
Gayle	San Francisco	(415) 555-1212
Kathleen	New York	(303) 411-5555
Jim	New York	(303) 555-1234
Susan	Rocklin	(916) 411-5678

On the `SE16` or General Table Display screen for the `ROLODEX` table, the following output would be displayed:

```
NAME                                X
CITY                                X
PHONE
```

If you wanted to display all the people who lived in New York, you would enter **New York** in the second column adjacent to the `CITY` field:

```
NAME                                X
CITY          New York              X
PHONE
```

The output from execution with this data selection criteria would be as follows:

```
Bob           New York
Kathleen      New York
Jim           New York
```

Notice that only the name and the city are output to the screen. In the initial selection screen, no `X` appears next to the `PHONE` field. If you click the green arrow button (Back) and put an `X` in the `PHONE` row, the phone numbers will also be listed.

A special ability of the second column is that you can use conditional operators along with the values. If you just enter a value in that box, the database assumes the "equal to" operator. You can also use other operators, as indicated in Table 7-4.

Table 7-4 Conditional Operators You Can Use with the General Table Display Utility

Conditional Operator	Syntax
Greater than	>
Less than	<
Greater than or equal to	>=, =>
Less than or equal to	<=, =<
Not equal to	<>, ><

All of these operators are used in the same context as with the `IF` statement described in Chapter 4, "Using Conditional Operators."

In version 3.0, SAP replaced the old `se16` transaction with a new version. The old `se16` transaction is the `se17` transaction just described. The new and improved `se16` command allows for a little more flexibility when searching directly through database tables. The initial screen is still the same as shown in Figure 7-4.

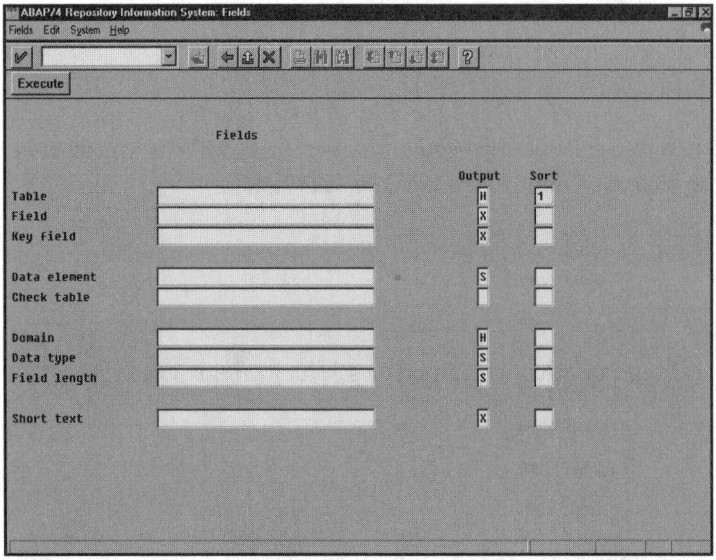

FIGURE 7-4

The Initial Screen of the 'se16' transaction

After entering the table name, **BSEG** in this case, hit the enter key or click the green check mark. This action brings us to the second screen where a selection screen is displayed. Each field in the table has a select-options range next to it. Values can be entered into these ranges in the format that is described in Chapter 1. The se17 command's options (the old se16 command) were a little cryptic as described above in the previous section. The new commands may appeal more to new users of SAP as they are more intuitive. As shown in Figure 7-5, you see that the width of the output list can now be set, as well as the maximum number of hits against the database.

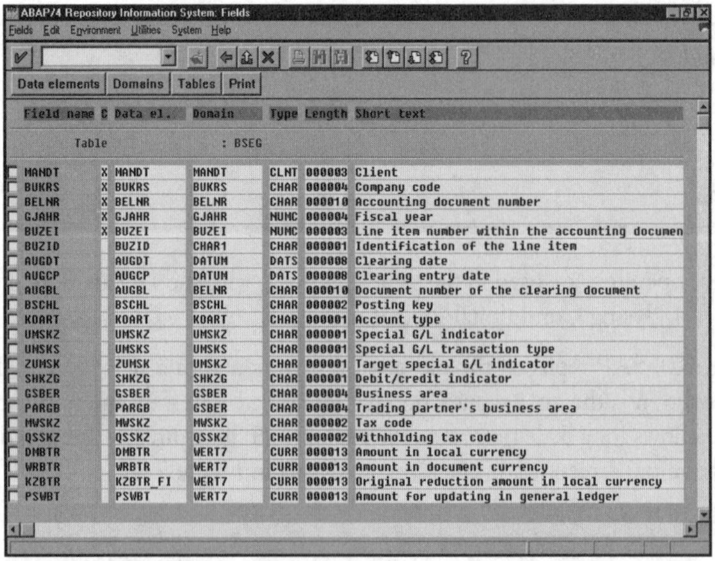

FIGURE 7-5

Table Selection Screen for transaction 'se16'

The fields represented by select-options can be chosen by the user. If you follow the menu path Settings | Fields for selection as shown in Figure 7-6, SAP brings up a list of fields with check boxes beside them, as shown in Figure 7-7.

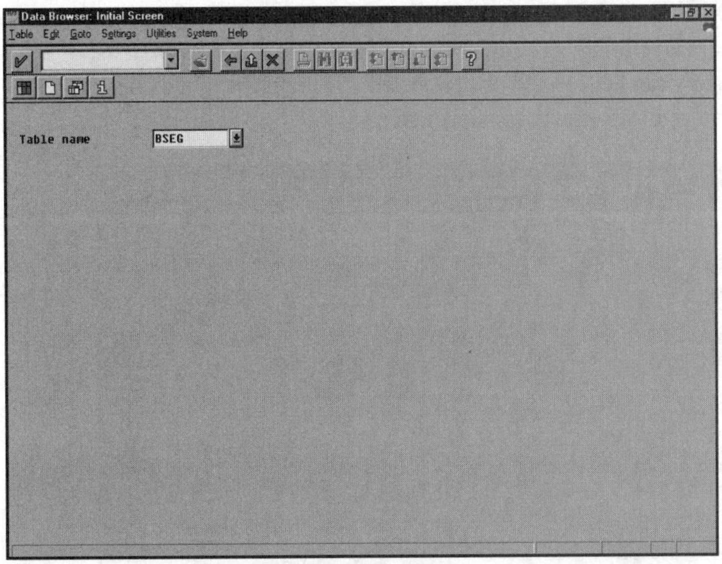

FIGURE 7-6

Menu path to select fields displayed

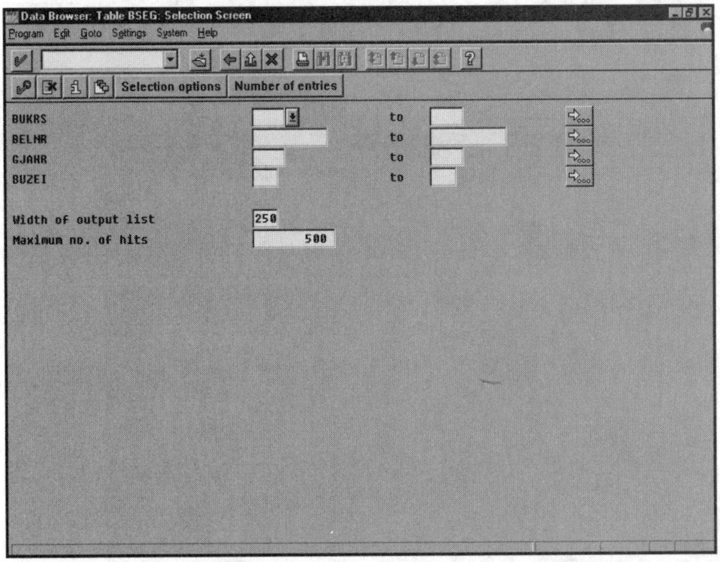

FIGURE 7-7

Selection screen for fields to be displayed transaction

Click on the fields you wish to select against, and then click on the green check button in the left corner. This action brings us back to our original screen shown in

Figure 7-5. Enter your specifications for the table, and then execute. A list of the data from the table is returned to the screen as shown in Figure 7-8.

Now, the output fields can also be specified and can be different from the input specifications. Follow the menu path shown in Figure 7-9, Settings | List Format | Choose fields to bring up a screen shown in Figure 7-10. Again a list of fields appears of which any can be selected or deselected. Click on the green check mark to exit this screen and return to the data output screen.

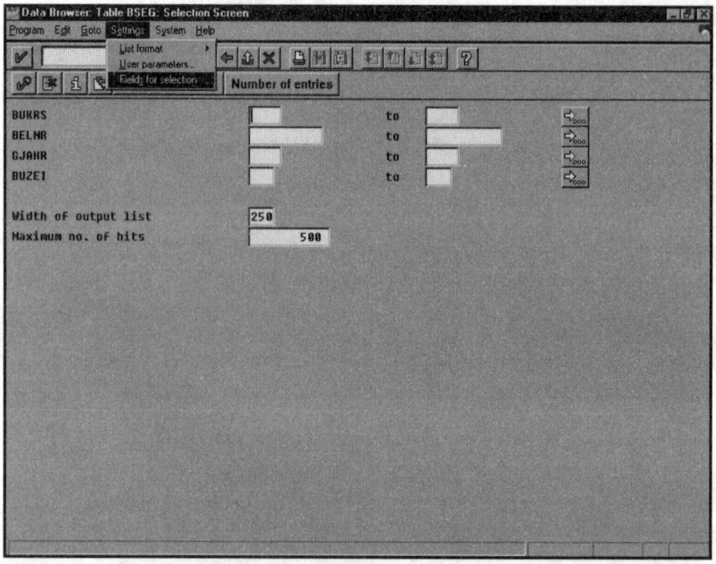

FIGURE 7-8

Output of general table display transaction

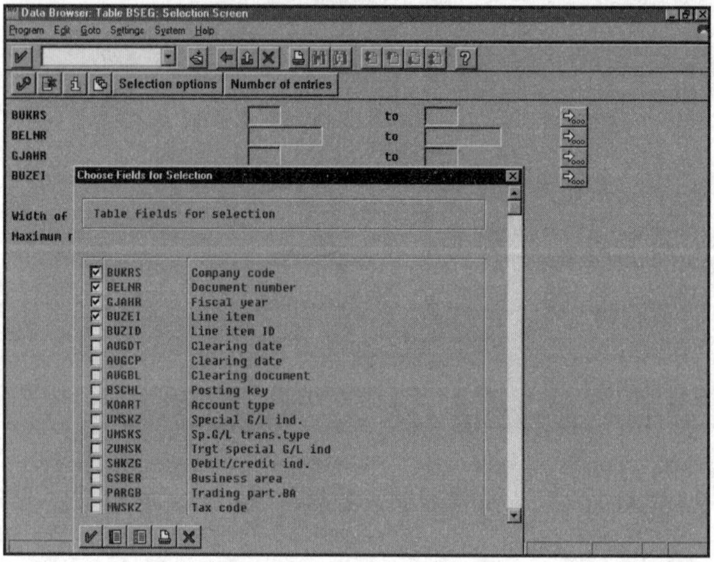

FIGURE 7-9

Menu path to change fields to be displayed

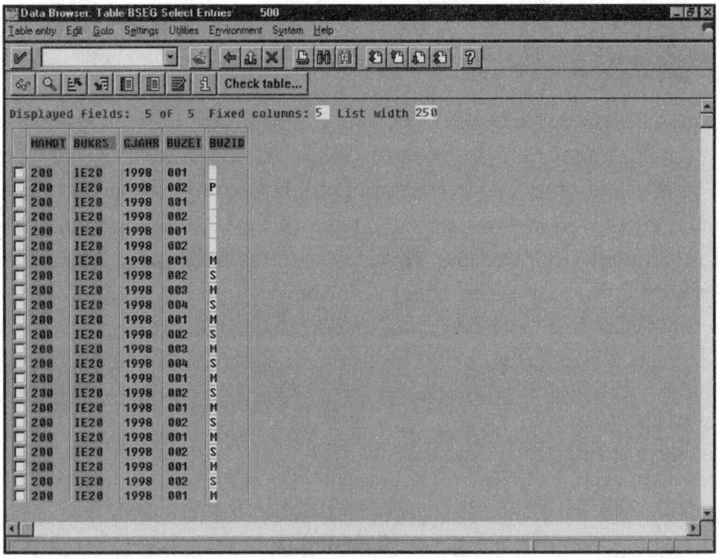

FIGURE 7-10

Selection screen for fields to be displayed

By double-clicking on a line in the output list, a screen displaying all the values of that record appears in the next screen. This output is displayed in Figure 7-11. This is a useful screen to look for individual data per record. Notice that in the initial selection screen and this last screen, that the fields have been displayed as field names, which are a bit cryptic. SAP allows you to change the display to show the field descriptions rather than following the menu path, Settings | User Settings. Select descriptions rather than field names to display the tables in a format that is easier to understand.

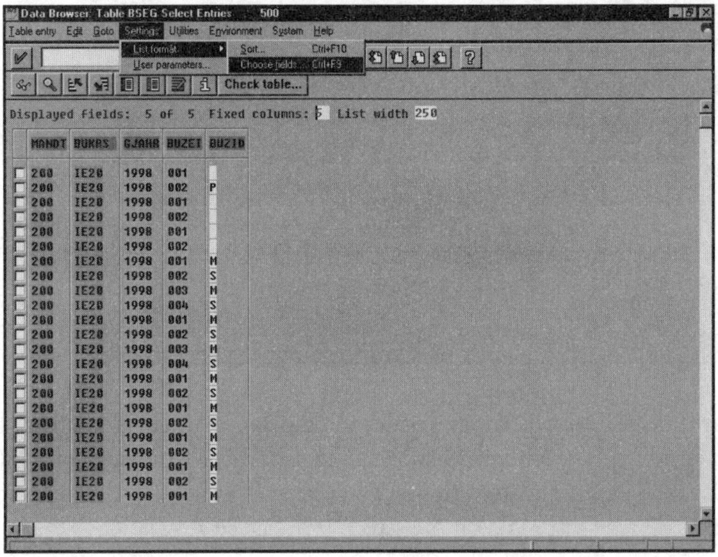

FIGURE 7-11

Display of one record after double-clicking an output record from general table display

Displaying Fields, Data Elements, and Domains (SE15 and DI03)

A useful data dictionary tool of the information systems feature is searching for tables with a certain field, data element, or domain. Certain fields exist in several tables, as do data elements and domains. If a certain field in the program specification is from a table that's generally known to be a large table, or a table that's hard to access, you'll want to find another table that has the same field with the same data, but which is easier to read. A good example of this instance is with the table `BSEG`. Besides being a very large table, it's a cluster table, and the database takes a long time to find the data in the table. A smaller table that holds much of the data in `BSEG`, but is a transparent table and therefore faster to read is `BSIS`. (In writing programs, the access time must be reduced in order to increase overall performance.)

How would you find `BSIS` if you didn't have past experience with that table? This section deals explicitly with that challenge. The data dictionary's *Information System* enables you to search for tables, fields, data elements, domains, and text throughout SAP's tables. To get to the screen, you can use the menu path Tools | Case | Data Dictionary | Display, or enter the fast transactions `SE15` or `DI03` (see Figure 7-12).

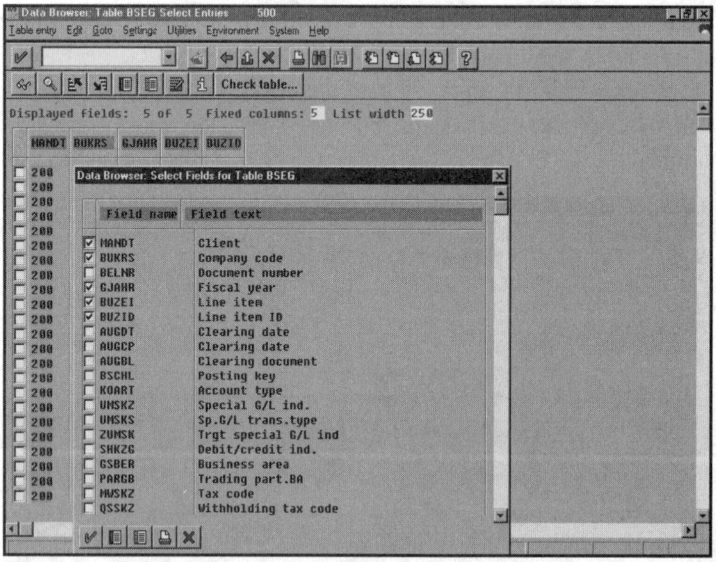

FIGURE 7-12

In this screen, you can specify the fields you want to see.

Let us use the `BSEG` example as our model. To find another field in another table that holds the same data as a field in `BSEG`, you must first display the fields in `BSEG`. Enter `BSEG` in the table line of the `DI03` transaction screen and click the Execute button. All of the fields are now displayed on the screen (see Figure 7-12).

On the screen, find the field you want and look for its corresponding data element. Write down the data element on a piece of paper. Click the green arrow key to go back one screen. Erase `BSEG` from the table line and type the data element of the desired field on the data element line. Now click Execute again. A list of tables comes up, along with the fields that are associated with that data element. Data elements always correspond to the same data, so any of the tables that appear will hold the same data as `BSEG` for that particular field. For example, if a data element is the same for two tables, the same data for that field will exist in those two tables.

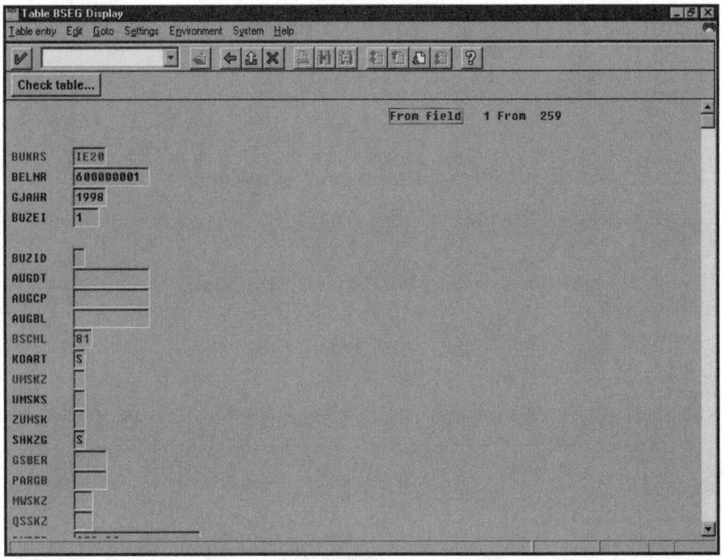

FIGURE 7-13

Here the screen displays the contents of the specified fields.

Now, you must only go through that list of tables and find the small transparent table that will make your program run at optimum speed. Searches can be done in the same way, looking for table names that use specific field names, domains, or text.

NOTE

Text is always a very long and tedious search and should be avoided if possible. Sometimes there's no choice, however, so do what you need to do to get the data for the client.

Summary

This chapter dealt with the definitions of what makes up the data structures of the database, and explanations of the tools used to search through that data. It's very important that you understand the difference between pool, cluster, transparent, and internal tables. The information system and general table display were discussed in this chapter; these tools and definitions are central to your understanding of SAP before you begin programming. I strongly recommend that you become familiar with them before proceeding with any further education in development.

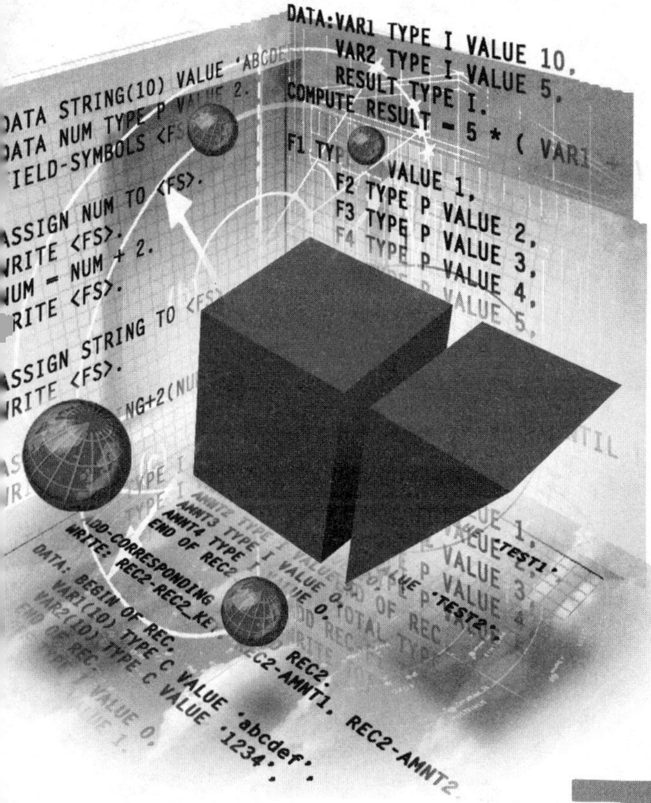

PART II

Accessing the Database

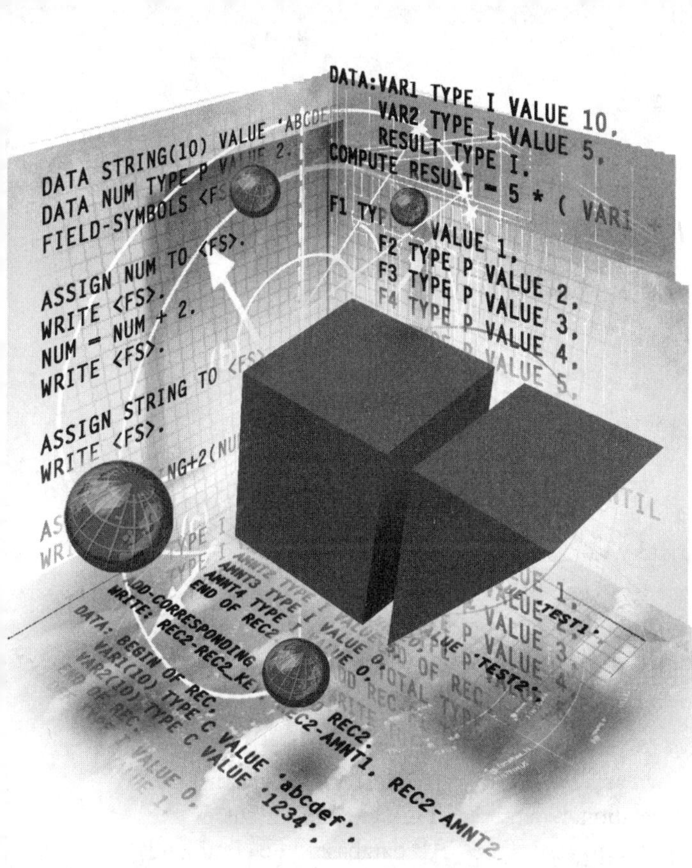

Chapter 8

Using SAP SQL to Access Database Tables

In This Chapter

- Using SQL to Access Tables and Views
- Using SQL with Transactions
- Reading Data from the Database (SELECT)
- Updating Tables (UPDATE)
- Inserting Data (INSERT)
- Deleting Rows (DELETE)
- Advanced Techniques in R/3 v3.x

The primary reason that Enterprise Resource Planning systems like SAP exist is to track and manipulate data. Like most modern client-server systems, SAP stores this data in a relational database. In order to write any practical ABAP/4 program, you must access this database.

One of the most important ways to read or manipulate the database is through *Structured Query Language*, also known as SQL. SQL is an industry standard that can be used to access any compliant relational database. This chapter discusses the ABAP/4 version of SQL, which is used to access the SAP database. The command set of SAP SQL is a limited subset of the standard version of SQL. Even if you already know SQL, it's important to become familiar with SAP's flavor of SQL because of its many limitations. With the introduction of version 3.0 of R/3 a number of enhancements were made to SAP SQL. These enhancements are discussed in the last section of this chapter.

NOTE

In this chapter, the term SQL refers to SAP SQL.

Although SAP SQL is a central topic in ABAP/4 programming because it accesses the data that SAP exists to track and manipulate, it comprises only four commands:

- `SELECT` reads data from a table or view.
- `UPDATE` changes data in a table.
- `INSERT` adds a new row of data to the table.
- `DELETE` removes a row or rows of data from a table.

Because `SELECT` is used on both `SAP` and user-created tables, it's the most important and useful of the commands, and I'll cover it first, followed by `UPDATE`, `INSERT`, and `DELETE`.

Using SQL to Access Tables and Views

As explained in Chapter 7, "Working with the Data Dictionary," a relational database is composed of many tables, each of which holds a specific set of data. A table is a physical object found in the database. The data in these tables can be thought of as a matrix of values. In a table of part data, for example, individual fields containing data such as part numbers and part descriptions make up the columns of the matrix, while individual entries such as the entry for a steel bolt make up a row of the matrix.

SQL allows a programmer to read rows, insert new rows, or change existing rows of data. In addition to tables, SAP supports *views*, which are a logical—not physical—set of data. In general, views combine data from several tables into a single logical object. For example, SAP uses one table for material data and another table to contain the description of the material. This setup allows a single type of material to have descriptions in multiple languages—English, French, and German, for example. You could create a view in the database to combine the material table and description table into a single view in which all of the information could be accessed together. Because a view is only a logical object, however, you can read but not change or add to the data in the view. To add a new part or change the English description, you must access the separate physical tables that provide the information for the view.

Note that views and tables appear identical to the programmer; they're both objects in the database.

Using SQL with Transactions

A major difference between the SAP database and generic relational databases is the fact that SAP provides thousands of built-in tables designed to support the SAP application. In addition to these SAP tables, users can create their own tables through the data dictionary.

The SAP application is composed of thousands of transactions; these transactions can be called from an ABAP/4 program in order to change data in SAP tables. However, although SQL can be used to *read* data from both SAP and *user-created* tables, it should be used to change or insert data only in user-created tables, not SAP tables. The SAP tables support the SAP application. In general, a program shouldn't be manipulating data in SAP tables by using SQL. In some special cases, SQL is used to make small changes to data in SAP tables, but this should be done only by programmers experienced not only in ABAP/4 but also in the details of the SAP application—those who know the impact these changes will have in SAP.

For example, suppose that you want to write a program to change the stock-on-hand quantity of a material. This quantity is stored in the SAP table `MARD`. You could use SQL to simply go in and change the quantity field in the table. But don't forget that SAP is an integrated package of financial, manufacturing, and human resources applications. If the quantity of a material has increased, it must have been purchased from a vendor. And if it was purchased from a vendor, there must be an invoice for payment. Accounts need to be credited and debited. The simple act of receiving new material can have a cascade effect throughout SAP. Simply using SQL to increase a single field in a single table isn't enough.

Now, if the program had called transaction `FB02`, material receipt, this transaction would have taken care of all the possible effects of receiving material. (Calling SAP transactions is discussed in Chapter 16, "Writing a BDC Session.") So it's important to remember only to *read* data from SAP tables.

Reading Data from the Database (SELECT)

Reading information from the database is probably the most common activity in ABAP/4. It's done in reports to extract the data to be formatted, interfaces to send data to external systems, and interactive programs to provide information to users. Because it's so common and can take up so much processing time, knowing the `SELECT` command backward and forward may be the most fundamental skill in ABAP/4 programming. In this first section, the basic form of the `SELECT` command is described. The basic form is compatible with versions 2.0–3.1 of R/3. Later in the chapter you will explore the more advanced techniques introduced in version 3.0 of R/3.

Here's the basic form:

```
SELECT * FROM tab [WHERE condition].
...
ENDSELECT.
```

`SELECT` is a looping command, as you can see by the presence of the `ENDSELECT` command. When a `SELECT` is issued against a table, it returns all rows of data contained in that table, one at a time. So the first row returned is available for processing during the first pass of the loop. The second row is available during the second pass of the loop, and so on, until all rows have been read from the table. If no data is found, the code within the `SELECT` loop won't be executed.

Now for an example of the SELECT command in action. This piece of code reads from table T001, which contains information on Company Codes, the smallest business unit in SAP for the purposes of external reporting. The company codes will be read and printed along with a description:

```
TABLES T001.      "Company Code

SELECT * FROM T001.    "Get all fields from T001

WRITE:  /, T001-BUKRS.  "Company Code
WRITE T001-BUTXT.   "Company Code Name

ENDSELECT.
```

A fictional company call Acme Tools might produce the following output for the preceding piece of code:

```
0100 Corporate
0200 Acme North America
0400 Acme Asia
0300 Acme Europe
```

The T001 table has many more fields than just BUKRS and BUTXT, and any of those fields could be used in the SELECT loop. SAP returns all data in the table; it's up to the programmer to decided which fields to use. Notice that the rows aren't returned in any particular order. Unlike standard SQL, SAP SQL doesn't allow the programmer to specify which fields of a table are returned by the SELECT statement. The command always returns *all* fields in a table. When the data is returned, it also isn't returned in any predictable order. (There is an option for processing the data in a certain order, which is discussed in the section titled "Using WHERE with ORDER BY".)

The return code SY-SUBRC tells you whether data has been returned. If one or more rows of data are returned to the SELECT loop, SY-SUBRC will be equal to 0 after the ENDSELECT command has executed. If no rows are returned and the loop isn't executed, SY-SUBRC will be set to 4.

When data is returned, it's available through the table work area. Thus, the fields can be used through the *table-field* notation, just like an internal table or record variable. Don't forget that all tables must be declared via the TABLES command before they're used in your program. (See Chapter 7 for more information about the TABLES command.)

Also, remember that each row is available for only one pass of the SELECT loop, so be prepared to store data in variables or internal tables if it will be needed later.

Using WHERE to Limit the Data Returned with SELECT

The basic SELECT command reads all data contained in a table and returns it to the program. But this isn't always what you want the program to do. A table can contain tens of thousands of rows of data. The program may be interested in only a tiny subset of that data. The question is, how do you limit the amount of data to only what you need? The mechanism used to do this in SQL is the where clause. The where clause allows the program to specify which rows of data are to be returned by the SELECT command.

In the earlier example for Acme Tools, the code printed all company codes. But what if the requirements had specified that the code for Corporate, 0100, was not to be printed? You could use the IF command to prevent display of Corporate if you know that the code for Corporate is 0100:

```
TABLES T001.        "Company Code

SELECT * FROM T001.    "Get all fields from T001

IF T001-BUKRS > '0100'.    "Don't Print Corp
  WRITE:  /, T001-BUKRS.  "Company Code
  WRITE T001-BUTXT.  "Company Code Name
ENDIF.

ENDSELECT.
```

Using IF would prevent code 0100 from being printed, so the program would be correct. But it wouldn't be efficient.

It's critical to remember that reading data from the database is very time consuming. Everything should be done to minimize the amount of data being read. In this case, you read a row of data, the Corporate code, which you know you aren't going to use. So instead of using an IF statement to exclude this data after reading it from the database, use a *where* clause to prevent it from being read in the first place. Using a *where* clause, the Acme Tools code would look like this:

```
TABLES T001.     "Company Code

SELECT * FROM T001 WHERE BUKRS > '0100'.

WRITE:  /, T001-BUKRS.  "Company Code
WRITE T001-BUTXT.  "Company Code Name

ENDSELECT.
```

Here's the output:

```
0200 Acme North America
0400 Acme Asia
0300 Acme Europe
```

In this case, the *where* clause tells SAP to go out to the `T001` table and return all rows of data where the field `BUKRS` is greater than `0100`; thus, the Corporate row is never returned to the program and won't be written out.

Preventing a single row from being read from the database won't speed up a program by any measurable degree, obviously, but it's easy to imagine another scenario. A second program might read and summarize thousands of financial transactions for the three Acme companies. If the *where* clause is used to exclude the thousands of transactions with a company code for Corporate, a significant performance boost would be seen.

Using Operators with WHERE

There are several ways that the condition of the `WHERE` clause can be assembled. Here's one:

```
WHERE field operator var.
```

When specifying a field in the *where* clause, the field name is used alone—you don't use the *table-field* format used in other statements. The operators available for use are the same ones seen in the `IF` statements (see Table 8-1). Either the abbreviated form or the symbol can be used but I recommend that you choose one form and stick to it to improve readability.

Table 8-1 Operators for the where Clause

Abbreviation	Symbol	Description
EQ	=	Equal to
NE	<>, ><	Not equal to
GT	>	Greater than
GE	>=	Greater than or equal to
LT	<	Less than
LE	<=	Less than or equal to

(Using AND and OR with WHERE

Here's another version of the `where` syntax:

```
WHERE condition1 AND condition2 ... AND conditionN.
```

For a row to be selected in this version, all the conditions in the list must be true. These individual conditions can include any of the options listed here. The `AND` operator can be combined with the `OR` operator, in which case the list is evaluated from left to right (unless parentheses are used).

Here's a version with `OR`:

```
WHERE condition1 OR condition2 ... OR conditionN.
```

In this version, for a row to be selected any one of the conditions in the list must be true. These individual conditions can any of the options listed here, but the database field involved in all conditions must be the same. For example, the statement

```
SELECT * FROM T001 WHERE BUKRS > '0100' OR BUKRS = '0000'.
```

is legal because the database field involved in both conditions is ***BUKRS***. But this next example would raise a syntax error:

```
SELECT * FROM T001 WHERE BUKRS BETWEEN '0000' AND '0500'
OR BUTXT <> 'CORPORATE'.
```

Because `BUKRS` is the field used in the first condition and `BUTXT` is used in the second, this statement wouldn't work.

The `OR` operator can be combined with `AND` in forming a `where` clause as long as those in the `OR` conditions are proper, as just discussed. The database fields used in the `AND` conditions aren't subject to any restrictions.

Using NOT with WHERE

The following syntax line shows how you can use NOT with WHERE:

```
WHERE field [NOT] BETWEEN var1 AND var2.
```

This condition is true if the contents of *field* are greater than or equal to *var1* and less than or equal to the contents of *var2*—unless modified by the NOT, in which case the opposite is true.

> **NOTE**
>
> The AND in this example is part of the BETWEEN operator and shouldn't be confused with the AND operator.

Another option for NOT:

```
WHERE field [NOT] IN (var1,var2,...,varN).
```

The condition is true if the value of *field* is equal to any of the variables in the list—unless modified by the NOT, in which case the opposite is true.

Now try this one:

```
WHERE field [NOT] LIKE string.
```

This operator allows you to compare a portion of the field to a character string. The string may contain wild-card characters for the comparison. The underscore (_) is a wild card that can stand for any single character. The percent sign (%) is a wild card that stands for any group of characters. These two wild cards can be used in the string in any combination. For example:

```
SELECT * FROM T001 WHERE BUTXT LIKE '%AMERICA'
                                             OR  BUTXT LIKE
'ADVANCED%MANUFACTURING'.
```

The first condition would be true for any company with a name ending in AMERICA—thus, NORTH AMERICA and SOUTH AMERICA would be selected, but CORPORATE wouldn't. The second condition would be true for any company with a name starting with ADVANCED and ending in MANUFACTURING—thus, ADVANCED FLIGHT MANUFACTURING would be selected, but CENTRAL MANUFACTURING wouldn't.

Here's one last version. Check it out:

```
WHERE field [NOT] IN sel.
```

The condition is true if the value of the field passes the conditions in the select-option or range `sel`. A *select-option* is a variable type covered in Chapter 1, "Data Types and Definitions." It's a parameter that allows the user to enter a set of one or more conditions at runtime. A *range* is also a variable type, but the programmer must populate it with a set of one or more conditions. These conditions, which act identically regardless of which of the two variable types is used, can be an inclusive or exclusive list, range, or single value. Basically, anything a programmer could define in a `where` clause, the user or programmer can specify in a single range or select-option. See Chapter 1 for more details on select-options and ranges.

NOTE

To work properly, the select-option or range should be defined for a database field with the same data type as *`field`*.

WHERE Clause Examples

Next, some examples of using a `WHERE` clause.

This first example demonstrates the use of several common operators such as equal, greater than, and less than. The table being read, `EKPO`, contains information on purchase orders:

```
SELECT * FROM EKPO WHERE EBELN > '0005000000'
                         AND WERKS = 'P002'
                         AND AEDAT < '19961201'.
```

In the next example, the `SELECT` statement reads from `EKPO` and uses `IN` and `BETWEEN` to restrict the rows returned. Notice that the first `IN` operator is a list and the second `IN` operator uses a `SELECT-OPTION`. In the case of the `IN` select-option, the user can enter as many conditions as needed and the programmer doesn't need to write any code to process it. The system evaluates the select-option and returns only those rows that meet the criteria entered by the user:

```
SELECT-OPTIONS S_AEDAT FOR EKPO-AEDAT.


SELECT * FROM EKPO WHERE EBELN BETWEEN '0005000000' AND '0005500000'
                         AND WERKS IN ('P002', 'P003', 'P005', 'P008')
                         AND AEDAT IN S_AEDAT.
```

The following example uses parentheses and the `OR` operator to limit the rows returned. This could have been done instead with the `IN` operator. Because of the limitation of the OR operator that the fields in the OR must be identical, OR and IN have the same effect in this case:

```
SELECT * FROM EKPO WHERE ( EBELN = '0005000000'
                         OR '0005000001'
                         OR '0005000002' )
                         AND WERKS = 'P002'
                         AND AEDAT < '19961201'.
```

Using the IN operator, this SELECT could be rewritten as follows:

```
SELECT * FROM EKPO WHERE EBELN IN ('0005000000', '0005000001', '0005000002')
                         AND WERKS = 'P002'
                         AND AEDAT < '19961201'.
```

Options for the SELECT Command

The SELECT command has several options that you can use to modify the SELECT behavior, as described in the following sections.

Inserting Records into an Internal Table (INTO TABLE)

When the INTO TABLE option is used, no ENDSELECT is required because all rows are inserted into the internal table specified by the programmer. Any data already in the internal table is lost. Here's the syntax:

```
SELECT * FROM tab INTO TABLE itab.
```

CAUTION

To avoid unpredictable results, make sure that the internal table you specify has the same structure as the database table from which you're selecting.

Appending Selected Records to a Table (APPENDING TABLE)

When the APPENDING TABLE option is used, no ENDSELECT is required because all rows are appended into the internal table specified by the programmer. In this case, any data already in the internal table is saved. Otherwise it's identical to using INTO TABLE. Here's how you use APPENDING TABLE:

```
SELECT * FROM tab APPENDING TABLE itab.
```

Selecting a Single Row (SELECT SINGLE)

You can use the `SELECT SINGLE` option when you want a single row of data. No `ENDSELECT` is needed because only one row is returned:

```
SELECT SINGLE * FROM tab WHERE where clause.
```

This is a very fast way to return a single row of data—for example, if you have a part number and want to look up the description for that single part.

In order to specify a single row, the `where` clause must include all the key fields. As discussed in Chapter 7, the primary key is the field or group of fields that uniquely identify all rows in a table. So if all key fields are in the `where` clause, only one row is returned. For example, if a table uses a key of *name* and *id*, the `where` clause would have to be `WHERE NAME = 'SMITH' AND ID = '19943'`. This would return only one row of data because only one row in the table has the combination of `SMITH` and `19943`. A syntax error is raised if the `where` clause doesn't contain all key fields in version 2.x of ABAP/4.

If you know that only one row of data will always be returned, use this option to improve performance over a `SELECT` loop.

Using ORDER BY to Sort Data

You can add `ORDER BY` to any of the other options except the `SELECT SINGLE` option. Using `ORDER BY` returns the results of a `SELECT` loop or fills the specified internal table in ascending order. The order can be determined by any field; if a table has a `LASTNAME` field, `ORDER BY LASTNAME` will return rows to the `SELECT` loop starting with `ADAMS`, `BORNE`, `DWELL`, and so on.

Use the following format:

```
SELECT * FROM tab [WHERE where clause] ORDER BY field1 field2 ... fieldn.
```

The following version returns the results of a `SELECT` loop or fills the specified internal table in ascending order by the primary key of the table. If the primary key consists of more than one field, then they're ordered left to right:

```
SELECT * FROM tab [WHERE where clause] ORDER BY PRIMARY KEY.
```

SELECT Examples

The following are several examples of the different options for use with the `SELECT` command.

The first example demonstrates the `INTO TABLE` option by selecting a set of rows out of the table `BSEG` (Financial Documents) and inserting it into an internal table in order by the field `AUGDAT`, a date field:

```
DATA BEGIN OF INT_BSEG OCCURS 1000.
       INCLUDE STRUCTURE BSEG.   "Duplicate the table BSEG
DATA END OF INT_BSEG.

SELECT * FROM BSEG WHERE BUKRS = 'SEUR'  "Company Code
                   AND GJAHR = '1995'  "Document Year
                  INTO TABLE INT_BSEG
                  ORDER BY AUGDAT.

    Notice no ENDSELECT is needed when using INTO TABLE
```

The next example demonstrates the use of `SELECT SINGLE`. The table being read is `MARD`, which stores information on the inventory quantities of materials. The key fields for this table are `MATNR` (material number), `WERKS` (plant), and `LGORT` (storage location). Remember that to use `SELECT SINGLE`, the entire key must be specified, so in this example parameters are defined and the `SELECT` uses them to look up a quantity and output it:

```
PARAMETERS:  P_MATNR LIKE MARD-MATNR,
P_WERKS LIKE MARD-WERKS,
P_LGORT LIKE MARD-LGORT.

SELECT SINGLE * WHERE MATNR = P_MATNR
                 AND WERKS = P_WERKS
                 AND LGORT = P_LGORT.

***Once again an ENDSELECT is not required
***because only one row will be returned
IF SY-SUBRC = 0.  "Only output if select succeeds
  WRITE:  'Quantity on hand is', MARD-LABST.
ELSE.
  WRITE 'Material does not exist at plant/location given.'.
ENDIF.
```

Updating Tables (UPDATE)

The UPDATE command in SAP SQL enables the programmer to change data within a database table. As stated earlier, this command isn't normally used to change data in SAP tables—only in user-defined tables. For the appropriate tables, this is a common activity. User tables often contain information that indicates when certain events occurred or will occur in the future.

The syntax for the UPDATE command comes in two different versions:

```
UPDATE tab [SET field1 = [field1 + ]var1 ... fieldN = [fieldN + ]varN]
        [WHERE condition].

UPDATE tab [FROM TABLE itab].
```

Using SET with UPDATE

In the first version of UPDATE, the SET option tells the system which of the fields to change. The where clause limits the rows to be changed, just like a where clause in a select statement limits the rows being read.

For example, suppose that you have a user table called ZJOB_LOG with a key field called Job_Id and these values:

Job_Id	Start	Doc#
WEEKLYGL	06/01/96	0054001000
AREXT	06/08/96	0073000500
APIMP	07/01/96	0030100000

The following statement is issued:

```
UPDATE ZJOB_LOG SET START = '08011996' DOC# = DOC# + 100.
```

The table would now contain these values:

Job_Id	Start	Doc#
WEEKLYGL	08/01/96	0054001100
AREXT	08/01/96	0073000600
APIMP	08/01/96	0030100100

Notice that the statement affected all rows. In the `Start` field, all rows were set to a constant value. The field `Doc#`, on the other hand, changed based on an equation.

This next statement demonstrates the effect of a `where` clause:

```
UPDATE ZJOB_LOG SET START = '12311999' WHERE JOB_ID = 'APIMP'.
```

The table would now contain these values:

Job_Id	Start	Doc#
WEEKLYGL	08/01/96	0054001100
AREXT	08/01/96	0073000600
APIMP	12/31/99	0030100100

Notice that only one row was affected by this statement because only one row met the requirements of the `where` clause.

It's also possible to issue an `UPDATE` without a `SET` or `WHERE` option:

```
UPDATE tab [FROM TABLE itab].
```

Remember this syntax line from a few paragraphs ago? In this case, the system looks at the values in the work area for the table and tries to find a row in the database that matches the values in the primary key field(s) of the work area. If found, it updates all fields in the table with the data in the work area. For example, suppose that a program needs to process 100 financial records every week and the table called `ZJOB_LOG` exists to keep track of the next time this job needs to run and the next document in the list to be processed. The following code updates this table with the correct information:

```
TABLES ZJOB_LOG    "User defined table for batch jobs
***
*** ZJOB_LOG Contains three fields:
*** Job_Id, C(8), Job Identifier, Primary Key
*** Start, D, Start Date
*** Doc#, C(12), Next Document
***


*** Get today's information
SELECT * SINGLE FROM ZJOB_LOG WHERE JOB_ID = 'WEEKLYGL'
                                START = SY-DATUM.
```

```
... <Process Data>

*** Update Job Log
ZJOB_LOG-START = ZJOB_LOG-START + 7.  "Schedule Next Job
ZJOB_LOG-DOC# = ZJOB_LOG-DOC# + 100.  "Set Next Document

UPDATE ZJOB_LOG.
IF SY-SUBRC <> 0.
  WRITE: /, 'Error on  Log Update!'.
ENDIF.
```

Because the `UPDATE` command here is issued with no `SET` or `WHERE` option, SAP uses the values in the work area for `ZJOB_LOG` and updates the row with the same key as the work area. In this case, the `SELECT` command populates the work area with the row where `Job_Id` is equal to `WEEKLYGL`. The field `Start` is changed to today's date plus seven days, and the `Doc#` field is increased by 100. Because `Job_Id` isn't changed, the `UPDATE` statement changes the same row that was originally selected.

In general, it's better if the update is issued with an explicit `WHERE` clause instead of using the work area, because it's easier to follow. This next code piece has the same effect as the one just examined, but notice how much easier it is to read:

```
TABLES ZJOB_LOG   "User defined table for batch jobs
***
*** ZJOB_LOG Contains three fields:
*** Job_Id, C(8), Job Identifier, Primary Key
*** Start, D, Start Date
*** Doc#, C(12), Next Document
***

*** Get today's information
SELECT * SINGLE FROM ZJOB_LOG WHERE JOB_ID = 'WEEKLYGL'

AND START = SY-DATUM.

... <Process Data>
```

```
*** Update Job Log
UPDATE ZJOB_LOG SET START = START + 7 DOC# = DOC# + 100
                                            WHERE JOB_ID = 'WEEKLYGL'.
IF SY-SUBRC <> 0.
  WRITE: /, 'Error on  Log Update!'.
ENDIF.
```

This example uses the `SET` option and the `where` clause to explicitly spell out what's changing. This is much easier to follow than the mysterious `UPDATE ZJOB_LOG`, which tells the reader nothing more than that something is changing about `ZJOB_LOG`.

Using the FROM TABLE Option with UPDATE

In the second version of `UPDATE`, there's an option called `FROM TABLE` that allows the programmer to submit an internal table with the same structure as the database table to be updated. No `SET` or `WHERE` clause is allowed with this option because the system takes the value stored in the primary key field(s) of the internal table and updates each corresponding row in the database table based on the value(s) stored in the internal table. If a row is present in the internal table with a key that isn't found in the database table, it's ignored, and processing continues with the next row in the internal table.

Suppose you want to reset the job log table. All interfaces should be set to run tomorrow, starting at the first appropriate document number. In SAP, most transaction-based data (for example, invoices, journal entries, and purchase requests) uses a document number as part of the key. Each transaction type can have a different valid range of document numbers—such as `0500000000` through `0650000000`. This next example demonstrates how to accomplish this objective:

```
TABLES ZJOB_LOG.

DATA      BEGIN OF ILOG OCCURS 10.     "Internal Table
     INCLUDE STRUCTURE ZJOB_LOG.       "Same Fields as zjob_log
DATA      END OF ILOG.

*** Initialize Internal Table
ILOG-JOB_ID = 'WEEKLYGL'.
ILOG-START = SY-DATUM + 1.        "Set date to tomorrow
```

```
ILOG-DOC# = '0050000000'.
APPEND ILOG.                         "Add record to Int Table

ILOG-JOB_ID = 'AREXT'.
ILOG-START = SY-DATUM + 1.          "Set date to tomorrow
ILOG-DOC# = '0060000000'.
APPEND ILOG.                         "Add record to Int Table

ILOG-JOB_ID = 'APEXT'.
ILOG-START = SY-DATUM + 1.          "Set date to tomorrow
ILOG-DOC# = '0030000000'.
APPEND ILOG.                         "Add record to Int Table

*** Update values in zjob_log
UPDATE ZJOB_LOG FROM TABLE ILOG.
```

Now suppose that ZJOB_LOG contained these values before this piece of code was run:

Job_Id	Start	Doc#
WEEKLYGL	08/01/96	0054001100
AREXT	08/01/96	0073000600
MMEXP	12/31/99	0020100100

If you ran the code and today's date was May 2, 1997, here's what you'd get:

Job_Id	Start	Doc#
WEEKLYGL	05/03/97	0050000000
AREXT	05/03/97	0060000000
MMEXP	12/31/99	0020100100

Notice that the third row didn't change because none of the rows in the internal table have a value for Job_Id that matches MMEXP. Also, the row in the internal table with a Job_Id of APEXT doesn't have any effect because no row in the database matches it.

The UPDATE command gives the programmer a great deal of flexibility in changing values in a database table. Always make it obvious what data is being changed by explicitly spelling it out with SET and the where clause.

Inserting Data (INSERT)

The INSERT command enables the programmer to add new data to a database table. As with UPDATE, the INSERT command shouldn't be used to add data to an SAP table—only to user-defined tables. This command isn't used as much as UPDATE because users manually entering data populate many tables. Each row in a database table must have a unique primary key. If a non-unique row is inserted into the table, the command fails and SY-SUBRC is set to 4. If the command succeeds, SY-SUBRC is set to 0, as usual.

The INSERT command uses one of two formats:

```
INSERT INTO tab VALUES rec.

INSERT tab [FROM TABLE itab].
```

The two different versions of the INSERT command are much like the versions of the UPDATE command. In one case, the data being added is provided explicitly; in the other, it's taken from the table work area or from an internal table.

Inserting Explicit Data

In the first option, the row to be inserted is first placed into a record *rec* that should have the same structure as the database table into which you're inserting. This is much akin to the SET option of the UPDATE command, where the new values are explicitly spelled out. Here's an example of this first version:

```
TABLES ZJOB_LOG.


DATA BEGIN OF LREC          .        "Log Record
       INCLUDE STRUCTURE ZJOB_LOG. "Same Fields as zjob_log
DATA END OF ILOG.


*** Initialize Internal Table
LREC-JOB_ID = 'WEEKLYGL'.
LREC-START = SY-DATUM + 1.          "Set date to tomorrow
LREC-DOC# = '0050000000'.


INSERT INTO ZJOB_LOG VALUES LREC.  "Insert Data
IF SY-SUBRC <> 0.
```

```
  WRITE: /, 'Error!  Duplicate Row Exists'.
ENDIF.

LREC-JOB_ID = 'AREXT'.
LREC-START = SY-DATUM + 1.        "Set date to tomorrow
LREC-DOC# = '0060000000'.

INSERT INTO ZJOB_LOG VALUES LREC.  "Insert Data
IF SY-SUBRC <> 0.
  WRITE: /, 'Error!  Duplicate Row Exists'.
ENDIF.

LREC-JOB_ID = 'AREXT'.
LREC-START = SY-DATUM + 1.        "Set date to tomorrow
LREC-DOC# = '0090000000'.

INSERT INTO ZJOB_LOG VALUES LREC.  "Insert Data
IF SY-SUBRC <> 0.
  WRITE: /, 'Error!  Duplicate Row Exists'.
ENDIF.
```

If `ZJOB_LOG` is empty when this piece of code is run, the first two rows of data would be inserted successfully into the table. But the third `INSERT` command would fail because it attempts to insert data with a value for `Job_Id` (`AREXT`) that had already been inserted. Even though the `Doc#` fields contain different values, the command fails because `Job_Id` is a duplicate.

Inserting Data with FROM TABLE

The second variation of the `INSERT` command allows you to use the table work area to insert new data into the table:

```
INSERT tab [FROM TABLE itab].
```

Much like the version of the `UPDATE` command that uses the table work area, it can be a little bit difficult to understand what's going on.

The `FROM TABLE` option acts just like the option of the same name in the `UPDATE` command. The system uses the values in the specified internal table and inserts the data into the database. Like `UPDATE`, if one row fails, in this case because of a duplicate key, it doesn't cause the entire command to fail. Those rows without duplicates are successfully inserted.

Deleting Rows (DELETE)

DELETE lets you remove rows of data from a database table. As stated earlier, this command isn't normally used to delete data in an SAP table—only in user-defined tables. Like INSERT and UPDATE, DELETE comes in two varieties:

```
DELETE tab WHERE condition.

DELETE tab [FROM TABLE itab].
```

The two different versions of the DELETE command are much like the versions of the UPDATE command. In one case, the data being removed is provided explicitly; in the other, it's taken from the table work area or from an internal table.

Using WHERE with DELETE

In the first version of DELETE, the row to be deleted is explicitly spelled out through use of the WHERE clause. Unfortunately, if you want to delete all rows from a table, you need to supply a WHERE clause that's true for all rows. A good one to use specifies an empty string:

```
WHERE primary key <> '' "
```

This is always true because primary keys can't be empty. If the command deletes at least one row from the specified table, the return code in SY-SUBRC is set to 0. If no rows are deleted, the return code is 4.

Here's an example of the first version of the DELETE command:

```
TABLES ZJOB_LOG.


DELETE FROM ZJOB_LOG WHERE START < SYS-DATUM.  "Assume today is 01/24/97
```

Suppose that table ZJOB_LOG contains these values before this piece of code is run:

Job_Id	Start	Doc#
WEEKLYGL	01/01/97	0054001100
AREXT	02/01/97	0073000600
MMEXP	12/31/96	0020100100

After running the code, here's what's left:

```
Job_Id      Start        Doc#
AREXT       02/01/97     0073000600
```

If you needed to make sure that all rows were deleted from the table every time, the following piece of code would accomplish just that:

```
TABLES ZJOB_LOG.
DELETE FROM ZJOB_LOG WHERE JOB_ID <> ''.
```

Because `Job_Id` is the key for the table, it will never be blank—thus, every row will meet the criteria for the `where` clause and be deleted.

Deleting Multiple Rows with FROM TABLE

The second variation of the `DELETE` command allows programmers to delete multiple rows using an internal table or use the table work area to specify a single row to be deleted:

```
DELETE tab [FROM TABLE itab].
```

Much like the version of the `UPDATE` command that uses the table work area, it can be confusing when someone else is trying to understand your program. The `FROM TABLE` option acts similar to the option of the same name in the `UPDATE` command. The system uses the values in the key field(s) to determine which rows to delete from the database. The non-key values are simply ignored.

Like `UPDATE`, if one row of the internal table fails, in this case because of a row with a matching key, it doesn't cause the entire command to fail. Those rows with matches are successfully deleted and failed rows are ignored.

Advanced Techniques in R/3 v3.x

When the 3.0 version of R/3 was released, it greatly enhanced the functionality of the `SELECT` command. The syntax of the command has become much more complicated so I will present a number of examples. Don't forget to take advantage of the online help in SAP if you need help with some of the details of the syntax.

By taking advantage of the 3.x enhancements, tremendous performance improvements can be made in ABAP/4 programs. The most import enhancement is the ability to limit the amount of data retrieved from the database. Before version 3.0, if you selected data from a table with 100 fields, you always returned all 100 fields even if you were only interested in two of them. Now the SELECT command has the option of specifying which fields should be returned from the database allowing the programmer to cut down unnecessary database and network activity.

Using Explicit Field Lists

Here's the advanced form of SELECT command:

```
SELECT [SINGLE] *¦f1 f2 f3 Ö [target] FROM tab [WHERE condition].
...
ENDSELECT.
```

The section of the command following the word "select" is referred to as the field list. Prior to version 3.0, the field list was always an asterisk. In order to improve performance, instead of using the * to indicate a return of all fields of a table, you should explicitly list each field you wish to be returned. Only when you are using an explicit field list does the target clause become important. You must ensure that each field has somewhere to be placed. The target can be one of a couple options:

```
INTO [CORRESPONDING FIELDS OF] rec
INTO (var1, var2, var3, Ö)
INTO [CORRESPONDING FIELDS OF] TABLE tab
APPENDING [CORRESPONDING FIELDS OF] TABLE tab
```

You must specify a target when using an explicit field list. The best way to do this is to place the results into the corresponding fields in the work area of the table from which the data is selected. For example:

```
SELECT PLNUM MATNR WERKS INTO CORRESPONDING FIELDS OF PLAF FROM PLAF.
```

The nice thing about this approach is that programs written under older versions of ABAP/4 can very easily be enhanced to improve their performance. Suppose an older program used this piece of code:

```
TABLES VBAK.
SELECT * FROM VBAK.
  WRITE: /, VBAK-VBELN, VBAK-ATULF, VBAK-AUART.
ENDSELECT.
```

This is not very effective because the table VBAK has over 70 different fields, yet only three of them are being used. By making a simple change to the select statement performance, it can be improved without changing the bulk of the code.

```
TABLES VBAK.
SELECT VBELN AUTLF AUART INTO CORRESPONDING FIELDS OF VBAK FROM VBAK.
  WRITE: /, VBAK-VBELN, VBAK-AUTLF, VBAK-AUART.
ENDSELECT.
```

When upgrading to version 3.x of R/3, simple changes such as these can be made to programs resulting in a general performance improvement across the system.

The other common approach is to define one or more variables and use them as the target as in this example.

```
TABLES VBAK.
DATA: XVBELN LIKE VBAK-VBELN,
      XAUART LIKE VBAK-AUART.
SELECT VBELN  AUART INTO ( XVBELN, XAUART ) FROM VBAK.
  WRITE: /, XVBELN, XAUART.
ENDSELECT.
```

Notice that there is no space between the variables and the beginning and ending parentheses. This exact syntax is required, and if a space is present it will result in a syntax error.

The next two examples are functionally identical but the second is more efficient. The first is written using the 2.x SAP SQL commands, and the second is written with the 3.x enhancements.

```
REPORT ZCTEST.


TABLES: VBAK, VBAP, VBUP, PLAF.


DATA: BEGIN OF INT_DAT OCCURS 2000,
        VBELN LIKE VBAK-VBELN,
        AUART LIKE VBAK-AUART,
        IHREZ LIKE VBAK-IHREZ,
        AUTLF LIKE VBAK-AUTLF,
        POSNR LIKE VBAP-POSNR,
        KWMENG LIKE VBAP-KWMENG,
        MATNR LIKE VBAP-MATNR,
        PLNUM LIKE PLAF-PLNUM,
        PSTTR LIKE PLAF-PSTTR,
      END OF INT_DAT.
```

```
SELECT-OPTIONS: S_VBELN FOR VBAK-VBELN DEFAULT '0600000000' OPTION GE,
                S_ERDAT FOR VBAK-ERDAT DEFAULT '19980101' OPTION GE.

* Read from sales order
SELECT  *  FROM VBAK WHERE VBELN IN S_VBELN
                      AND ERDAT IN S_ERDAT.
* Read from sales item
  SELECT * FROM VBAP WHERE VBELN = VBAK-VBELN
                      AND UEPOS = '000000'.
*   Read current item status
    SELECT * FROM VBUP WHERE VBELN EQ VBAP-VBELN
                        AND POSNR EQ VBAP-POSNR.

      CHECK VBUP-LFSTA NE 'C'.          "Delivery stat - Complete
*     read all planned order associated with the item
      SELECT * FROM PLAF WHERE KDAUF EQ VBAP-VBELN
                          AND KDPOS EQ VBAP-POSNR.

        INT_DAT-VBELN   =  VBAK-VBELN.
        INT_DAT-AUART   =  VBAK-AUART.
        INT_DAT-IHREZ   =  VBAK-IHREZ.
        INT_DAT-AUTLF   =  VBAK-AUTLF.
        INT_DAT-POSNR   =  VBAP-POSNR.
        INT_DAT-KWMENG  =  VBAP-KWMENG.
        INT_DAT-MATNR   =  VBAP-MATNR.
        INT_DAT-PLNUM   =  PLAF-PLNUM.
        INT_DAT-PSTTR   =  PLAF-PSTTR.
*       Save results in internal table
        APPEND INT_DAT.
      ENDSELECT.
    ENDSELECT.
  ENDSELECT.
ENDSELECT.
```

Here is the second example featuring the 3.x enhanced SAP SQL.

```
REPORT ZCTEST.

TABLES: VBAK, VBAP, VBUP, PLAF.

DATA: BEGIN OF IVBAK OCCURS 1000,
        VBELN LIKE VBAK-VBELN,
        IHREZ LIKE VBAK-IHREZ,
        AUTLF LIKE VBAK-AUTLF,
        AUART LIKE VBAK-AUART,
      END OF IVBAK.

DATA: BEGIN OF IVBAP OCCURS 10,
        VBELN LIKE VBAP-VBELN,
        POSNR LIKE VBAP-POSNR,
        KWMNG LIKE VBAP-KWMENG,
        MATNR LIKE VBAP-MATNR,
      END OF IVBAP.

DATA: BEGIN OF IPLAF OCCURS 10,
        PLNUM LIKE PLAF-PLNUM,
        PSTTR LIKE PLAF-PSTTR,
      END OF IPLAF.

DATA: BEGIN OF INT_DAT OCCURS 2000,
        VBELN LIKE VBAK-VBELN,
        AUART LIKE VBAK-AUART,
        IHREZ LIKE VBAK-IHREZ,
        AUTLF LIKE VBAK-AUTLF,
        POSNR LIKE VBAP-POSNR,
        KWMENG LIKE VBAP-KWMENG,
        MATNR LIKE VBAP-MATNR,
        PLNUM LIKE PLAF-PLNUM,
        PSTTR LIKE PLAF-PSTTR,
      END OF INT_DAT.
```

```
SELECT-OPTIONS: S_VBELN FOR VBAK-VBELN DEFAULT '0600000000' OPTION GE,
                S_ERDAT FOR VBAK-ERDAT DEFAULT '19980101' OPTION GE.

SELECT  VBELN AUART IHREZ AUTLF
             INTO CORRESPONDING FIELDS OF TABLE IVBAK
             FROM VBAK
             WHERE VBELN IN S_VBELN
               AND ERDAT IN S_ERDAT.

LOOP AT IVBAK.
* Loop at sales items
  SELECT VBELN POSNR KWMENG MATNR
                 INTO CORRESPONDING FIELDS OF TABLE IVBAP
                 FROM VBAP
                 WHERE VBELN = IVBAK-VBELN
                   AND UEPOS = '000000'.

  LOOP AT IVBAP.
    SELECT COUNT(*) FROM VBUP
           WHERE VBELN EQ VBAP-VBELN
             AND POSNR EQ VBAP-POSNR
             AND LFSTA EQ 'C'.         "Delivery stat - Complete
    CHECK SY-DBCNT = 0.

    SELECT PLNUM PSTTR INTO CORRESPONDING FIELDS OF TABLE IPLAF
                FROM PLAF WHERE KDAUF EQ VBAP-VBELN
                            AND KDPOS EQ VBAP-POSNR.
    LOOP AT IPLAF.
      INT_DAT-VBELN    =  IVBAK-VBELN.
      INT_DAT-AUART    =  IVBAK-AUART.
      INT_DAT-IHREZ    =  IVBAK-IHREZ.
      INT_DAT-AUTLF    =  IVBAK-AUTLF.
      INT_DAT-POSNR    =  IVBAP-POSNR.
      INT_DAT-KWMENG   =  IVBAP-KWMENG.
      INT_DAT-MATNR    =  IVBAP-MATNR.
```

```
        INT_DAT-PLNUM    =  IPLAF-PLNUM.
        INT_DAT-PSTTR    =  IPLAF-PSTTR.
APPEND INT_DAT.
    ENDLOOP.
  ENDLOOP.
ENDLOOP.
```

As these two examples show, with the 3.x enhancements you have much more control of database access in ABAP/4. In this case, you only require the information from nine fields out of the three tables accessed. In the first example, you must retrieve all data from those three tables (over 200 fields) even though you only require nine. So in the second example, you use explicit field lists to limit the fields returned to only those required. This provides a huge saving in terms of network utilization.

Also in the second example, you use the `INTO TABLE` option to fetch a single array of data instead of using a select loop. Retrieving data as a single array can be more efficient in many situations. SAP has difficulty with multiple-nested select loops such as those in the first example. When a program is executing, as long as a select loop is being processed, the application server must hold an open connection with the database server. When you have several nested select statements, such as in the first example, multiple connections must be held open. By using the `INTO TABLE` option, the program retrieves all requested data from the database at once and places it into an internal table. The programmer must use a `LOOP` command to loop through the internal table. Of course, if you know you will be looping through millions of rows of data, you do not want to wait for all of them to be transferred at once and then try to loop through all that data on the application server. In cases where large amounts of data is to be processed, it is better to use a select loop.

Using Aggregate Functions to Process Data

In addition to allowing you to specify individual fields, you can also use aggregate functions on fields. An aggregate function performs a certain mathematical function against an array of records. So, instead of returning all the records in the array, the database returns only the result of the mathematical function. The most common aggregate function is summation. Using the sum function on a quantity field, for example, would return the sum of the quantity of all records to be returned instead of the records themselves. When using aggregates, you use an explicit field list with the exception of the `COUNT(*)` aggregate. The syntax for using an aggregate is:

```
SELECT SINGLE funct( f1 ) [AS v1] funct( f2 ) [AS v2] ... INTO <target> from tab.
```

The addition of the SINGLE keyword may be used here because you know the aggregate always returns a single row. The target clause is required as in any case where an explicit field list is used. The AS option allows you to give a name to the aggregate function. Later I will demonstrate the use of AS with the INTO CORRESPONDING FIELDS option.

Here is a simple example of the use of aggregates. In this case, you will get the sum of the weight of all items in a delivery as well as the minimum and maximum weight of an item in the delivery.

```
TABLES LIPS.            "Delivery Items
DATA: XSUM LIKE LIPS-NTGEW, XMAX LIKE LIPS-NTGEW, XMIN LIKE LIPS-NTGEW.
SELECT SINGLE SUM( NTGEW ) MAX( NTGEW ) MIN( NTGEW )
       INTO (XSUM, XMAX, XMIN)
       FROM LIPS
       WHERE VBELN = '9234322'.
```

If you wish to use the INTO CORRESPONDING FIELDS option, you must use AS to rename the aggregate fields. By default, SAP does not recognize that NTGEW and SUM(NTGEW) are the same field. But if you use AS, you can rename the aggregate field back to NTGEW as seen in this example:

```
TABLES LIPS.
SELECT SINGLE SUM( NTGEW ) AS NTGEW
       INTO INTO CORRESPONDING FIELDS OF LIPS
       FROM LIPS
       WHERE VBELN = '9234322'.
```

Using GROUP BY to Subtotal Data

In this case, the field LIPS-NTGEW will show the sum of all the records returned by the select instead of a single value. Aggregates can also be used to generate subtotals instead of only totals. In this case, multiple rows are returned, one for each subtotal. Subtotals are created by placing the field you wish to subtotal in the field list and by adding an option called GROUP BY to the end of the select statement. Here is the syntax:

```
SELECT f1 f2 ... funct( f3 ) funct( f4 )  ...
       INTO <target> from tab [<where clause>]
       GROUP BY f1 f2 ...
ENDSELECT.
```

Notice that in this case, the SINGLE key word is not used. This is because you may get more than one subtotal; so, a select loop must be used instead. You can, of course, use any of the target options previously discussed. So if you use INTO TABLE, the results are placed into an internal table and a select loop is not required. Here is an example which returns the same aggregates as the first, but this time the plant (WERKS) subtotals them.

```
TABLES LIPS.            "Delivery Items
DATA: XSUM LIKE LIPS-NTGEW, XMAX LIKE LIPS-NTGEW, XMIN LIKE LIPS-NTGEW.
data: xwerks like lips-werks.
SELECT WERKS SUM( NTGEW ) MAX( NTGEW ) MIN( NTGEW )
       INTO (XWERKS, XSUM, XMAX, XMIN)
       FROM LIPS
       WHERE VBELN = '9234322'
       GROUP BY WERKS.
ENDSELECT.
```

Aggregates are very powerful and take full advantage of R/3's multi-tier architecture to balance the processing load between the database and the application servers. If you needed to sum a million rows in the past, you would have had to select those million rows, transfer them to the application server, and add them one at a time. This is slow and unnecessarily eats up a lot of network bandwidth. Using aggregates, the summation takes place very quickly at the database level and a single value is transported back to your program on the application server. The use of aggregates does increase the load on your database but, under normal conditions, the efficiency of aggregates is well worth it.

The following is a short program demonstrating the use of aggregates. The purpose of this program is to print a list of the total quantities of each material required by a planned order. It accepts the entry of a sales order number by the user and retrieves all planned orders associated with the sales orders entered. In SAP, a sales item can have one or more planned orders which tell how to build the item being sold. Each planned order is made up of the hierarchy of parts needed to make up the finished product. Within the planned order, a part may appear more than once. For example, a certain screw might secure the base of a chair as well as each armrest. This program reads the entire planned order and sums all of the parts in order to present a subtotal of the quantity required for each part.

```
REPORT ZCRLTST .


TABLES: VBAP,                   "Sales Items
```

```
        PLAF,                       "Planned Orders
        RESB.                       "Planned Order Components

DATA: BEGIN OF IDAT OCCURS 50,
        MATNR LIKE RESB-MATNR,                 "Material
        BDMNG LIKE RESB-BDMNG,                 "Quantity
      END OF IDAT.

SELECT-OPTIONS S_VBELN FOR VBAP-VBELN.

SELECT VBELN POSNR INTO CORRESPONDING FIELDS OF VBAP
                    FROM VBAP WHERE VBELN IN S_VBELN
                                 AND UEPOS EQ '000000'.
* Write Order and Item numbers
  WRITE: /, VBAP-VBELN, VBAP-POSNR.
  SELECT PLNUM RSNUM INTO CORRESPONDING FIELDS OF PLAF
                FROM PLAF WHERE KDAUF = VBAP-VBELN
                             AND KDPOS = VBAP-POSNR.
*   Write Planned order number
    WRITE: / PLAF-PLNUM.
    SELECT MATNR SUM( BDMNG ) AS BDMNG
                                INTO CORRESPONDING FIELDS OF TABLE IDAT
                                FROM RESB
                                WHERE RSNUM = PLAF-RSNUM
                                  AND SHKZG NE 'S'
                                  AND POSTP EQ 'L'
                                  AND DUMPS NE 'X'
                                GROUP BY MATNR.
    LOOP AT IDAT.
*     Write material and quantity
      WRITE: / IDAT-MATNR, IDAT-BDMNG.
    ENDLOOP.
  ENDSELECT.
ENDSELECT.
```

Using INNER JOIN to Access Multiple Tables

One of the more significant shortcomings of SAP SQL has been its lack of a join command. In standard SQL, the programmer can retrieve data from multiple tables at the same time. This is referred to as a *table join* and is part of the syntax of the SELECT command. In order to perform a table join, the tables must have a relationship that tells the database how to combine the data from the multiple tables into a single result set. For example, two tables, one with header data and the second with item data might be joined to retrieve both head and item data at the same time. Without using a join in the program, it would have to retrieve all the header data, then retrieve all the item data, and then combine it. Although SAP did not have a join command, it did allow the creation of views, which can include data from multiple tables, but views are data dictionary objects and must be set up ahead of time.

This situation changed with version 3.0 of R/3. In 3.0, an undocumented command was added which allowed table joins to be performed in ABAP/4. Because this command is undocumented and unsupported by SAP, it should be used with extreme care. There is no guarantee that the command will be present in future versions of ABAP/4, so any program which uses joins may not work after an upgrade. With this caveat in mind, here is the syntax of SELECT command with the INNER JOIN option.

```
select tab1~f1 tab1~f2 tab2~f3 ... into (target)
       from (tab1 inner join tab2 on tab1~key1 = tab2~key1
                                  and tab1~key2 = tab2~key2 ...
             inner join tab3 on tab1~key1 = tab3~key1
                                  and tab1~key2 = tab3~key2
             ...)
       [WHERE whereclasue]
       [ORDER BY tab1~f1 tab2~f2 ...].
```

The syntax of this form of the SELECT command is very different from a standard select. As you can see, the table name and field name are not separated by a dash (—) but instead by a tilde (~). With this option it is possible to select from more than two tables but it is very important to choose the correct main table. The main table is the table in the FROM clause of the select. The other tables are referred to as *join tables*. The main table must have a relationship with all of the join tables. If the relationships in the join are not specified correctly, the select will return incorrect data and may cause a tremendous load on the system and result in incorrect results.

In this first example, you select data from two tables. The first is PLAF, which holds data about planned orders. The second is VBAP, which holds data about sales items.

The planned orders are associated with a sales item, so the join relationship is the order number and item number.

```
TABLES PLAF.
DATA: XVBELN LIKE VBAP-VBELN,
      XPOSNR LIKE VBAP-POSNR,
      XMATNR LIKE VBAP-MATNR,
      XPLNUM LIKE PLAF-PLNUM.

  SELECT VBAP~VBELN VBAP~POSNR VBAP~MATNR PLAF~PLNUM
       INTO (XVBELN, XPOSNR, XMATNR, XPLNUM)
       FROM ( PLAF INNER JOIN VBAP ON PLAF~KDAUF = VBAP~VBELN
                                   AND PLAF~KDPOS = VBAP~POSNR )
       WHERE VBAP~VBELN = '1231311'
       ORDER BY VBAP~MATNR.
  ENDSELECT.
```

This last example demonstrates joining three tables. Notice in this case that, instead of using a select loop, you use the `INTO TABLE` option to place the results of the select directly into an internal table.

```
REPORT ZCTEST1 .

TABLES: VBAK,        "Sales Order Header
        VBAP,        "Sales Item
        VBUK.        "Document Status

DATA: BEGIN OF IDAT OCCURS 100,
      VBELN LIKE VBAK-VBELN,
      POSNR LIKE VBAP-POSNR,
      MATNR LIKE VBAP-MATNR,
      LFGSK LIKE VBUK-LFGSK,
      END OF IDAT.

  SELECT VBAK~VBELN VBAP~POSNR VBAP~MATNR VBUK~LFGSK
       INTO  CORRESPONDING FIELDS OF TABLE IDAT
```

```
        FROM ( VBAK INNER JOIN VBUK ON VBAK~VBELN = VBUK~VBELN
                   INNER JOIN VBAP ON VBAK~VBELN = VBAP~VBELN )
        WHERE VBUK~LFSTK <> 'C'           "Documents not complete
        ORDER BY MATNR.

LOOP AT IDAT.
     WRITE: /, IDAT.
ENDLOOP.
```

The use of the `INTO TABLE` option demonstrates that any of the common select options will also work with the `INNER JOIN` option.

All of these enhancements demonstrated add a great deal of power and flexibility to ABAP/4. It is important to take advantage of them in both new and existing programs when moving to the latest version of R/3.

Summary

This chapter has been an introduction to SAP SQL. Later in the book, when you get into detailed business cases and examples, you'll be able to see clearly the importance of SAP SQL. Almost every program makes use of SAP SQL to some extent, especially the `SELECT` command.

The `GET` command is a second method used to read information from the database, the pros and cons of which are detailed in Chapter 13, "Working with Logical Databases." Because the database is the heart of SAP, the SAP SQL commands that give a programmer access to that heart are of paramount importance.

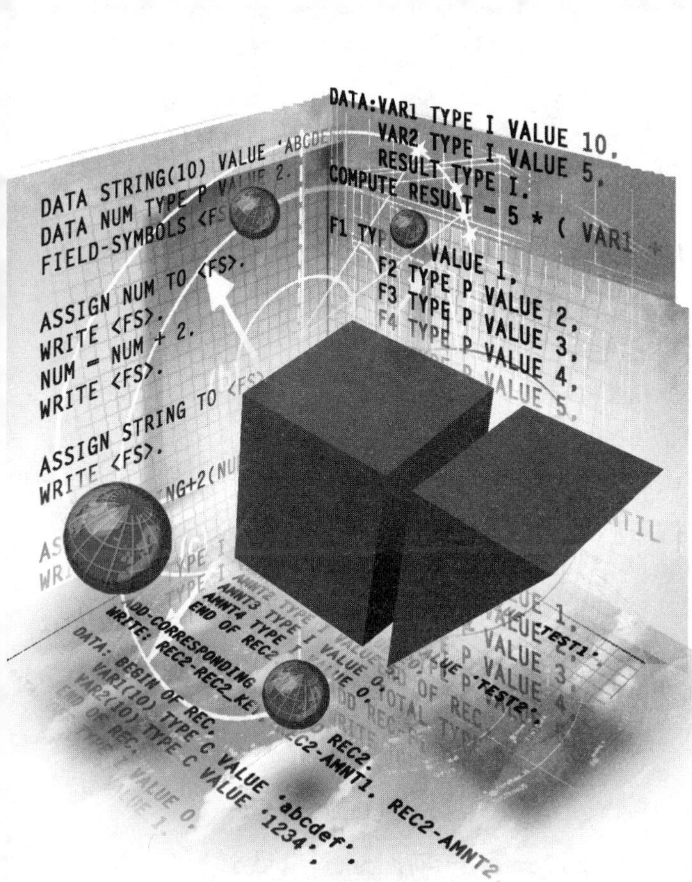

Chapter 9

Working with External Files

In This Chapter

- Data Mapping
- Establishing the Path and Filename
- Opening the File (`OPEN DATASET`)
- Adding a System Message (`MESSAGE`)
- Sending a Command to the Server (`FILTER`)
- Writing the Data to the Server (`TRANSFER`)
- Reading the Data from the Data File (`READ`)
- Closing the File (`CLOSE DATASET`)

This chapter deals with how ABAP code imports and exports external files from and to the application server. The application server is the machine on which all the compiled code is being executed, and the format of the file is either an ASCII text or binary.

The importance of external files can be highlighted by two examples:

- When SAP is implemented, the old system isn't just shut off and SAP started up. SAP is too large and complex a system for that, so SAP is brought online piece by piece, with pieces of the old system being replaced by the new pieces of SAP. To maintain this coexistence between the old system and SAP, some data must be shared between the two systems. The data is generally transferred in text format in a file that's either produced by the old system and read into SAP, or produced by SAP and copied to the old system. Transferring files between systems allows the SAP implementation to progress step by step with relatively few growing pains.
- The second important purpose of external files is for additional processing by one of the users. Essentially, the user might not want a *hard copy* (paper copy) version of the data in a report, so in addition to the paper copy, an electronic version is created. The electronic version can be imported into third-party software such as Microsoft's Excel spreadsheet, or a form-generation tool such as Fantasia. The electronic copy allows users to process the data in a custom format that SAP might not supply. Also, the file can be attached to an e-mail message and read by a number of users, rather than having copies printed and sent throughout the company. The electronic version essentially saves paper and allows users to utilize third-party software tools to analyze the data from SAP.

External files can be read or written directly using ABAP/4 code, or processed using one of SAP's included function modules. These function modules can read and write external files to and from the application server as well as directly to the user's PC. These helpful functions are discussed in the latter portion of this chapter.

Data Mapping

When data is transferred from a system to SAP or vice versa, the source of the data and its final destination must be determined. *Data mapping* is the term used to describe the "travel plans" of the data being transferred. One of the primary purposes of coding ABAP is coding *interfaces*. An interface is the regular transfer of data from an older system to SAP, or vice versa.

This chapter is more concerned with the format of the output data. The term *format* refers to the fact that all fields pulled from SAP or brought in from an outside file should be of type C, character fields. Particular attention must be paid to the length of these fields, incoming or outgoing.

The best way to achieve good mapping from one system to another is to construct an internal table that has the desired format for the incoming or outgoing data. To accomplish this task, ask a functional analyst for a sample file that will be used by the program. Then mark the separate fields and count how many spaces each field takes. Examine the following "file" (for visual purposes, each space in the file's contents is represented by a period):

```
apple.....fruit..........500....
banana....fruit..........600....
squash....vegetable......20.....
```

To hold this data in an internal table, you must count the spaces for each field. The first field can be identified as `description`, or `DESC` for short, and it holds 10 characters. The second field can be characterized as `type` and it is called just that. It holds 15 characters. The last field is regarded as the `quantity`, or shortened as `QTY`. It holds 7 characters. Now that you've specified the lengths and what kind of data each field holds, you can create an internal table that would hold each record (shown next):

```
DATA:     BEGIN OF INT_TAB OCCURS 100,
                DESC(10) TYPE C,          "description
                TYPE(15) TYPE C,          "type
                QTY(7) TYPE C.            "quantity
DATA:     END OF INT_TAB.
```

This internal table is now set to read data from an external text file. If you put data into this internal table, on the other hand, it could be written as an external text file. This practice of setting up a structure to hold the incoming or outgoing data is a very good idea in order to separate fields from each other and to keep the incoming or outgoing data in a consistent format.

When setting up tables for data transfer, remember these two rules:

- All the fields in the internal table must be character fields to make sure that the right number of spaces from the data are read in or written out. Character fields will read in the defined number of spaces; some other fields won't. Character fields always work, so stick with them for transferring data. Once the data is read into SAP, the character field can be transferred to another field that's more appropriate. For example, the `QTY` field can be transferred to a field of type I (integer), which would allow for quantitative analysis on the field.
- The second rule is essentially mentioned in the first rule. Make sure that the right number of spaces is used to define the fields in the internal table. Get a preview copy of the file and count out the spaces for each field. Although the process may seem tedious, it gives you results that are accurate and reliable.

This preliminary data mapping saves time and headaches later, when you come down to actually processing the data. The first goal is to get the data in or out cleanly. If no mistakes are encountered in the transfer process for the incoming or outgoing data, you can count on data integrity when the time comes to process the data.

Establishing the Path and Filename

The first actual step of accessing an external text file is establishing the path and filename of that file. The path and the filename should be declared as separate parameters in the data declaration section of your code. A separate data field should also be created to store the concatenation of the path and filename.

Here's an example:

```
PARAMETERS:     P_PATH(50) TYPE C lower case,
                P_FILE(20) TYPE C lower case.


DATA:          W_DATA(70) TYPE C.
```

```
MOVE P_PATH TO W_DATA.
MOVE P_FILE TO W_DATA+50(20).
CONDENSE W_DATA NO-GAPS.
```

The screen that this code would generate is shown in Figure 9-1.

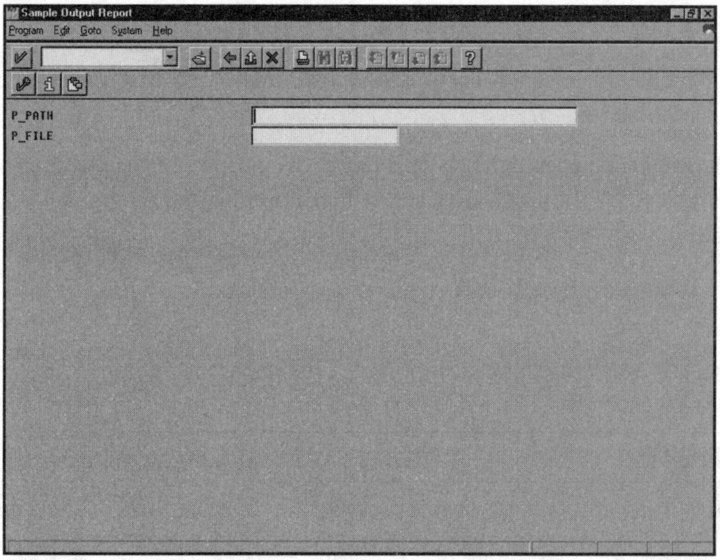

FIGURE 9-1

The sample selection screen for path and filename input

Let's say that the path entered is `/users/finance/`. The filename will be `audit.txt`. The path is moved to the data field, `W_DATA`. The filename is moved to the offset position in `W_DATA`, starting at the 50th position. The `CONDENSE / NO-GAPS` code then removes all spaces between the path and the filename to make `W_DATA` contain the full path and filename for that file.

TIP

By using parameters for the path and the filename, you've made the program modular. The program can change as path structures or filenames change. Path and filename should never be hard-coded into the program.

Opening the File (OPEN DATASET)

Once the full path and filename are stored in one field, a command is issued to open that file for reading, writing, or appending. To open the file, use the `OPEN DATASET` command:

```
OPEN DATASET path plus filename FOR [[OUTPUT,INPUT,APPENDING]
                                                        [IN [TEXT, BINARY]
MODE.]
```

The following sections discuss the options used with the `OPEN DATASET` command.

Marking a File for Output (FOR OUTPUT)

In `OUTPUT` mode, the program opens the file (if it exists) and writes over it, or creates the file (if it doesn't exist).

If the following code is executed, a zero-length file appears in the directory specified by `/users/zuser/` on the application server that's running the program. The filename is `abap.txt`:

```
DATA:     W_PATH(40) TYPE C VALUE '/users/zuser/abap.txt'.


OPEN DATASET W_PATH FOR OUTPUT.
```

> **NOTE**
>
> If the path is incorrect, or if the path is protected, `SY-SUBRC` is set to be greater than 0. Generally, it's a good rule of thumb to make the path and the filename separate parameters to be entered at runtime. That way, if a path changes, the program can adapt.

Because the file has no data transferred to it in the current program, it's "zero-length." If you don't want to overwrite your previous week's file with the same name, make the new filename dynamic by incorporating the date or some other variable. In case of a system shutdown or catastrophe, keeping data on hand from previous weeks is a good idea in order to restore the system.

Marking a File for Input (FOR INPUT)

To read an external file, the `FOR INPUT` addition is needed at the end of the `OPEN DATASET` statement. The file must already exist on the application server in the specified path.

To see this command in action, look at the following sample code—it's explained later in the section called "Reading the Data from the Data File (`READ`)":

```
DATA:     END OF INT_TAB.
```

```
DATA:  W_DATASET(50) VALUE '/users/abap.txt'.

OPEN DATASET W_DATASET FOR INPUT IN TEXT MODE.
DO.
     IF SY-SUBRC <> 0.
          EXIT.
     ENDIF.
     READ DATASET W_DATASET INTO INT_TAB.
     APPEND INT_TAB.
     CLEAR INT_TAB.
ENDDO.
CLOSE DATASET W_DATASET.
```

Selecting a Transfer Mode (IN TEXT MODE / IN BINARY MODE)

When text is transferred to a file, it can be transferred in one of two ways: text mode or binary mode. In text mode, the data is transferred line by line, or field by field, with a carriage return inserted into the file after each line or field transferred. The data displayed from a text file would appear in the following format, if printed out:

```
1    2    3    4    5
6    7    8    9    10
11   12   13   14   15
```

After each line (five numbers), a carriage return is inserted in the text file and the next piece of data appears on the next line.

If data is transferred in binary mode, no carriage return is inserted after each field or line. The data keeps adding to the file as it progresses. The file from the preceding section would appear in the following format if written in binary mode:

```
1   2   3   4   5   6   7   8   9   10   11   12   13   14   15
```

No carriage return is inserted after each line, so the data appears line after line.

The general rule is that if the data is written in binary mode, you need to make sure that the other program reads the file in binary mode. The same rule applies for text mode. Generally, write the file and read the file in the same mode to avoid problems when dealing with external files.

TIP

Check what the file looks like when it's printed out. If it looks like a binary file (no carriage returns), read the file `IN BINARY MODE`. If it looks like a text file (carriage returns present after each line), read the file `IN TEXT MODE`.

Writing to the End of a File (FOR APPENDING)

The `FOR APPENDING` addition to the `OPEN DATASET` command opens a file for the purpose of writing at the end of the file. The file must exist for the program to write to the end of the file; if the file doesn't exist, a new file is created. No example for this command is really necessary. If a file exists, records are added to the end of the file. If it doesn't exist, a new file is created. Otherwise, this addition to the `OPEN DATASET` command acts just like the addition `FOR OUTPUT`.

Indicating the Start of the Read (AT POSITION)

The `AT POSITION` addition to the `OPEN DATASET` command specifies a file position at which the read starts (counting from the start of the file). The next read or write will start at this position. The general syntax for this addition is as follows:

```
OPEN DATASET FOR INPUT AT POSITION position number.
```

The position is a byte marker and is marked explicitly as a number. *`position number`* can be any number from `0` to the end of the file. Obviously, you can't specify a position before the start of the file.

Adding a System Message (MESSAGE)

The `MESSAGE` command places a system message from the operating system into the field *`msg`*. This data field must be declared in the data declaration portion of the program; the field is generally of type character with a length of around 60 to 80 spaces:

```
DATA:     W_DATASET(50) VALUE '/users/abap.txt',
                W_MESSAGE(100),
                 W_RECORD(100).


OPEN DATASET W_DATASET FOR INPUT IN TEXT MODE MESSAGE W_MESSAGE.
DO.
```

```
    IF SY-SUBRC <> 0.
        WRITE W_MESSAGE.
        EXIT.
    ENDIF.
READ DATASET W_DATASET INTO W_RECORD.
ENDDO.
CLOSE DATASET W_DATASET.
```

Let's say, for example, that the file doesn't exist. If you try to open a file that doesn't exist, a system error message is placed in W_MESSAGE and displayed. If programs fail, it's nice to have a message indicating why—in this case, whether opening the file was or wasn't a problem. The more messages in your program, the easier it is to decipher what's causing a problem (assuming the messages are meaningful).

Sending a Command to the Server (FILTER)

The FILTER command allows SAP to issue an operating system command to the application server, provided that the application server is running a UNIX or Windows NT operating system. The general syntax for this command is:

```
OPEN DATASET dataset FOR OUTPUT FILTER filter command.
```

filter command can be any UNIX or NT command. For example, the value of *filter command* could be zip. The file would then be saved and *zipped* (compressed). When you need to open the file and read it again, you can use a *filter command* equal to unzip. The file is then *unzipped* (uncompressed) and read into SAP.

The FILTER command can be used with the OPEN DATSET command FOR OUTPUT and FOR INPUT.

Writing the Data to the Server (TRANSFER)

TRANSFER is the command used to write the data from SAP to the opened datafile on the application server. Logically, the TRANSFER command is associated with the OPEN DATASET *dataset* FOR OUTPUT command. Following is the general syntax:

```
TRANSFER field TO path and filename.
```

`path and filename` here is the same as the dataset name used to open the file. `field` can be any data field declared in the data declarations portion of the program. The field can be an internal table name as well as just a field name.

The following program first reads all of the records from the financial accounting detail table, BSEG, into an internal table, INT_TAB. Then, once all the records have been transferred, the file is opened for output. The LOOP AT command loops through to read all the records of INT_TAB. As each record is read, it's transferred to the file:

```
TABLES: BSEG.
DATA:      BEGIN OF INT_TAB OCCURS 1000.
                     INCLUDE STRUCTURE BSEG.
DATA:      END OF INT_TAB.

DATA:      W_DATASET(50) VALUE '/users/abap.txt'.

SELECT * FROM BSEG INTO TABLE INT_TAB WHERE
                                                              GJAHR =
'1996'.

OPEN DATASET W_DATASET FOR OUTPUT IN TEXT MODE.
LOOP AT INT_TAB.
TRANSFER INT_TAB TO W_DATASET.
ENDLOOP.
CLOSE DATASET W_DATASET.
```

After all the records have been processed, the file is closed with the CLOSE DATASET command, which is covered in the later section "Closing the File (CLOSE DATASET)". If the transfer was not successful for some reason, SY-SUBRC will have a value other than zero in it.

Essentially, the TRANSFER command takes a data field or internal table record and writes it to an external file, providing that the file has been opened for output.

Reading the Data from the Data File (READ)

The READ command is the command used to read the data from the opened data file on the application server into SAP. The read command transfers the current line of the file, or just the right number of characters if the read is done in binary mode, into the field or internal table record. The general syntax of the READ statement used with external files is

```
READ path and filename INTO fieldname.
```

path and filename refers to the dataset that was opened using the OPEN DATASET command FOR INPUT. *fieldname*, exactly as with the TRANSFER command, can refer to any field or internal table record that was declared in the data declaration portion of the program.

If the file is opened in text mode, the line is transferred to the field or internal table record. If the line exceeds the number of spaces for either, the end of the line is dropped off. If the file is opened in binary mode, only the number of spaces allocated to the field or to the internal table record is transferred from the file. While binary mode sounds better, it's just a better idea to count out exactly how many spaces each field will take in the file and make your field(s) of an internal table match those spaces. In binary mode, it's possible to read half of a piece of data into one field and the other half into another field.

The following program reads in the data file that's output just above the code. Notice that the internal table has been precisely configured to read in just the right number of letters to fill the records properly. After the data is declared, the dataset is opened and the reading process begins:

```
DATAFILE
Doolittle          Bob       Truck Driver
Smith              Sally     CEO
Morgan             Stephanie Lawyer

DATA:      BEGIN OF INT_TAB OCCURS 10,
               LAST(19),
               FIRST(10),
               OCCUPATION(15).
DATA:      END OF INT_TAB.

DATA:  W_DATASET(50) VALUE '/users/abap.txt'.

OPEN DATASET W_DATASET FOR INPUT IN TEXT MODE.
DO.
```

```
        IF SY-SUBRC <> 0.
            EXIT.
        ENDIF.
        READ DATASET W_DATASET INTO INT_TAB.
        APPEND INT_TAB.
        CLEAR INT_TAB.
ENDDO.
CLOSE DATASET W_DATASET.
```

Because the program essentially is "dumb" and doesn't know how many records are in this file, the `IF` statement tells the program to exit if an error is encountered. An error is encountered if the program attempts to read a record that doesn't exist. An error is denoted by the system field, `SY-SUBRC` not being equal to `0`. Each time the data is read into the internal table record, it must be appended to the table. Then the header record of the internal table is cleared in preparation for the next input. The `CLEAR` statement makes sure that no duplicate records are copied to the file.

Closing the File (CLOSE DATASET)

The final command issued is the `CLOSE DATASET` command:

```
CLOSE DATASET path plus filename.
```

This command closes the file. It must be used after writing, appending to, or reading the file.

Summary

In every SAP implementation, moving files to and from external systems is very important. SAP systems are not brought up at 100 percent; normally, part of the system is brought up and is run in parallel with the old system. For this to happen, external files must serve as communications between the new and old systems. This chapter covered how to read, write, and modify these files. External files are used extensively in Chapter 15, "Writing a Data Extract," and Chapter 16, "Writing a BDC Program."

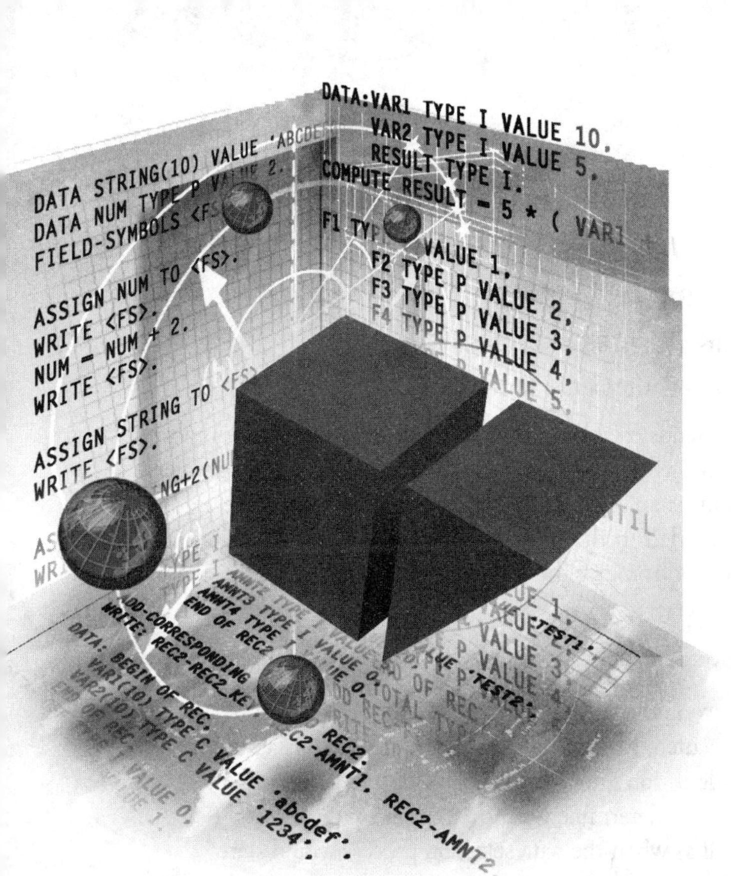

Chapter 10

Advanced Data Output

In This Chapter

- Processing Events in ABAP/4
- Hiding Field Contents with `HIDE`
- Using Field Groups as an Alternative to Internal Tables

This chapter defines the commands in ABAP that cover events, interactive reporting, and a substitute for internal tables. Whereas all three of these topics are very important in your development as an ABAPer, it's important that you have a good grasp of the fundamentals presented in the previous chapters before launching into these areas. If you're a bit shaky on some of the topics covered in the chapters before this one, please reread the chapters.

These are the major topics covered in this chapter:

- *Events* are markers in code that define when the code following the `EVENT` label will be executed. For example, `AT USER-COMMAND` is an event that specifies what code to run after a user clicks a button or presses a function key. Other events determine what the output might be on the selection screen, as well as when the data selection process would start.
- The `HIDE` statement, used in conjunction with events and the `WRITE` statement, allows interactive reporting. In *interactive reporting*, the report is written to the screen. The user can double-click a certain line to get more information, or to process a certain line of information.
- Generally, interactive reporting is handled by developing *module pools* using the screen and menu painter, but it's possible to use ABAP commands in the editor screen to do a little interactive reporting. Module pools are a different type of program developed in SAP. They are developed using the screen and menu painter—editors outside of the ABAP/4 editor that's introduced in this book. The generation of screens and menus is not covered in this book.
- *Field groups* are another method used to store data. Field groups enable you to store more data than in internal tables and to sort and process the records in a new and efficient fashion. Contractors debate whether field groups are faster or slower than internal tables in regard to access time, but the superior storage capacity is a definite plus for field groups.

You don't need to read this chapter in order; read any sections, in any order, that interest you. Again, make sure that you have a good basic understanding of topics from previous chapters; otherwise, comprehending these new and advanced topics might be difficult.

Processing Events in ABAP/4

Events are markers that define certain code that is to occur at certain times in the program. They help define how your programs should run. Certain events governed by the AT command, for example, are used extensively in interactive reporting. Other events, such as INITIALIZATION and START-OF-SELECTION, define at what times the data selection occurs or what default values appear on the selection screen before the program is run. Basically, the events tell the application server when to process certain parts of code. Events govern the timing of the program.

The events covered in this chapter include:

- INITIALIZATION.
- START-OF-SELECTION.
- END-OF-SELECTION.
- AT USER-COMMAND.
- AT LINE-SELECTION.
- AT PF*function* key number.
- AT SELECTION-SCREEN.
- AT NEW *field*.
- AT END OF *field*.
- AT FIRST.
- AT LAST.
- AT *field-group*.

Setting Initial Values (INITIALIZATION)

The INITIALIZATION event occurs after the data declaration portion of the program. The code under this event defines the initial values of the parameters and select-options before the initial selection screen appears. Here's an example:

```
REPORT ZABAPER.

TABLES:     MARC,
            MARD,
            MSEG,
            VBFA.
```

```
PARAMETERS:      P_NAME LIKE SY-UNAME,
                 P_DATE LIKE SY-DATUM.

SELECT-OPTIONS: S_MATNR FOR MSEG-MATNR.

INITIALIZATION.
P_NAME = SY-UNAME.
P_DATE = SY-DATUM - 1.

S_MATNR-LOW = '1'.
S_MATNR-HIGH = '10'.
S_MATNR-OPTION = 'BT'.
S_MATNR-SIGN = 'I'.
APPEND S_MATNR.
CLEAR S_MATNR.

START-OF-SELECTION.
WRITE 'START OF PROGRAM'.
```

Before the selection screen comes up, in the code between the two events `INITIALIZATION` and `START-OF-SELECTION`, the parameters for the user name, date, and the selection-screen range for material number are all blank (see Figure 10-1). However, if you include the code lines just shown, the new selection screen appears with values already filled in (see Figure 10-2).

Essentially, the code that appears after the event `INITIALIZATION` and before the next event, usually `START-OF-SELECTION`, is used to define the default or initial values of the `PARAMETERS` and `SELECT-OPTIONS`. The difference between defining default values in the actual `PARAMETER` definition, using the `DEFAULT` addition, and defining the value after the `INITIALIZATION` event, is that the default values can be calculated with `INITIALIZATION`. The values defined after the `INITIALIZATION` event are also present in background processing, where the application is run in background mode. Background mode is used when a program is not run online, but in a batch. The program is scheduled to run automatically without a user clicking an Execute button, and the `INITIALIZATION` values appear automatically in the selection screen.

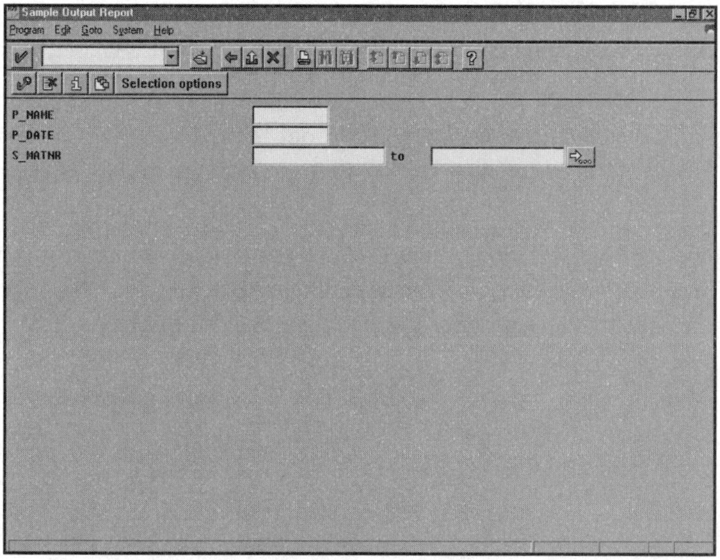

FIGURE 10-1

The selection screen with parameters and select-options initialized, but without values

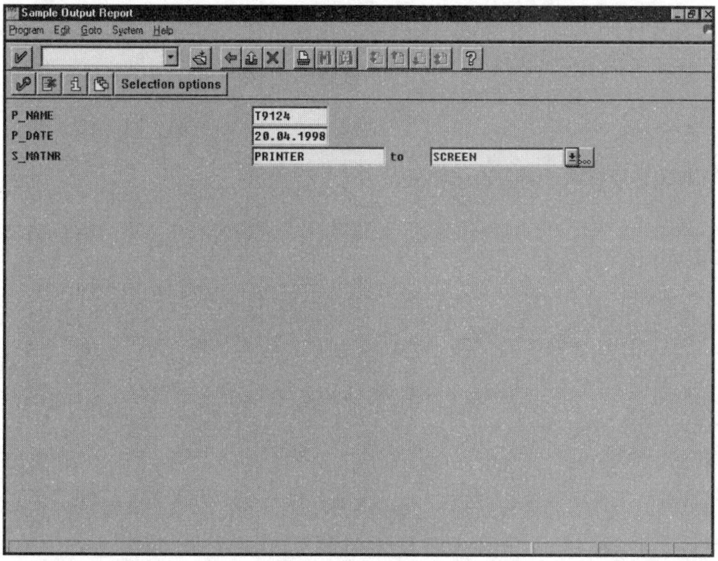

FIGURE 10-2

The selection screen with parameters and select-options initialized, with values

Using the START-OF-SELECTION and END-OF-SELECTION Markers

The START-OF-SELECTION event defines the code that will be processed initially—before any logical database access. This means that when the GET command is executed to utilize logical databases, the data extraction from that logical database occurs by looping through the code defined between the START-OF-SELECTION and END-OF-SELECTION markers. (See Chapter 13, "Working with Logical Databases," for details.)

Essentially, the START-OF-SELECTION and END-OF-SELECTION combination marks the place in the code that the data is read from the database and processed. The START-OF-SELECTION event also marks when another event has ended, such as INITIALIZATION.

In the following example, the INITIALIZATION event is performed first. The selection screen appears next. After the data is entered or changed, the next piece of code to run is the code that appears after the START-OF-SELECTION event:

```
REPORT ZABAPER.

TABLES:     MARC,
            MARD,
           MSEG,
            VBFA.

PARAMETERS:     P_NAME LIKE SY-UNAME,
                P_DATE LIKE SY-DATUM.

SELECT-OPTIONS: S_MATNR FOR MSEG-MATNR.

INITIALIZATION.
P_NAME = SY-UNAME.
P_DATE = SY-DATUM - 1.

S_MATNR-LOW = '1'.
S_MATNR-HIGH = '10'.
S_MATNR-OPTION = 'BT'.
S_MATNR-SIGN = 'I'.
APPEND S_MATNR.
CLEAR S_MATNR.

START-OF-SELECTION.
WRITE 'START OF PROGRAM'.
```

```
PERFORM SAMPLE_SUBROUTINE.
END-OF-SELECTION.

FORM SAMPLE_SUBROUTINE.
ENDFORM.
```

START-OF-SELECTION and END-OF-SELECTION, like INITIALIZATION, help with the timing of the code being run in ABAP. The code after END-OF-SELECTION is triggered after all logical database records are read, or after a STOP command is executed somewhere in the code.

Triggering Code with AT event

There are certain times when events can trigger certain code in the program to run. These events are governed by the AT event command. The event is an event defined by the commands that follow the AT event. If the specified event occurs (for example, a function key is pressed), the code after the AT event command is executed. The ENDAT command defines the end of the code that must be executed if the event occurs.

The following sections explore some of the events used with AT event.

Executing User Commands (AT USER-COMMAND and AT LINE-SELECTION)

The USER-COMMAND event is used in interactive reporting. The code between the AT USER-COMMAND and the ENDAT command is executed when the user enters data into the OK code field (the upper-left entry field on the screen where you enter transactions) or when a function key is pressed. The data entered into the OK code field is stored in the system field SY-UCOMM.

The following code generates a crude report on-screen. If the user selects a line with the cursor and types DETA for detail, the program checks the detail table BSEG for the details associated with that document number and prints them to the screen. If no data is found, a message is printed saying NO DATA FOUND. Finally, if the user types END, the message END OF REPORT is written to the screen:

```
REPORT ZABAP2.

TABLES:     BKPF,
            BSEG.
```

```
START-OF-SELECTION.
SELECT * FROM BKPF.
     WRITE BKPF.
     HIDE BKPF-BELNR.
ENDSELECT.
END-OF-SELECTION.

AT USER-COMMAND.
     CASE SY-UCOMM.
          WHEN 'DETA'.
               SELECT * FROM BSEG WHERE  BELNR = BKPF-BELNR.
                    IF SY-SUBRC <> 0.
                         WRITE ' NO DATA FOUND'.
                    ENDIF.
                    WRITE BSEG.
               ENDSELECT.
          WHEN 'END'.
               WRITE 'END OF REPORT'.
     ENDCASE.
```

The `AT LINE-SELECTION` command defines the code that's executed after a user double-clicks a line or presses the F2 function key:

```
REPORT ABAP3.

TABLES:      BKPF,
             BSEG.

START-OF-SELECTION.
GET BKPF.
     WRITE BKPF.
     HIDE BKPF-GJAHR.
END-OF-SELECTION.

AT LINE-SELECTION.
     CHECK BKPF-GJAHR <> ' '.
```

```
SELECT * FROM BSEG WHERE GJAHR = BKPF-GJAHR.
IF SY-SUBRC <> 0.
     WRITE 'NO DATA EXISTS FOR THAT FISCAL YEAR'.
ENDIF.
     WRITE BSEG.
ENDSELECT.
```

The `HIDE` command in this example temporarily stores the contents of the fields displayed to the screen. (See the later section "Hiding Field Contents with `HIDE`" for details.) The `CHECK` statement makes sure that a valid line is selected (a line is selected that contains data from `BKPF`).

Essentially, the `LINE-SELECTION` event is specific to the double-click or the F2 function key. The function key can be changed, but that should be a rare occurrence—you have to use screen and menu painter logic that isn't covered in this book.

Controlling Function Keys (AT PFfunction key number)

The event `AT PF`*`function_key number`* governs function keys that the user would press in interactive reporting. *`function key number`* is a number from 1 to 24. The number can't be a variable. Essentially, a report is displayed and then the processor "waits" for the user to press a function key. When this function key is pressed, the code after the `AT` command is executed. Here's a very simple version of code demonstrating this event:

```
REPORT ZABAP MESSAGE-ID ZZ.

TABLES:     PBIM,
            PBED.

SELECT * FROM PBIM WHERE MATNR LIKE '64%'.
     WRITE PBIM.
ENDSELECT.

AT PF8.
     MESSAGE I999 WITH 'FUNCTION KEY 8 IS PRESSED'.

AT PF10.
     MESSAGE I999 WITH 'FUNCTION KEY 10 IS PRESSED'.
```

This code checks the independent requirements table, `PBIM`, for all material numbers beginning with 64, and writes them to the screen. The `AT` commands aren't related precisely to the first code, but they exemplify exactly what the `AT PF`*`function key number`* command does. The code after the `AT` command could be any code, including the interactive reporting code demonstrated in the preceding sections. Any commands can be executed after the function key is pressed that represents the code after the `AT` command.

Processing Screen Input (AT SELECTION-SCREEN)

The `AT SELECTION-SCREEN` event is processed after the selection screen from a program is processed. For example, the selection screen is brought up on-screen, the user enters the data, and then clicks the Execute button. Before any code starts, the code after the `AT SELECTION-SCREEN` command is executed. Generally this `AT` command is used to check for errors so that the user can reprocess the screen if the initial data input was invalid. Here's an example:

```
REPORT ZABAP.

PARAMETERS:      P_NAME LIKE SY-UNAME.

AT SELECTION-SCREEN.
     IF P_NAME <> ' '.
          MESSAGE I999 WITH 'Please enter some data'.
     ENDIF.

WRITE: 'The current user is', P_NAME.
```

If the user doesn't enter any data but clicks the Execute button anyway, the `Please enter some data` message pops up, and the selection screen is reprocessed.

Triggering Events with Field Changes (AT NEW field and AT END OF field)

The `AT NEW` *`field`* command covers a field changing in an internal table. If a new value is encountered in *`field`*, the commands after the `AT` command are executed.

The following program loops through the internal table `INT_PBIM`, created by a data extract from the database table `PBIM`. Every time a new material number appears, the program writes `NEW MATERIAL NUMBER`. Essentially, if a new value appears in *`field`*, the `AT` event is triggered.

```
REPORT ZABAP.
TABLES:     PBIM.

DATA:       BEGIN OF INT_PBIM OCCURS 1000.
           INCLUDE STRUCTURE PBIM.
DATA:       END OF INT_PBIM.

SELECT * FROM PBIM INTO TABLE INT_PBIM.

LOOP AT INT_PBIM.

     AT NEW MATNR.
          WRITE 'NEW MATERIAL NUMBER'.
     ENDAT.
     WRITE INT_PBIM.
ENDLOOP.
```

The AT END OF *field* command is almost exactly the same as AT NEW *field*—except that the event is triggered after the last encounter of the value in the field. This code waits until the last instance of a material number is reached and then writes a message to the screen indicating how many instances of that material number were processed:

```
REPORT ZABAP.
TABLES:     PBIM.

DATA:       BEGIN OF INT_PBIM OCCURS 1000.
           INCLUDE STRUCTURE PBIM.
DATA:       END OF INT_PBIM.

DATA:       W_INDEX LIKE SY-TABIX.

SELECT * FROM PBIM INTO TABLE INT_PBIM.

LOOP AT INT_PBIM.
     W_INDEX = W_INDEX + 1.
     AT END OF MATNR.
```

```
            WRITE W_INDEX, 'INSTANCES OF ', INT_PBIM-MATNR.
WRITE:
            CLEAR W_INDEX.
      ENDAT.
      WRITE INT_PBIM.
ENDLOOP.
```

NOTE

The AT *field-group* command, although it's one of the AT commands, is covered in the later section on field groups, "Using Field Groups as an Alternative to Internal Tables." (You need to understand field groups before AT *field-group* will make sense to you. To explain the purpose and use of this event here would be putting the cart before the horse.)

Hiding Field Contents with HIDE

The HIDE command stores the contents of a field in memory, if the line is selected via cursor position. The syntax for this command is pretty simple:

```
HIDE field.
```

If a line is double-clicked or selected and then a function key is pressed, *field* is populated with the data from the current line holding that field. For example, if a selected line has the three fields *name*, *address*, and *phone number*, and a HIDE ADDRESS command has been issued, the address on the selected line is put into the field ADDRESS.

The following program loops through the customer data table, KNA1, and prints the contents to the screen. When it's finished, the user selects a line and double-clicks and the program writes the customer number of that line to the screen.

```
REPORT ZABAP.
TABLES: KNA1.

SELECT * FROM KNA1.
     WRITE KNA1.
     HIDE KNA1-KUNNR.
ENDSELECT.
```

```
AT LINE-SELECTION.
     CHECK KNA1-KUNNR <> ' '.
     WRITE KNA1-KUNNR.
```

Using Field Groups as an Alternative to Internal Tables

Field groups combine fields from the data declaration portion of the program into one group; in other words, several fields are grouped together under one field-group name. At runtime, the `INSERT` command is used to define which data fields are assigned to which field group. There should always be a `HEADER` field group that defines how the extracted data will be sorted; the data is sorted by the fields grouped under the `HEADER` field group.

Defining Field Groups

The syntax for defining the field groups is very simple:

```
FIELD-GROUPS:      field group 1, field group 2.
```

Now look at an example of how a field group is defined and which fields are assigned to it:

```
REPORT:      ZABAP.

TABLES: ZCUSTOMERS.

DATA:      NAME(10) TYPE C,
           ADDRESS(50) TYPE C,
           PHONE(10) TYPE C.

FIELD-GROUPS:      HEADER,
                  ITEM.

INSERT NAME INTO HEADER.
INSERT ADDRESS PHONE INTO ITEM.
```

Every time the HEADER is referenced, it points to the data field NAME. Also, if you attempt to sort the data extract, it will be sorted by the field NAME, which is the only field in the field group HEADER. Make sure you always define a header because this is the group that SORT works from. To store a lot of records, the data must be copied to a storage area using the EXTRACT command (see the next section).

Extracting Data

As the data fields are populated, you'd probably like to save them. To do this, you use the EXTRACT command. The EXTRACT command copies the contents of the fields to a sequential dataset in the paging area of memory. The syntax of the field is:

```
EXTRACT field group
```

This command takes all the values of all the fields and copies them to a place in memory. As you move through the new data, each record is copied to memory. (Take a look at the last example in this chapter for a complete description and demonstration of how the entire process works.)

Sorting the Records (SORT)

The SORT command sorts all the records by the HEADER field group. The syntax for this command is just this:

```
SORT.
```

Because no internal table is referenced by the SORT command, the processor takes the SORT command and points it at the field groups. The SORT command is very simple.

It's possible to sort by a field group other than HEADER. If you want to do this, type the following command, specifying the *field group* you want to use:

```
SORT BY field groupj.
```

The program sorts all the records by the fields contained in *field group*.

Copying Records to Fields with LOOP

The LOOP command is similar to the SORT command. The general syntax is

```
LOOP.
      code
ENDLOOP.
```

The LOOP command essentially copies the records found in the paging area of memory, one by one, to the current fields in memory. As each pass of the loop is processed, a new record is copied to those fields.

Triggering an Event with a New Value (AT field-group)

The AT *field group* command is an event that triggers when a new value is encountered in the referenced *field group*. The code following the AT statement and enclosed by the ENDAT statement is executed if a new value is found in *field group*.

```
REPORT ZABAP.

DATA:       NAME(10)          TYPE C,
            ADDRESS(50)       TYPE C,
            CITY(30)          TYPE C,
            PHONE(10)         TYPE C.

FIELD-GROUPS:    HEADER, DATA.

INSERT NAME                    INTO HEADER.
INSERT ADDRESS CITY PHONE      INTO DATA.

NAME = 'BOB'.
ADDRESS =       '1900 PENNSYLVANIA AVENUE'     .
CITY =          'WASHINGTON DC'.
PHONE =         '212-555-2345'.
EXTRACT HEADER.
EXTRACT DATA.
ADDRESS =      '789 LOS HOLTAS DRIVE'.
CITY =         'NEW HAVEN'.
PHONE =        '314-555-8934'.
EXTRACT DATA.
NAME = 'SKIP'.
ADDRESS =      '134 LOS COLTAS ST'      .
CITY =         'MARYSVILLE'.
```

```
PHONE =         '893-555-1245'.
EXTRACT HEADER.
EXTRACT DATA.
ADDRESS =       '9999 HENLEY STREET'.
CITY =          'REGENTS STREET'.
PHONE =         '987-555-1212'.
EXTRACT DATA.
NAME = 'ANNA'.
ADDRESS =       '3290 CITY DR.'.
CITY =          'SLIDELL'.
PHONE =         '916-555-1212'.
EXTRACT HEADER.
EXTRACT DATA.

SORT.

LOOP.
     AT HEADER.
          WRITE: / NAME.
     ENDAT.
     AT DATA.
          WRITE:/ ADDRESS, CITY, PHONE.
          WRITE:/.
     ENDAT.
ENDLOOP.
```

The program defines the field groups and the data in the data declaration portion of the program. Then, as the data is copied to the fields, copies of the data are made to the paging area by the `EXTRACT` command. Notice that the `HEADER` isn't always extracted at the same time as the `DATA` is extracted. If the records are unchanged in the header, there's no reason to extract that data again because the extract on the `DATA` field group copies all the information.

The output (on-screen) of this data would be:

```
BOB
1900 PENNSYLVANIA AVENUE                         WASHINGTON DC
212-555-2345
```

```
789 LOS HOLTAS DRIVE                              NEW HAVEN
314-555-8934

SKIP
9999 HENLEY STREET                                REGENTS STREET
987-555-1212

134 LOS COLTAS ST                                 MARYSVILLE
893-555-1245


ANNA
3290 CITY DR                                   SLIDELL
916-555-1212
```

As the code loops through the fields copied to the paging area, the data is displayed to the screen. On encountering a new name, the program outputs that name with the addresses, phone numbers, and cities associated with that name. Then another new name is found and output to the screen, along with all the pertinent information associated with that name.

Summary

This chapter discussed the advanced issues in creating output—working with events related to selection screen initialization and to interactive reporting. Working with events such as `AT` enables you to make the selection screen more dynamic and easier for the user to use. The `HIDE` command lets you print fields to the screen and save other fields in memory, waiting for the user to call them up via a function key or by some other means of selection.

This chapter also introduced the concept of field groups as an alternative to internal tables. Because field groups are stored in the paging area of memory and can hold much more information than internal tables, this is a very useful feature of ABAP/4.

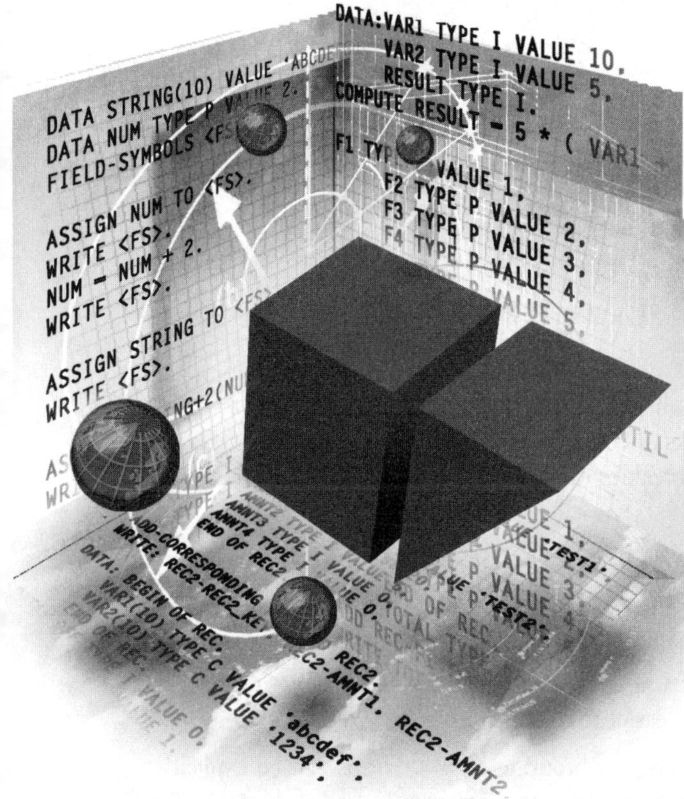

Chapter 11

Adding Subroutines to Your Program

In This Chapter

- Executing Subroutines (`PERFORM`)
- Defining Subroutines (`FORM`)
- Understanding the Scope of Local and Global Variables
- Form Examples

Like all modern programming languages, ABAP/4 allows the programmer to break programs into self-contained blocks of code. These blocks of code are often referred to as *subroutines*. The practice of breaking down a large program into smaller subroutines offers many advantages:

- Because the subroutines are self-contained, they can be debugged independently of each other.
- Changes in one subroutine don't affect any other part of the program.
- The overall complexity of a program can be hidden by breaking it into smaller pieces that may be easier to understand.

ABAP/4 calls the most basic type of a subroutine a *form*. Forms can be explicitly defined in a program, or can be made available to a program by use of the `INCLUDE` command. Forms are defined using the `FORM` command and invoked with the `PERFORM` command. A program can pass data to and from a form with parameters, variables, or constants, which are included in the `PERFORM` statement and can be used inside the form. With ABAP/4, parameters can be constants, variables, records, or internal tables.

A final subroutine issue is *variable scope*. The *scope* of a variable determines whether a subroutine can access that particular variable.

Using the information in this chapter, you should be able to use subroutines to develop large, complex programs while still maintaining readability and efficiency.

Executing Subroutines (PERFORM)

The `PERFORM` command executes a form that has been defined in the program by using the `FORM` command. The `PERFORM` statement can occur in the code prior to the physical location of the `FORM`—that is, a form doesn't need to be defined before you can use it with `PERFORM`.

The basic syntax for the `PERFORM` command is as follows:

```
PERFORM form   [USING     p1 p2 p3 ...]
               [CHANGING     p1 p2 p3 ...]
               [TABLES    itab1 itab2 itab3 ...].
```

When a PERFORM is issued, the system executes the named form and then continues execution with the next command following the PERFORM.

You use forms to break up programs into logical groups. For example, here's a program to write a simple report:

```
***  Report ZOFIM000

***  02/01/97


REPORT ZOFIM000 LINE-SIZE 132 MESSAGE-ID ZZ.

TABLES:  ...          "Table List Goes Here

DATA:    ...          "Global Variables Go Here


*** Start Execution


PERFORM INITIALIZATION.

PERFORM EXTRACT_DATA.

PERFORM PROCESS_DATA.

PERFORM PRINT_DATA.


*** End Program


*** Forms


FORM INITIALIZATION.       "Forms Go Here

...
```

Instead of an imposing list of raw code, someone looking at the program for the first time can immediately see the structure of the program. If a change needs to be made to the selection criteria for the report, you could tell immediately that the EXTRACT_DATA form is the section of the program where you need to look. The value of using this modular approach to programming can't be overstated.

Using Parameters to Pass Data (USING, TABLES, and CHANGING)

Data can be explicitly passed to and from a form with the USING and TABLES options. USING passes a single variable to a form. The CHANGING option has nearly the same effect (it's discussed later, in the forms section). If the value of the parameter is changed during the execution of the form, that new value is passed back on completion of the form when using the CHANGING option, or is immediately changed with the USING option. The TABLES option passes an internal table—with all its rows of data—to the form. As is the case with USING, if any of the rows in the internal tables are changed during the execution of the form, the new values are immediately changed. For example:

```
REPORT ZOMMR00 LINE-SIZE 80.


DATA:      BEGIN OF MATL_EXTRACT  OCCURS 1000,
             MATL#(18),            "Material Number
             MATL_QTY(8),          "Material Plant
             PLANT(4),             "Plant
           END OF MATL_EXTRACT.


DATA WS_RETURN_CODE LIKE SY-SUBRC.  "Return Code


*** Start Execution


PERFORM INITIALIZATION.
PERFORM EXTRACT_DATA TABLES MATL_EXTRACT
                     USING WS_RETURN_CODE.


IF WS_RETURN_CODE <> 0.
  EXIT.                        "Quit Program if Error
ENDIF.


PERFORM PROCESS_DATA TABLES MATL_EXTRACT
                     USING WS_RETURN_CODE.
```

```
IF WS_RETURN_CODE <> 0.
  EXIT.                     "Quit Program if Error
ENDIF.

PERFORM PRINT_DATA TABLES MATL_EXTRACT.

*** End Program

*** Forms

FORM INITIALIZATION.      "Forms Go Here
...
```

This program is similar to the one in the preceding section, but by using parameters it's obvious what the major data structure is for the program MATL_EXTRACT. You can see how this internal table is passed from subroutine to subroutine, and get a sense of how the data flows in the program. The use of parameters in forms becomes more important as programs grow in complexity, necessitating several internal tables and many variables.

Executing Multiple PERFORMs with Different Parameters

The following example executes the STRING_CONCATENATE form five times, using the parameters supplied:

```
*** Here are five PERFORM statements
PERFORM STRING_CONCATENATE USING 'PART' WS_TEMP1 VAR1.
PERFORM STRING_CONCATENATE USING 'PART' WS_TEMP2 VAR2.
PERFORM STRING_CONCATENATE USING 'PART' WS_TEMP3 VAR3.
PERFORM STRING_CONCATENATE USING 'PART' WS_TEMP4 VAR4.
PERFORM STRING_CONCATENATE USING 'PART' WS_TEMP5 VAR5.
```

Another way to write these five commands is as a single statement using the colon notation (see Chapter 1, "Data Types and Definitions," for details on the colon notation). Used with PERFORM, the colon notation allows multiple PERFORMs to take place, each one using a different set of parameters:

```
*** Here is a single statement that is functionally the same
PERFORM STRING_CONCATENATE:   USING 'PART' WS_TEMP1 VAR1,
```

```
USING 'PART' WS_TEMP2 VAR2,
USING 'PART' WS_TEMP3 VAR3,
USING 'PART' WS_TEMP4 VAR4,
USING 'PART' WS_TEMP5 VAR5.
```

Use the colon notation to improve readability when executing several PERFORMs at the same time with different parameters.

Defining Subroutines (FORM)

Now that you have seen a few simple examples of the PERFORM command in action, let's turn to the FORM command. This command defines the statements that make up a form. The block of code beginning with FORM must conclude with the statement ENDFORM.

NOTE

A form can't be defined within another form, but *recursive calls* or a form that calls itself are allowed. Also, you can declare new variables in a form, but this data is reinitialized each time the form is called—unless it's a recursive call, which can be a drag on performance.

The syntax for the FORM command is rather lengthy:

```
FORM form     [TABLES  itab1 itab2 itab3 ...]
[USING p1 [TYPE typ] p2 p3 ...]
[USING     VALUE(p1) [TYPE typ] VALUE(p2) VALUE(p3)...]
[CHANGING VALUE(p1) [TYPE typ] VALUE(p2) VALUE(p3)...]
[p STRUCTURE struct].
```

Forms should be grouped together at the end of the program, one after another. The only statement that can be placed after a FORM...ENDFORM block is another FORM statement. The name of a form can be up to 30 characters in length and should be descriptive as to the purpose of the form.

This is a simple example of the use of a form:

```
PERFORM PAGE_FOOTER.
...
```

```
PERFORM PAGE_HEADER.


FORM PAGE_FOOTER.
  WRITE:  1(10) SY-SUBRC, 72(6) WS_PAGE#.
ENDFORM.

FORM PAGE_HEADER.
  WRITE: 31(18) 'GL JOURNAL ENTRY'.
ENDFORM.
```

In this example, two simple forms print information for the header and footer of a page. They might be called hundreds of times in the execution of the program, and their purpose is very clear.

Using Parameters to Pass Data

The best way to make data available to a form to be used or changed is by passing it to the form as a parameter. Parameters must be defined in both the FORM and the PERFORM command. They are passed by location, so the first parameter listed in the PERFORM is passed to the first parameter listed in the FORM. Because of this scheme, you need to take care when using forms. It's very easy to make a mistake and get the parameters mixed up.

ABAP/4 does not require you to define a type for parameters in a subroutine, but it is advisable to do so. When you specify a data type for a form parameter, the ABAP/4 compiler can optimize the code it produces to handle the parameter in the most efficient way possible. Also, if you define a type for your parameters, the syntax check has a better chance to find errors made in the calling of forms.

The next sections discuss the types of parameters allowed in a form.

Passing Internal Tables by Reference (TABLES)

The TABLES parameter enables you to pass internal tables to subroutines by reference (you can't pass internal tables by value):

```
TABLES  itab1 itab2 itab3 ...
```

The TABLES parameter must always appear first in the FORM statement—before any USING or CHANGING.

To access any of the individual fields with the syntax `tab-field` (for example, `MARD-MATNR`), you must also use the `STRUCTURE` option. Without `STRUCTURE`, only line-oriented statements can be used, such as `WRITE itab`—you wouldn't be able to say `WRITE itab-FIELD1`. (See the later section "Indicating the Structure of the Incoming Parameter (STRUCTURE)" for details on using the `STRUCTURE` option.)

Passing Parameters by Reference or Value (USING)

This option defines the parameters *p1*, *p2*, *p3* and so on that are passed to the subroutine when it's called by a `PERFORM` statement:

```
USING p1 [TYPE typ] p2 p3 ...
```

The parameters are passed by reference, which means that any changes to the parameter during the execution of the subroutine immediately change the variable passed in by the `PERFORM` statement.

This option tells the system to define the parameters *p1*, *p2*, *p3* and so on that are passed to the subroutine by value:

```
USING VALUE(p1) [TYPE typ] VALUE(p2) VALUE(p3) ...
```

Passing by value means that any changes to the parameter during the execution of the subroutine won't affect the original variable.

NOTE

Reference parameters and value parameters can be combined in the same `USING` statement.

Returning Changes to the Original Variables (CHANGING VALUE)

The `CHANGING VALUE` option passes parameters by value, but also transfers any change of a parameter value back to the original variables when `ENDFORM` is reached:

```
CHANGING VALUE(p1) [TYPE typ]  VALUE(p2) VALUE(p3) ...
```

This is appropriate for recursive subroutine calls, for which the variable shouldn't be changed immediately—only when the subroutine ends. If the subroutine is canceled due to an error, no changes are made to the parameters specified by `CHANGING VALUE`.

Indicating the Structure of the Incoming Parameter (STRUCTURE)

The STRUCTURE option follows any parameter that refers to a record or an internal table. It tells the system what the field layout of the incoming parameter is going to be:

```
STRUCTURE struct
```

You can reference any of the individual fields of that structure in the subroutine. STRUCTURE also allows you to pass both data dictionary structures and internal structures (for example, internal tables or records). If you are going to access any of the fields within the record, you must include the STRUCTURE option.

Here's an example:

```
DATA:      BEGIN OF WS_REC,   "Record Variable
             F1(10) TYPE C,
             F2(4) TYPE N,
             F3(1) TYPE C,
           END OF WS_REC.

DATA BEGIN OF ITAB OCCURS 1000."Internal Table
  INCLUDE STRUCTURE BSEG.    "Financial Documents Table
DATA END OF ITAB.

...
PERFORM TEST   TABLES ITAB
                USING WS_REC.
...

FORM TEST      TABLES P_ITAB STRUCTURE BSEG
                USING P_REC STRUCTURE WS_REC.

  LOOP AT P_ITAB.                  "This is allowed with or without STRUCTURE
    WRITE:  /, P_ITAB-BELNR,     "This is allowed only with STRUCTURE
                P_REC-F1.
```

```
    WRITE:  /, P_ITAB,          "This is allowed with or without STRUCTURE
               P_REC.
  ENDLOOP.

ENDFORM.
```

Without the STRUCTURE option, the subroutine can't access any of the individual fields in a record or internal table.

Understanding the Scope of Local and Global Variables

When I talk about the *scope* of a variable, I'm referring to the areas of the program in which the variable can be used. ABAP/4 has only two types of scopes:

- Any variable defined in the main portion of a program is considered *global* and can be used anywhere in the program.
- Any variable defined in a subroutine is *local* and can be used only in that specific subroutine—nowhere else in the program.

Look at this code:

```
REPORT ZTEST1.

DATA:     GLOBAL1(10) TYPE C,     "These are global variables
          GLOBAL2(10) TYPE C.

***Start Main Program
GLOBAL1 = 'TEST'.

PERFORM FORM1.
***End Main Program

FORM FORM1.
  DATA:   W_FORM1(10) TYPE C,     "These are local because they are defined in a
form
          W2_FORM1(10) TYPE C.    "These can only be used in this form
```

```
  W_FORM1 = GLOBAL1.              "This is allowed because GLOBAL1 is global
  PERFORM FORM2 USING W_FORM1.

ENDFORM.

FORM FORM2 USING VALUE(P_1) TYPE C.     "Notice the name is different in the form

  GLOBAL2 = P_1.                           "This works because P_1 is passed
into this form
  W2_FORM1 = GLOBAL2.              "This would raise an error because W2_FORM1
                                                "is local to
FORM1 and can only be used there
ENDFORM.
```

This example has two global variables and two forms. In the first form, two variables are defined. Because the variables are defined in a form, they're local in scope and can be used only in FORM1. To use the variable W_FORM1 in FORM2, it's passed in as a parameter.

This program would raise an error because W2_FORM1 is referenced in FORM2. To use the variable without raising an error, it should be passed to FORM2 as a parameter, in the same way as W_FORM1 is passed.

As you can see, variable-scope rules in ABAP/4 are fairly straightforward. It's best to limit the number of global variables used and stick with local variables, which are passed as parameters to only those forms that need to use them.

Persistent Local Variables (STATICS)

Instead of using the DATA command to define local variables within a form, the STATICS command can be used. The syntax of the STATICS command is identical to that of DATA but the local variables defined by it persist after a form has been executed. When a local variable is defined with the data statement in a form, it is re-created each time the form is called. Re-creating the variable is slow and any value held by the variable is lost. On the other hand, a variable defined with STATICS is not re-created the second time a form is called. It persists between PERFORM commands and retains its value much like a global variable would. Despite this persistence, the scoping rules of a local variable still are in effect so the variable can only be accessed from within the form it was defined in. The following examples show the difference between STATICS and DATA variables.

```
REPORT ZTEST.

  PERFORM F1.
  PERFORM F1.

*Begin Forms
FORM F1.
  STATICS V1 TYPE I.
  ADD 1 TO V1.
  WRITE V1.
ENDFORM.
```

Here is the Output:

```
         1           2
```

In this first example, the local variable `V1` is defined by the `STATICS` command. The first time the form `F1` is called, `V1` is defined and initialized to a value of zero. After the add command, `V1` has a value of one. The second time `F1` is called, `V1` is still equal to one, so after the add command, it is now equal to two.

```
REPORT ZTEST2.

PERFORM F1.
PERFORM F1.

*Begin Forms
FORM F1.
  DATA V1 TYPE I.
  ADD 1 TO V1.
  WRITE V1.
ENDFORM.
```

Here is the Output:

```
         1           1
```

In this second example, the local variable V1 is defined by the DATA command. The first time the form F1 is called, V1 is defined and initialized to a value of zero. After the add command, V1 has a value of one. The second time F1 is called, V1 is redefined and initialized to a value of zero. So, after the add command, V1 is now equal to one again.

Form Examples

In this section, you'll take a look at some examples of using forms in programs. Forms aren't *required* in any program, but they're a great way to improve them.

The first example demonstrates the difference between passing parameters by reference and passing by value:

```
REPORT ZTEST.


DATA:      VAR1 TYPE I,
           VAR2 TYPE I.


***Begin Main Program
  VAR1 = 10.
  VAR2 = 25.


  PERFORM FORM1 USING VAR1 VAR2.


  WRITE:  VAR1, VAR2.
***End Main Program


FORM FORM1 USING P1 TYPE I VALUE(P2) TYPE I.


DATA LOCAL1 TYPE I VALUE 30.


  P1 = LOCAL1 + P2.
  PERFORM FORM2 USING LOCAL1 P1.


  P2 = LOCAL1.


ENDFORM.              "End FORM1
```

```
FORM FORM2 USING VALUE(P1) TYPE I P2 TYPE I.

  P1 = 50 + P2.
  P2 = P1.

ENDFORM.          "End FORM2
```

This example is confusing on purpose. It's an example of mixing value and reference; the output would be `105 25`. Despite the confusion, all you need to remember is that value parameters can't be changed in the subroutine; reference parameters can.

The next example shows how an internal table can be passed into subroutines. Remember that internal tables can be passed only by reference—not by value:

```
REPORT ZTEST.

DATA:     BEGIN OF ITAB OCCURS 100,
           FIELD1(10) TYPE C,
           FIELD2 TYPE I,
           END OF ITAB.
DATA VAR1 TYPE I VALUE 5.

***Begin Main Program
  ITAB-FIELD1 = 'ONE'.
  ITAB-FIELD2 = 100.
  APPEND ITAB.

  ITAB-FIELD1 = 'TWO'.
  ITAB-FIELD2 = 200.
  APPEND ITAB.

  ITAB-FIELD1 = 'THREE'.
  ITAB-FIELD2 = 300.
  APPEND ITAB.

  PERFORM FORM1 TABLES ITAB
                USING VAR1.
***End Main Program
```

```
FORM FORM1        TABLES PTAB STRUCTURE ITAB
                  USING P1.

  LOOP AT PTAB.
    PTAB-FIELD2 = PTAB-FIELD2 * P1.
    MODIFY PTAB.
  ENDLOOP.

ENDFORM.          "End FORM1
```

After the program is run, this would be the value of the internal table ITAB:

```
FIELD1      FIELD2
ONE         500
TWO         1000
THREE       1500
```

The next example demonstrates the use of the CHANGING parameter in a recursive function call. Remember that a recursive form is a form that calls itself. USING parameters can't be used with recursive functions because they change the value of parameters immediately. For recursive forms, the parameters should be changed only after the form has ended, which is exactly how CHANGING operates. This example calculates N!, which is the classic example of a recursive subroutine. The answer to N! is calculated as 1 * 2 * 3 * 4 *...* N—or, put another way, N * (N – 1)! Because the same function is used over and over again, it's perfect for a recursive form:

```
REPORT ZTEST.

DATA W_RESULT TYPE I.  "Result of Calculation

PARAMETER P_NUM TYPE I.  "Number to be calculated

*** Begin Main Processing
  PERFORM CALC_POWER CHANGING P_NUM W_RESULT.

  WRITE: 'The answer is ', W_RESULT.
*** End Main Processing
```

```
***  Form CALC_POWER
***  This form will calculate ! for the input
***  and return the result in output.
FORM CALC_POWER CHANGING VALUE(P_INPUT) VALUE(P_OUTPUT).

DATA: W_TEMP_IN TYPE I,   "Holds temp value for calculation
      W_TEMP_OUT TYPE I.  "Holds temp result of calculation

  IF P_INPUT <> 1.                          "Call form until input is one
    W_TEMP_IN = P_INPUT - 1.
    PERFORM CALC_POWER CHANGING W_TEMP_IN W_TEMP_OUT.
  ELSE.                                     "Output is one when input is one
    W_TEMP_OUT = 1.
  ENDIF.

  P_OUTPUT = P_INPUT * W_TEMP_OUT.        "Calculate answer

ENDFORM.  "End CALC_POWER
```

When this program is run, it prompts the user to enter a number and then returns the result. So if a user enters **4**, the result returned is 1 * 2 * 3 * 4 or 24. The program calculates this by passing the value `4` into the `CALC_POWER` form. In the form, the input value of `4` is multiplied by the result from calling itself—using `4 -1` or `3` as the input value. Each time the form calls itself, the current values are saved. The form keeps calling itself until the input is `1`, at which point the result is set to `1` as well, and the form ends, which causes the `CHANGING` parameter to be passed back to the calling form with the answer.

The use of recursion in forms isn't a common operation, but for some tasks like the example just shown, it can provide extremely elegant solutions.

This final example is another demonstration of recursion. In this case, you call the same form repeatedly to read the nested structure of a sales order. Within R/3, a sales order can be made up of multiple materials. In some cases, the materials may be part of a hierarchical structure. For example, the first material might be a car and below that in the hierarchy would be an engine and below that a piston. In this example, you read the entire hierarchy and look up the product division of each material and then produce a report of materials sorted by the division.

```
REPORT ZC LINE-SIZE 132 LINE-COUNT 65 MESSAGE-ID ZZ.

TABLES: VBAP,       "Sales Item Table
    MARA.                   "Material Master

DATA: BEGIN OF IORD OCCURS 10,
        POSNR LIKE VBAP-POSNR,          "Sales Item
        MATNR LIKE VBAP-MATNR,       "Material
        SPART LIKE MARA-SPART,          "Division
      END OF IORD.

PARAMETERS: P_VBELN LIKE VBAP-VBELN,  "Sales Order
            P_POSNR LIKE VBAP-POSNR.  "Sales Item

* Begin Program
START-OF-SELECTION.
* Get Top of Hierarchy from Input Parameters
  SELECT SINGLE MATNR INTO IORD-MATNR
                       FROM VBAP
                       WHERE VBELN = P_VBELN
                         AND POSNR = P_POSNR.
  IF SY-SUBRC EQ 0.
    SELECT SINGLE SPART INTO IORD-SPART
                         FROM MARA
                         WHERE MATNR = IORD-MATNR.
*   Record Top-Level item
    IORD-POSNR = P_POSNR.
    APPEND IORD.

*   Get all nested items
    PERFORM GET_CHILD_ITEMS USING P_POSNR.

*   Print results
    SORT IORD BY SPART MATNR.
    LOOP AT IORD.
```

```
      WRITE: / IORD-SPART,
               IORD-MATNR,
               IORD-POSNR,
               P_VBELN.
    ENDLOOP.
  ENDIF.

*---------------------------------------------------------------------*
*       FORM GET_CHILD_ITEMS
*---------------------------------------------------------------------*
*       Get any lower level items                                     *
*---------------------------------------------------------------------*
*  —>  HIGH_ITEM                                                      *
*---------------------------------------------------------------------*
FORM GET_CHILD_ITEMS USING PARENT LIKE VBAP-POSNR.

*   UEPOS hold's the parent item number
  SELECT POSNR MATNR INTO CORRESPONDING FIELDS OF VBAP
                                            FROM VBAP WHERE VBELN =
P_VBELN

AND UEPOS = PARENT.

    IORD-POSNR = VBAP-POSNR.
    IORD-MATNR = VBAP-MATNR.
    SELECT SINGLE SPART INTO IORD-SPART
                        FROM MARA
                        WHERE MATNR = IORD-MATNR.

*   Record Current Item
    APPEND IORD.
*   Get any children items of current item
    PERFORM GET_CHILD_ITEMS USING VBAP-POSNR.
  ENDSELECT.
ENDFORM.                              " GET_CHILD_ITEMS
```

The output of this report might look like this:

```
A1          9123-A52     000010  6002300
A1          9123-B62     000050  6002300
A4          9143-A52     000020  6002300
B1          9223-Z52     000040  6002300
B1          9124-Z52     000030  6002300
B1          9123-Z62     000100  6002300
B1          9223-Z72     000090  6002300
B1          9123-Z54     000060  6002300
C2          9173-F52     000070  6002300
C2          9133-F52     000080  6002300
```

Summary

The process of breaking down a large program into smaller, more manageable blocks of code is a standard programming technique. This technique is supported in ABAP/4 through the `FORM` and `PERFORM` commands. By breaking down programs into smaller subroutines, you make them easier to understand, maintain, and enhance. Instead of using global variables throughout a program, it's better to pass variables from one form to another as parameters. Variables can be passed by reference, where changes to the variable in the form are permanent, or by value, where variables can't be changed in the form. Programming examples in future chapters make extensive use of forms and parameters.

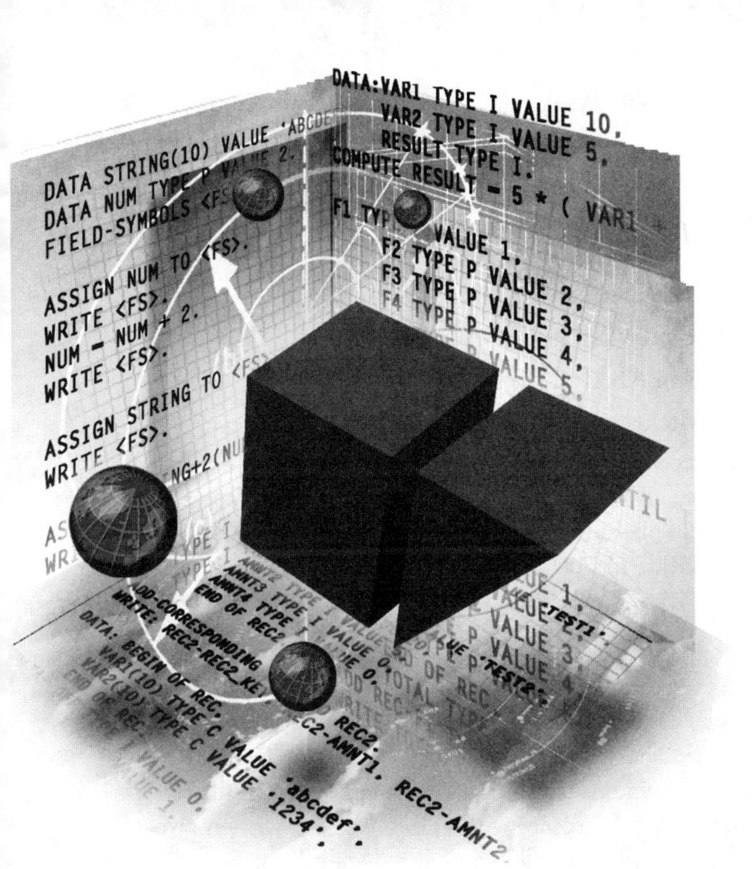

Chapter 12

Using Function Modules

In This Chapter

- Using the Function Modules Screen
- Creating a Custom Function Module
- Using Function Modules in ABAP Code
- Some Useful Function Modules

Imagine for a moment that you receive your first sheet of specifications for your first program—and then SAP America calls and says that they'll write half the code for you. Not only would you be ecstatic because there's less work to do, but you would also know that the code they provide has been tested extensively. To some extent, SAP has already done this by providing ready-to-use function modules along with their software package.

A *function module* is a separate program that can be called from your ABAP code to perform a specific task. Examples of such tasks include uploading and downloading files between the application server and your PC, calculating whether a date falls on a Sunday or a Monday, or perhaps rounding a number with decimals in it to the second place. The software provided by SAP comes with a library of pre-written programs that can be called to do these tasks, as well as a multitude of others.

These function modules are called by the ABAP code using the CALL statement. You, the programmer, provide the fields that hold the necessary information for the function module to do its work, as well as fields to receive the results of the work from the function calls. This chapter introduces you to the function module maintenance screen, where you can search for function modules by keywords, test function modules, examine what input and output parameters must be used, and view the source code SAP has used to program these function calls.

NOTE

Function calls are the code that makes a "call" from the ABAP/4 code to the function module. The function module is the actual code and characteristics of the function module.

Using the Function Modules Screen

The Maintain Function Modules screen has quite a few features. To navigate to the screen, follow the menu path Tools|Applications|Development|Function Library Button. The quick transaction code is SE37 entered in the command line on top of any screen.

Within the Maintain Function Modules screen, you can view several features of the function module (see Figure 12-1). The screen has an input line to enter the function module name. By clicking one of the option buttons on the screen, you can display or modify the import/export parameters, the exceptions list, the documentation, the notes, the source code, and several other items of the selected module.

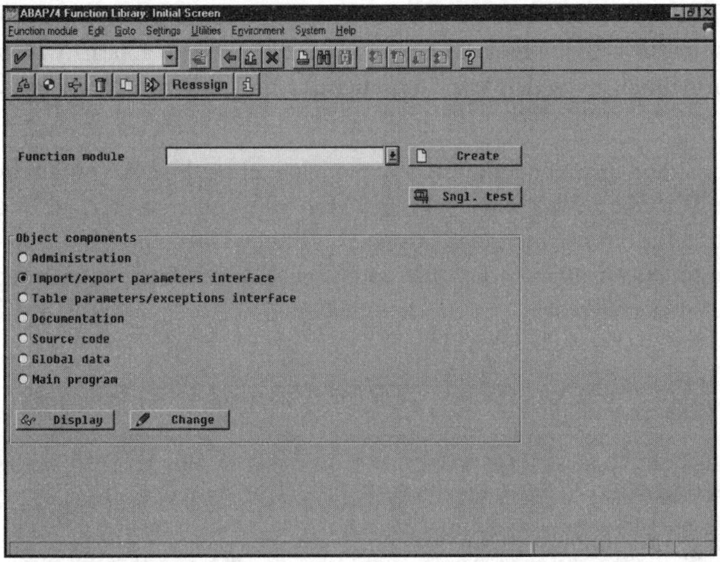

FIGURE 12-1

The Maintain Function Modules screen

An important item to note is the import/export parameters, which represent the data that your ABAP/4 code sends into the function module and receives from the function module. Documentation provides important criteria for searching. The source code lets you view what the function module is doing when you call it.

TIP

Remember that the function module isn't magic; it's just another ABAP/4 program written by SAP or a third party to accomplish a certain task. You can gain a great deal of programming knowledge by viewing the code used in function modules. By clicking the Test button, you can run the function module in test mode with sample data to see whether it provides the output you need.

The hardest part about starting to learn ABAP/4 is that the lack of experience with the SAP system puts you at a disadvantage. Seasoned ABAPers have used many function modules and usually have some favorites that they use quite often in their programs. For your convenience, a list of favorite function modules used by the authors is provided at the end of this chapter. You should learn how these function modules work and how best to use them. For now, the next section demonstrates how to search for a function module that you need.

Searching for a Specific Function Module

To search for a function module, click the Find button on the Maintain Function Modules screen (`se37`). The Find Function Modules screen appears with a variety of search methods by which you can search for the desired function module (see Figure 12-2).

The best method to search for a function module is either by entering a string in the Function Name box along with asterisks (*) for wild-card characters, or by entering key words in the Short Description box (in the "Search Documentation For" section). After the processor returns a list, just double-click the desired function module to bring it up and analyze it.

> **NOTE**
>
> For a beginner ABAPer, there's no guarantee that a desired function module exists, but SAP has covered almost everything a programmer could desire. If the exact function module you need doesn't exist, maybe you can alter the output to fit the program specifications, or alter the function module and make your own version of it to get the correct results.

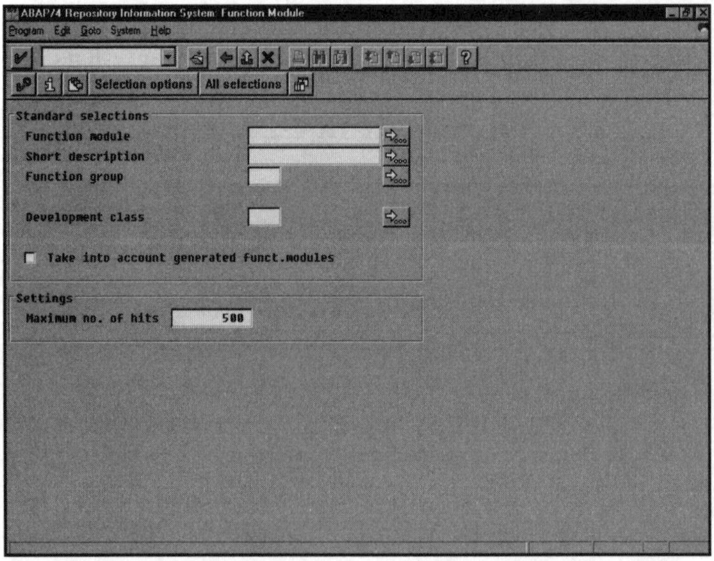

FIGURE 12-2

Searching for Function Modules. Enter your search criteria, and click 'Execute'.

Testing Individual Function Modules

At the Maintain Function Modules screen, you can click the Test button to test a function module. A screen appears in which you can enter sample input data, and the function module will show the output fields, using the sample data (see Figure 12-3).

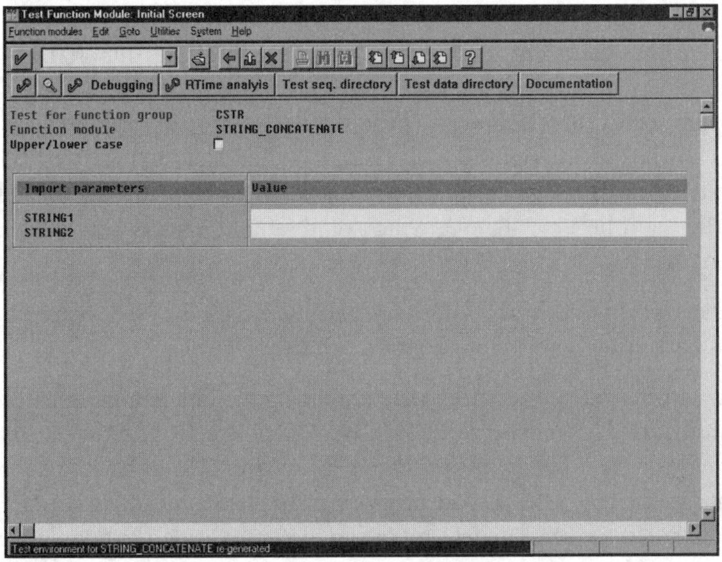

FIGURE 12-3

The Test Environment for Function Modules screen

After filling in the list of input parameters, click the Execute button. The output parameters will be filled on the lower half of the screen.

Creating a Custom Function Module

If you find certain programs that you have created are using identical code, perhaps it's time that you develop your own function modules. It's a very simple process in which you create simple ABAP code and just define the input and output parameters.

Defining Input/Output Parameters

The first step is to open the Maintain Function Modules screen. Now you need to give a name to your function module. Pick any name that hasn't been used before, but be sure to start the name with the letter Z to denote that this function module was created by a third party. Type the desired name in the Function Module combo box.

When you eventually click the Create button to begin creating the function module (don't do it yet), the screen that appears will be related to your choice of option buttons below the function name. The two most important aspects of the function module are the import/export parameter interface and the source code. The third important aspect is the table fields, if you're using a table, and defining the exceptions or errors.

To start creating your function module, click the Interface Import/Export Parameters button and then click Create. A screen will appear where you can define your import and export parameters. Type the names of your desired fields in these boxes. In the box to the right of each field, type the data dictionary or table fields in which to define these parameters. For example, if you typed `Year`, the field to the right of it might be `BKPF-GJAHR`, which represents the fiscal year field from the accounting header.

Create the export fields in the same way, and then click the Next Screen button or the green back arrow to work on the source code.

Import parameters are passed from the program to the function module. Their path is one way, from the program to the function module code. Export parameters are exactly the opposite. They are passed from the function module back to the program. Note, that in the code, the import parameters are listed under "exporting" and the export parameters are listed under "importing" because the descriptions are relative to where the variables are. Table parameters are not restricted to one-way traffic. They are passed back and forth between the code and the function module.

Developing the ABAP Code

When you're ready to work on the source code for your function module, you reach it by using the Source Code button on the Maintain Function Modules screen. The ABAP/4 editor screen (`se38`) will open.

Because you've already defined the input and output parameters, these are defined as variables in your program—even though no formal data declarations are found in the source code. The procedure is very simple from here on. Just assume that the input parameters contain data, and manipulate the data in whatever way you need to obtain the output you want. Store that output in the parameters you define as the output parameters. The ABAP code that calls your program will output the parameters needed by your function module and receive the data from your function module. Let's say that you use the string concatenate function module (which takes two strings and makes them into one). Your program would export the two strings, and the function module would send back one string. If you sent out `'abc'` and `'def'` you would get back `'abcdef'` in this example.

Defining Tables and Handling Errors

The next part of the process allows you to define the tables that you will be importing or exporting with the function module, and set up error-handling for errors your function module might encounter with data being input.

To define tables and errors, go back to the Maintain Function Modules screen and click the option button named Interface Table Parameters/Exceptions and then click Create.

To define tables, simply list the name by which you want to call your incoming or outgoing table. Then type the name of a data dictionary structure or internal table that has already been defined, to define the structure of your table. (If you have a unique table, be sure to use the data dictionary to declare and define your new table before writing the function module.) This process is exactly the same as defining the import and export parameter interface, except that you are now declaring tables rather than fields.

Because this program will be a remote program, you need to define the possible errors that the program might encounter. For example, if your function module is a program to read in the name of a customer and output the address from the database, one error might be that the customer referenced by the code doesn't exist. The code used to raise the event that activates that error is the `MESSAGE` command with a unique addition for function modules. The syntax is as follows:

```
MESSAGE Xnumber RAISING event.
```

`X` represents the type of message—`E`, `A`, `I`, or `S`—just like the regular `MESSAGE` command. *`number`* is the general message number. *`event`* is the exception that you define. When this event is raised, the definition that associates that event with a number for the `SY-SUBRC` puts that number in the return code. This definition is set when you call the function under `EXCEPTIONS`. (See the next section, on using function modules in ABAP/4 code.)

Simply brainstorm the most likely errors you will encounter and assign codes to them. The output of the `SY-SUBRC` (system return-code field) will be associated with these codes. `0` always represents a positive (no errors) result.

TIP

Try not to exceed five return codes so that the programmer doesn't get bogged down in return codes when using your function module.

Activating the Function Module

The final step in creating a function module is to click the Activate button. This step checks the function module for errors and compiles your ABAP code. If you encounter any errors, recheck your steps and your source code.

Using Function Modules in ABAP Code

The first step in using function modules is to search through the function library (using the Find Function Modules screen) for the function module you want to use. For this example, you'll use the function module `G_POSTING_DATE_OF_PERIOD_GET`. This function module is actually an `FI` (finance) function module to get the ending date of the current fiscal period.

To insert a function into your code, click the Insert Statement button on the ABAP/4 Editor Edit Program screen while you are in the editor. In the resulting dialog box, click the `CALL FUNCTION` option button and type the function module's name into the box (see Figure 12-4).

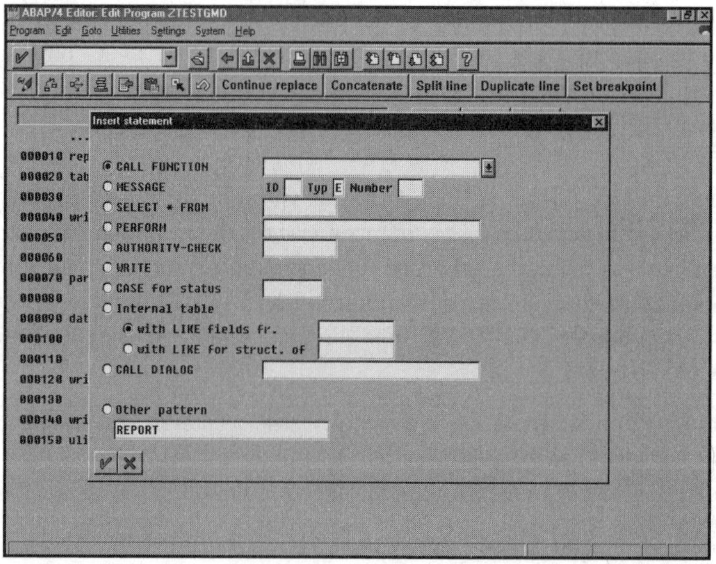

FIGURE 12-4

Inserting a function into code

For this example, type in `G_POSTING_DATE_OF_PERIOD_GET` and click OK. The code inserted into the program looks like this:

```
CALL FUNCTION 'G_POSTING_DATE_PERIOD_GET'
     EXPORTING
```

```
          PERIOD                    =
          VARIANT                   =
          YEAR                      =
     IMPORTING
          TO_DATE                   =
     EXCEPTIONS
          PERIOD_NOT_DEFINED        = 1
          VARIANT_NOT_DEFINED       = 2.
```

It's up to you, the programmer, to fill in the appropriate fields in this template that SAP conveniently inserts into your program. Once your code is inserted, along with the incoming and outgoing variables, you can use the function module to get the data you need. In this case, the incoming data consists of the fiscal period, a fiscal year variant, and the current year. The fiscal year period is a unique key used by SAP to define when your fiscal year begins and ends.

The subsequent code demonstrates how a function call is coded into an ABAP/4 program:

```
REPORT ZABAP.
MESSAGE-ID ZZ.

PARAMETERS:     P_PERIOD(3) TYPE N OBLIGATORY.

DATA:           W_VARIANT(2) TYPE C VALUE 'AM',
                W_ENDDATE LIKE SY-DATUM,
                W_YEAR(4) TYPE N.

MOVE SY-DATUM+0(4) TO W_YEAR.
CALL FUNCTION 'G_POSTING_DATE_OF_PERIOD_GET'
     EXPORTING
          PERIOD                    = P_PERIOD
          VARIANT                   = W_VARIANT
          YEAR                      = W_YEAR
     IMPORTING
          TO_DATE                   = W_ENDDATE
     EXCEPTIONS
          PERIOD_NOT_DEFINED        = 1
          VARIANT_NOT_DEFINED       = 2.
```

```
CASE SY-SUBRC.
     WHEN 1.
          MESSAGE E999 WITH 'PERIOD NOT DEFINED'.
     WHEN 2.
          MESSAGE E999  WITH 'VARIANT NOT DEFINED'.
     WHEN OTHERS.
          SHIFT W_ENDDATE BY 4 PLACES CIRCULAR.
ENDCASE.

WRITE W_ENDDATE.
```

The function module is now defined with input and output parameters, along with what the SY-SUBRC field will contain upon reaching the two exceptions defined.

Processing Input/Output Parameters

The program defines what the input data is by putting the appropriate data into the incoming fields. Notice that the parameter P_PERIOD is obligatory, meaning that the user can't get past the selection screen without entering a value into that field. The program then defines what the year and variant are, and the function module accepts these three values as the input parameters. Once processed, the code in the function module outputs the ending date into the output parameter, W_ENDDATE.

Defining Errors Encountered in Function Calls

If an error occurs in the function module, one of the two exception events are raised, and the SY-SUBRC field is populated with a value. The code after the function module then checks to see what the return code is, and outputs an appropriate message relating to that code. If there are no errors, the program modifies the output from the function module and then outputs it to the screen. In a regular program, the output would be used to retrieve more data from the database or something of that nature, but to keep the examples concise, it's just output to the screen here.

Some Useful Function Modules

- This set of function modules is used to download and upload files to and from your PC:

WS_DOWNLOAD	Automatically downloads a file to a PC
WS_UPLOAD	Automatically uploads a file to a PC

DOWNLOAD	Downloads a file, but prompts the user for name and path
UPLOAD	Uploads a file, but prompts the user for name and path

- This set of function modules works with fields and strings and manipulates them in useful ways:

STRING_CENTER	Transports a string into the target field in centered format

- This group of function modules generates random numbers:

QF05_RANDOM	Generates a random number
QF05_RANDOM_INTEGER	Generates a random integer
QF05_RANDOM_SAVE_SEED	Saves the initial value for the function modules
ROUND	Rounds a number to the correct place

- Useful Function Modules:

DATE_CONVERT_TO_FACTORYDATE	Intuitively, this function module converts a regular date to the factory date. Factory dates will take into account working holidays, and special days.
FACTORYDATE_CONVERT_TO_DATE	This is the reverse of the above function module.

- Fun Function Modules:

SAPGUI_PROGRESS_INDICATOR	This function call is the one that is responsible for creating the little progress indicator on the bottom left portion of the screen when programs are

generated, or a new transaction is compiled.

This function call can be added to your program to show the percent completion of the program. Be careful not to add this function module to programs that will be run over a modem line because the network time to ping the progress back and forth will extend the length of the program by hours, especially if the modem is 28.8 or slower. See the following example subroutine for some useful code.

```
FORM STATUS_INDICATOR USING COUNT-MAX    TYPE I
                            COUNT-ACTUAL TYPE I
                            TEXT TYPE C.
  DATA: BEGIN OF PERCENT,
          ACTUAL TYPE I,
          DISPLAY(3),
        END   OF PERCENT.

  DATA: MOD TYPE I.
  DATA: STRING(80).
  MOD = COUNT-ACTUAL MOD 05.            "jede 5. Lieferung
  CHECK MOD = 0.
  PERCENT-ACTUAL = 100 * COUNT-ACTUAL / COUNT-MAX.
  WRITE PERCENT-ACTUAL TO PERCENT-DISPLAY.
  STRING = TEXT.
  REPLACE '&' WITH PERCENT-DISPLAY INTO STRING.
  CONDENSE STRING.
  CALL FUNCTION 'SAPGUI_PROGRESS_INDICATOR'
       EXPORTING
            PERCENTAGE = PERCENT-ACTUAL
```

```
            TEXT         = STRING
        EXCEPTIONS
            OTHERS       = 1.

ENDFORM.                                  " PROCESS_INDICATOR
```

For example, say you are displaying records in an internal table. A describe command gets you the total number of records in the table, and looping through the table, you know the current record by the system variable SY-TABIX. The text could consist of something to the effect of '& Percent. Pass the total number of records to the COUNT-MAX, and the current record number to the COUNT-ACTUAL, and the text to the text field. Put the call to this form inside the loop through the table, and the indicator will show up on the bottom, along with a changing percentage! Have fun with this one.

Summary

This chapter introduced and explained how to program with function modules—code already written by SAP—in your ABAP/4 projects. It showed how you can develop your own function modules and how to utilize them in code as well.

A function module has import fields supplied by the program to the function module. The function module takes these fields, uses them, and produces export fields to send back to the program. Function modules are very useful—why write extra code if it already has been written for you?

Several useful function modules were listed; once you start programming in ABAP/4, you'll want to explore these modules to find out just how useful they really are.

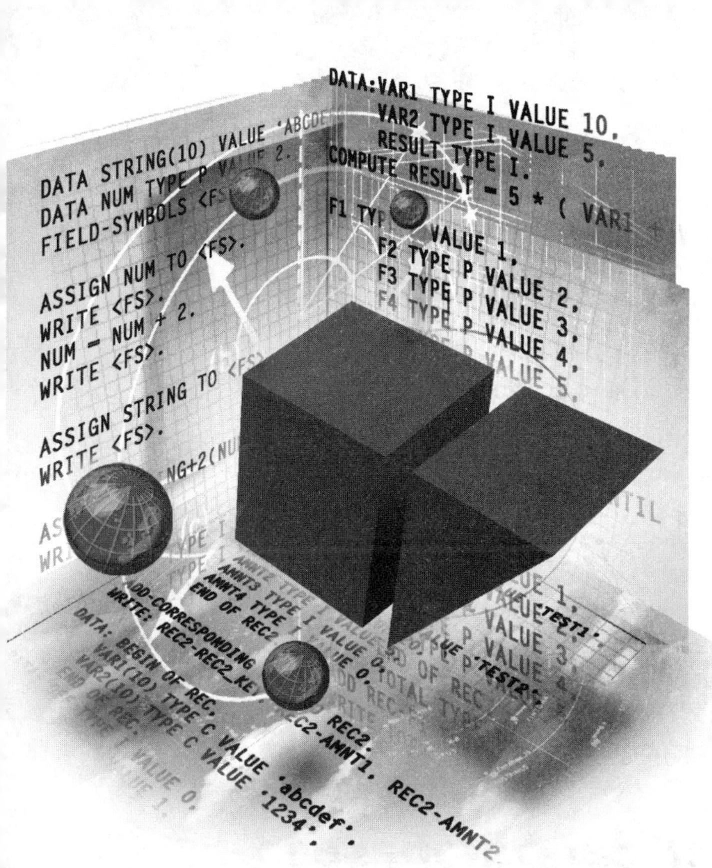

Chapter 13

Working with Logical Databases

In This Chapter

- Advantages of Logical Databases
- Using the GET Event to Retrieve Data
- Limiting Data with Logical Database Parameters

Chapter 8, "Using SAP SQL to Access Database Tables," introduced SAP SQL, a set of statements that allows the programmer to read and change data stored in the SAP database. In order to read data from a table, the SELECT command was used in that chapter. Another method that allows the programmer to read data from a table is through the use of a *logical database*. A logical database is actually a separate program, usually written by SAP, although user-created logical databases are allowed. A logical database provides read-only access to a group of related tables to an ABAP/4 program. When a program that calls a logical database is run, the program behind the logical database runs as well. The logical database issues the SELECT commands and returns the data to the calling program.

Advantages of Logical Databases

SAP uses a relational database to store data. Therefore, in order to read a single business object, such as a purchase order, the programmer must read from several tables. These tables are typically assembled in a parent-child relationship, where a single parent record in one table has zero or more child records in another table. In this case, the purchase order header information is in the database table EKKO, and each line item of the purchase order is stored in the database table EKPO.

The programmer must know the primary key for each table and use the key values to read from each table. The logical database hides this complexity from the programmer because it knows how the different tables relate to each other, and can issue the SELECT command with the proper where clause to retrieve the data. Because you don't have access to the where clause that the logical database uses, the logical database has its own selection screen with the typical criteria from which you might want the user to select. When you use a logical database in your program, this selection screen is called automatically, and the user can enter information to limit the data returned by the logical database. The developer can also use the CHECK command to limit what data the program processes, as described later in this chapter.

Using the GET Event to Retrieve Data

SAP includes a number of events that a programmer can use to enable the processing of data from a logical database. An *event* is a keyword that defines a block of code to be executed when the system detects the appropriate occurrence. The most important event for logical databases is the `GET table` event.

`GET` isn't a command like `SELECT` or `WRITE`; instead, it's an event. It can be confusing because ABAP/4 has no `ENDGET`; all code following the `GET` keyword is considered part of the `GET` event until another event keyword is reached—such as a different `GET table` or an `END-OF-SELECTION`. The syntax of the `GET` event is:

```
GET table [LATE].
```

Using events to access data in a logical database can be confusing at first, so you'll start with a simple example. All logical databases have three-character identifiers; for example, the logical database for material is `MSM`. A logical database is composed of several tables that form a *hierarchy*. The logical database makes data from that hierarchy available to an ABAP/4 program. A portion of the hierarchy for the `MSM` logical database is made up of these tables:

- `MARAV` (Material header)
- `MARM` (Quantity unit)
- `MBEWV` (View for logical database)
- `MVKE` (Material Master: Sales Data)
- `MARCV` (View table for the logical database `MGM`)
- `PROPF` (Forecast parameters)
- `MARD` (Material Master: Storage Location/Batch Segment)

`MARAV` is at the top of the hierarchy. Below it are `MARM`, `MBEWV`, `MVKE`, and `MARCV`. `MARCV` has two more tables below it: `PROPF` and `MARD`.

To access these tables via a `SELECT` command, the programmer would need to know how all these tables are related to each other. The material type is stored in `MARAV`, but the material location is in `MARD`, so to include both these values in a report would be a chore. When using a logical database, however, no knowledge of the relationships is required. Unfortunately, because ABAP/4 has no `ENDGET` command, reading code with multiple `GET` events can be confusing. You simply have to remember that a code block associated with an event ends with the next event statement, such as another `GET` or an `END-OF-SELECTION`:

```
REPORT ZOMMT00000.
```

```
TABLES:     MARAV,     "Material Header
MARD.     "Material Storage Location

START-OF-SELECTION.
  WRITE:  /, 'Extracting Materials and locations'.
  WRITE:  /, /, 'Material Number', 16 'Material Type'.

GET MARAV.
  WRITE:  /, /, (15) MARAV-MATNR,       "Material#
          16 MARAV-MTART.      "Material Type

GET MARD.
  WRITE:  /,      2(4) MARD-WERKS,      "Plant Code
          7 MARD-LGORT.          "Storage Location

END-OF-SELECTION.
  WRITE: /, /, 'Report Complete'.
```

NOTE

Notice that nowhere in the program is the logical database MSM mentioned. Unfortunately, logical databases are assigned in the program attributes, not directly in the ABAP/4 code. If you see the GET event in the program, however, you know that the program is using a logical database.

Now suppose that this report is run for Acme Tools, which currently has only three materials in SAP, and those materials can be allocated to any of three plants. The output of the report would look something like this:

```
Extracting Materials and locations

Material Number Material Type

0050000100        M001
  PLNA 0001
  PLNA 0002
  PLEU 0001
```

```
0050000200          M001
  PLNA 0002
  PLAS 0001

0050000300          T001
  PLAS 0001
  PLEU 0001

Report Complete
```

In the traditional top-down method of flow, you would expect a list of all the rows of data from MARAV, followed by all the rows of data from MARD. But events in a ABAP/4 program don't execute in a top-down manner; they execute when appropriate. When looking at a program that uses events, it's important not to try to read the code in a top-down manner. Each event is a separate subroutine that's executed when the system detects a certain condition.

In the example code, the logical database MSM reads data from the hierarchy of tables previously mentioned and makes this data available one row at a time. The first event triggered in the program is START-OF-SELECTION, which occurs just before any data is read. Next, the database is accessed by MSM. The first table in the hierarchy is MARAV, so the first row of this table is provided to the program triggering the GET MARAV event.

MSM continues to read through the tables in the hierarchy after MARAV—it reads from MBEWV, MVKE, MARCV, PROPF, and MARD, which again triggers an event in the program (GET MARD). For each record in MARD that's a child to the record read from the top of the hierarchy, MARAV, the GET MARD event is triggered.

When all rows have been read by MSM, control returns to MARAV. The program gets the next row. This action triggers the GET MARAV event, which prints the second material number.

From this point, the process repeats itself with the data being read from the tables lower in the hierarchy until all records that are children of the current MARAV record have been read. So the simple report is actually doing a great deal of work. This is often the case in ABAP/4, where much of the complexity can be hidden from a programmer. But this also means that a simple mistake can produce wildly wrong answers. A simple GET statement may in fact access four or more database tables if the GET specifies a table at the bottom of a logical database hierarchy. The overhead of reading from all those tables isn't obvious from looking at a single statement.

Using GET LATE

The modifier LATE changes the conditions that trigger the GET event. Instead of being triggered when a new row is made available to a program by a logical database, it's triggered after all records lower in the hierarchy have been processed. So if your first example is changed to use GET LATE like this:

```
REPORT ZOMMT00000.

TABLES:     MARAV,      "Material Header
MARD.      "Material Storage Location

START-OF-SELECTION.
  WRITE:  /, 'Extracting Materials and locations'.
  WRITE:  /, /, 'Material Number', 16 'Material Type'.

GET MARAV LATE.
  WRITE:  /, (15) MARAV-MATNR,       "Material#
          16 MARAV-MTART, /.      "Material Type

GET MARD.
  WRITE:  /,       2(4) MARD-WERKS,      "Plant Code
          7 MARD-LGORT.          "Storage Location

END-OF-SELECTION.
  WRITE: /, /, 'Report Complete'.
```

The resulting output would look like this:

```
Extracting Materials and locations

Material Number Material Type

  PLNA 0001
  PLNA 0002
  PLEU 0001
0050000100        M001
```

```
  PLNA 0002
  PLAS 0001
0050000200        M001

  PLAS 0001
  PLEU 0001
0050000300        T001

Report Complete
```

It's possible to use both `GET` and `GET LATE` events for the same table in the same program.

Limiting Data with Logical Database Parameters

Each logical database has its own selection screen with parameters that can be used at runtime to enter a set of criteria for the data returned to the program. For example, the Financial Documents logical database, `BRM`, uses the screen shown in Figure 13-1.

When a user enters values into the selection screen, those values are used as criteria when the logical database returns data to the calling program. Only rows of data that meet the criteria specified by the user are returned.

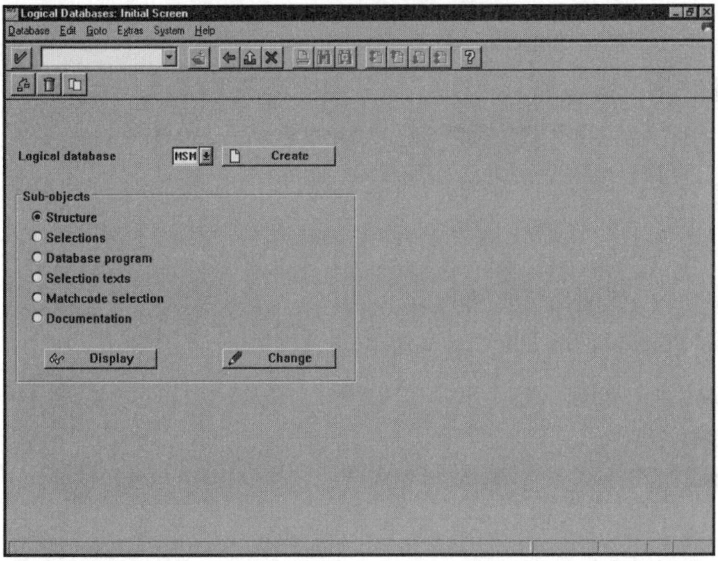

FIGURE 13-1

The selection screen for the logical database BRM

If other parameters are present in the program using the logical database, they'll be added to the end of the selection screen. This works well for entering criteria at runtime, but what if a program is required to apply criteria to the rows processed—*without* a user entering criteria at runtime? The basic way to accomplish this is by using a CHECK statement.

CHECK includes a conditional statement; if that condition fails, CHECK acts like an EXIT statement. When a CHECK statement fails in a logical database, processing for the current table stops and no subordinate table is read. For example, suppose that the report from the preceding example should list only data with a material type of T001:

```
REPORT ZOMMT00000.



TABLES:     MARAV,      "Material Header
MARD.     "Material Storage Location


START-OF-SELECTION.
  WRITE:  /, 'Extracting Materials and locations'.
  WRITE:  /, /, 'Material Number', 16 'Material Type'.


GET MARAV.
  CHECK MARAV-MTART = 'T001'.
  WRITE:  /, /, (15) MARAV-MATNR,       "Material#
          16 MARAV-MTART.      "Material Type


GET MARD.
  WRITE:  /,       2(4) MARD-WERKS,      "Plant Code
          7 MARD-LGORT.            "Storage Location


END-OF-SELECTION.
  WRITE: /, /, 'Report Complete'.
```

This would produce the following output:

```
0050000300        T001
  PLAS 0001
  PLEU 0001
```

Not only are the records from MARAV for which the material type isn't T001 not processed, but the child records from MARD for those records also aren't processed.

The CHECK command seems simple—and it really is. Use it to limit the amount of data returned from the database. When you use a SELECT statement without a where clause, it returns all rows from a single table. But when you use a GET event without a CHECK, the system not only must access all rows in that table, but also all rows in all tables above it in the logical database hierarchy. This can be a serious drain on performance. Remember the first rule of client-server programming: Limit database access as much as possible to improve performance.

Summary

Logical databases can be a convenient way of reading information from the database. Much of the complexity of a relational database is hidden from the programmer, resulting in programs that are simpler and easier to maintain. But this simplicity comes with a tradeoff in efficiency when using a logical database. Because the programmer has no access to the where clauses that the logical database uses to retrieve data, in some cases a program using a SELECT statement may give you better performance.

In general, if you're reading a small number of records from large tables and can make use of indexes other than the primary key, SELECTs are more efficient. But if you can use CHECKs at high levels in the table hierarchy to limit the amount of data being returned, logical databases can be efficient. Chapter 14, "Writing a Report," provides more examples of the tradeoffs from using SELECT versus logical databases.

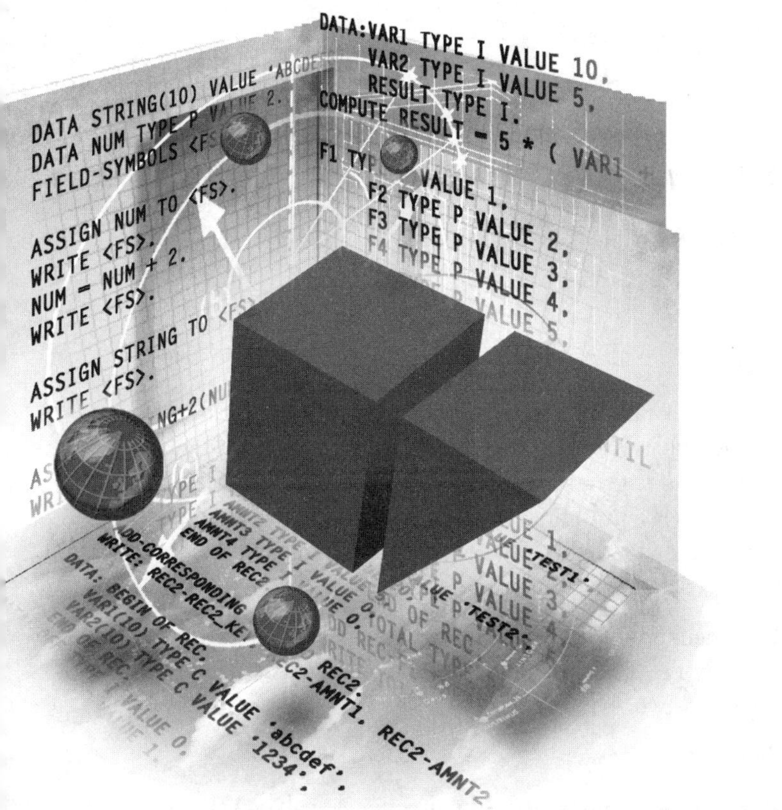

Chapter 14

Writing a Report

In This Chapter

- Functional Specifications
- Data Selection
- Output
- The Complete Program

One of the most basic and complex tasks of a programmer is to write a program that extracts data from the database tables and outputs the data in a format that's usable by the user population. The output is generally printed to the screen, from which it can easily be transferred to paper via a print function. This program is called a *report*. Simply put, a report is a program that reads data from the database, manipulates that data, and outputs the processed data to the screen and printer(s).

Reports are one of the three main programs written by ABAPers. Data extracts and BDC sessions (or interfaces) are the other two main programs. These two programs are discussed in detail in the next two chapters.

To write a report, you follow these basic steps:

1. Review the functional specifications provided by the functional analyst. You must review this document closely, checking these items:

   - What the report covers
   - Where the data comes from
   - Whether it's possible to fit all the data the user wants on the screen

2. After reviewing and altering the functional specs as necessary, write the code.

TIP

You might assume that you would first define the data tables to hold the extracted data, but it's best to first attempt to code the SELECT statements to extract the data from the database tables. Once the SQL code is worked out, you have a better idea of how much data is coming in, and in what format. Then you can define the data fields and internal tables that will be used to process the data.

Functional Specifications

Table 14-1 is an example of what you could expect in a functional spec. Use this spec to write a report in this chapter:

Table 14-1 Functional Specifications

```
REPORT NAME: Income Tax Report
DESCRIPTION: This report provides the details of shipments by
             state if in the US, and by destination country if
             outside the US. This report will only display
             transactions that have been recognized on the
             general ledger (G/L), therefore postings to the
             balance sheet, and deferred revenue are not
             selected.
FREQUENCY:   This report will be run by the users as needed, preferably, online.
```

Number	Table/ Field Name	Description	Field Type/ Length	Data Source
1	BKPF-BUKRS	Company Code	Char 4	Selection Criteria
2	KNA1-REGIO	State	Char 2	
3	KNA1-LAND1	Country / State	Char 2	
4	BSEG-SGTXT	Sales Order No.	Char 10	
5	BSEG-BELNR	Invoice No.	Char 10	
6	BKPF-BLART	Document Type	Char 2	
7	BKPF-BUDAT	Posting Date	Char 10	
8	BSEG-HKONT	G/L Account(5*)	Char 10	
9	BSEG-DMBTR	Amount (US $)	Char 13	
10	BSEG-GSBER	Business Area	Char 4	Selection Criteria
11	KNA1-ORT01	City	Char 35	
12	KNA1-ORT02	County	Char 35	

Sort Criteria

- Sort the internal table by company code and then by country or state.
- Start a new page for each new company code and new location (country or state).

Selection Criteria

- Company Code (as a range)
- Business Area (as a range)
- Posting Date (as a range)
- Document Types (as a range)

Default Values

Posting Date Last fiscal period (use function module)

Document Types ZZ.

NOTE

Lines in this layout have been condensed to fit within the printed margins of this book.

Sample Layout for Income Tax Report

```
PROGRAM:      12345678          Income Tax Report          Page: 1234
DATE:      MM/DD/YY
CO. CODE:      1234        Date Range From: MM/DD/YY      To: MM/DD/YY
TIME:      HH:MM:SS

STATE/ CUSTOMER S/O NO. INVOICE   DOC DATE   G/L   AMOUNT   BUS   CITY COUN-
TRY /
COUNTY     NO.            TYPE               ACCOUNT  (US $)  AREA  STATE
```

Review this spec and see what you would do or how you would plan on writing this program.

There are several steps you must walk through to write this program correctly and cover all options. The steps are covered later in this chapter; however, the first step is to review the tables that hold the data for this report and compare those tables against the specs. For a better analysis, all tables that you'll use are listed in the next section. Some of these tables aren't listed in the specs, but the reason for their presence in the list will become apparent as you compare what the specs require and what the system can provide in a later section.

Tables Used in the Sample Report

The following tables from SAP are provided for reference in researching how to write this report. I'll be referencing these tables throughout this chapter, so please look over the following pages. These are the actual table listings from an SAP client:

Table 14-2 BKPF

Table 14-3 BSEG

Table 14-4 KNA1

Table 14-5 VBPA

Table 14-6 VBRP

Table 14-7 BSIS

Table 14-2 BKPF

Field name	C	Data el.	Domain	Type	Length	Short text
_ MANDT	X	MANDT	MANDT	CLNT	000003	Client
_ BUKRS	X	BUKRS	BUKRS	CHAR	000004	Company code
_ BELNR	X	BELNR	BELNR	CHAR	000010	Document reference number
_ GJAHR	X	GJAHR	GJAHR	NUMC	000004	Fiscal year
_ BLART		BLART	BLART	CHAR	000002	Document type
_ BLDAT		BLDAT	DATUM	DATS	000008	Date of the document
_ BUDAT		BUDAT	DATUM	DATS	000008	Posting date in the document
_ MONAT		MONAT	MONAT	NUMC	000002	Fiscal period
_ CPUDT		CPUDT	DATUM	DATS	000008	Accounting document entry date
_ CPUTM		CPUTM	UZEIT	TIMS	000006	Time of entry
_ AEDAT		AEDAT_BKPF	DATUM	DATS	000008	Date of the last doc ument change by transaction
_ UPDDT		UPDDT	DATUM	DATS	000008	Date of the last document update
_ WWERT		WWERT	DATUM	DATS	000008	Translation date
_ USNAM		USNAM	USNAM	CHAR	000012	User name
_ TCODE		TCODE_BKPF	CHAR4	CHAR	000004	Transaction code
_ BVORG		BVORG	BVORG	CHAR	000016	Intercompany posting procedure number
_ XBLNR		XBLNR	XBLNR	CHAR	000016	Reference document number
_ DBBLG		DBBLG	BELNR	CHAR	000010	Recurring entry docu ment number

(continued)

Table 14-2 BKPF **(continued)**

Field name	C Data el.	Domain	Type	Length	Short text
_ STBLG	STBLG	BELNR	CHAR	000010	Reverse document number
_ STJAH	STJAH	GJAHR	NUMC	000004	Reverse document fiscal year
_ BKTXT	BKTXT	TEXT25	CHAR	000025	Document header text
_ WAERS	WAERS	WAERS	CUKY	000005	Currency key
_ KURSF	KURSF	KURSF	DEC	000009	Exchange rate
_ KZWRS	KZWRS	WAERS	CUKY	000005	Currency key of the group currency
_ KZKRS	KZKRS	KURSF	DEC	000009	Group currency exchange rate
_ BSTAT	BSTAT	BSTAT	CHAR	000001	Document status
_ XNETB	XNETB	XFELD	CHAR	000001	Indicator: Document posted net ?
_ FRATH	FRATH	WERT7	CURR	000013	Freight amount in local currency
_ XRUEB	XRUEB	XFELD	CHAR	000001	Indicator: Document is posted to a previous period
_ GLVOR	GLVOR	CHAR4	CHAR	000004	G/L business activity
_ GRPID	APQ_GRPN	CHAR12	CHAR	000012	Queue group name
_ DOKID	DOKID_BKPF	CHAR40	CHAR	000040	Document name in the archive system
_ ARCID	EXTID_BKPF	CHAR10	CHAR	000010	Extract ID document header
_ IBLAR	IBLAR	IBLAR	CHAR	000002	Internal document type for document control
_ AWTYP	AWTYP	AWTYP	CHAR	000005	Application type (interface information)
_ AWKEY	AWKEY	AWKEY	CHAR	000020	Application key (interface information)
_ FIKRS	FIKRS	FIKRS	CHAR	000004	Financial Management Area
_ HWAER	HWAER	WAERS	CUKY	000005	Local currency

(continued)

Table 14-2 BKPF *(continued)*

Field name	C Data el.	Domain	Type	Length	Short text
_ HWAE2	HWAE2	WAERS	CUKY	000005	Currency key of second local currency
_ HWAE3	HWAE3	WAERS	CUKY	000005	Currency key of third local currency
_ KURS2	KURS2	KURSF	DEC	000009	Exchange rate for the second local currency
_ KURS3	KURS3	KURSF	DEC	000009	Exchange rate for the third local currency
_ BASW2	CURSR	CURSR	CHAR	000001	Source currency for the currency translation
_ BASW3	CURSR	CURSR	CHAR	000001	Source currency for the currency translation
_ UMRD2	UMRD2	CURDT	CHAR	000001	Translation date type for second local currency
_ UMRD3	UMRD3	CURDT	CHAR	000001	Translation date type for third local currency
_ XSTOV	XSTOV	XFELD	CHAR	000001	Indicator: Document is flagged for reversal
_ STODT	STODT	DATUM	DATS	000008	Date planned for the posting to a prior period
_ XMWST	XMWST	XFELD	CHAR	000001	Indicator: Tax calcu-lated automatically
_ CURT2	CURT2	CURTP	CHAR	000002	Currency type of second local currency
_ CURT3	CURT3	CURTP	CHAR	000002	Currency type of third local currency
_ KUTY2	KURST	KURST	CHAR	000004	Exchange rate type
_ KUTY3	KURST	KURST	CHAR	000004	Exchange rate type
_ XSNET	XSNET	XFELD	CHAR	000001	G/L account amounts are net amounts

(continued)

Table 14-2 BKPF **(continued)**

Field name	C	Data el.	Domain	Type	Length	Short text
_ AUSBK		AUSBK	BUKRS	CHAR	000004	Source company code
_ XUSVR		XUSVR_BKPF	XFELD	CHAR	000001	Indicator: US taxes changed at detail level ?

Table 14-3 BSEG

Field name	C	Data el.	Domain	Type	Length	Short text
_ MANDT	X	MANDT	MANDT	CLNT	000003	Client
_ BUKRS	X	BUKRS	BUKRS	CHAR	000004	Company code
_ BELNR	X	BELNR	BELNR	CHAR	000010	Document reference number
_ GJAHR	X	GJAHR	GJAHR	NUMC	000004	Fiscal year
_ BUZEI	X	BUZEI	BUZEI	NUMC	000003	Line item number within the accounting document
_ BUZID		BUZID	CHAR1	CHAR	000001	Identification of the line item
_ AUGDT		AUGDT	DATUM	DATS	000008	Clearing date
_ AUGCP		AUGCP	DATUM	DATS	000008	Clearing entry date
_ AUGBL		AUGBL	BELNR	CHAR	000010	Document number of the clearing document
_ BSCHL		BSCHL	BSCHL	CHAR	000002	Posting key
_ KOART		KOART	KOART	CHAR	000001	Account type
_ UMSKZ		UMSKZ	UMSKZ	CHAR	000001	Special G/L indicator
_ UMSKS		UMSKS	UMSKS	CHAR	000001	Special G/L transaction type
_ ZUMSK		ZUMSK	UMSKZ	CHAR	000001	Target special G/L indicator
_ SHKZG		SHKZG	SHKZG	CHAR	000001	Debit/credit indicator
_ GSBER		GSBER	GSBER	CHAR	000004	Business area
_ PARGB		PARGB	GSBER	CHAR	000004	Trading partner's business area
_ MWSKZ		MWSKZ	MWSKZ	CHAR	000002	Tax code
_ QSSKZ		QSSKZ	QSSKZ	CHAR	000002	Withholding tax code

(continued)

Table 14-3 BSEG ***(continued)***

Field name	*C Data el.*	*Domain*	*Type*	*Length*	*Short text*
_ DMBTR	DMBTR	WERT7	CURR	000013	Amount in local currency
_ WRBTR	WRBTR	WERT7	CURR	000013	Amount in document currency
_ KZBTR	KZBTR	WERT7	CURR	000013	Amount in group currency
_ PSWBT	PSWBT	WERT7	CURR	000013	Amount for updating in general ledger
_ PSWSL	PSWSL	WAERS	CUKY	000005	Transaction currency key for monthly debits and credits
_ TXBHW	TXBHW	WERT7	CURR	000013	Original tax base amount in local currency
_ TXBFW	TXBFW	WERT7	CURR	000013	Original tax base amount in document currency
_ MWSTS	MWSTS	WERT7	CURR	000013	Tax amount in local currency
_ WMWST	WMWST	WERT7	CURR	000013	Tax amount in docu-ment currency
_ HWBAS	HWBAS	WERT7	CURR	000013	Tax base amount in local currency
_ FWBAS	FWBAS	WERT7	CURR	000013	Tax base amount in document currency
_ HWZUZ	HWZUZ	WERT7	CURR	000013	Provision amount in local currency
_ FWZUZ	FWZUZ	WERT7	CURR	000013	Additional tax in document currency
_ SHZUZ	SHZUZ	CHAR1	CHAR	000001	Debit/credit addition for cash discount
_ STEKZ	CHAR2	CHAR2	CHAR	000002	Char2
_ MWART	MWART	MWART	CHAR	000001	Tax type
_ TXGRP	TXGRP	NUM03	NUMC	000003	Group indicator for tax line items

(continued)

Table 14-3 BSEG *(continued)*

Field name	C	Data el.	Domain	Type	Length	Short text
KTOSL	_	KTOSL	CHAR3	CHAR	000003	Internal processing key
QSSHB	_	QSSHB	WERT7	CURR	000013	Withholding tax base amount
KURSR	_	KURSR	KURSP	DEC	000009	Hedged exchange rate
GBETR	_	GBETR	WERT7	CURR	000013	Hedged amount in foreign currency
BDIFF	_	BDIFF	WRTV7	CURR	000013	Valuation difference
BDIF2	_	BDIF2	WRTV7	CURR	000013	Valuation difference for the second local currency
VALUT	_	VALUT	DATUM	DATS	000008	Value date
ZUONR	_	ZUONR	ZUONR	CHAR	000018	Allocation number
SGTXT	_	SGTXT	TEXT50	CHAR	000050	Line item text
ZINKZ	_	ZINKZ	ZINKZ	CHAR	000002	Exception from interest calculation
VBUND	_	RASSC	RCOMP	CHAR	000006	Trading partner ID
BEWAR	_	RMVCT	RMVCT	CHAR	000003	Transaction type
ALTKT	_	ALTKT	ALTKT	CHAR	000010	Account number in group
VORGN	_	VORGN	VORGN	CHAR	000004	Transaction type for general ledger
FDLEV	_	FDLEV	FDLEV	CHAR	000002	Planning level
FDGRP	_	FDGRP	FDGRP	CHAR	000010	Planning group
FDWBT	_	FDWBT	WERT7	CURR	000013	Planning amount in document currency
FDTAG	_	FDTAG	DATUM	DATS	000008	Planning date
FKONT	_	FIPLS	FIPLS	NUMC	000003	Financial budget item
KOKRS	_	KOKRS	CACCD	CHAR	000004	Controlling area
KOSTL	_	KOSTL	KOSTL	CHAR	000010	Cost center
PROJN	_	PROJN	PROJN	CHAR	000016	Project number
AUFNR	_	AUFNR	AUFNR	CHAR	000012	Order number
VBELN	_	VBELN_VF	VBELN	CHAR	000010	Billing document
VBEL2	_	VBELN_VA	VBELN	CHAR	000010	Sales document
POSN2	_	POSNR_VA	POSNR	NUMC	000006	Sales document item
ETEN2	_	ETENR	ETENR	NUMC	000004	Schedule line

(continued)

Table 14-3 BSEG *(continued)*

Field name	C Data el.	Domain	Type	Length	Short text
_ ANLN1	ANLN1	ANLN1	CHAR	000012	Asset main number
_ ANLN2	ANLN2	ANLN2	CHAR	000004	Asset sub-number
_ ANBWA	ANBWA	BWASL	CHAR	000003	Asset transaction type
_ BZDAT	BZDAT	DATUM	DATS	000008	Asset value date
_ PERNR	PERNR	PERNR	NUMC	000008	Personnel number
_ XUMSW	XUMSW	XFELD	CHAR	000001	Indicator: Sales-related item ?
_ XHRES	XHRES	XFELD	CHAR	000001	Indicator: Resident G/L account ?
_ XKRES	XKRES	XFELD	CHAR	000001	Indicator: line item display via account possible ?
_ XOPVW	XOPVW	XFELD	CHAR	000001	Indicator: Open item management ?
_ XCPDD	XCPDD	XFELD	CHAR	000001	Indicator: One-time data or alternative payee set ?
_ XSKST	XSKST	XFELD	CHAR	000001	Indicator: Statistical posting to cost center
_ XSAUF	XSAUF	XFELD	CHAR	000001	Indicator: Posting to order is statistical
_ XSPRO	XSPRO	XFELD	CHAR	000001	Indicator: Posting to project is statistical
_ XSERG	XSERG	XFELD	CHAR	000001	Indicator: Posting to prof.analysis is statistical
_ XFAKT	XFAKT	XFELD	CHAR	000001	Indicator: Billing document update successful ?
_ XUMAN	XUMAN	XFELD	CHAR	000001	Indicator: Transfer posting from down payment ?
_ XANET	XANET	XFELD	CHAR	000001	Indicator: Down payment in net procedure ?

(continued)

Table 14-3 BSEG *(continued)*

Field name	C Data el.	Domain	Type	Length	Short text
_ XSKRL	XSKRL	XFELD	CHAR	000001	Indicator: Line item not liable to cash discount ?
_ XINVE	XINVE	XFELD	CHAR	000001	Indicator: Investment goods concerned ?
_ XPANZ	XPANZ	XFELD	CHAR	000001	Indicator: display item
_ XAUTO	XAUTO	XFELD	CHAR	000001	Indicator: line item automatically created
_ XNCOP	XNCOP	XFELD	CHAR	000001	Indicator: Items can not be copied ?
_ XZAHL	XZAHL	XFELD	CHAR	000001	Indicator: Is it a payment transaction ?
_ SAKNR	SAKNR	SAKNR	CHAR	000010	G/L account number
_ HKONT	HKONT	SAKNR	CHAR	000010	G/L accounting general ledger account
_ KUNNR	KUNNR	KUNNR	CHAR	000010	Customer number
_ LIFNR	LIFNR	LIFNR	CHAR	000010	Vendor account number
_ FILKD	FILKD	MAXKK	CHAR	000010	Account number of the branch
_ XBILK	XBILK	XFELD	CHAR	000001	Indicator: Account is balance sheet account ?
_ GVTYP	GVTYP	CHAR2	CHAR	000002	P+L statement account type
_ HZUON	HZUON	ZUONR	CHAR	000018	Allocation number for special G/L accounts
_ ZFBDT	ZFBDT	DATUM	DATS	000008	Baseline date for due date calculation
_ ZTERM	ZTERM	ZTERM	CHAR	000004	Terms of payment key
_ ZBD1T	ZBD1T	ZBDXT	DEC	000003	Cash discount days 1
_ ZBD2T	ZBD2T	ZBDXT	DEC	000003	Cash discount days 2
_ ZBD3T	ZBD3T	ZBDXT	DEC	000003	Net payment terms period
_ ZBD1P	ZBD1P	PRZ23	DEC	000005	Cash discount percentage 1

(continued)

Table 14-3 BSEG *(continued)*

Field name	C Data el.	Domain	Type	Length	Short text
_ ZBD2P	ZBD2P	PRZ23	DEC	000005	Cash discount percentage 2
_ SKFBT	SKFBT	WERT7	CURR	000013	Amount qualifying for cash discount (in document currency)
_ SKNTO	SKNTO	WERT7	CURR	000013	Cash discount amount in local currency
_ WSKTO	WSKTO	WERT7	CURR	000013	Cash discount amount in document currency
_ ZLSCH	SCHZW_ BSEG	ZLSCH	CHAR	000001	Payment method
_ ZLSPR	ZLSPR	ZAHLS	CHAR	000001	Payment block key
_ ZBFIX	ZBFIX	ZBFIX	CHAR	000001	Fixed payment terms
_ HBKID	HBKID	HBKID	CHAR	000005	Short key for a house bank
_ BVTYP	BVTYP	BVTYP	CHAR	000004	Partner bank type
_ NEBTR	NEBTR	WERT7	CURR	000013	Net payment amount
_ MWSK1	MWSKX	MWSKZ	CHAR	000002	Tax code for distribution
_ DMBT1	DMBTX	WRTV7	CURR	000013	Amount in local currency for tax distribution
_ WRBT1	WRBTX	WRTV7	CURR	000013	Amount in foreign currency for tax breakdown
_ MWSK2	MWSKX	MWSKZ	CHAR	000002	Tax code for distribution
_ DMBT2	DMBTX	WRTV7	CURR	000013	Amount in local currency for tax distribution
_ WRBT2	WRBTX	WRTV7	CURR	000013	Amount in foreign currency for tax breakdown
_ MWSK3	MWSKX	MWSKZ	CHAR	000002	Tax code for distribution

(continued)

Table 14-3 BSEG *(continued)*

Field name	C Data el.	Domain	Type	Length	Short text
_ DMBT3	DMBTX	WRTV7	CURR	000013	Amount in local currency for tax distribution
_ WRBT3	WRBTX	WRTV7	CURR	000013	Amount in foreign currency for tax breakdown
_ REBZG	REBZG	BELNR	CHAR	000010	Doc.no.of the invoice to which the transaction belongs
_ REBZJ	REBZJ	GJAHR	NUMC	000004	Fiscal year of the relevant invoice (in credit memo)
_ REBZZ	REBZZ	BUZEI	NUMC	000003	Line item in the relevant invoice
_ REBZT	REBZT	REBZT	CHAR	000001	Following document type
_ ZOLLT	ZOLLT	ZOLLT	CHAR	000008	Customs tariff number
_ ZOLLD	ZOLLD	DATUM	DATS	000008	Customs date
_ LZBKZ	LZBKZ	LZBKZ	CHAR	000003	State central bank indicator
_ LANDL	LANDL	LAND1	CHAR	000003	Supplying country
_ DIEKZ	DIEKZ	DIEKZ	CHAR	000001	Service indicator (foreign payment)
_ SAMNR	SAMNR	SAMNR	NUMC	000008	Invoice list number
_ ABPER	ABPER_RF	BUPER	ACCP	000006	Settlement period
_ VRSKZ	VRSKZ	CHAR1	CHAR	000001	Insurance indicator
_ VRSDT	VRSDT	DATUM	DATS	000008	Insurance date
_ DISBN	DISBN	BELNR	CHAR	000010	Bill of exchange usage document number (discount document)
_ DISBJ	DISBJ	GJAHR	NUMC	000004	Bill of exchange usage document fiscal year
_ DISBZ	DISBZ	BUZEI	NUMC	000003	Line item within the bill of exchange usage document

(continued)

Table 14-3 BSEG *(continued)*

Field name	C Data el.	Domain	Type	Length	Short text
_ WVERW	WVERW	WVERW	CHAR	000001	Bill of exchange usage type
_ ANFBN	ANFBN	BELNR	CHAR	000010	Document number of the bill of exchange payment request
_ ANFBJ	ANFBJ	GJAHR	NUMC	000004	Fiscal year of the bill of exchange pay-ment request document
_ ANFBU	ANFBU	BUKRS	CHAR	000004	Company code in which bill of exch.payment request is posted
_ ANFAE	ANFAE	DATUM	DATS	000008	Bill of exchange pay-ment request due date
_ BLNBT	BLNBT	WERT7	CURR	000013	Base amount for determining the pref-erence amount
_ BLNKZ	BLNKZ	BLNKZ	CHAR	000002	Subsidy indicator for determining the reduction rates
_ BLNPZ	BLNPZ	PRZ52	DEC	000007	Preference percentage rate
_ MSCHL	MSCHL	MSCHL	CHAR	000001	Dunning key
_ MANSP	MANSP	MANSP	CHAR	000001	Dunning block
_ MADAT	MADAT	DATUM	DATS	000008	Date of the last dunning notice
_ MANST	MAHNS	MAHNS	NUMC	000001	Dunning level
_ MABER	MABER	MABER	CHAR	000002	Dunning area
_ ESRNR	ESRNR	ESRNR	CHAR	000011	POR subscriber number
_ ESRRE	ESRRE	ESRRE	CHAR	000027	POR reference number
_ ESRPZ	ESRPZ	CHAR2	CHAR	000002	POR check digit
_ KLIBT	KLIBT	WERT7	CURR	000013	Credit control amount
_ QSZNR	QSZNR	CHAR10	CHAR	000010	Certificate number of the withholding tax exemption

(continued)

Table 14-3 BSEG *(continued)*

Field name	C Data el.	Domain	Type	Length	Short text
_ QBSHB	QBSHB	WERT7	CURR	000013	Withholding tax amount (in document currency)
_ QSFBT	QSFBT	WERT7	CURR	000013	Withholding tax-exempt amount (in document currency)
_ NAVHW	NAVHW	WERT7	CURR	000013	Nondeductible input tax (in local currency)
_ NAVFW	NAVFW	WERT7	CURR	000013	Nondeductible input tax (in document currency)
_ MATNR	MATNR	MATNR	CHAR	000018	Material number
_ WERKS	WERKS	WERKS	CHAR	000004	Plant
_ MENGE	MENGE	MENG13	QUAN	000013	Quantity
_ MEINS	MEINS	MEINS	UNIT	000003	Base unit of measure
_ ERFMG	ERFMG	MENG13	QUAN	000013	Quantity in unit of entry
_ ERFME	ERFME	MEINS	UNIT	000003	Unit of entry
_ BPMNG	BPMNG	MENG13	QUAN	000013	Quantity in order price unit
_ BPRME	BPRME	MEINS	UNIT	000003	Order price unit (purchasing)
_ EBELN	EBELN	EBELN	CHAR	000010	Purchasing document number
_ EBELP	EBELP	EBELP	NUMC	000005	Item number of purchasing document
_ ZEKKN	ZEKKN	NUM02	NUMC	000002	Serial number of account assignment
_ ELIKZ	ELIKZ	XFELD	CHAR	000001	"Delivery completed" indicator
_ VPRSV	VPRSV	VPRSV	CHAR	000001	Price control indicator
_ PEINH	PEINH	PACK3	DEC	000005	Price unit
_ BWKEY	BWKEY	BWKEY	CHAR	000004	Valuation area
_ BWTAR	BWTAR	BWTAR	CHAR	000010	Valuation type
_ BUSTW	BUSTW	BUSTW	CHAR	000004	Posting string for values

(continued)

Table 14-3 BSEG ***(continued)***

Field name	C Data el.	Domain	Type	Length	Short text
_ REWRT	REEWR	WRTV7	CURR	000013	Invoice value entered (in local currency)
_ REWWR	REFWR	WRTV7	CURR	000013	Invoice value in foreign currency
_ BONFB	BONFB	WERT7	CURR	000013	Amount qualifying for bonus in local currency
_ BUALT	BUALT	WERT7	CURR	000013	Amount posted in alternative price control
_ PSALT	PSALT	VPRSV	CHAR	000001	Alternative price control
_ NPREI	NPREI	WERT11	CURR	000011	New price
_ TBTKZ	TBTKZ	TBTKZ	CHAR	000001	Indicator: subsequent debit/credit
_ SPGRP	SPGRP	XFELD	CHAR	000001	Blocking reason: Price
_ SPGRM	SPGRM	XFELD	CHAR	000001	Blocking reason: Quantity
_ SPGRT	SPGRT	XFELD	CHAR	000001	Blocking reason: Date
_ SPGRG	SPGRG	XFELD	CHAR	000001	Blocking reason: Order Price Quantity
_ SPGRV	SPGRV	XFELD	CHAR	000001	Blocking reason: Project Budget
_ SPGRQ	SPGRQ	XFELD	CHAR	000001	Indicator: manual blocking reason
_ STCEG	STCEG	STCEG	CHAR	000020	VAT registration number
_ EGBLD	EGBLD	LAND1	CHAR	000003	Country of destination for delivery of goods
_ EGLLD	EGLLD	LAND1	CHAR	000003	Supplying country for delivery of goods
_ RSTGR	RSTGR	CHAR3	CHAR	000003	Reason code for payments
_ RYACQ	RYACQ	CHAR4	CHAR	000004	Year of acquisition

(continued)

Table 14-3 BSEG **(continued)**

Field name	C Data el.	Domain	Type	Length	Short text
_ RPACQ	RPACQ	NUM03	NUMC	000003	Period of acquisition
_ RDIFF	RDIFF	WRTV7	CURR	000013	Exchange rate gain/loss realized
_ RDIF2	RDIF2	WRTV7	CURR	000013	Exchange rate diffe-rence realized for second local currency
_ PRCTR	PRCTR	PRCTR	CHAR	000010	Profit center
_ XHKOM	XHKOM	XFELD	CHAR	000001	Indicator: G/L account assigned manually ?
_ VNAME	JV_NAME	JV_NAME	CHAR	000006	Joint Venture
_ RECID	JV_RECIND	JV_RECIND	CHAR	000002	Recovery indicator
_ EGRUP	JV_EGROUP	JV_EGROUP	CHAR	000003	Equity group
_ VPTNR	JV_PART	KUNNR	CHAR	000010	Joint venture partner
_ VERTT	RANTYP	RANTYP	CHAR	000001	Contract type
_ VERTN	RANL	RANL	CHAR	000013	Contract number
_ VBEWA	SBEWART	VSBEWART	CHAR	000004	Transaction type
_ DEPOT	RLDEPO	VRLDEPO	CHAR	000010	Deposit title
_ TXJCD	TXJCD	TXJCD	CHAR	000015	Jurisdiction for tax calculation tax juris-diction code
_ IMKEY	IMKEY	IMKEY	CHAR	000008	Internal key for property object
_ DABRZ	DABRBEZ	DDAT	DATS	000008	Reference date for account settlement
_ POPTS	POPTSATZ	POPTSATZ	DEC	000009	Property option record
_ FIPOS	FIPOS	FIPOS	CHAR	000014	Commitment item
_ KSTRG	KSTRG	KSTRG	CHAR	000012	Process manufacturing cost object
_ NPLNR	NPLNR	AUFNR	CHAR	000012	Network number for account assignment
_ AUFPL	CO_AUFPL	AUFPL	NUMC	000010	Routing number of operations in the order

(continued)

Table 14-3 BSEG *(continued)*

Field name	C Data el.	Domain	Type	Length	Short text
_ APLZL	CIM_COUNT	CIM_COUNT	NUMC	000008	Counter which numbers data base entries consecutively
_ PROJK	PS_PSP_PN	PS POSNR	NUMC	000008	Account assignment to WBS element
_ PAOBJNR	RKEOBJNR	RKEOBJNR	NUMC	000010	Business segment number (CO-PA)
_ PASUBNR	RKESUBNR	RKESUBNR	NUMC	000004	Business segment changes (CO-PA)
_ SPGRS	SPGRS	XFELD	CHAR	000001	Block.reason: Others
_ SPGRC	SPGRC	XFELD	CHAR	000001	Block.reason: Quality
_ BTYPE	JV_BILIND	JV_BILIND	CHAR	000002	Billing indicator
_ ETYPE	JV_ETYPE	JV_ETYPE	CHAR	000003	Equity type
_ XEGDR	XEGDR	XFELD	CHAR	000001	Indicator: Triangular deal within the EC ?
_ LNRAN	LNRAN	LNRAN	NUMC	000005	Current number of asset line items in fiscal year
_ HRKFT	HRKFT	HRKFT	CHAR	000004	Origin as subdivision of cost element
_ DMBE2	DMBE2	WERT7	CURR	000013	Amount in second local currency
_ DMBE3	DMBE3	WERT7	CURR	000013	Amount in third local currency
_ DMB21	DMB2X	WRTV7	CURR	000013	Amount in second local currency for tax breakdown
_ DMB22	DMB2X	WRTV7	CURR	000013	Amount in second local currency for tax breakdown
_ DMB23	DMB2X	WRTV7	CURR	000013	Amount in second local currency for tax breakdown
_ DMB31	DMB3X	WRTV7	CURR	000013	Amount in third local currency for tax breakdown

(continued)

Table 14-3 BSEG ***(continued)***

Field name	C Data el.	Domain	Type	Length	Short text
_ DMB32	DMB3X	WRTV7	CURR	000013	Amount in third local currency for tax breakdown
_ DMB33	DMB3X	WRTV7	CURR	000013	Amount in third local currency for tax breakdown
_ MWST2	MWST2	WERT7	CURR	000013	Tax amount in second local currency
_ MWST3	MWST3	WERT7	CURR	000013	Tax amount in third local currency
_ NAVH2	NAVH2	WERT7	CURR	000013	Nondeductible input tax in second local currency
_ NAVH3	NAVH3	WERT7	CURR	000013	Nondeductible input tax in third local currency
_ SKNT2	SKNT2	WERT7	CURR	000013	Cash discount amount in second local currency
_ SKNT3	SKNT3	WERT7	CURR	000013	Cash discount amount in third local currency
_ BDIF3	BDIF3	WRTV7	CURR	000013	Valuation difference for the third local currency
_ RDIF3	RDIF3	WRTV7	CURR	000013	Exchange rate difference realized for third local currency
_ HWMET	HWMET	HWMET	CHAR	000001	Method with which the local currency amount was determined
_ GLUPM	GLUPM	GLUPM	CHAR	000001	Selection of transaction currency for G/L update
_ XRAGL	XRAGL	XFELD	CHAR	000001	Indicator: Clearing was reversed

(continued)

Table 14-3 BSEG *(continued)*

Field name	C Data el.	Domain	Type	Length	Short text
_ UZAWE	UZAWE	UZAWE	CHAR	000002	Payment method supplement
_ LOKKT	LOKKT	SAKNR	CHAR	000010	Account number in the local chart of accounts
_ FISTL	FISTL	FISTL	CHAR	000016	CF center
_ GEBER	BP_GEBER	BP_GEBER	CHAR	000010	Sponsor
_ STBUK	STBUK	BUKRS	CHAR	000004	Tax company code
_ TXBH2	TXBH2	WERT7	CURR	000013	Original tax base amount in second local currency
_ TXBH3	TXBH3	WERT7	CURR	000013	Original tax base amount in third local currency
_ PPRCT	PPRCTR	PRCTR	CHAR	000010	Partner profit center

Table 14-3 KNA1

Field name	C Data el.	Domain	Type	Length	Short text
_ MANDT	X MANDT	MANDT	CLNT	000003	Client
_ KUNNR	X KUNNR	KUNNR	CHAR	000010	Customer number
_ ADRNR	ADRNR	ADRNR	CHAR	000010	Address
_ ANRED	ANRED	TEXT15	CHAR	000015	Title
_ AUFSD	AUFSD_X	KAUFS	CHAR	000002	Central order block for customer
_ BAHNE	BAHNE	BAHNH	CHAR	000025	Express train station
_ BAHNS	BAHNS	BAHNH	CHAR	000025	Train station
_ BBBNR	BBBNR	NUM07	NUMC	000007	Standard company number
_ BBSNR	BBSNR	NUM05	NUMC	000005	Standard company number (supplement)
_ BEGRU	BRGRU	BRGRU	CHAR	000004	Authorization group
_ BRSCH	BRSCH	BRSCH	CHAR	000004	Industry key
_ BUBKZ	BUBKZ	NUM01	NUMC	000001	Check digit for the standard company number

(continued)

Table 14-4 KNA1 *(continued)*

Field name	C Data el.	Domain	Type	Length	Short text
_ DATLT	DATLT	TEXT14	CHAR	000014	Number of data communication line
_ ERDAT	ERDAT_RF	DATUM	DATS	000008	Date on which the record was created
_ ERNAM	ERNAM_RF	USNAM	CHAR	000012	Name of the user who created the object
_ EXABL	EXABL	XFELD	CHAR	000001	Indicator: Unloading points exist
_ FAKSD	FAKSD_X	FAKSP	CHAR	000002	Central billing block for customer
_ FISKN	FISKN_D	KUNNR	CHAR	000010	Account number of the master record with the fiscal address
_ KNAZK	KNAZK	WFCID	CHAR	000002	Customer factory calendar
_ KNRZA	KNRZA	KUNNR	CHAR	000010	Account number of an alternative payer
_ KONZS	KONZS	KONZS	CHAR	000010	Group key
_ KTOKD	KTOKD	KTOKD	CHAR	000004	Customer account group
_ KUKLA	KUKLA	KUKLA	CHAR	000002	Customer classification
_ LAND1	LAND1_GP	LAND1	CHAR	000003	Country key
_ LIFNR	LIFNR	LIFNR	CHAR	000010	Vendor account number
_ LIFSD	LIFSD_X	LIFSP	CHAR	000002	Central delivery block for the customer
_ LOCCO	LOCCO	LOCCO	CHAR	000010	Standard point location code
_ LOEVM	LOEVM_X	XFELD	CHAR	000001	Central delete flag for master record
_ NAME1	NAME1_GP	NAME	CHAR	000035	Name 1
_ NAME2	NAME2_GP	NAME	CHAR	000035	Name 2
_ NAME3	NAME3_GP	NAME	CHAR	000035	Name 3
_ NAME4	NAME4_GP	NAME	CHAR	000035	Name 4
_ NIELS	NIELS	NIELS	CHAR	000002	Nielsen indicator
_ ORT01	ORT01_GP	TEXT35	CHAR	000035	City
_ ORT02	ORT02_GP	TEXT35	CHAR	000035	District
_ PFACH	PFACH	PFACH	CHAR	000010	Post office box

(continued)

Table 14-4 KNA1 ***(continued)***

Field name	*C*	*Data el.*	*Domain*	*Type*	*Length*	*Short text*
PSTL2	_	PSTL2	PSTLZ	CHAR	000010	Postal code of PO box
PSTLZ	_	PSTLZ	PSTLZ	CHAR	000010	Postal code
REGIO	_	REGIO	REGIO	CHAR	000003	Region
COUNC	_	COUNC	COUNC	CHAR	000003	County code
CITYC	_	CITYC	CITYC	CHAR	000004	City code
RPMKR	_	RPMKR	RPMKR	CHAR	000005	Regional market
SORTL	_	SORTL	CHAR10	CHAR	000010	Sort field
SPERR	_	SPERB_X	XFELD	CHAR	000001	Central posting block
SPRAS	_	SPRAS	SPRAS	LANG	000001	Language key
STCD1	_	STCD1	STCD1	CHAR	000016	Tax number 1
STCD2	_	STCD2	STCD2	CHAR	000011	Tax number 2
STKZA	_	STKZA	STKZA	CHAR	000001	Indicator: Business partner subject to equalization tax ?
STKZU	_	STKZU	XFELD	CHAR	000001	Indicator: Business partner subject to tax on sales/purch. ?
STRAS	_	STRAS_GP	TEXT35	CHAR	000035	Street and house number
TELBX	_	TELBX	TEXT15	CHAR	000015	Telebox number
TELF1	_	TELF1	TEXT16	CHAR	000016	1st telephone number
TELF2	_	TELF2	TEXT16	CHAR	000016	Second telephone number
TELFX	_	TELFX	TEXT31	CHAR	000031	Fax number
TELTX	_	TELTX	TEXT30	CHAR	000030	Teletex number
TELX1	_	TELX1	TEXT30	CHAR	000030	Telex number
LZONE	_	LZONE	ZONE	CHAR	000010	Transportation zone to which the goods are delivered
XCPDK	_	XCPDK	XFELD	CHAR	000001	Indicator: Is the account a one-time account ?
XZEMP	_	XZEMP	XFELD	CHAR	000001	Indicator: Alternative payee in document allowed ?

(continued)

Table 14-4 KNA1 ***(continued)***

Field name	C Data el.	Domain	Type	Length	Short text
_ VBUND	RASSC	RCOMP	CHAR	000006	Trading partner ID
_ STCEG	STCEG	STCEG	CHAR	000020	VAT registration number
_ DEAR1	DEAR1	XFELD	CHAR	000001	Competitor ID
_ DEAR2	DEAR2	XFELD	CHAR	000001	Sales partner indicator
_ DEAR3	DEAR3	DEAR3	CHAR	000001	Sales prospect ID
_ DEAR4	DEAR4	XFELD	CHAR	000001	Indicator for customer type 4
_ DEAR5	DEAR5	XFELD	CHAR	000001	Customer type 5
_ GFORM	GFORM	GFORM	CHAR	000002	Legal status
_ BRAN1	BRAN1	BRACO	CHAR	000010	Industry code 1
_ BRAN2	BRAN2	BRACO	CHAR	000010	Industry code 2
_ BRAN3	BRAN3	BRACO	CHAR	000010	Industry code 3
_ BRAN4	BRAN4	BRACO	CHAR	000010	Industry code 4
_ BRAN5	BRAN5	BRACO	CHAR	000010	Industry code 5
_ EKONT	EKONT	VBELN	CHAR	000010	Initial contact
_ UMSAT	UMSAT	UMSAT	CURR	000008	Annual sales
_ UMJAH	UMJAH	JAHR	NUMC	000004	Year for which sales are given
_ UWAER	UWAER	WAERS	CUKY	000005	Currency of sales figure
_ JMZAH	JMZAH	JMZAH	NUMC	000006	Number of employees for the year
_ JMJAH	JMJAH	JAHR	NUMC	000004	Year for which the number of employees is given
_ KATR1	KATR1	ATTR1	CHAR	000002	Attribute 1
_ KATR2	KATR2	ATTR2	CHAR	000002	Attribute 2
_ KATR3	KATR3	ATTR3	CHAR	000002	Attribute 3
_ KATR4	KATR4	ATTR4	CHAR	000002	Attribute 4
_ KATR5	KATR5	ATTR5	CHAR	000002	Attribute 5
_ KATR6	KATR6	ATTR6	CHAR	000003	Attribute 6
_ KATR7	KATR7	ATTR7	CHAR	000003	Attribute 7
_ KATR8	KATR8	ATTR8	CHAR	000003	Attribute 8
_ KATR9	KATR9	ATTR9	CHAR	000003	Attribute 9

(continued)

Table 14-4 KNA1 *(continued)*

Field name	C Data el.	Domain	Type	Length	Short text
_ KATR10	KATR10	ATTR10	CHAR	000003	Attribute 10
_ STKZN	STKZN	STKZN	CHAR	000001	Indicator: Business partner a sole proprietor ?
_ UMSA1	UMSA1	UMSA1	CURR	000015	Annual sales
_ TXJCD	TXJCD	TXJCD	CHAR	000015	Jurisdiction for tax calculation tax jurisdiction code
_ MCOD1	MCDD1	CHAR25	CHAR	000025	Search string for using matchcodes
_ MCOD2	MCDD2	CHAR25	CHAR	000025	Search string for using matchcodes
_ MCOD3	MCDD3	CHAR25	CHAR	000025	Search string for using matchcodes

Table 14-5 VBPA

Field name	C Data el.	Domain	Type	Length	Short text
_ MANDT	X MANDT	MANDT	CLNT	000003	Client
_ VBELN	X VBELN	VBELN	CHAR	000010	Sales and distribu-tion document number
_ POSNR	X POSNR	POSNR	NUMC	000006	Item number of SD document
_ PARVW	X PARVW	PARVW	CHAR	000002	Partner function ID (e.g. SH for ship-to party)
_ KUNNR	KUNNR	KUNNR	CHAR	000010	Customer number
_ LIFNR	LIFNR	LIFNR	CHAR	000010	Vendor account number
_ PERNR	PERNR	PERNR	NUMC	000008	Personnel number
_ PARNR	PARNR	PARNR	NUMC	000010	Number of contact person
_ ADRNR	ADRNR	ADRNR	CHAR	000010	Address
_ ABLAD	ABLAD	TEXT25	CHAR	000025	Unloading point
_ LAND1	LAND1	LAND1	CHAR	000003	Country key

(continued)

Table 14-5 VBPA *(continued)*

Field name	C Data el.	Domain	Type	Length	Short text
_ ADRDA	ADRDA	ADRDA	CHAR	000001	Address indicator
_ XCPDK	XCPDK	XFELD	CHAR	000001	Indicator: Is the account a one-time account ?
_ HITYP	HITYP_KH	HITYP	CHAR	000001	Customer hierarchy type
_ PRFRE	PRFRE	XFELD	CHAR	000001	Relevant for pricing ID
_ BOKRE	BOKRE	XFELD	CHAR	000001	ID: Customer is to receive rebates
_ HISTUNR	HISTUNR	NUM2	NUMC	000002	Level number within hierarchy

Table 14-6 VBRP

Field name	C Data el.	Domain	Type	Length	Short text
_ MANDT	X MANDT	MANDT	CLNT	000003	Client
_ VBELN	X VBELN_VF	VBELN	CHAR	000010	Billing document
_ POSNR	X POSNR_VF	POSNR	NUMC	000006	Billing item
_ UEPOS	UEPOS	POSNR	NUMC	000006	Higher-level item in bill of material structures
_ FKIMG	FKIMG	MENG13	QUAN	000013	Actual invoiced quantity
_ VRKME	VRKME	MEINS	UNIT	000003	Sales unit
_ UMVKZ	UMVKZ	UMBSZ	DEC	000005	Numerator (factor) for conversion of sales quantity into SKU
_ UMVKN	UMVKN	UMBSN	DEC	000005	Denominator (divisor) for conversion of sales qty. into SKU
_ MEINS	MEINS	MEINS	UNIT	000003	Base unit of measure
_ SMENG	SMENG	MENG13	QUAN	000013	Scale quantity in base unit of measure

(continued)

Table 14-6 VBRP ***(continued)***

Field name	C Data el.	Domain	Type	Length	Short text
_ FKLMG	FKLMG	MENG13	QUAN	000013	Billing quantity in stockkeeping unit
_ LMENG	LMENG	MENG13	QUAN	000013	Required quantity for mat.management in base units
_ NTGEW	NTGEW_15	MENG15	QUAN	000015	Net weight
_ BRGEW	BRGEW_15	MENG15	QUAN	000015	Gross weight
_ GEWEI	GEWEI	MEINS	UNIT	000003	Unit of weight
_ VOLUM	VOLUM_15	MENG15	QUAN	000015	Volume
_ VOLEH	VOLEH	MEINS	UNIT	000003	Volume unit
_ GSBER	GSBER	GSBER	CHAR	000004	Business area
_ PRSDT	PRSDT	DATUM	DATS	000008	Date for pricing and exchange rate
_ FBUDA	FBUDA	DATUM	DATS	000008	Date on which ser-vices rendered
_ KURSK	KURSK	KURRF	DEC	000009	Exchange rate for pricing and statistics
_ NETWR	NETWR_FP	WERTV8	CURR	000015	Net value of the billing item in docu-ment currency
_ VBELV	VBELV	VBELN	CHAR	000010	Originating document
_ POSNV	POSNV	POSNR	NUMC	000006	Originating item
_ VGBEL	VGBEL	VBELN	CHAR	000010	Document number of the reference document
_ VGPOS	VGPOS	POSNR	NUMC	000006	Item number of the reference item
_ VGTYP	VBTYP	VBTYP	CHAR	000001	SD document category
_ AUBEL	VBELN_VA	VBELN	CHAR	000010	Sales document
_ AUPOS	POSNR_VA	POSNR	NUMC	000006	Sales document item
_ AUREF	AUREF	XFELD	CHAR	000001	Sales document has resulted from reference
_ MATNR	MATNR	MATNR	CHAR	000018	Material number
_ ARKTX	ARKTX	TEXT40	CHAR	000040	Short text for sales order item

(continued)

Table 14-6 VBRP ***(continued)***

Field name	C Data el.	Domain	Type	Length	Short text
_ PMATN	PMATN	MATNR	CHAR	000018	Pricing reference material
_ CHARG	CHARG	CHARG	CHAR	000010	Batch number
_ MATKL	MATKL	MATKL	CHAR	000009	Material group
_ PSTYV	PSTYV	PSTYV	CHAR	000004	SD document item category
_ POSAR	POSAR	POSAR	CHAR	000001	Item type
_ PRODH	PRODH	PRODH	CHAR	000018	Product hierarchy
_ VSTEL	VSTEL	VSTEL	CHAR	000004	Shipping point
_ ATPKZ	ATPKZ	XFELD	CHAR	000001	Replacement part
_ SPART	SPART	SPART	CHAR	000002	Division
_ POSPA	POSPA	POSNR	NUMC	000006	Item number in the partner segment
_ WERKS	WERKS	WERKS	CHAR	000004	Plant
_ ALAND	ALAND	LAND1	CHAR	000003	Delivering country (country from which the goods are sent)
_ WKREG	WKREG	REGIO	CHAR	000003	Region of the plant
_ WKCOU	WKCOU	CHAR3	CHAR	000003	County in which the plant is located
_ WKCTY	WKCTY	CHAR4	CHAR	000004	City of the plant
_ TAXM1	TAXM1	TAXKM	CHAR	000001	Tax classification for this material
_ TAXM2	TAXM2	TAXKM	CHAR	000001	Tax classification 2 for this material
_ TAXM3	TAXM3	TAXKM	CHAR	000001	Tax classification 3 for this material
_ TAXM4	TAXM4	TAXKM	CHAR	000001	Tax classification 4 for this material
_ TAXM5	TAXM5	TAXKM	CHAR	000001	Tax classification 5 for material
_ TAXM6	TAXM6	TAXKM	CHAR	000001	Tax classification 6 for this material
_ TAXM7	TAXM7	TAXKM	CHAR	000001	Tax classification 7 for this material

(continued)

Table 14-6 VBRP ***(continued)***

Field name	***C Data el.***	***Domain***	***Type***	***Length***	***Short text***
_ TAXM8	TAXM8	TAXKM	CHAR	000001	Tax classification 8 for this material
_ TAXM9	TAXM9	TAXKM	CHAR	000001	Tax classification 9 for this material
_ KOWRR	KOWRR	XFELD	CHAR	000001	Statistical values
_ PRSFD	PRSFD	XFELD	CHAR	000001	Carry out pricing
_ SKTOF	SKTOF	XFELD	CHAR	000001	Cash discount indicator
_ SKFBP	SKFBT	WERT7	CURR	000013	Amount qualifying for cash discount (in document currency)
_ KONDM	KONDM	KONDM	CHAR	000002	Material pricing group
_ KTGRM	KTGRM	KTGRM	CHAR	000002	Account determination group for this material
_ KOSTL	KOSTL	KOSTL	CHAR	000010	Cost center
_ BONUS	BONUS	BONUS	CHAR	000002	Volume rebate group
_ PROVG	PROVG	PROVG	CHAR	000002	Commission group
_ EANNR	EANNR	CHAR13	CHAR	000013	European article number
_ VKGRP	VKGRP	VKGRP	CHAR	000003	Sales group
_ VKBUR	VKBUR	VKBUR	CHAR	000004	Sales office
_ SPARA	SPART_AK	SPART	CHAR	000002	Division for order header
_ SHKZG	SHKZG_VA	XFELD	CHAR	000001	Returns item
_ ERNAM	ERNAM	USNAM	CHAR	000012	Name of the user who created the object
_ ERDAT	ERDAT	DATUM	DATS	000008	Date on which the record was created
_ ERZET	ERZET	UZEIT	TIMS	000006	Entry time
_ BWTAR	BWTAR	BWTAR	CHAR	000010	Valuation type
_ LGORT	LGORT	LGORT	CHAR	000004	Storage location
_ STAFO	STAFO	STAFO	CHAR	000006	Update group for statistics updating

(continued)

Table 14-6 VBRP *(continued)*

Field name	C Data el.	Domain	Type	Length	Short text
_ WAVWR	WAVWR	WERTV7	CURR	000013	Cost in document currency
_ KZWI1	KZWI1	WERTV7	CURR	000013	Subtotal 1 from pric-ing procedure for condition
_ KZWI2	KZWI2	WERTV7	CURR	000013	Subtotal 2 from pric-ing procedure for condition
_ KZWI3	KZWI3	WERTV7	CURR	000013	Subtotal 3 from pric-ing procedure for condition
_ KZWI4	KZWI4	WERTV7	CURR	000013	Subtotal 4 from pric-ing procedure for condition
_ KZWI5	KZWI5	WERTV7	CURR	000013	Subtotal 5 from pric-ing procedure for condition
_ KZWI6	KZWI6	WERTV7	CURR	000013	Subtotal 6 from pric-ing procedure for condition
_ STCUR	STCUR_AP	KURRF	DEC	000009	Exchange rate for statistics (Exch.rate at time of creation)
_ UVPRS	UVPRS	XFELD	CHAR	000001	Incomplete with respect to pricing
_ UVALL	UVALL	XFELD	CHAR	000001	Generally incomplete
_ EAN11	EAN11	EAN11	CHAR	000018	International Article Number/Universal Product Code
_ PRCTR	PRCTR	PRCTR	CHAR	000010	Profit center
_ KVGR1	KVGR1	KVGR1	CHAR	000003	Customer Group 1
_ KVGR2	KVGR2	KVGR2	CHAR	000003	Customer Group 2
_ KVGR3	KVGR3	KVGR3	CHAR	000003	Customer Group 3
_ KVGR4	KVGR4	KVGR4	CHAR	000003	Customer Group 4
_ KVGR5	KVGR5	KVGR5	CHAR	000003	Customer Group 5

(continued)

Table 14-6 VBRP *(continued)*

Field name	C Data el.	Domain	Type	Length	Short text
_ MVGR1	MVGR1	MVGR1	CHAR	000003	Material Pricing Group 1
_ MVGR2	MVGR2	MVGR2	CHAR	000003	Material Pricing Group 2
_ MVGR3	MVGR3	MVGR3	CHAR	000003	Material Pricing Group 3
_ MVGR4	MVGR4	MVGR4	CHAR	000003	Material Pricing Group 4
_ MVGR5	MVGR5	MVGR5	CHAR	000003	Material Pricing Group 5
_ MATWA	MATWA	MATNR	CHAR	000018	Original material
_ BONBA	BONBA	WERTV7	CURR	000013	Rebate basis 1
_ KOKRS	KOKRS	CACCD	CHAR	000004	Controlling area
_ PAOBJNR	RKEOBJNR	RKEOBJNR	NUMC	000010	Business segment number (CO-PA)
_ PS_PSP_PNR	PS_PSP_PNR	PS_POSNR	NUMC	000008	Account assignment to WBS element
_ AUFNR	AUFNR	AUFNR	CHAR	000012	Order number
_ TXJCD	TXJCD	TXJCD	CHAR	000015	Jurisdiction for tax calculation tax jurisdiction code
_ CMPRE	CMPRE	WERTV6	CURR	000011	Item credit price
_ CMPNT	CMPNT	XFELD	CHAR	000001	ID: Item participates at credit functions
_ CUOBJ	CUOBJ_VA	CUOBJ	NUMC	000018	Internal object number for SD variant processing
_ CUOBJ_CH	CUOBJ_CH	CUOBJ	NUMC	000018	Internal object number for batch classification
_ KOUPD	KOUPD	XFELD	CHAR	000001	Conditions update
_ UECHA	UECHA	POSNR	NUMC	000006	Higher-level item of batch split item
_ XCHAR	XCHAR	XFELD	CHAR	000001	Batch management indicator (internal)

Table 14-7 BSIS

Field name	C	Data el.	Domain	Type	Length	Short text
_ MANDT	X	MANDT	MANDT	CLNT	000003	Client
_ BUKRS	X	BUKRS	BUKRS	CHAR	000004	Company code
_ HKONT	X	HKONT	SAKNR	CHAR	000010	G/L accounting general ledger account
_ AUGDT	X	AUGDT	DATUM	DATS	000008	Clearing date
_ AUGBL	X	AUGBL	BELNR	CHAR	000010	Document number of the clearing document
_ ZUONR	X	ZUONR	ZUONR	CHAR	000018	Allocation number
_ GJAHR	X	GJAHR	GJAHR	NUMC	000004	Fiscal year
_ BELNR	X	BELNR	BELNR	CHAR	000010	Document reference number
_ BUZEI	X	BUZEI	BUZEI	NUMC	000003	Line item number within the accounting document
_ BUDAT		BUDAT	DATUM	DATS	000008	Posting date in the document
_ BLDAT		BLDAT	DATUM	DATS	000008	Date of the document
_ WAERS		WAERS	WAERS	CUKY	000005	Currency key
_ XBLNR		XBLNR	XBLNR	CHAR	000016	Reference document number
_ BLART		BLART	BLART	CHAR	000002	Document type
_ MONAT		MONAT	MONAT	NUMC	000002	Fiscal period
_ BSCHL		BSCHL	BSCHL	CHAR	000002	Posting key
_ SHKZG		SHKZG	SHKZG	CHAR	000001	Debit/credit indicator
_ GSBER		GSBER	GSBER	CHAR	000004	Business area
_ MWSKZ		MWSKZ	MWSKZ	CHAR	000002	Tax code
_ FKONT		FIPLS	FIPLS	NUMC	000003	Financial budget item
_ DMBTR		DMBTR	WERT7	CURR	000013	Amount in local currency
_ WRBTR		WRBTR	WERT7	CURR	000013	Amount in document currency
_ MWSTS		MWSTS	WERT7	CURR	000013	Tax amount in local currency
_ WMWST		WMWST	WERT7	CURR	000013	Tax amount in document currency
_ SGTXT		SGTXT	TEXT50	CHAR	000050	Line item text

(continued)

TTable 14-7 BSIS *(continued)*

Field name	C Data el.	Domain	Type	Length	Short text
_ PROJN	PROJN	PROJN	CHAR	000016	Project number
_ AUFNR	AUFNR_NEU	AUFNR	CHAR	000012	Order number
_ WERKS	WERKS	WERKS	CHAR	000004	Plant
_ KOSTL	KOSTL	KOSTL	CHAR	000010	Cost center
_ ZFBDT	ZFBDT	DATUM	DATS	000008	Baseline date for due date calculation
_ XOPVW	XOPVW	XFELD	CHAR	000001	Indicator: Open item management ?
_ VALUT	VALUT	DATUM	DATS	000008	Value date
_ BSTAT	BSTAT	BSTAT	CHAR	000001	Document status
_ BDIFF	BDIFF	WRTV7	CURR	000013	Valuation difference
_ BDIF2	BDIF2	WRTV7	CURR	000013	Valuation difference for the second local currency
_ VBUND	RASSC	RCOMP	CHAR	000006	Trading partner ID
_ PSWSL	PSWSL	WAERS	CUKY	000005	Transaction currency key for monthly debits and credits
_ WVERW	WVERW	WVERW	CHAR	000001	Bill of exchange usage type
_ DMBE2	DMBE2	WERT7	CURR	000013	Amount in second local currency
_ DMBE3	DMBE3	WERT7	CURR	000013	Amount in thrid local currency
_ MWST2	MWST2	WERT7	CURR	000013	Tax amount in second local currency
_ MWST3	MWST3	WERT7	CURR	000013	Tax amount in third local currency
_ BDIF3	BDIF3	WRTV7	CURR	000013	Valuation difference for the third local currency
_ RDIF3	RDIF3	WRTV7	CURR	000013	Exchange rate difference realized for third local currency
_ XRAGL	XRAGL	XFELD	CHAR	000001	Indicator: Clearing was reversed

(continued)

Table 14-7 BSIS *(continued)*

Field name	C Data el.	Domain	Type	Length	Short text
_ PROJK	PS_PSP_PNR	PS_POSNR	NUMC	000008	Account assignment to WBS element
_ PRCTR	PRCTR	PRCTR	CHAR	000010	Profit center
_ XSTOV	XSTOV	XFELD	CHAR	000001	Indicator: Document is flagged for reversal

Verifying the Data

The first step of writing a report is checking data that the functional analyst specifies against what the database actually holds. You must see whether the fields he or she has specified are correct and are from viable tables in the database, and then determine whether those tables are the optimal source for that data.

Data Selection

Data selection is a very important part of writing a report. It consists of a number of steps:

1. Choosing the tables from which the data will be drawn.
2. Determining the order in which the data will be selected.
3. Deciding whether an internal table or a field group is the best method for the report.
4. Specifying the data types that you plan to use for the data.

These topics are covered in the following sections.

Choosing the Tables

If you look at the existing specs for this sample project, you'll notice that the table `BSEG` is mentioned. The authors know from experience (which you will gain with time) that this table holds many records, is a cluster table, and represents a performance issue if you use it in your data access. Now, you know of a different table—one that contains the same G/L data that the `BSEG` table holds: the `BSIS` table. This information is found through experience with using the tables of the

FI module, or by a careful search using the information system of the data dictionary (the di03 transaction).

If you look at the BSIS table (refer to the tables in the preceding section), you'll see that all the data that you must read from the BKPF table is also listed in the BSIS table. You've just killed two birds with one stone: The BKPF and BSEG tables have now been replaced with the BSIS table. Don't expect your functional analyst to know this information. It's your job to know or find this out. (And now you know!)

The KNA1 table doesn't pose a threat to performance, and it's a transparent table in the database. Because you've changed from the BKPF table access to the BSIS table access, you now don't have a link from the billing data to the KNA1 data through the field KUNNR. In order to make the link, you must use the tables VBPA (the Sales Document: Partner table) and VBRP (the Billing Item Data table). Generally, as a new programmer, you would notice this fact as you attempt to retrieve the information from KNA1 and then search for tables to link BSIS and KNA1. The facts mentioned here are for you to reference as you think about the program and how to accomplish it.

Determining the Order of Data Selection

The order of data selection plays an important role in how efficient your code is for your report. For this report, it isn't an issue, as we've replaced the major tables, BSEG and BKPF, with only one table. KNA1 is a table from which to get supplemental data, as are VBPA and VBRP. If you didn't have the BSIS table, however, the order of data reads from the tables would be from BKPF first, which holds all the header data for that document, and then to BSEG to get the line item data.

Choosing Field Groups Versus Internal Tables

The last step before actually starting to code the report is to determine how many records will typically be retrieved, and whether an internal table or field groups would be appropriate for the report. Use transaction SE16 to get the general table display for BSIS, and enter 5% for the G/L Account field. Then click Execute to do a full read on the table. If your system is set to read only 100 records at a time from the production machine, write a quick ABAP/4 program to fill an internal table, and track the number of records using a field for a counter.

This ABAP code will give you an initial count of how many records the code will extract from the database:

```
REPORT ZABAP.


TABLES:     BSIS.
```

```
DATA:      BEGIN OF INT_BSIS OCCURS 10000.
           INCLUDE STRUCTURE BSIS.
DATA:      END OF INT_BSIS.

DATA:      W_COUNTER(6) TYPE N.

SELECT * FROM BSIS WHERE HKONT LIKE '005%'.
MOVE BSIS TO INT_BSIS.
APPEND INT_BSIS.
CLEAR INT_BSIS.
W_COUNTER = W_COUNTER + 1.
ENDSELECT.

WRITE:      'THERE ARE ', W_COUNTER, 'RECORDS IN BSIS'.
```

Of course, we'd like to restrict the table read by dates and document types, so include that in your initial ABAP program so that you limit the number of records retrieved from the database. For the sample, assume that only 8,000 records are retrieved, so make the internal table `OCCURS` statement with a limit of 10,000 to cover the 8,000 records and give it some space to grow in the future.

You should use field groups if the record number returned is in the hundreds of thousands. In this case, only 8,000 records (for your purposes) were retrieved. So an internal table is appropriate.

Eight thousand records will be retrieved, and three other tables (`VBPA`, `VBRP`, and `KNA1`) have to be read to fill the additional fields for that internal table. You must decide whether to do the three reads as the `BSIS` table is read, or to read all the records from `BSIS` into an internal table directly, loop through that internal table, and then do the other reads. Because sequential reads are slow, and you're searching through `BSIS` with the condition of one of the first digits of an account number being `5`, the best idea in this case is not to limit the read on `BSIS` by adding on extra processing time in the middle of it. Nested select loops are also generally a performance issue, so the best choice for this report is to read the `BSIS` table directly into an internal table and then loop through that table:

```
SELECT        * FROM  BSIS INTO TABLE *BSIS
       WHERE  BUKRS        IN S_BUKRS
       AND    HKONT      LIKE '005%'
       AND    GJAHR         IN S_GJAHR
```

```
AND    BELNR        IN S_BELNR
AND    BUDAT        IN S_DATUM
AND    BLART        IN S_SDART
AND    GSBER        IN S_GSBER.
```

The first thing you might see here is that, in addition to the hard-coded `005` in the G/L account, I've picked select-options for all the fields that are used as search criteria for the table `BSIS`. The specs indicate that in the selection screen only company code (`BUKRS`), business area (`GSBER`), posting date (`BUDAT`), and document type (`BLART`) are given to the user as ranges.

However, if you look at the `BSIS` table, the primary index also contains fiscal year (`GJAHR`), and document number (`BELNR`). You can figure out what the fiscal year is if you have the posting date; and if the user happens to know the document number, that will be a more specific and faster read. Note that for this example I assume 12 posting periods. The actual number is stored in table T009. By including these two additional ranges in the search criteria, the database sees that most of the primary key is used, and uses the primary index to search through `BSIS`, rather than using a slower index or just a plain sequential search:

```
SELECT-OPTIONS: S_BUKRS FOR BSIS-BUKRS,"Company Code
                S_GSBER FOR BSIS-GSBER,"Business Area
                S_BELNR FOR BSIS-BELNR,"Document Numbers
                S_DATUM FOR BSIS-BUDAT,"Posting Date
                S_GJAHR FOR BSIS-GJAHR,"Fiscal Year
                S_SDART FOR BSIS-BLART."Doc types for SD I/F

INITIALIZATION.

  S_SDART-LOW = 'RX'.
  APPEND S_SDART.

  PERFORM DETERMINE_PERIOD USING SY-DATUM CHANGING W_GJAHR W_MONAT.
  IF W_MONAT <> 1.
    W_MONAT = W_MONAT - 1.
  ELSE.
    W_MONAT = 12.
  ENDIF.
```

```
S_GJAHR-LOW = W_GJAHR.
APPEND S_GJAHR.

PERFORM DETERMINE_DATES.
APPEND S_DATUM.
```

In the data declaration portion of the program, the select-options are defined for the corresponding `BSIS` fields. The default values are determined after the `INITIALIZATION` event. Certain dates are determined by utilizing function calls inside subroutines being called in the program.

Specifying the Data Types

Now that you've determined which tables to use, and that an internal table must be used to store the incoming data, it's time to describe that internal table, which will hold the data to be printed out.

In addition to the internal table that holds the data for display, you must also define the internal table to hold all the `BSIS` records that match your criteria:

```
TABLES:
        KNA1,
        BSIS,
        VBRP,
        VBAP.
DATA: BEGIN OF *BSIS OCCURS 10000.
         INCLUDE STRUCTURE BSIS.
DATA: END OF *BSIS.

DATA: BEGIN OF INTAB OCCURS 10000,
              BUKRS LIKE BKPF-BUKRS,
              LAND1 LIKE KNA1-LAND1,
              LANDKEY(2) TYPE C,
              NAME1 LIKE KNA1-NAME1,
              SONO  LIKE BSIS-BELNR,
              BELNR LIKE BSIS-BELNR,
              BLART LIKE BKPF-BLART,
              BUDAT LIKE BKPF-BUDAT,
              HKONT LIKE BSIS-HKONT,
```

```
                DMBTR LIKE BSIS-DMBTR,
                GSBER LIKE BSIS-GSBER,
                 ORT01 LIKE KNA1-ORT01,
                 ORT02 LIKE KNA1-ORT02,
                 SGTXT LIKE BSIS-SGTXT.
DATA: END OF INTAB.

DATA: W_LINNO LIKE SY-LINNO.
DATA: W_SONO LIKE VBRP-AUBEL.
DATA: W_ZEROS TYPE N.
DATA: W_LENGTH TYPE N.
DATA: W_SUBTOTAL LIKE BSIS-DMBTR,
      W_TOTAL    LIKE BSIS-DMBTR.

DATA: W_BUZEI(3) TYPE N,                "Line item number
      W_SPERIOD(1) TYPE C,
      W_MONAT(2) TYPE N,                "Fiscal Period
      W_GJAHR(4) TYPE N.                "Fiscal Year

DATA: W_GJAHR1 LIKE BKPF-GJAHR,
      W_GJAHR2 LIKE BKPF-GJAHR,
      W_MONAT1 LIKE BKPF-MONAT,
      W_MONAT2 LIKE BKPF-MONAT.
```

The `*BSIS` table is essentially an internal table with the same structure as `BSIS`. The program will use this internal table to store all the records extracted from the `BSIS` database table that match the user's selection criteria.

The internal table, `INTAB`, contains all the fields that the specs define as output. Once the records from `BSIS` are read into `*BSIS`, the program will loop through `*BSIS`, moving the corresponding fields over to `INTAB`. As the program loops record by record through `*BSIS`, it reviews the current record and looks up the other required data from the tables `KNA1`, `VBPA`, and `VBRP`. When the record is full, the record is appended to `INTAB`:

```
LOOP AT *BSIS.

    PERFORM GET_DATA.
    APPEND INTAB.
```

```
    CLEAR INTAB.
  ENDLOOP.
LOOP AT INTAB.

* Get company name and address for the details printout
    IF INTAB-BLART IN S_SDART.
      PERFORM GET_SHIP_TO_SD.             "For SD Doc types
    ENDIF.

    MODIFY INTAB.

  ENDLOOP.
*---------------------------------------------------------------------*
*       FORM GET_DATA                                                 *
*---------------------------------------------------------------------*
*       moves appropriate data from bsis into internal tables
*       and makes debit values negative.
*---------------------------------------------------------------------*
FORM GET_DATA.

  CASE *BSIS-SHKZG.
    WHEN 'S'.
      *BSIS-DMBTR = *BSIS-DMBTR - 2 * *BSIS-DMBTR.
    WHEN 'H'.
*ABSOLUTE VALUE, SO NO CHANGE (ALREADY POSITIVE (CREDIT)).
  ENDCASE.

*Detail Internal Table Report
  MOVE *BSIS-BUKRS TO INTAB-BUKRS.
  MOVE *BSIS-BELNR TO INTAB-BELNR.
  MOVE *BSIS-BLART TO INTAB-BLART.
  MOVE *BSIS-BUDAT TO INTAB-BUDAT.
  MOVE *BSIS-HKONT TO INTAB-HKONT.
  MOVE *BSIS-DMBTR TO INTAB-DMBTR.
  MOVE *BSIS-GSBER TO INTAB-GSBER.
  MOVE *BSIS-SGTXT TO INTAB-SGTXT.
```

```
ENDFORM.
*---------------------------------------------------------------------*
*       FORM GET_SHIP_TO_SD                                           *
FORM GET_SHIP_TO_SD.

  CLEAR VBPA.
  CLEAR VBRP.

  SELECT         * FROM  VBRP UP TO 1 ROWS
         WHERE  VBELN        = INTAB-BELNR
            AND AUBEL <> ' '.
  ENDSELECT.

  MOVE VBRP-AUBEL TO INTAB-SONO.

  SELECT         * FROM VBPA  UP TO 1 ROWS
       WHERE VBELN = VBRP-AUBEL

       AND   PARVW = 'WE'.
  ENDSELECT.

  IF SY-SUBRC NE 0.
    EXIT.
  ENDIF.
PERFORM GET_KNA1_ADDRESS USING VBPA-KUNNR.


ENDFORM.
*---------------------------------------------------------------------*
*       FORM GET_KNA1_ADDRESS                                         *
*---------------------------------------------------------------------.
FORM GET_KNA1_ADDRESS USING W_KUNNR.
  SELECT  SINGLE * FROM KNA1
       WHERE KUNNR = W_KUNNR.
```

```
    IF SY-SUBRC <> 0.
      EXIT.
    ENDIF.

    CASE KNA1-LAND1.
      WHEN 'US'.
        MOVE KNA1-REGIO TO INTAB-LAND1.
        MOVE 'US'       TO INTAB-LANDKEY.
      WHEN OTHERS.
        MOVE KNA1-LAND1 TO INTAB-LAND1.
    ENDCASE.
*
    MOVE KNA1-NAME1 TO INTAB-NAME1.
    MOVE KNA1-ORT01 TO INTAB-ORT01.
    MOVE KNA1-ORT02 TO INTAB-ORT02.

ENDFORM.
```

The program first loops through `*BSIS` and moves the appropriate data from `*BSIS` to `INTAB`. Then the program loops through `INTAB` and checks the tables `VBPA`, `VBRP`, and `KNA1` for the address information for each associated account. Once all of the data is moved from these tables to the record in `INTAB`, the record in `INTAB` is modified to include the additional information. You end up with an internal table, `INTAB`, that holds all the data that now needs to be output to the screen and subsequently to the printer.

If the specs required that this program write a flat file to UNIX or download the file to the user's PC, you would have no problem, as the program could just loop through `INTAB` and place the information in those two places. In this case, however, the information must be printed. The next section discusses how the information in the internal table is written to the screen and printer.

Output

Per specifications, the program must sort the internal table by company code and then by state or country:

```
* Sort internal tables via user specified criteria.
  SORT INTAB  BY BUKRS LAND1 BELNR.
```

Notice that the sort criteria is by company code first, location second, and then by document number. Try to think for the users if you can. Try to picture yourself reading this report and think about how easy it would be to read. By sorting last by document number, the program makes the final report much easier to read in its final product. The user can look at a page and find the appropriate document number easily. The user won't know the difference, but he will come back to you later if you don't make these adjustments, and ask you to make them. Try to put yourself in the user's shoes and solve problems before they happen.

Setting Up Titles and Headers

Output is probably the most tedious part of writing code to generate a report. All the data is nicely tucked away in an internal table, and now your job is to make it appear in a presentable format on the media of your choice—in this case the screen and the printer. The first code should be to generate the header of the page. This code prints out the page number, column headings, and report title for each new page. It's generally incorporated in a subroutine that's called if the code detects that the end of the page has been reached:

```
 PERFORM WRITE_HEADER.
*&---------------------------------------------------------------------*
*&       Form  WRITE_HEADER
*&---------------------------------------------------------------------*
FORM WRITE_HEADER.

  WRITE: /55           'WALTHERs GAS AND OIL COMPANY.'.
  WRITE:/              'Program:',
              12       SY-REPID.
  WRITE:/              'Date:',

              12       SY-DATUM.
  WRITE:/              'Company:',
              12       INTAB-BUKRS,
              47       'Posting Date From:',
              66       S_DATUM-LOW,
              77       'To:',
              81       S_DATUM-HIGH.
  WRITE:/              'Time:',
```

```
                12         SY-UZEIT.
  SKIP 2.
  WRITE:/                  TEXT-001,
                09         TEXT-002,
                30         TEXT-003,
                41         TEXT-004,
                52         TEXT-005,
                57         TEXT-006,
                76         TEXT-008,
                68         TEXT-007,
                94         TEXT-009,
                99         TEXT-010,
                116        TEXT-011.

  WRITE:/                  TEXT-021,
                09         TEXT-022,
                52         TEXT-025,
                57         TEXT-026,
                76         TEXT-028,
                68         TEXT-027,
                94         TEXT-029.

  ULINE.
  ULINE.
ENDFORM.                                       " WRITE_HEADER
```

Table 14-8 lists the text elements for this program.

The next code outputs the data to the screen. It also checks which line number the data is output on, and, if the end of the page is reached, calls the subroutine to generate a new page with the appropriate headers and titles:

```
LOOP AT INTAB.
*   IF SY-TABIX <> 1.
    ON CHANGE OF INTAB-BUKRS OR INTAB-LAND1.
      IF SY-TABIX <> 1.
        WRITE:/77 '---------'.
        WRITE:/60 'Subtotal:',
```

TABLE 14-8 Text Elements for the Tax Report

No.	Text
001	State /
002	Customer
003	S/O #
004	INVOICE
005	DOC
006	POST
007	G/L
008	AMOUNT
009	BUS
010	CITY
011	COUNTY
012	COUNTRY
022	
025	Type
026	Date
027	Account
028	US $
029	Area
052	The Fiscal Year Range does not match the Date Range

```
                76 W_SUBTOTAL.
        W_SUBTOTAL = 0.
      ENDIF.
      NEW-PAGE.
      PERFORM WRITE_HEADER.
    ENDON.

    WRITE:/
                     INTAB-LAND1,
                09   INTAB-NAME1+0(20),
                30   INTAB-SONO,
                41   INTAB-BELNR,
                52   INTAB-BLART,
                57   INTAB-BUDAT,
                76   INTAB-DMBTR,
```

```
          68   INTAB-HKONT,
          94   INTAB-GSBER,
          99   INTAB-ORT01,
          116  INTAB-ORT02.

    W_SUBTOTAL = W_SUBTOTAL + INTAB-DMBTR.
    W_TOTAL    = W_TOTAL    + INTAB-DMBTR.


  ENDLOOP.

TOP OF PAGE.

WRITE: /119 'CONTINUED....'.
      NEW-PAGE.
      PERFORM WRITE_HEADER.
```

For each new company code or new location, a new page is generated. Also, if a new page is reached, the header of the page is printed. This could change as the user specifies landscape or portrait mode. If a new company code or location is found, a subtotal of the dollar amounts is printed at the bottom of the page for summary purposes.

The hardest and most tedious part of writing the report is positioning the text appropriately across the page. The best (and most boring) way is to use the mouse to click and count the number of spaces over for each column, one by one, and then change the code to reflect that column position. Just run the program over and over and make sure that the column headings are aligned along with the data beneath them. Also make sure that enough of the data output to the screen in that column is showing. Make sure that your code doesn't cut the data short.

Printing the Report

The final step of the reporting process is to send the output to a printer. If the report is run online, once the data appears on-screen, click the Print button that automatically appears on the menu bar.

If the program is executed in background mode or as a job, you must create a job print definition. First, type the name of your program into the ABAP editor screen and click Execute. The selection screen appears. Enter the appropriate data and choose Program | Execute in Background. A screen appears that looks like Figure 14-1.

Type the printer name. To print immediately, select the option Print Immed. Deselect the option Delete After Print, and select New Spool Request. Then click the Save button. A background job will be scheduled to run. Once it's finished, the report will automatically print out at that printer station.

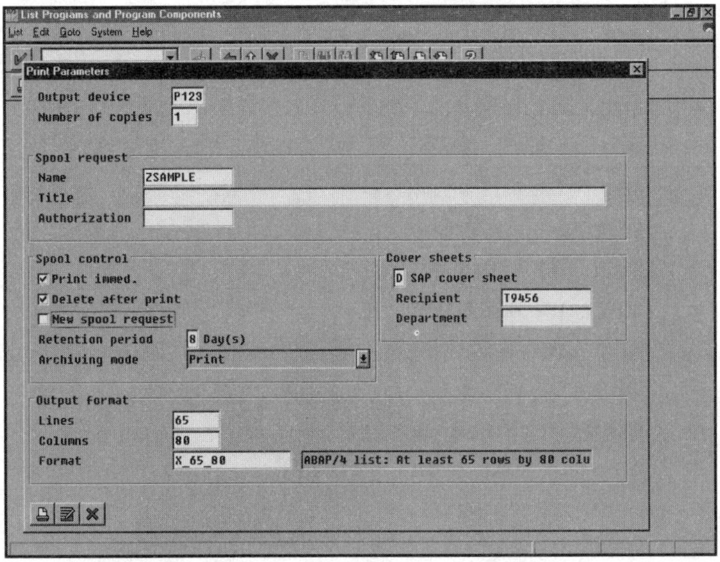

FIGURE 14-1

Print specifications for a background job

The Complete Program

This code represents the completed report in its full form, from start to finish. Separate pieces have been introduced throughout the chapter, so this last part of the chapter contains the code in its entirety:

```
REPORT ZREPORT
LINE-SIZE 132
LINE-COUNT 65
MESSAGE-ID ZZ.


TABLES: BSIS,              "Accounting: Secondary index for G/L Accounts
        KNA1,              "General Data in Customer Master
        VBPA,              "Sales Document:Partner
        VBRP.              "Billing: Item Data
```

```
DATA: BEGIN OF *BSIS OCCURS 10000.
        INCLUDE STRUCTURE BSIS.
DATA: END OF *BSIS.

DATA: BEGIN OF INTAB OCCURS 10000,
               BUKRS LIKE BKPF-BUKRS,
               LAND1 LIKE KNA1-LAND1,
               LANDKEY(2) TYPE C,
               NAME1 LIKE KNA1-NAME1,
               SONO  LIKE BSIS-BELNR,
               BELNR LIKE BSIS-BELNR,
               BLART LIKE BKPF-BLART,
               BUDAT LIKE BKPF-BUDAT,
               HKONT LIKE BSIS-HKONT,
               DMBTR LIKE BSIS-DMBTR,
               GSBER LIKE BSIS-GSBER,
               ORT01 LIKE KNA1-ORT01,
               ORT02 LIKE KNA1-ORT02,
               SGTXT LIKE BSIS-SGTXT.
DATA: END OF INTAB.

DATA: W_LINNO LIKE SY-LINNO.
DATA: W_SONO LIKE VBRP-AUBEL.
DATA: W_ZEROS TYPE N.
DATA: W_LENGTH TYPE N.
DATA: W_SUBTOTAL LIKE BSIS-DMBTR,
      W_TOTAL    LIKE BSIS-DMBTR.

DATA: W_BUZEI(3) TYPE N,                "Line item number
      W_SPERIOD(1) TYPE C,
      W_MONAT(2) TYPE N,                "Fiscal Period
      W_GJAHR(4) TYPE N.                "Fiscal Year

DATA: W_GJAHR1 LIKE BKPF-GJAHR,
      W_GJAHR2 LIKE BKPF-GJAHR,
      W_MONAT1 LIKE BKPF-MONAT,
```

```
      W_MONAT2 LIKE BKPF-MONAT.
SELECT-OPTIONS: S_BUKRS FOR BSIS-BUKRS,"Company Code
                S_GSBER FOR BSIS-GSBER,"Business Area
                S_BELNR FOR BSIS-BELNR,"Document Numbers
                S_DATUM FOR BSIS-BUDAT,"Posting Date
                S_GJAHR FOR BSIS-GJAHR,"Fiscal Year
                S_SDART FOR BSIS-BLART."Doc types for SD I/F

INITIALIZATION.

  S_SDART-LOW = 'RX'.
  APPEND S_SDART.

  PERFORM DETERMINE_PERIOD USING SY-DATUM CHANGING W_GJAHR W_MONAT.
  IF W_MONAT <> 1.
    W_MONAT = W_MONAT - 1.
  ELSE.
    W_MONAT = 12.
  ENDIF.

  S_GJAHR-LOW = W_GJAHR.
  APPEND S_GJAHR.

  PERFORM DETERMINE_DATES.
  APPEND S_DATUM.
*---------------------------------------*
START-OF-SELECTION.
 PERFORM DETERMINE_PERIOD USING S_DATUM-LOW  CHANGING W_GJAHR1 W_MONAT1.
 PERFORM DETERMINE_PERIOD USING S_DATUM-HIGH CHANGING W_GJAHR2 W_MONAT2.

*Check to make sure that the fiscal year range matches the posting range
  IF W_GJAHR1 <> S_GJAHR-LOW.
    MESSAGE E999 WITH TEXT-052.
  ELSEIF S_GJAHR-HIGH = 0 AND S_GJAHR-LOW  <> W_GJAHR2.
    MESSAGE E999 WITH TEXT-052.
  ELSEIF S_GJAHR-HIGH <> 0 AND S_GJAHR-HIGH <> W_GJAHR2.
```

```
    MESSAGE E999 WITH TEXT-052.
  ENDIF.

* Combine the two select-options for doc type into one select option
* to run agains the table.

END-OF-SELECTION.


*------------------------------------------------------------------*
* Move the selected data from BSIS into an internal table for faster
*      processing.
*------------------------------------------------------------------*
  SELECT       * FROM  BSIS INTO TABLE *BSIS
         WHERE  BUKRS        IN S_BUKRS
         AND    HKONT        LIKE '005%'
         AND    GJAHR        IN S_GJAHR
         AND    BELNR        IN S_BELNR
         AND    BUDAT        IN S_DATUM
         AND    BLART        IN S_sdART
         AND    GSBER        IN S_GSBER.
*------------------------------------------------------------------*
* Move the data from internal table *BSIS into an internal table
*      and add other pertinent data.
*------------------------------------------------------------------*
  LOOP AT *BSIS.

    PERFORM GET_DATA.
    APPEND INTAB.
    CLEAR INTAB.
  ENDLOOP.
*------------------------------------------------------------------*
* Loop through the internal table to add customer details and move
*      summary data into seperate tables for output.
*------------------------------------------------------------------*
  LOOP AT INTAB.
```

```
* Get company name and address for the details printout
    IF INTAB-BLART IN S_SDART.
      PERFORM GET_SHIP_TO_SD.              "For SD Doc types
    ENDIF.

    MODIFY INTAB.

  ENDLOOP.

END-OF-SELECTION.

* Sort internal tables via user specified criteria.
  SORT INTAB  BY BUKRS LAND1 BELNR.
*-----------------------------------------------------------------.*
* O U T P U T
  NEW-PAGE.
  W_TOTAL = 0.
  W_SUBTOTAL = 0.
* DETAIL REPORT
 PERFORM WRITE_HEADER.
  LOOP AT INTAB.
*   IF SY-TABIX <> 1.
    ON CHANGE OF INTAB-BUKRS OR INTAB-LAND1.
      IF SY-TABIX <> 1.
        WRITE:/77 '----------'.
        WRITE:/60 'Subtotal:',
                76 W_SUBTOTAL.
        W_SUBTOTAL = 0.
      ENDIF.
      NEW-PAGE.
      PERFORM WRITE_HEADER.
    ENDON.
*   ENDIF.

    WRITE:/
                  INTAB-LAND1,
```

```
                09    INTAB-NAME1+0(20),
                30    INTAB-SONO,
                41    INTAB-BELNR,
                52    INTAB-BLART,
                57    INTAB-BUDAT,
                76    INTAB-DMBTR,
                68    INTAB-HKONT,
                94    INTAB-GSBER,
                99    INTAB-ORT01,
                116   INTAB-ORT02.

    W_SUBTOTAL = W_SUBTOTAL + INTAB-DMBTR.
    W_TOTAL    = W_TOTAL    + INTAB-DMBTR.



  IF SY-SUBRC <> 0.
    WRITE:/42 'N O   A C C O U N T S   F O U N D'.
  ELSE.
    WRITE:/77 '————————'.
    WRITE:/60 'Subtotal:',
           76 W_SUBTOTAL.
    ULINE.
    WRITE:/60 'TOTAL:',
           76 W_TOTAL.
  ENDIF.

  WRITE:/.
  WRITE: /48 'E N D   O F  P R I N T   R E P O R T'.
TOP OF PAGE.
NEW-PAGE.
      PERFORM WRITE_HEADER.
*---------------------------------------------------------------------*
*       FORM DETERMINE_PERIOD                                          *
*---------------------------------------------------------------------*
*       ........                                                       *
```

```
*-----------------------------------------------------------------------.*
FORM DETERMINE_PERIOD USING W_DATUM CHANGING W_GJAHR W_MONAT.
  CALL FUNCTION 'PERIOD_DETERMINE'
       EXPORTING
            I_DATUM                = W_DATUM
            I_MONAT                = '00'
            I_PERIV                = 'AM'
            I_XM016                = ' '
       IMPORTING
            E_GJAHR                = W_GJAHR
            E_MONAT                = W_MONAT
       EXCEPTIONS
            ERROR_PERIOD          = 01
            ERROR_PERIOD_NUMBER  = 02
            ERROR_SPECIAL_PERIOD = 03
            ERROR_T009            = 04.

ENDFORM.
*-----------------------------------------------------------------------.*
*        FORM DETERMINE_DATES                                            *
*-----------------------------------------------------------------------.*
*        ........                                                         *
*-----------------------------------------------------------------------.*
FORM DETERMINE_DATES.

  CALL FUNCTION 'PERIOD_DAY_DETERMINE'
       EXPORTING
            I_GJAHR                = W_GJAHR
            I_MONAT                = W_MONAT
            I_PERIV                = 'BB'
       IMPORTING
            E_FDAY                 = S_DATUM-LOW
            E_LDAY                 = S_DATUM-HIGH
            E_SPERIOD              = W_SPERIOD
       EXCEPTIONS
```

```
             ERROR_PERIOD          = 01
             ERROR_PERIOD_VERSION = 02
             FIRSTDAY_NOT_DEFINED = 03
             PERIOD_NOT_DEFINED    = 04.

ENDFORM.
*---------------------------------------------------------------------*
*       FORM GET_SHIP_TO_SD                                            *
*---------------------------------------------------------------------*
*       ........                                                       *
*---------------------------------------------------------------------*
FORM GET_SHIP_TO_SD.

  CLEAR VBPA.
  CLEAR VBRP.

  SELECT        * FROM  VBRP UP TO 1 ROWS
         WHERE  VBELN       = INTAB-BELNR
            AND AUBEL <> ' '.
  ENDSELECT.

  MOVE VBRP-AUBEL TO INTAB-SONO.

  SELECT        * FROM VBPA  UP TO 1 ROWS
       WHERE VBELN = VBRP-AUBEL
*      AND   POSNR = VBRP-AUPOS.
       AND   PARVW = 'AA'.
  ENDSELECT.

  IF SY-SUBRC NE 0.
    EXIT.
  ENDIF.
PERFORM GET_KNA1_ADDRESS USING VBPA-KUNNR.


ENDFORM.
```

```
*&---------------------------------------------------------------------*
*&      Form  WRITE_HEADER
*&---------------------------------------------------------------------*
FORM WRITE_HEADER.

  WRITE: /55          'WALTHERs GAS AND OIL COMPANY.'.
WRITE:/              'Program:',
               12      SY-REPID.
  WRITE:/             'Date:',

               12      SY-DATUM.
  WRITE:/             'Company:',
               12      INTAB-BUKRS,
               47      'Posting Date From:',
               66      S_DATUM-LOW,
               77      'To:',
               81      S_DATUM-HIGH.
  WRITE:/             'Time:',
               12      SY-UZEIT.
  SKIP 2.
  WRITE:/            TEXT-001,
               09     TEXT-002,
               30     TEXT-003,
               41     TEXT-004,
               52     TEXT-005,
               57     TEXT-006,
               76     TEXT-008,
               68     TEXT-007,
               94     TEXT-009,
               99     TEXT-010,
               116    TEXT-011.

  WRITE:/            TEXT-021,
               09     TEXT-022,
               52     TEXT-025,
```

```
              57      TEXT-026,
              76      TEXT-028,
              68      TEXT-027,
              94      TEXT-029.
  ULINE.
  ULINE.
ENDFORM.                                    " WRITE_HEADER

*---------------------------------------------------------------------*
*       FORM GET_KNA1_ADDRESS                                         *
*---------------------------------------------------------------------
FORM GET_KNA1_ADDRESS USING W_KUNNR.
  SELECT  SINGLE * FROM KNA1
       WHERE KUNNR = W_KUNNR.

  IF SY-SUBRC <> 0.
    EXIT.
  ENDIF.

  CASE KNA1-LAND1.
    WHEN 'US'.
      MOVE KNA1-REGIO TO INTAB-LAND1.
      MOVE 'US'       TO INTAB-LANDKEY.
    WHEN OTHERS.
      MOVE KNA1-LAND1 TO INTAB-LAND1.
  ENDCASE.
*
  MOVE KNA1-NAME1 TO INTAB-NAME1.
  MOVE KNA1-ORT01 TO INTAB-ORT01.
  MOVE KNA1-ORT02 TO INTAB-ORT02.

ENDFORM.

*---------------------------------------------------------------------*
*       FORM GET_DATA                                                 *
*---------------------------------------------------------------------*
```

```
*       moves appropriate data from dbtab BSIS into internal tables
*       *BSIS and makes debit values negative.
*---------------------------------------------------------------------.*
FORM GET_DATA.

  CASE *BSIS-SHKZG.
    WHEN 'S'.
      *BSIS-DMBTR = *BSIS-DMBTR - 2 * *BSIS-DMBTR.
    WHEN 'H'.
*ABSOLUTE VALUE, SO NO CHANGE (ALREADY POSITIVE (CREDIT)).
  ENDCASE.

*Detail Internal Table Report
  MOVE *BSIS-BUKRS TO INTAB-BUKRS.
  MOVE *BSIS-BELNR TO INTAB-BELNR.
  MOVE *BSIS-BLART TO INTAB-BLART.
  MOVE *BSIS-BUDAT TO INTAB-BUDAT.
  MOVE *BSIS-HKONT TO INTAB-HKONT.
  MOVE *BSIS-DMBTR TO INTAB-DMBTR.
  MOVE *BSIS-GSBER TO INTAB-GSBER.
  MOVE *BSIS-SGTXT TO INTAB-SGTXT.

ENDFORM.
```

Summary

Congratulations—you've just learned one of the three most important programs to write for SAP in ABAP/4! The next two chapters on data extracts and BDC sessions are more complex, so be sure to review this chapter and the previous chapters to solidify your basic knowledge before you continue.

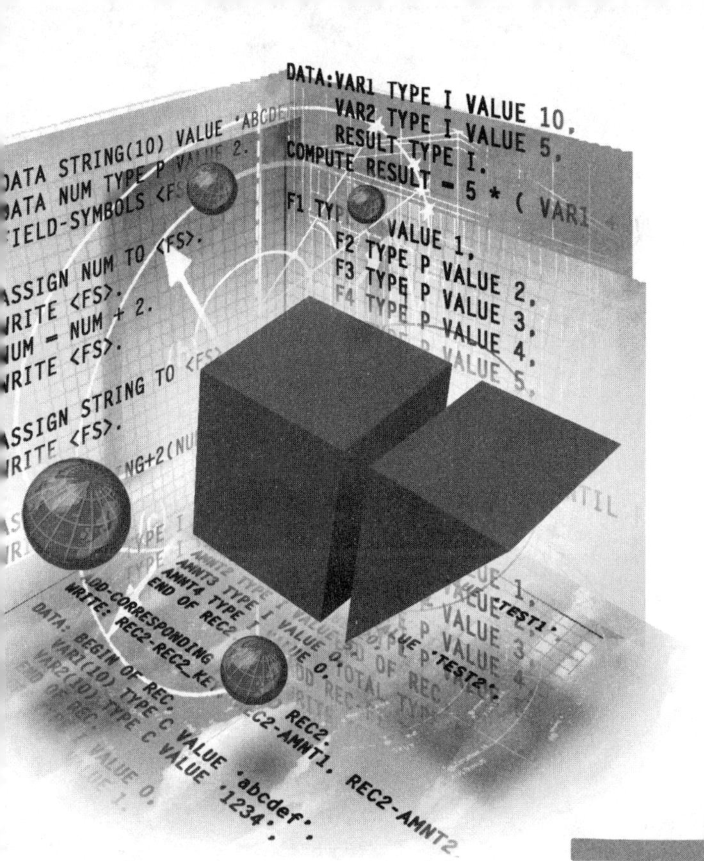

PART III

Advanced Technical Issues

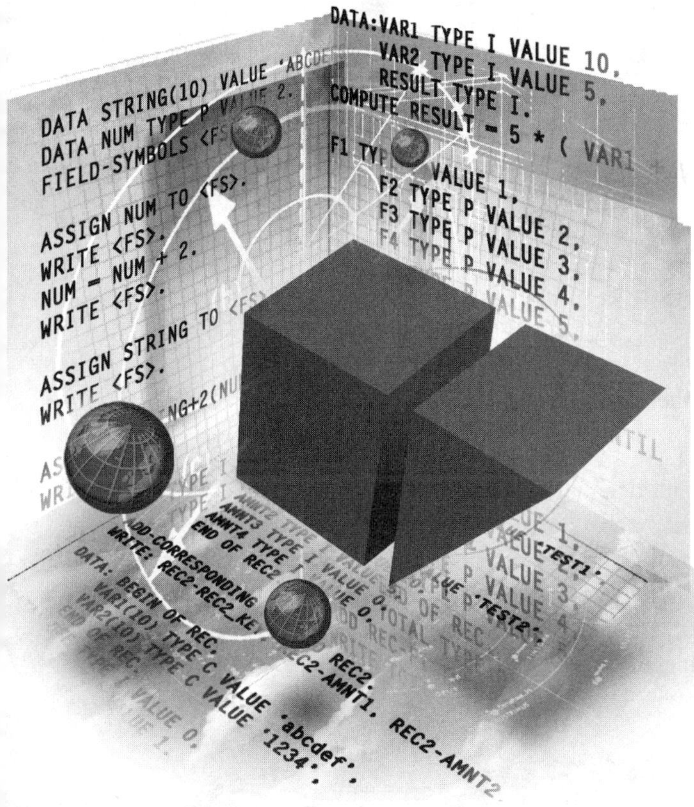

Chapter 15

Writing a Data Extract

In This Chapter

- Steps in a Data Extract
- Determining the Data to be Extracted
- Extracting the Data
- Writing the Data to a File
- Transferring the File to the Target System
- Example Extracts

A *data extract* is a program that pulls data out of a system on a periodic basis so that it can be transferred to an external system for processing. In the case of SAP, data extracts are often used to keep legacy or other external systems in sync with SAP by passing data from SAP to those systems. For example, a legacy manufacturing system might need weekly extracts of material inventory levels from SAP. This chapter goes through the steps of designing and writing a data extract.

Steps in a Data Extract

Several steps are commonly used to design and write a data extract:

1. The first step is to determine what data to extract by looking for the database tables that hold the information.

2. The second step is to extract the correct data from those database tables identified.

3. The third step is to write that data—in the proper format—to a file.

4. The final step is to transfer the file to the target system.

Once each of these steps is complete, the final program can be scheduled for future use.

Determining the Data to Be Extracted

The first step in the process is to determine what data is to be extracted. You'll be given a set of program requirements that could range from "We need some information on materials" to a detailed breakdown of exactly which database tables, which fields in those tables, and the criteria to be used to determine which rows of data to select. Normally, the requirements you get will fall somewhere in the middle.

Usually the requirements are written by business analysts who have no knowledge of relational databases and will simply list the information they need in business terms.

So the requirements might call for extracting all purchase orders that include purchase order number, date, name of requester, and material numbers for items ordered. The programmer's job is to take those business terms and translate them into specific tables and fields in those tables.

Using Logical Databases to Find Tables

A number of ways exist in SAP to find the tables that hold the information you need. One of the simplest ways is to look at the logical databases SAP has already created for the business object that interests you. As discussed in Chapter 13, "Working with Logical Databases," a logical database is a group of tables that SAP has put together to allow a program to use the `GET` event to read information from the database. Simply look at the list of logical databases for the business object in which you are interested (see Figure 15-1). This list is found in the logical database information transaction, `SE36`.

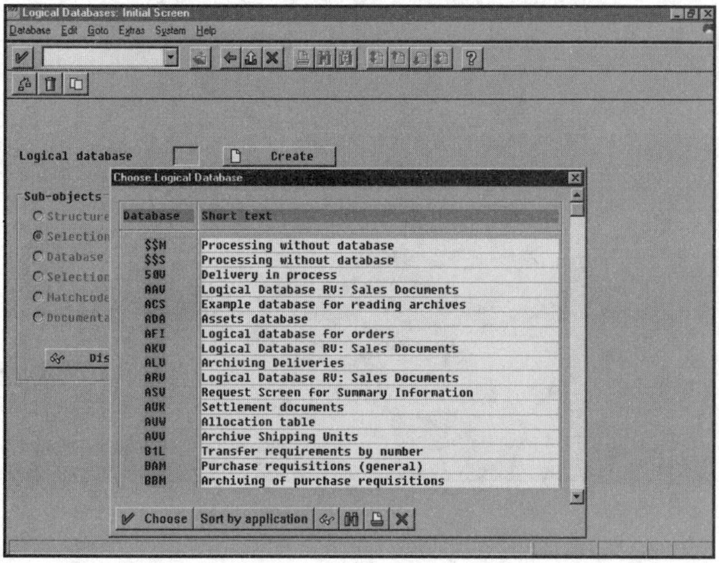

FIGURE 15-1

The list of logical databases

For example, the logical database for purchase orders is `KSM`. By using the Display Structure button on the logical database information screen, you can view the table hierarchy that includes the database tables `EKKO` and `EKPO`. The structure gives descriptions for each table; from there, you can use the data dictionary to get a list of the individual fields in each table.

Using SAP Transactions to Find Tables

Another way to find the tables that hold the attributes of specific business objects is to look at the SAP transactions. As you may recall, a *transaction* is a group of screens used by end users to maintain or view data—so transactions will correspond to the business terms that the analysts use. SAP provides transactions for all business objects in the system. For purchase orders, there are transactions to create, change, or view the purchase orders. For example, the transaction `ME23`, would display a single purchase order over several screens.

Remember that most fields on a screen correspond with a field in the database. The system provides the database field name in the Technical Information dialog box (see Figure 15-2). To access the dialog box for a particular field, click the field, press F1, and then choose Technical Information.

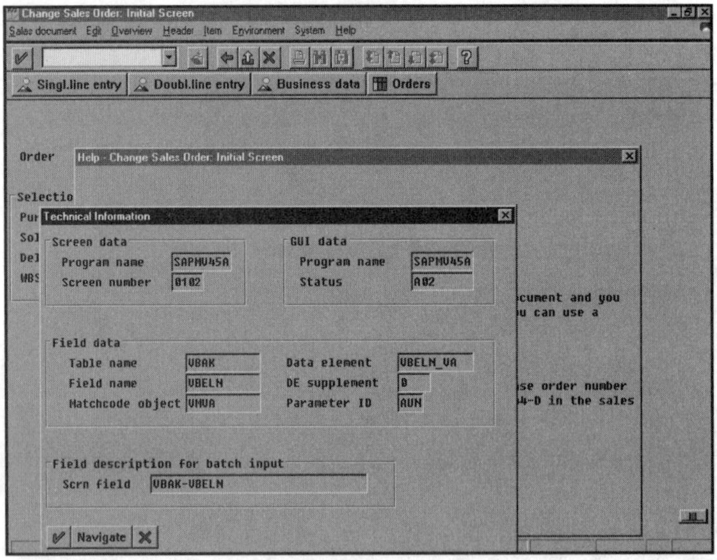

FIGURE 15-2

Technical information for a database field

NOTE

For some screen fields, the technical information won't provide a corresponding field in the database. In these cases, look at the other fields that appear on the screen and determine which database tables they come from. Most attributes of business objects can be found in three or four tables at most.

Choosing Specific Fields

Once the database fields have been mapped to the business requirements, you can determine which specific fields need to be read and whether there are any criteria to limit the amount of rows. Periodic extracts of data normally don't want the same data read twice, so programs need criteria to limit the extract to new data only. All data entered into SAP is date stamped with the date of entry recorded in a database table; so, the date stamp is often a good criterion.

Another possible criterion is the document number—a number that's assigned to most transactions and is incremented each time a new transaction occurs. For example, each time a new purchase order is created, the purchase order number (`EKKO-EBAN`) is increased. So if the last purchase order number extracted is saved, each time the program is run that last number can be recalled and used as a starting point.

Extracting the Data

Once the database tables and fields have been identified, you need to write a program to read the data. As you should know by now, you can read information from the database with either of two techniques:

- To read the tables directly, you use the `SELECT` command. In this case, the programmer must understand the relationships between the many tables.
- The second technique is to use a logical database and the `GET` statement. This is easier to use but often not as efficient as `SELECT` statements.

Regardless of the technique used, the fields will be read and any criteria needed should be applied through a `where` clause or `CHECK` statement.

Writing the Data to a File

After the information is read from the database, it needs to be written to a system file. The `TRANSFER` command moves data from SAP to a system file. The first step is to determine the directory path and name of the system file you'll use.

A common approach to naming such a file is to mix a static name with a date stamp so that each file has a unique name. For example, a daily extract of purchase order information might use a file name such as `poextract.04.18.97`; the next time the interface is run, the file name would be `poextract.04.19.97`. By using unique names, you avoid the possibility of overwriting a file that failed to transfer.

Once the file name is built, use the `OPEN` command to ready the file for writing.

When the information has been read from the database, the program can process or format the data. When giving the requirements for an extract, those requirements contain the necessary format for the extract file. The typical format is to specify each field by its position in the file. For example, the purchase order number might occupy the first ten positions of a file, the creation date might be in the next eight positions, and so on. Another possibility is a format where each field is followed by a separator, such as a comma or a pound sign.

CAUTION

When using separators, be very careful of long description fields because they may contain any type of character, including the separator. For example, the description of a part might be `Bolt, Steel, 7 inch`. If you used the comma as a separator, this description would throw off the entire file because the target system would think that the description field was two different fields. Use the `REPLACE` command to remove any separators that might be in description fields before transferring them to the file.

Transferring the File to the Target System

After the system file has been built, the final step is to send that file to the target system. ABAP/4 has the ability to create a system file and transfer data to and from it, but it has very limited ability to deal with the operating system. No ABAP/4 command exists to move or copy files at the operating-system level; each SAP site must set up its own way of moving files into and out of SAP.

Some of the common techniques used are a daemon or the `CALL FUNCTION` command. A *daemon* is a program that runs in the background of the operating system, written in a low-level language such as C, watching for files and sending them to the proper target. As explained in Chapter 11, "Adding Subroutines to Your Program," the `CALL FUNCTION` command can be used to make operating system calls if your operating system is UNIX. For example, `CALL FUNCTION` can be used to execute the UNIX `rcp` (remote copy) command to move files to another server. Because moving files into and out of SAP is such a common operation, all sites will have a solution to this problem. You should find this solution and use it in all your programs.

Example Extracts

Next, you'll look at three examples of data extract programs:

- The first example extracts documents created by the SAP automated check runs and writes them to a file. SAP automatically creates checks for payments to vendors.
- The second example extracts purchase order information (a *purchase order* is an order to buy one or more items).
- The final example is an extract of material inventories.

In each example, the requirements are provided, followed by the ABAP/4 program to accomplish them.

Check Payments

The first program, called ZCHECK, extracts documents created by the SAP automated check runs and writes them to a file. SAP automatically creates checks for payments to vendors and records these checks as financial documents in the BKPF and BSEG tables. For each document, a record is placed in BKPF with general information such as document number and date created. Then each line item of the document is placed in BSEG with information such as the amount, vendor, and general ledger account.

This data extract will be run by end users on demand and should allow the user to enter the following parameters:

- A range of document numbers
- A range of document dates
- A company code
- The path and file name of the output file

These checks can be identified by a document type (BKPF-BLART) of KZ and a payment indicator (BSEG-ZLSCH) of C. Once the check information is read, determine the bank account of the check by using the G/L Account (BSEG-SAKNR) to retrieve the bank ID (T042I-HBKID) and then the bank account (T012K-BANKN).

The output file should have the format shown in Table 15-1.

Table 15-1 ZCHECK Output File

Field Name	Position	Data Type	Length	Source: SAP table-field
Check number	1	C	10	BSEG-BELNR
Date of issue "MMDDYY"	11	C	06	BSEG-VALUT
Bank account number	17	C	17	T012K-BANKN,
Amount "00000000000"	34	C	11	BSEG-WRBTR
Name Vendor	45	C	30	LFA1-NAME1
Filler	75		06	

Here's the program:

```
*------------------------------------------------------------.*
* Program Name:                              Date      : 12/11/96 *
* SAP Name     : ZCHECK                                        *
*                                                              *
*------------------------------------------------------------.*
* Description : This program will extract Check Documents on demand   *
*               from the BBSEG table which contains different financial *
*               documents.  Look ups will be done to retrieve the      *
*               vendor name and bank account of the check.             *
***********************************************************************
REPORT ZCHECK          NO STANDARD PAGE HEADING
                        LINE-SIZE 132
                        LINE-COUNT 65
                        MESSAGE-ID ZZ.

***********************************************************************
*-------------------------------------------------------------------*
* Tables                                                          *
*-------------------------------------------------------------------*
***********************************************************************

TABLES : BSEG,                          "Financial Documents Header
         BKPF,                          "Financial Documents Item
         LFA1,                          "Vendor Master
```

```
        T042I,                          "Account determination
        T012K.                          "House Bank Accounts

*************************************************************************
*_______________________________________________________________________
__________*
* Variables                                                             *
*-----------------------------------------------------------------------*
*************************************************************************

DATA:
       WS_BUF(15),                      "Temporary Buffer
       WS_AMNT(11) TYPE N,              "Temporary Field For Amount
       WS_REC# TYPE I VALUE 0.          "Record Count


DATA: BEGIN OF REC_OUT OCCURS 0,        "Output File
        CHECT(10),                        "Check Number
        ZALDT(6),                         "Check Date
        BANKN(18),                        "Bank Account
        AMNT(11),                         "Check Amount
        NAME1(30),                        "Vendor Name
        FILLER(6),
      END OF REC_OUT.

*-----------------------------------------------------------------------*
* Select Options/Parameters                                             *
*-----------------------------------------------------------------------*

PARAMETERS: P_BUKRS LIKE BSEG-BUKRS OBLIGATORY.  "Company Code

SELECT-OPTIONS:   S_BUDAT FOR BKPF-BUDAT,    "Date Created
            S_BELNR FOR BKPF-BELNR.          "Document Number

PARAMETERS: P_FILE(45) OBLIGATORY LOWER CASE  "UNIX Output File Name
                       DEFAULT '/interfaces/outbound/checkdata.txt'.
```

```
************************************************************************
*-----------------------------------------------------------------------*
* Main Processing
*-----------------------------------------------------------------------*
************************************************************************

START-OF-SELECTION.
  PERFORM OPEN_DATASET.
  PERFORM EXTRACT_DATA.
  PERFORM CLOSE_DATASET.
****** End Program

*----------------------------------------------------------------------- *
*       FORM OPEN_DATASET                                               *
*-----------------------------------------------------------------------.*
*       Read data from BKPF, financial documents header table, and    *
*       BSEG, financial documents line items, then look up vendor name*
*       and bank account before transferring data to file.           *
*-----------------------------------------------------------------------.*
FORM OPEN_DATASET.

****** build unix filename to write
  OPEN DATASET P_FILE FOR OUTPUT IN TEXT MODE.
  IF SY-SUBRC NE 0.
    MESSAGE E999 WITH 'Error Creating File ' P_FILE.
  ENDIF.

ENDFORM.                                "End Form Open_Dataset

*-----------------------------------------------------------------------.*
*       FORM EXTRACT_DATA                                               *
*-----------------------------------------------------------------------.*
*       Read data from BKPF, financial documents header table, and    *
*       BSEG, financial documents line items, then look up vendor name*
*       and bank account before transferring data to file.            *
*-----------------------------------------------------------------------.*
```

```
FORM EXTRACT_DATA.

*** Select Header Documents
SELECT * FROM BKPF WHERE BELNR IN S_BELNR       "Check Document#
                        AND BUDAT IN S_BUDAT     "Check Posting Date
                        AND BUKRS = P_BUKRS      "Company Code
                        AND BLART = 'KZ'.        "Document Type
  SELECT * FROM BSEG WHERE BUKRS = BKPF-BUKRS   "Get Void Line Items
                        AND BELNR = BKPF-BELNR
                        AND GJAHR = BKPF-GJAHR
                        AND ZLSCH = 'C'.          "Indicates Check
      CLEAR REC_OUT.

      WRITE BSEG-WRBTR USING EDIT MASK 'RR___________'       "Get Amount
                TO REC_OUT-AMNT.
      PERFORM PAD_FIELD USING REC_OUT-AMNT.

      MOVE BKPF-BUDAT TO WS_BUF.       "get date 'DDMMYY'
      MOVE WS_BUF+4(4) TO REC_OUT-ZALDT.
      MOVE WS_BUF+2(2) TO REC_OUT-ZALDT+4.
      MOVE BSEG-BELNR(10) TO REC_OUT-CHECT.         "Check#

      SELECT SINGLE * FROM LFA1
                  WHERE LIFNR = BSEG-LIFNR.
        MOVE LFA1-NAME1 TO REC_OUT-NAME1.

      SELECT * FROM T042I                            "Get Bank Account
            WHERE UKONT = BSEG-HKONT.
        SELECT SINGLE * FROM T012K
              WHERE BUKRS = T042I-ZBUKR
                AND HBKID = T042I-HBKID
                AND HKTID = T042I-HKTID.
        IF SY-SUBRC EQ 0.
          MOVE T012K-BANKN(18) TO REC_OUT-BANKN.     "Bank Account
          PERFORM PAD_FIELD USING REC_OUT-BANKN.
        ELSE.
```

```
          MESSAGE E999 WITH T042I-HBKID T042I-HKTID
                                'Bank Account missing from T012K'.
        ENDIF.
      ENDSELECT.
      TRANSFER REC_OUT TO P_FILE.        "Save Record to File
    ENDSELECT.
  ENDSELECT.

  WS_REC# = WS_REC# + 1.

ENDFORM.

*---------------------------------------------------------------------*
*       FORM CLOSE_DATASET                                            *
*---------------------------------------------------------------------*
*       Close dataset and report totals                               *
*---------------------------------------------------------------------*
FORM CLOSE_DATASET.

  CLOSE DATASET P_FILE.
  IF SY-SUBRC NE 0.
    MESSAGE E999 WITH 'Error Closing file ' P_FILE.
  ENDIF.
  IF WS_REC# > 0.
    MESSAGE I999 WITH  WS_REC# 'records written to File.'.
  ELSE.
    MESSAGE I999 WITH 'No records found.  No file created.'.
  ENDIF.
ENDFORM.                                  "End form Close_Dataset

*---------------------------------------------------------------------*
*       FORM PAD_FIELD                                                *
*---------------------------------------------------------------------*
*       Pad number with leading zeros                                 *
*---------------------------------------------------------------------*
FORM PAD_FIELD USING P_NUM.
```

```
  SHIFT P_NUM RIGHT.
  WHILE SY-SUBRC = 0.
    REPLACE ' ' WITH '0' INTO P_NUM. "Zero Pad
  ENDWHILE.

ENDFORM.
```

This first example demonstrates a simple extract program run at user demand. The following examples demonstrate more of the attributes for extracts.

Purchase Orders

The second program extracts information about new purchase orders created in SAP. It reads the Purchase Order Line Item table, EKPO. The tracking number, together with the purchase order number and purchase order line item number, is used to retrieve the material requisition number from table EBAN. The custom table ZOUT_DOC stores the last document number read during the last time the extract was run. After the extract is run, the last document read is replaced in the ZOUT_DOC table.

The following parameters are allowed:

- Starting Purchase Order Number
- Ending Purchase Order Number
- Path and File name of Output File

The user will supply a file name for the extract data set. Assume that the program won't have to transfer the file to an external system. Table 15-2 shows the format for the output file.

Once the requirements have been determined, the next step is to develop the ABAP/4 program to extract the data:

```
***********************************************************************
* Program Name:                               Date:  10/01/96       *
* SAP Name     : ZPOEXT                                               *
*                                                                   *
*-------------------------------------------------------------------*
* Description : Extract New Purchase Order Data.                    *
*                                                                   *
***********************************************************************
```

Table 15-2 ZPOEXT Output File

Field Name	Position	Data Type	Length	Source: SAP table-field
PO Number	1	C	10	EKPO-EBELN
PO Line Number	11	C	5	EKPO- EBELP
Request Number	18	C	10	EKPO-EDNR
Request Line Number	28	C	5	EBAN-BNFPO
Item Quantity	33	C	18	EKPO-MENGE
PO Date	51	C	10	EKKO-AEDAT
Item Description	61	C	40	EKPO-TXZ01
Item Amount '0000000000'	101	C	10	EKPO-NETWR

```
REPORT ZPOEXT        NO STANDARD PAGE HEADING
                        LINE-SIZE 132
                        LINE-COUNT 65
                        MESSAGE-ID ZZ.

*-----------------------------------------------------*
* Tables                                              *
*-----------------------------------------------------*

TABLES :     ZOUT_DOC ,    "Interface Document Log
             EKKO, "Purchase Order Headers
             EKPO, "Purchase Order Line Item Detail
             EBAN. "Purchase Requisitions

*-----------------------------------------------------*
* Variables                                           *
*-----------------------------------------------------*

DATA:
     WS_TEMP(18),                                   "Temp field for con-
version
     WS_AMOUNT(13) TYPE N,                   "Temp field for amount
     WS_MAX LIKE EKPO-EBELN,             "Max Doc# Processed
     BEGIN OF REC_OUT,
```

```
            EBELN LIKE EKPO-EBELN,
            EBELP LIKE EKPO-EBELP,
            BEDNR LIKE EKPO-BEDNR,
            BNFPO LIKE EBAN-BNFPO,
            MENGE LIKE EKPO-MENGE,
            AEDAT LIKE EKKO-AEDAT,
            TXZ01 LIKE EKPO-TXZ01,
            AMOUNT(10) TYPE C,
        END OF REC_OUT.


*_____________________________________________________________________*
* Select Options/Parameters                                           *
*_____________________________________________________________________*
PARAMETERS:
            P_BELNR LIKE EKPO-EBELN,      "Starting PO to process
            P_LIMIT LIKE EKPO-EBELN    "Upper Limit of  PO's to process
               DEFAULT '9999999999',
            P_FILE(45) OBLIGATORY LOWER CASE    "UNIX Output File
                        DEFAULT '/interfaces/outbound/podata.txt'.

***********************************************************************
*_____________________________________________________________________*
* Main Processing
*_____________________________________________________________________
___________*
***********************************************************************
INITIALIZATION.


START-OF-SELECTION.
  PERFORM OPEN_DATASET.
  PERFORM EXTRACT_DATA.
  PERFORM CLOSE_DATASET.
  PERFORM UPDATE_ZOUT_DOC.
```

```
****** End Program
*---------------------------------------------------.*
*       FORM OPEN_DATASET                           *
*---------------------------------------------------.*
*       Read data from BKPF, financial documents header table, and    *
*       BSEG, financial documents line items, then look up vendor name*
*       and bank account before transferring data to file.           *
*---------------------------------------------------.*
FORM OPEN_DATASET.

  OPEN DATASET P_FILE FOR OUTPUT IN TEXT MODE.
  IF SY-SUBRC NE 0.
    MESSAGE E999 WITH 'Error Creating File ' P_FILE.
  ENDIF.

ENDFORM.  "End Form Open_Dataset


*---------------------------------------------------*
*       FORM EXTRACT_DATA                           *
*---------------------------------------------------*
* Extract Purchase Order data from SAP and transfer to file.       *
*---------------------------------------------------*
FORM EXTRACT_DATA.

  IF P_BELNR IS INITIAL.  "Look up next PO# if parameter is blank
    SELECT SINGLE * FROM ZOUT_DOC           "Get First PO#
                 WHERE  ID = 'POEXT'.
      P_BELNR =  ZOUT_DOC-BELNR.            "Assign Starting PO#
  ENDIF.

  WS_MAX = P_BELNR.                          "Store Current PO#

* Extract new PO items
  SELECT * FROM EKPO WHERE EBELN <= P_LIMIT
                       AND EBELN > P_BELNR.
```

```
    IF EKPO-EBELN > WS_MAX.
      MOVE EKPO-EBELN TO WS_MAX.           "Keep max PO# processed
    ENDIF.
    CLEAR REC_OUT.                       "Clear Buffer

    MOVE EKPO-EBELN TO REC_OUT-EBELN.         "Get PO#
    MOVE EKPO-EBELP TO REC_OUT-EBELP.         "Get PO Line#
    MOVE EKPO-BEDNR TO REC_OUT-BEDNR.   "Requisition Number

    SELECT * FROM EBAN WHERE EBELN = EKPO-EBELN
                             AND EBELP = EKPO-EBELP
                             AND BEDNR = EKPO-BEDNR.
      MOVE EBAN-BNFPO TO REC_OUT-BNFPO.         "Get Requisition line#
    ENDSELECT.

    MOVE EKPO-MENGE TO REC_OUT-MENGE.           "Get Item Qty
    MOVE EKPO-TXZ01 TO REC_OUT-TXZ01.           "Get Item Description
    MOVE EKPO-NETWR TO WS_AMOUNT.               "Get Order Amount
    WS_AMOUNT = WS_AMOUNT * 100.                "Remove Decimal

    PERFORM PAD_FIELD USING WS_AMOUNT.            "Format Amount
    MOVE WS_AMOUNT to REC_OUT-AMOUNT.           "Save Amount

    SELECT SINGLE * FROM EKKO WHERE EBELN = EKPO-EBELN.
      MOVE EKKO-AEDAT TO REC_OUT-AEDAT.         "Get PO Transaction Date

      TRANSFER REC_OUT TO P_FILE.             "Write buffer to file
  ENDSELECT.
ENDFORM.  "End Form Extract_Data

*-----------------------------------------*
*       FORM CLOSE_DATASET                *
*-----------------------------------------*
*  Close Dataset and report any errors    *
*-----------------------------------------*
```

```
FORM CLOSE_DATASET.

  CLOSE DATASET P_FILE.
  IF SY-SUBRC NE 0.
    MESSAGE E999 WITH 'Error Closing file ' P_FILE.
  ENDIF.

ENDFORM.  "End form Close_Dataset

*---------------------------------------------------------------------*
*       FORM UPDATE_ZOUT_DOC                                          *
*---------------------------------------------------------------------*
*  Update ZOUT_DOC with last document processed
*---------------------------------------------------------------------*
FORM UPDATE_ZOUT_DOC.
  UPDATE  ZOUT_DOC SET BELNR = WS_MAX      "Update Last Document
                WHERE  ID = 'POEXT'.
  IF SY-DBCNT NE 1.              "If # of rows update <> 1 Raise Error
      MESSAGE E999 WITH 'Error Updating Table ZOUT_DOC'.
  ENDIF.
ENDFORM.  "End Form Update_ZOUT_DOC

*---------------------------------------------------------------------*
*       FORM PAD_FIELD                                                *
*---------------------------------------------------------------------*
*       Pad number with leading zeros                                 *
*---------------------------------------------------------------------*
FORM PAD_FIELD USING P_NUM.
  SHIFT P_BELNR RIGHT.
  WHILE SY-SUBRC = 0.
    REPLACE ' ' WITH '0' INTO P_BELNR. "Zero Pad
  ENDWHILE.

ENDFORM.
```

Inventory Changes

SAP records changes to materials as *material movements*. Each movement is recorded in a material document in the MKPF and MSEG tables, much like the financial documents stored in the BKPF and BSEG tables discussed in the preceding sections. The type of movement can be determined by the document type. This program reads through the material documents in the MSEG table. If a new document has a storage location MSEG-LGORT, it indicates that the available quantity has changed since the last time the extract has been run. Only one document needs to be reported for each combination of Material, Plant, and Storage Location because the program will look up the current quantity directly. Once all appropriate documents have been identified, extract the current material quantity from the MARD table. The last material document number read will be updated in ZOUT_DOC and used to restrict the search next time it's run to new documents.

The following parameters are allowed:

- Target system to which you're sending the extract
- User ID on target system
- File name and path for target system

The user will supply the parameters at runtime. Assume that a custom function call has been written that will transfer the extracted file to the target system, called ZUNIX_FILE_TRANSFER. Table 15-3 shows the format for the output.

Here's the program:

```
************************************************************************
* Program Name:                                       Date   : 10/01/96 *
* SAP Name     : ZMATQTY                                                *
*                                                                       *
*________________________________________________________________________ *
* Description : Extract Material Movements and Current Quantities.      *
*                                                                       *
*                                                                       *
************************************************************************

REPORT ZMATQTY          NO STANDARD PAGE HEADING
LINE-SIZE 132
LINE-COUNT 65
MESSAGE-ID ZZ.
```

Table 15-3 ZMATEXT Output File Format

Field Name	Position	Data Type	Length	Source: SAP table-field
Material number	1	CHAR	18	MARD-MATNR
Plant	19	CHAR	4	MARD-WERKS
Storage location	23	CHAR	4	MARD-LGORT
Quantity	27	CHAR	14	MARD-LABST
Material Document	41	C	10	MSEG-MBLNR
Document Year	51	C	4	MSEG-MJAHR
Document Line Number	55	C	4	MSEG-ZEILE

```
*----------------------------------------*
* Tables                                 *
*----------------------------------------*

TABLES :    ZOUT_DOC,     "Interface Document Log
            MARD, "Material Quantity on Hand
            MSEG. "Material Movement Documents



*----------------------------------------*
* Variables                              *
*----------------------------------------*

DATA:
        WS_DSN(85)              "Filename
          VALUE '/interfaces/outbound/matqty.txt',
        WS_MAX LIKE MSEG-MBLNR,       "Max Document Processed
        WS_MBLNR LIKE MSEG-MBLNR.      "Starting Document to Process

DATA:  BEGIN OF ITAB OCCURS 0,
MATNR LIKE MSEG-MATNR,             "Material Number
          WERKS LIKE MSEG-WERKS,            "Plant Code
          LGORT LIKE MSEG-LGORT,            "Storage Location
          LABST LIKE MARD-LABST,            "Material Quantity
```

```
         MBLNR LIKE MSEG-MBLNR,              "Document #
         MJAHR LIKE MSEG-MJAHR,              "Doc Year
         ZEILE LIKE MSEG-ZEILE,              "Doc Line#
       END OF ITAB.

*---------------------------------------------------------------*
* Select Options/Parameters                                     *
*---------------------------------------------------------------*
PARAMETERS:  P_DEST(30),    "Target System for Extract
             P_USER(30),    "User Id on Target
             P_TARGET(85). "Target File and Path

SELECT-OPTIONS:  S_WERKS FOR MSEG-WERKS,          "Plant Code
                           S_MATNR FOR MSEG-MATNR.         "Material Number

*---------------------------------------------------------------*
* Main Processing
*---------------------------------------------------------------*

START-OF-SELECTION.
  PERFORM OPEN_DATASET.
  PERFORM EXTRACT_DATA.
  PERFORM CLOSE_DATASET.
  PERFORM UPDATE_ZOUT_DOC.
****** End Program

*---------------------------------------------------------------*
*       FORM OPEN_DATASET                                       *
*---------------------------------------------------------------*
* Open dataset and check for errors
*---------------------------------------------------------------*
FORM OPEN_DATASET.

  OPEN DATASET WS_DSN FOR OUTPUT IN TEXT MODE.
  IF SY-SUBRC NE 0.
```

```
    MESSAGE E999 WITH 'Error Creating File ' WS_DSN.
  ENDIF.

ENDFORM.  "End Form Open_Dataset

*-----------------------------------------------------------------*
*       FORM EXTRACT_DATA                                         *
*-----------------------------------------------------------------*
* Extract data and Transfer it to the internal table, itab.       *
* Movement Documents are read and stored in an internal table only if *
* no other document for that Material, Plant, Location combination    *
* has not been read before.                                       *
*                                                                 *
* After all new documents have been read look up the current quantity  *
* from MARD.
* If documents have been read transfer file to target system.     *
*-----------------------------------------------------------------*
FORM EXTRACT_DATA.

  SELECT SINGLE * FROM ZOUT_DOC            "Get First Document#
                 WHERE  ID = 'MATEXT'.
      WS_MBLNR =  ZOUT_DOC-BELNR.            "Assign Starting PO#

  WS_MAX = WS_MBLNR.                         "Save Max Document

*** Get Material Movement (Change) Documents
  SELECT * FROM MSEG WHERE MBLNR > WS_MBLNR
                           AND LGORT NE '    '
                           AND MATNR IN S_MATNR
                           AND WERKS IN S_WERKS.

    IF MSEG-MBLNR > WS_MAX.
      MOVE MSEG-MBLNR TO WS_MAX.        "Keep max document# processed
    ENDIF.
```

```
*   Insert Werks/Matnr into Itab if it is not already there
    READ TABLE ITAB WITH KEY MATNR = MSEG-MATNR
                             WERKS = MSEG-WERKS
                             LGORT = MSEG-LGORT
                    TRANSPORTING NO FIELDS.
    IF SY-SUBRC NE 0.                    "If no rows found append new data
      CLEAR ITAB.
      MOVE MSEG-MBLNR TO ITAB-MBLNR.
      MOVE MSEG-MJAHR TO ITAB-MJAHR.
      MOVE MSEG-ZEILE TO ITAB-ZEILE.
      MOVE MSEG-MATNR TO ITAB-MATNR.
      MOVE MSEG-WERKS TO ITAB-WERKS.
      MOVE MSEG-LGORT TO ITAB-LGORT.
      APPEND ITAB.
    ENDIF.
  ENDSELECT.

*** Get Quantities for selected materials
  LOOP AT ITAB.
    SELECT SINGLE * FROM MARD WHERE MATNR = ITAB-MATNR
                                AND WERKS = ITAB-WERKS
                                AND LGORT = ITAB-LGORT.
    IF SY-SUBRC EQ 0.
      ITAB-LABST = MARD-LABST.
      TRANSFER ITAB TO WS_DSN.       " Transfer Data to File
    ENDIF.
  ENDLOOP.
  IF SY-SUBRC <> 0.
    MESSAGE I999 WITH 'No Documents Found'.
  ELSE.
***** Send the UNIX file to system specified at runtime
  CALL FUNCTION 'ZUNIX_FILE_TRANSFER'
     EXPORTING
          I_DEST_SYSTEM              = P_DEST
          I_USER_ID                  = P_USER
```

```
          I_TARGET_FILE                 = P_TARGET
          I_FILENAME                    = WS_DSN
     EXCEPTIONS
          CAN_NOT_CONNECT               = 01
          SYNTAX_ERROR                  = 02.
  IF SY-SUBRC = 0.
    MESSAGE I999 WITH 'Outbound transfer successful with'
                      WS_DSN.
  ELSE.
    MESSAGE E999 WITH 'Outbound transfer failed with '
                      WS_DSN 'ERROR' SY-SUBRC.
  ENDIF.
ENDIF.

ENDFORM.     "End Form Extract_Data

*_____________________________________________*
*       FORM CLOSE_DATASET                    *
*_____________________________________________*
*  Close Dataset and report any errors        *
*_____________________________________________*
FORM CLOSE_DATASET.

  CLOSE DATASET WS_DSN.
  IF SY-SUBRC NE 0.
    MESSAGE E999 WITH 'Error Closing file '.
  ENDIF.


ENDFORM.  "End form Close_Dataset

*_____________________________________________*
*       FORM UPDATE_ZOUT_DOC                  *
*_____________________________________________*
*  Update ZOUT_DOC with last document processed
*_____________________________________________*
```

```
FORM UPDATE_ZOUT_DOC.
  UPDATE  ZOUT_DOC SET BELNR = WS_MAX      "Update Last Document
                 WHERE  ID = 'MATEXT'.
  IF SY-DBCNT NE 1.                  "If # of rows update <> 1 Raise Error
      MESSAGE E999 WITH 'Error Updating Table ZOUT_DOC'.

  ENDIF.
ENDFORM.  "End Form Update_ZOUT_DOC
```

Summary

The data extract is one of the most common programs that is coded on an SAP system. No company uses SAP exclusively, so the ability to move information into and out of SAP, to integrate SAP into a heterogeneous network of systems, is critical. Data extracts are half of that equation. The other half, moving information into SAP, is addressed in Chapter 16, "Writing a BDC Program."

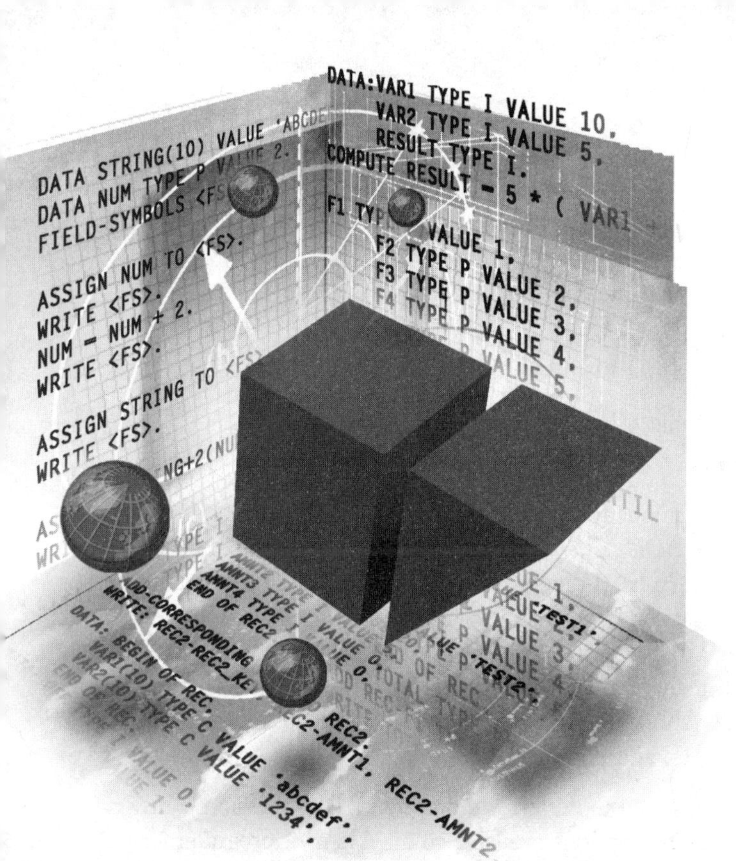

Chapter 16

Writing a BDC Program

In This Chapter

- Steps in a BDC Session
- Identifying Screens in a Transaction
- Building the BDC Table
- Submitting the BDC Table
- Example BDC Sessions

ABAP/4 has a programming technique for loading data into SAP, known as a *Batch Data Communications Session* or *BDC session*. A BDC session is a combination of ABAP/4 programming and built-in SAP functionality. It simulates the act of a user entering data into an SAP transaction. The system takes the data from an ABAP/4 program and feeds it to an SAP transaction screen by screen, much like a user would. The programmer can choose to have SAP process a batch of several transactions immediately or at a later time. Also a single transaction can be executed directly by the programmer with more control and better error handling.

Either way, several steps must be taken to design and program a BDC session. This chapter explains those steps and the options available to an ABAP/4 programmer who wants to use a BDC session to load data into SAP.

Steps in a BDC Session

The first step in a BDC session is to identify the screens of the transaction that the program will process. Next, you write a program to build the BDC table that is used to submit the data to SAP. The final step is to submit the BDC table to the system in batch mode or as a single transaction through the `CALL TRANSACTION` command. Once these steps are completed, the program can be scheduled for periodic execution. The following sections examine the individual steps in the process, and then two examples are provided for you to review.

Identifying Screens in a Transaction

When a user enters data into SAP, he or she uses transactions for the data entry. Each transaction has several screens, identified by a program name and a screen number, into which that data is entered. Information on the current screen can be found by choosing the System | Status command from any menu (see Figure 16-1).

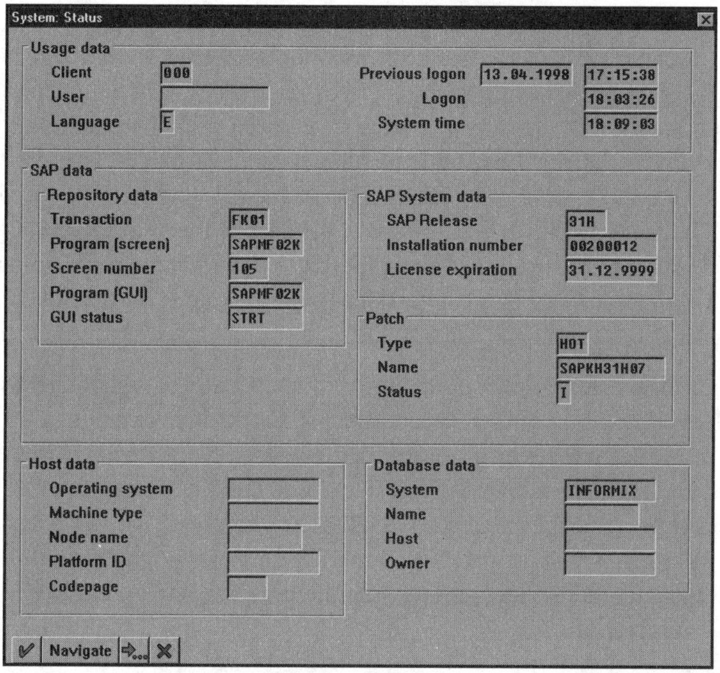

FIGURE 16-1

The system status screen

Each screen has fields that correspond with fields in the database. These field names are used when building the BDC table that submits the data to SAP. Clicking a screen field, pressing the Help key (F1), and then clicking the Technical Info button (see Figure 16-2) can retrieve the field name.

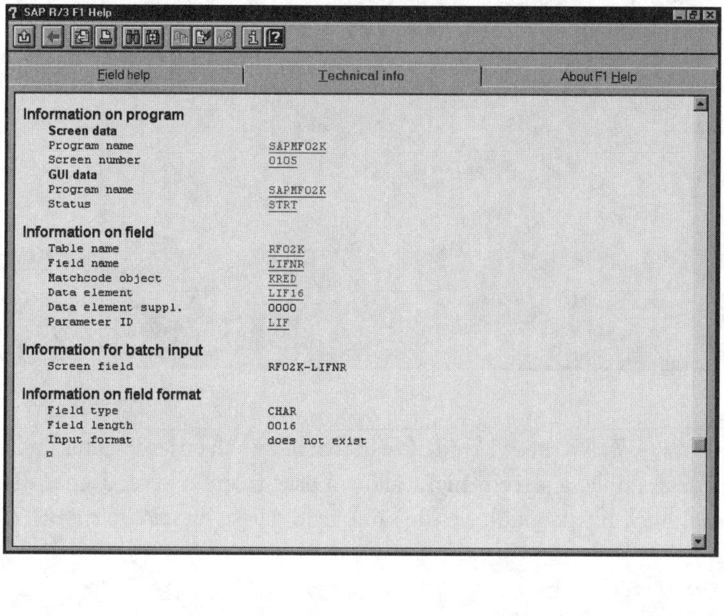

FIGURE 16-2

Reviewing the technical information for a database field

Screens also have function buttons that may bring up other screens. One function code may be called per screen—the most common being F11 (Save). To get a list of available function codes from any screen, right-click the screen. Submitting a function code is identical to submitting a value for a screen field. The value `BDC_OKCODE` is used in place of a field name, and the function code is used in place of the field value, in the form `/XX`, where `XX` is the number of the function code. So the last entry into all BDC tables, which is always to save the data, is the field name `BDC_OKCODE` and a field value of `/11`. In some cases you need to duplicate the act of a user selecting a field with the cursor. This can be done using the value `BDC_CURSOR` in place of the field name. Then place the name of the field you wish to select in the field value.

To design a BDC session, you need to map out the path of which screens will be used in the transaction, which fields must be populated, and which function buttons are used to move from screen to screen. For example, the transaction `MK02`, which changes a purchasing vendor, has several screens. The first screen number is `0100` and the program name for the screen is `SAPMF02K`. This screen has two fields, `RF02K-LIFNR` and `RF02K-EKORG`, plus several check boxes (see Figure 16-3). Once all screens are identified, the next step to write the program is to build the BDC table, using that information.

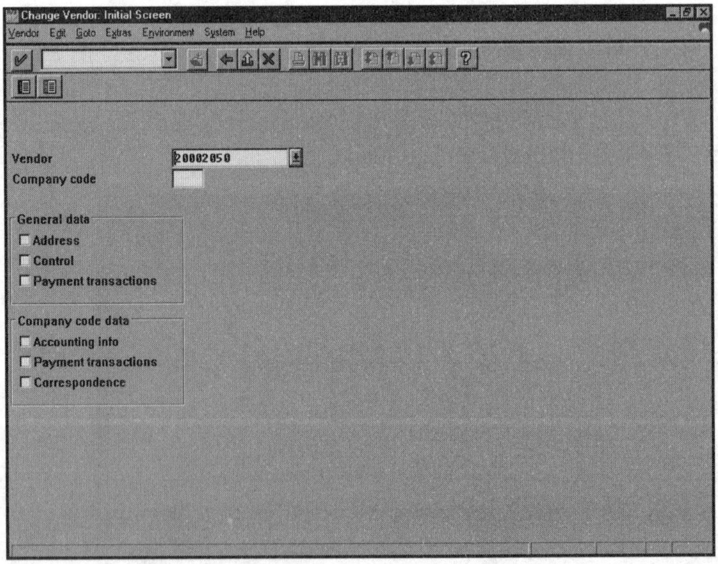

FIGURE 16-3

The initial screen of the Change Vendor program

A *multiple-line field* is a special kind of field that allows the user to enter multiple lines of data. For example, a screen might allow a user to enter several lines of text as a description. Each line would have the same field name, for example `MARA-LTEXT`. In order to populate data to this type of field, an index is added to the field name to indicate which line is to be populated by the BDC session. The first line of text would be populated as `MARA-LTEXT(1)`, the second as `MARA-LTEXT(2)`, and so on. Many times, only the first line is used in a BDC session, but if multiple lines are required, a counter should be used to track which line will be populated.

Usually a screen has several fields with multiple lines. For example, the screen to create a purchase order has fields for line number, material number, quantity, amount, and others. Each line corresponds to a separate item. Figure 16-4 shows an example of a screen that uses multiple lines for several fields. This screen allows multiple year/total U.S. dollar combinations to be entered.

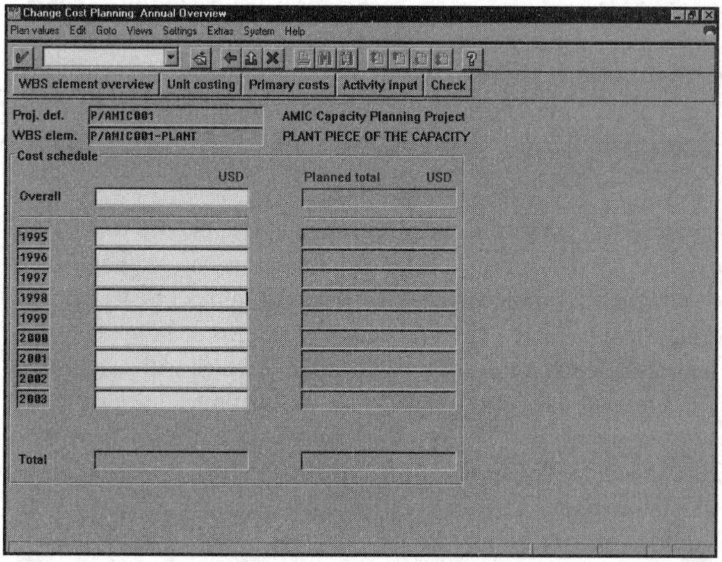

FIGURE 16-4

An example of multiple-line fields

Building the BDC Table

The BDC table is an internal table with a specific structure that's filled with the data to be submitted. The program should fill the BDC table with values for fields, one row in the internal table per record. An additional record to provide information about the screen itself must precede the rows of field data. Table 16-1 shows the structure of the BDC table.

Table 16-1 BDC Table Structure

Field	Type	Description
program	Char(8)	Program name of transaction
dynpro	Char(4)	Screen number of transaction
dynbegin	Char(1)	Indicator for new screen
fnam	Char(35)	Name of database field from screen
fval	Char(80)	Value to submit to field

Before data for fields can be entered, a screen record is added to the BDC table with the program name in the `program` field, the screen name in the `dynpro` field, and an `X` in the `dynbegin` field, which tells the system that a new screen is beginning. Then a record is added for each field on the screen for which you want to submit data. For field records, the `program`, `dynpro`, and `dynbegin` fields should be left blank. Instead, the name of the field is placed in the `fnam` field and the value for that field is placed in the `fval` field. For example, to submit data for the first screen of the Change Vendor transaction, the row of data added to the BDC table would have `SAPMF02K` in the `program` field, `0100` in the `dynpro` field, and `X` in the `dynbegin` field.

Once these fields are populated, the record should be appended to the table. The next record would be the data for the first field on the screen, `Vendor`. For this field, `RF02K-LIFNR` would be placed in the `fnam` field. The vendor number to be changed, for example `0010010`, would be placed in `fval`, and the record would be appended to the BDC table. The next field to be entered is `RF02K-EKORG`, which will be populated with the value `CNTL`. Once all fields are populated for the first screen, a new screen is started in the same way as the first. The process repeats until all screens have been completed for this transaction. The final entry into the BDC table is always the function code F11 to save the completed transaction. Table 16-2 shows the values for this example, as they would be placed in the fields.

Table 16-2 BDC Table Values

program	dynpro	dynbegin	fnam	fval
SAPMF02K	0100	X	RF02K-LIFNR	0010010
			RF02K-EKORG	CNTL
SAPMF02K	0200	X		

A typical BDC program may process three to six screens each, with anywhere from two to ten fields. The code to build the BDC table is straightforward, consisting mainly of `MOVE` and `APPEND` commands. Because the process to build the BDC table is repeated dozens of times, it's a good candidate for a subroutine.

Following are two examples of building a BDC table. The first example doesn't use forms:

```
REPORT ZBDCVEND.
*** Example to build part of a BDC table for the Change Vendor Transaction
DATA BEGIN OF INT_BDC OCCURS 100.       "BDC Table
  INCLUDE STRUCTURE BDCDATA.
DATA END OF INT_BDC.

*** Start of Main Program

*** Start Screen 100
MOVE 'SAPMF02K' TO INT_BDC-PROGRAM.
MOVE '0100' TO INT_BDC-DYNPRO.
MOVE 'X' TO INT_BDC-DYNBEGIN.
APPEND INT_BDC.

***
MOVE 'RF02K-LIFNR' TO INT_BDC-FNAM.
MOVE '0010010' TO INT_BDC-FVAL.
APPEND INT_BDC.

***
MOVE 'RF02K-EKORG' TO INT_BDC-FNAM.
MOVE 'CNTL' TO INT_BDC-FVAL.
APPEND INT_BDC.

*** And so on until the BDC Table is complete
```

This example shows the repetitive nature of building a BDC table; anything repetitive can usually be done better with a subroutine. In this next example, two forms are created. The first, `BDC_SCREEN`, is used when a new screen is to be started; the second, `BDC_FIELD`, is used when a new field is to be added to the BDC table:

```
REPORT ZBDCVEND.
*** Example to build part of a BDC table for the Change Vendor Transaction
DATA BEGIN OF INT_BDC OCCURS 100.       "BDC Table
  INCLUDE STRUCTURE BDCDATA.
```

```
DATA END OF INT_BDC.

*** Start of Main Program

*** Start Screen 100
PERFORM BDC_SCREEN      TABLES INT_BDC
USING 'SAPMFO2K' '0100'.

PERFORM BDC_FIELD TABLES INT_BDC:
                      USING 'RF02K-LIFNR' '0010010',
                      USING 'RF02K-EKORG' 'CNTL'.

*** And so on until the BDC Table is complete
...

*** End of Main Program

*** Form BDC_SCREEN
*** This form takes two parameters and makes an entry into a BDC table specified
*** for a new screen.
FORM BDC_SCREEN TABLES P_BDC STRUCTURE BDCDATA
                      USING P_PROGRAM P_SCREEN.
  CLEAR P_BDC.           "Clears table work area

  P_BDC-PROGRAM = P_PROGRAM.
  P_BDC-DYNPRO = P_SCREEN.
  P_BDC-DYNBEGIN = 'X'.
  APPEND P_BDC.

ENDFORM.

*** Form BDC_FIELD
*** This form takes two parameters and makes an entry into a BDC table specified
*** for a new field
```

```
FORM BDC_FIELD TABLES P_BDC STRUCTURE BDCDATA
                   USING P_NAME P_VALUE.

  CASE P_VALUE.
    WHEN ' '.                               "Don't move if value is blank
    WHEN OTHERS.                            "Move value
      MOVE P_NAME TO P_BDC-FNAM.
      MOVE P_VALUE TO P_BDC-FVAL.
      APPEND P_BDC.
  ENDCASE.

ENDFORM.
```

Although you have to write two forms for this second example, the main portion of the program is made much simpler through the use of PERFORM and the colon notation. As you can imagine, if you had a program with six screens and fifty fields, the first method of building the BDC table would be quite complicated and unnecessarily verbose.

Submitting the BDC Table

Once the BDC table has been built, it needs to be submitted to SAP for processing. There are two ways to submit a BDC table. The first is through the CALL TRANSACTION command, which allows a single transaction to be processed by SAP. The second is to use the BDC_INSERT function, which allows multiple transactions to be processed. There are a number of factors to consider before deciding which technique to use to submit the BDC table.

Processing Data with CALL TRANSACTION

The CALL TRANSACTION command allows a single BDC table to be processed immediately by the system. The data in the BDC table is used to execute the transaction; the return code for the statement tells the program whether the transaction executed successfully. When using CALL TRANSACTION, it's the programmer's responsibility to handle failed transactions, but this method is a very efficient way to process transactions. The syntax for the command is as follows:

```
CALL TRANSACTION trans [USING bdctab MODE mode] [UPDATE upd]
                       [MESSAGES INTO messtab].
```

The mode allows the programmer to control what happens when the BDC table is submitted. These are the possible entries:

`A`	Show all screens
`E`	Show only screens with errors
`N`	Show no screens

The `A` and `E` modes are normally used for debugging. When the program is executed in `A` or `E` mode, the screens from the transaction appear populated with data from the BDC table, and the user must step through each screen—and can correct errors, in some cases. Mode `N` is the only mode that can be used in a program that's run in the background, without user attention. In this case, no screens appear. If an error occurs, the transaction fails, and the return code is not `0`. In addition to the return code, the system error message is available through a set of `SY` fields: `SY-MSGNO`, `SY-MSGID`, `SY-MSGV1`, `SY-MSGV2`, `SY-MSGV3`, and `SY-MSGV4`.

The update option controls how changes are made to the database. The values are 'A' for asynchronous updates or 'S' for synchronous updates. In the case of a synchronous update, the command will wait for changes to be made. For an asynchronous update, the command will not wait. This effect of this option varies with the exact transaction called.

The messages option will cause SAP to capture any error or success messages and place them in the internal table specified. See the second example for usage of the messages option.

This approach processes a single transaction faster than using `BDC_INSERT` (discussed in the next section). Because the results of the transaction are returned to the calling program, error handling can be implemented in the program. It may be possible to correct certain errors and resubmit the data, or a separate error report could be created. Also, it's possible to use `CALL TRANSACTION` without a BDC table. In this case, the current program is suspended, the transaction specified is brought up, and a user must enter data into the screens.

Processing Data with BDC INSERT

The second way to process a BDC session is by submitting it to the system for batch processing. With this method, several transactions can be processed together. But unlike `CALL TRANSACTION`, the data isn't processed immediately; instead, it's placed into the SAP batch queue for later processing. Thus, the results of processing a transaction aren't returned to the program that created the BDC session. (However, the SAP transaction `SM35` allows a user to view the results of a batch job that has been processed by the system.)

There are three SAP function modules that need to be called from the BDC program to submit the transactions for processing (the functions are executed with the `CALL FUNCTION` command, discussed in Chapter 11, "Adding Subroutines to Your Program"):

- `BDC_OPEN_GROUP`

  This function opens the BDC session and must be called before any processing is done.
- `BDC_INSERT`

  This function is called for each transaction in the batch. The BDC table is filled with data, as previously discussed for a transaction. Then the `BDC_INSERT` function is called and the BDC table is passed to it. This process is repeated for each transaction in the batch.
- `BDC_CLOSE_GROUP`

  This final function closes the session and submits it to SAP for processing.

Using the BDC_OPEN_GROUP Function

The function module `BDC_OPEN_GROUP` opens a BDC *session*. A BDC session is a batch of several transactions that will be processed together. Only one session can be open at a time. The following parameters should be exported to the function when called:

CLIENT	The SAP client in which the session is processed. Usually left blank, which causes it to default to the current client.
GROUP	A name used to identify the BDC session to be processed. This name doesn't need to be unique.
HOLDDATE	Suspends processing of the BDC session until after this date has passed.
KEEP	Keeps the session in the system after processing until it's deleted by an administrator, when the field is set to X.
USER	The name used to execute the session in batch mode. You can't supply an online user name for this field.

Using the BDC_INSERT Function

The `BDC_INSERT` function adds a transaction to the BDC session that's currently open. The following parameters should be exported to the function when called:

`TCODE`	The transaction code for the transaction that should be used to process the data in the BDC table being inserted. For example, `MK02` for the change vendor transaction.
`DYNPROTAB`	The name of the internal table being used as the BDC table for the current program.

Using the BDC_CLOSE_GROUP Function

Use the `BDC_CLOSE_GROUP` function to close the current BDC session, once all transactions to be processed have been inserted. There are no parameters needed for this function. When the session is closed, it's ready to be processed by the system.

Example BDC Sessions

This section presents three examples of BDC sessions. These examples are for reference only—they won't run on just any SAP installation. Because SAP is so customizable, the screens for a given transaction can vary wildly between installations. For example, when creating a new vendor (a company from which materials may be purchased), Company X may need to supply a tax code, but at Company Y, no tax code field will even appear in the Create Vendor transaction. Thus, every company using SAP will write BDC programs based on their unique installation of SAP. This is great for programmers, because it means all BDC programs must be customized for each unique installation of SAP.

A BDC Program to Change a Vendor's Address

This first program changes address information for a vendor. The transaction that does this is `MK02`. (The transaction allows you to change much more information about a vendor than simply the address, obviously, but that's all this example program will do.) There are two screens to this transaction that you'll be using. (Remember that the first step to writing a BDC session is to identify all screens, fields, and function codes that will be used.) Figure 16-5 shows the first screen for transaction `MK02`. Here the program must supply the vendor number that is to be changed and select the address box to indicate the type of data that you want to change.

The second screen looks like Figure 16-6. Here's where the address information goes. Once the information has been passed to the screen, the final step is to save the changes. All transactions use the function code F11 to save, and a save always ends a transaction. Using the Help system to identify the field name for each field would produce the list shown in Table 16-3.

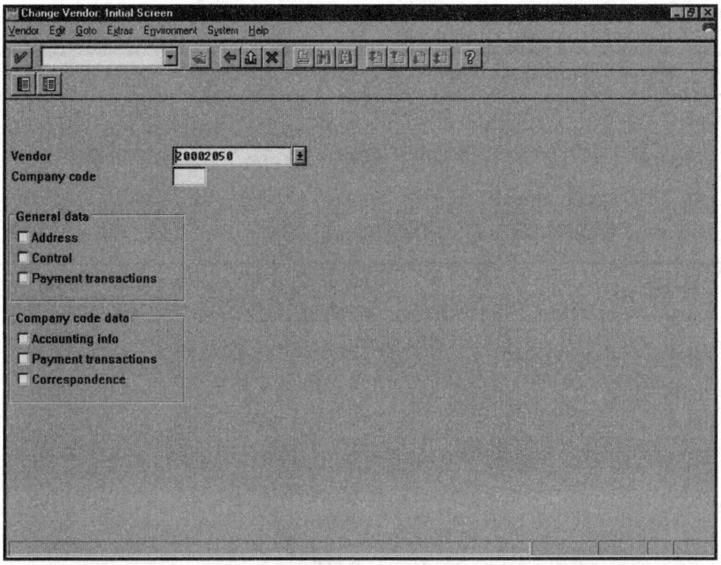

FIGURE 16-5

Change Vendor, screen 1

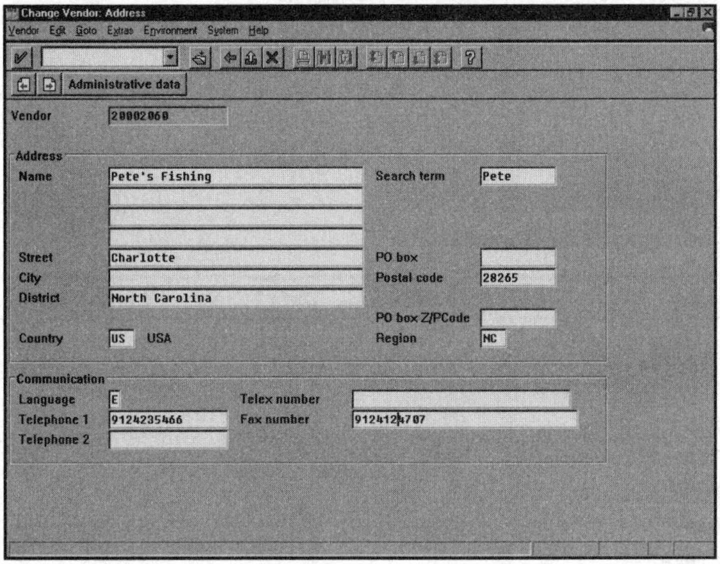

FIGURE 16-6

Change Vendor, screen 2

The program should read a data file and use the information to execute the Change Vendor transaction as many times as needed. The `CALL TRANSACTION` command should be used to submit each transaction for processing. All errors encountered during processing of the file should be written out in a report at the end of the program. The program reads the information to be loaded into SAP via the BDC session, from an external text file with the file format shown in Table 16-4.

Table 16-3 Field Names for the Change Vendor Transaction

Field	Contents
	Field Names for Screen 0100
Vendor Number	RF02K-LIFNR
Purchasing Organization	RF02K-EKORG
Change Address Check Box	RF02K-D0110
	Field Names for Screen 0200
Vendor Name 1	LFA1-NAME1
Vendor Name 2	LFA1-NAME2
Vendor Name 3	LFA1-NAME3
Vendor Name 4	LFA1-NAME4
Vendor Street	LFA1-STRAS
Vendor City	LFA1-ORT01
Vendor Region	LFA1-REGIO
Vendor Zip	LFA1-PSTLZ
Vendor Country	LFA1-LAND1
Vendor Phone 1	LFA1-TELF1
Vendor Phone 2	LFA1-TELF2

Table 16-4 Input File Format

Field Name	Position	Data Type	Length
Vendor Number	1	C	10
Purchasing Organization	11	C	4
Vendor Name 1	16	C	35
Vendor Name 2	51	C	35
Vendor Name 3	86	C	35
Vendor Name 4	111	C	35
Vendor Street	146	C	35
Vendor City	181	C	35
Vendor Region	216	C	3
Vendor Zip	219	C	10
Vendor Country	229	C	3
Vendor Phone 1	232	C	16
Vendor Phone 2	248	C	16

And here at last is the code for this example:

```
*---------------------------------------------------------*
* Program Name: Change Vendor      Date:    08/21/96*
* SAP Name    : ZBDCVEND  Version: 1.0      *
*                                                       *
* Programmer  : Bob Lyfareff       Last Update:    10/01/96 *
*                                                       *
*---------------------------------------------------------*
*                                                      *
REPORT ZPAIPLLD  LINE-SIZE 80
LINE-COUNT 65
MESSAGE-ID ZZ.
*---------------------------------------------------------*
* Tables                                               *
*---------------------------------------------------------*
* None                                                 *
*---------------------------------------------------------*
* Variables                                            *
*---------------------------------------------------------*
DATA:       WS_EOF(1)     TYPE C,  " End of File Indicator
            WS_INDEX(2)   TYPE N,  " General work index
            WS_LOOP(2)    TYPE N.  " Loop calculation
*---------------------------------------------------------*
* Internal Tables                                      *
*---------------------------------------------------------*
**** BDC Processing
DATA BEGIN OF INT_BDC OCCURS 100.
        INCLUDE STRUCTURE BDCDATA.
DATA END OF INT_BDC.

**** Vendor In File
DATA: BEGIN OF REC_VEND,
  LIFNR LIKE RF02K-LIFNR,
  EKORG LIKE RF02K-EKORG,
```

```
  NAME1 LIKE LFA1-NAME1,
  NAME2 LIKE LFA1-NAME2,
  NAME3 LIKE LFA1-NAME3,
  NAME4 LIKE LFA1-NAME4,
  STRAS LIKE LFA1-STRAS,
  ORT01 LIKE LFA1-ORT01,
  REGIO LIKE LFA1-REGIO,
  PSTLZ LIKE LFA1-PSTLZ,
  LAND1 LIKE LFA1-LAND1,
  TELF1 LIKE LFA1-TELF1,
  TELF2 LIKE LFA1-TELF2,
END OF REC_VEND.

DATA: BEGIN OF INT_ERROR OCCURS 50,
  MSG LIKE SY-MSGV1,
  LIFNR LIKE LFA1-LIFNR,
END OF INT_ERROR.

*-----------------------------------------*
* Parameters                              *
*-----------------------------------------*
PARAMETERS:  P_INFILE(80) TYPE C LOWER CASE.  "Input file name and path


*-----------------------------------------*
*     Main Processing                     *
*-----------------------------------------*
START-OF-SELECTION.
  PERFORM INITIALIZATION.
  PERFORM PROCESS_FILE.


END-OF-SELECTION.
  PERFORM ERROR_REPORT.
```

```
*---------------------------------------------------------------------*
*       Form  INITIALIZATION                                          *
*---------------------------------------------------------------------*
*       This opens the Inbound file of Vendor Change Data.            *
*       If the open of the file is not successful an error            *
*       message is produced                                           *
*---------------------------------------------------------------------*
FORM INITIALIZATION.

* <<< Open the inbound file for input >>>

  OPEN DATASET P_INFILE FOR INPUT IN TEXT MODE.

* <<< If file not opened then show Error message >>>
  IF SY-SUBRC <> 0.
    MESSAGE E999 WITH 'Error opening ' P_INFILE.
  ENDIF.

ENDFORM.                                " INITIALIZATION

*---------------------------------------------------------------------*
*       Form  PROCESS_FILE                                            *
*---------------------------------------------------------------------*
*       This form will read the vendor file and build the BDC table   *
*       For each record.  It will then submit each transaction and    *
*       save any errors recorded.                                     *
*---------------------------------------------------------------------*
FORM PROCESS_FILE.
  DO.
    READ DATASET P_INFILE INTO REC_VEND.
    IF SY-SUBRC <> 0.
      EXIT.
    ENDIF.

    PERFORM BUILD_BDC.
```

```
    PERFORM SUBMIT_BDC.
  ENDDO.

ENDFORM.                                    " PROCESS_FILE

*-----------------------------------------------------------------*
*       Form  BUILD_BDC                                            *
*-----------------------------------------------------------------*
*       This form will build the BDC table for each transaction.   *
*                                                                  *
*-----------------------------------------------------------------*
FORM BUILD_BDC.
REFRESH INT_BDC.
*** Build Screen 100
  PERFORM BDC_SCREEN TABLES INT_BDC
                      USING 'SAPMFO2K' '0100'.

  PERFORM BDC_FIELD TABLES INT_BDC:
                  USING 'RF02K-LIFNR' REC_VEND-LIFNR,  "Vendor
                  USING 'RF02K-EKORG' REC_VEND-EKORG,  "Purchase Org
                  USING 'RF02K-D0110' 'X'.       "Select Address

*** Build Screen 200
  PERFORM BDC_SCREEN TABLES INT_BDC
                      USING 'SAPMFO2K' '0200'.

  PERFORM BDC_FIELD TABLES INT_BDC:
                  USING 'LFA1-NAME1' REC_VEND-NAME1,  "Vendor Name1
                  USING 'LFA1-NAME2' REC_VEND-NAME2,  "Vendor Name2
                  USING 'LFA1-NAME3' REC_VEND-NAME3,  "Vendor Name3
                  USING 'LFA1-NAME4' REC_VEND-NAME4,  "Vendor Name4
                  USING 'LFA1-STRAS' REC_VEND-STRAS,  "Vendor Street
                  USING 'LFA1-ORT01' REC_VEND-ORT01,  "Vendor City
                  USING 'LFA1-REGIO' REC_VEND-REGIO,  "Vendor Region
                  USING 'LFA1-PSTLZ' REC_VEND-PSTLZ,  "Vendor Zip
```

```
                    USING 'LFA1-LAND1' REC_VEND-LAND1,  "Vendor Country
                    USING 'LFA1-TELF1' REC_VEND-TELF1,  "Vendor Phone 1
                    USING 'LFA1-TELF2' REC_VEND-TELF2., "Vendor Phone 2
                    USING 'BDC_OKCODE' '/11' .           "Save and End

ENDFORM.                                   "BUILD_BDC

*---------------------------------------------------------------------*
*       Form  SUBMIT_BDC                                              *
*---------------------------------------------------------------------*
*       This form will submit the BDC table using CALL TRANSACTION.  *
*                                                                     *
*---------------------------------------------------------------------*
FORM SUBMIT_BDC.

  CALL TRANSACTION 'MK02' USING INT_BDC MODE 'N'.
  IF SY-SUBRC <> 0.  "If error record vendor and error msg
    MOVE SY-MSGV1 TO INT_ERROR-MSG.
    MOVE REC_VEND-LIFNR TO INT_ERROR-LIFNR.
    APPEND INT_ERROR.
  ENDIF.

ENDFORM.                                   "SUBMIT_BDC

*---------------------------------------------------------------------*
*       Form  ERROR_REPORT                                            *
*---------------------------------------------------------------------*
*       This form will write out any errors to the screen.           *
*                                                                     *
*---------------------------------------------------------------------*
FORM ERROR_REPORT.

  WRITE 'Vendor Records with Errors!'.
  WRITE: /, 'VENDOR', 11 'ERROR MESSAGE'.
```

```
  LOOP AT INT_ERROR.
    WRITE: /, INT_ERROR-LIFNR, 11 INT_ERROR-MSG.
  ENDLOOP.

ENDFORM.                                       "ERROR_REPORT

*_______________________________________________________________.*
*      Form BDC_SCREEN
*_______________________________________________________________.*
*      This form takes two parameters and makes an entry into a BDC *
*      table specified for a new screen.                            *
*_______________________________________________________________.*
FORM BDC_SCREEN TABLES P_BDC STRUCTURE BDCDATA
                USING P_PROGRAM P_SCREEN.
  CLEAR P_BDC.                                 "Clears table work area

  P_BDC-PROGRAM = P_PROGRAM.
  P_BDC-DYNPRO = P_SCREEN.
  P_BDC-DYNBEGIN = 'X'.
  APPEND P_BDC.

ENDFORM.

*_______________________________________________________________.*
*      Form BDC_FIELD
*_______________________________________________________________.*
*      This form takes two parameters and makes an entry into a BDC *
*      table specified for a new field.                             *
*_______________________________________________________________.*
FORM BDC_FIELD TABLES P_BDC STRUCTURE BDCDATA
               USING P_NAME P_VALUE.

  CASE P_VALUE.
    WHEN ' '.                                  "Don't move if value is blank
    WHEN OTHERS.                               "Move value
      MOVE P_NAME TO P_BDC-FNAM.
```

```
        MOVE P_VALUE TO P_BDC-FVAL.
        APPEND P_BDC.
    ENDCASE.

ENDFORM.
```

Comparing Different Processing Techniques

This second example allows the programmer to compare three different techniques to process a transaction. The transaction, which will be processed, is the *Planned Order Action Control* or *MDAC*. A planned order is a plan to manufacture a product. It contains all the parts that make up the product, the quantities needed, and the dates when the product will be produced. Typically a planned order will have a start date and a finish date. The planned order action control transaction allows certain actions to be performed against a planned order. Some examples of actions available are: checking the availability of the materials required to determine a start date, uncommitting the material reservation of a planned order, and explode the bill of materials of a product to determine the parts required for a planned order. Transaction MDAC consists of one screen only. See Figure 16-7 for the MDAC screen.

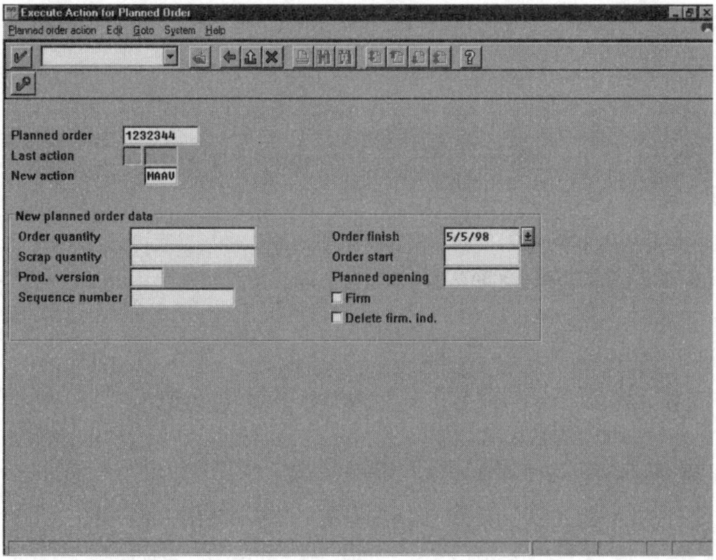

FIGURE 16-7

The initial screen of the program to change the planning costs

The example program allows the person executing it to determine how the MDAC transaction will be processed. You can choose from processing via `CALL TRANSACTION` or a BDC session. Also in the case of the MDAC transaction, there is a function module, which performs the same activity. Some simple transactions like MDAC have an associated function call but not all. By allowing the user to choose how to process the transaction, the three techniques can be compared. For example, you might want to time each to see which technique gives you the best performance. Table 16-5 lists the fields we will be populating for screen one of transaction MDAC.

Table 16-5 Field names for the change transaction

Field	Contents
	Field Names for Screen 1
Planned Order Number	PLAF-PLNUM
Total Qty	MDCD-GSMNG
Scrap Qty	MDCD-AVMNG
Production Version	MDCD-VERID
Sequence Number	MDCD-SEQNR
Open Date	MDCD-PERTR
Start Date	MDCD-PSTTR
Finish Date	MDCD-PEDTR
Action	T46AC-ACCTO

```
REPORT ZCBDCTST MESSAGE-ID ZZ LINE-SIZE 170 LINE-COUNT 58.


TABLES: PLAF,                              "Planned Orders
        T100.                              "System Error Messages

DATA: BEGIN OF BD OCCURS 200.            "Batch input data table
        INCLUDE STRUCTURE BDCDATA.
DATA: END OF BD.


DATA: BEGIN OF XMDCD.                    "Action Handler input
        INCLUDE STRUCTURE MDCD.
DATA: END OF XMDCD.


DATA BEGIN OF MESSTAB OCCURS 10.        "Message table for errors
        INCLUDE STRUCTURE BDCMSGCOLL.
DATA END OF MESSTAB.
```

```
DATA: WS_TEMP1 LIKE BDCDATA-FVAL,       "Temp field for dates
      WS_TEMP2 LIKE BDCDATA-FVAL.       "Temp field for quantities

SELECT-OPTIONS P_PLN FOR PLAF-PLNUM NO INTERVALS.  "Planned Order#

PARAMETERS:  P_ACTION LIKE PLAF-MDACC  "Planned Order Action
                       DEFAULT 'MAAV',  "Check Availability
             P_CALL DEFAULT 'B'.        "Type of Processing
                                          "        B - BDC Session
                                          "        C - Call Trasaction
                                          "        F - Function Call

PARAMETERS:  P_ORIDE AS CHECKBOX,       "Override dates in database
             P_DATE1 TYPE D,            "Pln Order Open
             P_DATE2 TYPE D,            "Pln Order Start
             P_DATE3 TYPE D.            "Plan Order Finish

PARAMETERS:  P_BDC LIKE APQI-GROUPID   "Name of BDC Session
                   DEFAULT 'BDC01'.

PARAMETERS:  P_UPDATE DEFAULT 'S',      "Update Mode
             P_MODE DEFAULT 'N'.        "Screen Mode

* Begin main program
START-OF-SELECTION.

  IF P_CALL EQ 'B'.
*   Process in a BDC session so open a new one
    CALL FUNCTION 'BDC_OPEN_GROUP'
         EXPORTING
              GROUP                 = P_BDC
              KEEP                  = 'X'
              USER                  = SY-UNAME
         EXCEPTIONS
```

```
                CLIENT_INVALID      = 1
                DESTINATION_INVALID = 2
                GROUP_INVALID       = 3
                GROUP_IS_LOCKED     = 4
                HOLDDATE_INVALID    = 5
                INTERNAL_ERROR      = 6
                QUEUE_ERROR         = 7
                RUNNING             = 8
                SYSTEM_LOCK_ERROR   = 9
                USER_INVALID        = 10
                OTHERS              = 11.
    IF SY-SUBRC NE 0.
      MESSAGE E999 WITH 'Error Opening BDC Session!'.
    ENDIF.
  ENDIF.

* Loop at planned order numbers entered by user
  LOOP AT P_PLN.

    SELECT SINGLE * FROM PLAF WHERE PLNUM = P_PLN-LOW.
    IF SY-SUBRC NE 0.
      MESSAGE I999 WITH 'Pln Order does not exist:' P_PLN-LOW.
*     Skip this entry
      CONTINUE.
    ENDIF.

*   Override dates in database if user requested
    IF P_ORIDE NE SPACE.
      PLAF-PERTR = P_DATE1.
      PLAF-PSTTR = P_DATE2.
      PLAF-PEDTR = P_DATE3.
    ENDIF.

*   Date Sequence must be correct if not blank
    IF NOT ( PLAF-PSTTR IS INITIAL ) AND NOT ( PLAF-PEDTR IS INITIAL ).
```

```
    IF PLAF-PSTTR >= PLAF-PEDTR.      "Should be Start < Finish
      CLEAR PLAF-PSTTR.
    ENDIF.
  ENDIF.

  IF NOT ( PLAF-PSTTR IS INITIAL ) AND NOT ( PLAF-PERTR IS INITIAL ).
    IF PLAF-PERTR > PLAF-PSTTR.       "Should be Open <= Start
      CLEAR PLAF-PERTR .
    ENDIF.
  ENDIF.

  IF P_CALL NE 'F'.
*   If this is not a function call then build BDC table
    PERFORM BUILD_BDC.
  ENDIF.

  CASE P_CALL.
    WHEN 'C'.
*     Process via a call transaction immediatly
      CALL TRANSACTION 'MDAC' USING BD MODE
                                   P_MODE UPDATE P_UPDATE
                                   MESSAGES INTO MESSTAB.
      IF SY-SUBRC EQ 0.
        WRITE: /, 'MDAC execute successfully!', P_PLN-LOW.
      ELSE.
        WRITE: /, 'MDAC Failed!', SY-SUBRC, P_PLN-LOW.
      ENDIF.
*     Print results from message table
      PERFORM PRINT_RESULTS.
    WHEN 'B'.
*     Process in batch via BDC session
      CALL FUNCTION 'BDC_INSERT'
           EXPORTING
                TCODE          = 'MDAC'
           TABLES
```

```
                DYNPROTAB       = BD
          EXCEPTIONS
                INTERNAL_ERROR = 1
                NOT_OPEN        = 2
                QUEUE_ERROR     = 3
                TCODE_INVALID   = 4
                OTHERS          = 5.
    IF SY-SUBRC EQ 0.
      WRITE: /, 'BDC Insert successful!', P_PLN-LOW.
    ELSE.
      WRITE: /, 'BDC Insert Failed!' , SY-SUBRC, P_PLN-LOW.
    ENDIF.
  WHEN 'F'.
*       Process immidiately via a call function, no BDC table required

*       Fill XMDCD record for planned order
    XMDCD-PSTTR = PLAF-PSTTR.      "Start date in planned ord
    XMDCD-PEDTR = PLAF-PEDTR.      "Finish date in planned ord
    XMDCD-PERTR = PLAF-PERTR.      "Opening date in planned ord
    XMDCD-VERID = PLAF-VERID.      "Production version
    XMDCD-SEQNR = PLAF-SEQNR.      "Sequence number order

*       Call function to execute action immediately
    CALL FUNCTION 'MD_SET_ACTION_PLAF'
          EXPORTING
                IPLNUM          = P_PLN-LOW
                IACCTO          = P_ACTION
                IAENKZ          = 'X'
                IMDCD           = XMDCD
          EXCEPTIONS
                ERROR_MESSAGE = 1.
    IF SY-SUBRC EQ 0.
      WRITE: /, 'Function Call successful!', P_PLN-LOW.
    ELSE.
      WRITE: /, 'Function Call failed!', SY-SUBRC, P_PLN-LOW.
```

```
        ENDIF.
      ENDCASE.
    ENDLOOP.

    IF P_CALL EQ 'B'.
*     CLOSE BDC SESSION
      CALL FUNCTION 'BDC_CLOSE_GROUP'
           EXCEPTIONS
                NOT_OPEN    = 1
                QUEUE_ERROR = 2
                OTHERS      = 3.
      IF SY-SUBRC EQ 0.
        WRITE: /, 'BDC Close successful!'.
      ELSE.
        WRITE: /, 'BDC Close Failed!', SY-SUBRC.
      ENDIF.
    ENDIF.


*** Start Forms
*---------------------------------------------------------------------*
*       FORM BUILD_BDC                                                *
*---------------------------------------------------------------------*
*       Build BDC Table for current planned order                     *
*---------------------------------------------------------------------*
FORM BUILD_BDC.

* Clear header and internal table
  CLEAR BD. REFRESH BD.

* Screen start.
  PERFORM BDC_SCREEN TABLES BD USING 'SAPMM61P' '0300'.

  MOVE  P_PLN-LOW TO WS_TEMP2.
* Customer purchase order number.
```

```
  PERFORM BDC_FIELD TABLES BD
          USING 'PLAF-PLNUM' WS_TEMP2.

* Convert planned order total quantity to character field
  WRITE PLAF-GSMNG NO-SIGN LEFT-JUSTIFIED TO WS_TEMP2.
  PERFORM BDC_FIELD TABLES BD
          USING 'MDCD-GSMNG' WS_TEMP2.

* Convert planned order scrap quantity to character field
  WRITE PLAF-AVMNG NO-SIGN LEFT-JUSTIFIED TO WS_TEMP2.
  PERFORM BDC_FIELD TABLES BD
          USING 'MDCD-AVMNG' WS_TEMP2.

* Convert Production version to character field
  WRITE PLAF-VERID NO-SIGN LEFT-JUSTIFIED TO WS_TEMP2.
  PERFORM BDC_FIELD TABLES BD
          USING 'MDCD-VERID' WS_TEMP2.

* Convert Sequence Number to character field
  WRITE PLAF-SEQNR NO-SIGN LEFT-JUSTIFIED TO WS_TEMP2.
  PERFORM BDC_FIELD TABLES BD
          USING 'MDCD-SEQNR' WS_TEMP2.

* Fill open date
  IF NOT ( PLAF-PERTR IS INITIAL ).
    WRITE PLAF-PERTR MM/DD/YYYY TO WS_TEMP1.
    PERFORM BDC_FIELD TABLES BD
            USING 'MDCD-PERTR' WS_TEMP1.
  ENDIF.

* Fill Start Date
  IF NOT ( PLAF-PSTTR IS INITIAL ).
    WRITE PLAF-PSTTR MM/DD/YYYY TO WS_TEMP1.
    PERFORM BDC_FIELD TABLES BD
            USING 'MDCD-PSTTR' WS_TEMP1.
  ENDIF.
```

```
* Fill Finish Date
  IF NOT ( PLAF-PEDTR IS INITIAL ).
    WRITE PLAF-PEDTR MM/DD/YYYY TO WS_TEMP1.
    PERFORM BDC_FIELD TABLES BD
            USING 'MDCD-PEDTR' WS_TEMP1.
  ENDIF.

  MOVE P_ACTION TO WS_TEMP2.
* Fill Planned Order Action
  PERFORM BDC_FIELD TABLES BD
          USING 'T46AC-ACCTO' WS_TEMP2.

* Execute Action
  PERFORM BDC_OKCODE TABLES BD USING '/8'.

ENDFORM.

*---------------------------------------------------------------------*
*       FORM PRINT_RESULTS                                            *
*---------------------------------------------------------------------*
*       The power of Call Transaction is that it executes the BDC     *
*       in real time and the results can be captured in an internal   *
*       table.  This allows you to give real time feedback to the     *
*       person executing the transaction.  The results are in the    *
*       the for of system messages.  Only the message id and number   *
*       are captured in the results table.  A look up must be done    *
*       using the table T100 to get the english text of the message.  *
*       Both success and error messages will be capture.              *
*       This results functionality is only found in Call Transaction  *
*---------------------------------------------------------------------*
FORM PRINT_RESULTS.

  DATA WS_TEXT(100).                   "English text of results

  LOOP AT MESSTAB.                     "Loop at results table
```

```
*    Get english text of current message
     SELECT SINGLE TEXT INTO (WS_TEXT)
                   FROM T100 WHERE SPRSL = SY-LANGU
                              AND ARBGB = MESSTAB-MSGID
                              AND MSGNR = MESSTAB-MSGNR.
*   Some message have variables.  Replace the & with the variable
    REPLACE '&' WITH MESSTAB-MSGV1 INTO WS_TEXT.
    REPLACE '&' WITH MESSTAB-MSGV2 INTO WS_TEXT.
    REPLACE '&' WITH MESSTAB-MSGV3 INTO WS_TEXT.
    REPLACE '&' WITH MESSTAB-MSGV4 INTO WS_TEXT.

    WRITE: / MESSTAB-MSGID,
             MESSTAB-MSGNR,
             WS_TEXT(100).
    CLEAR WS_TEXT.
  ENDLOOP.

  CLEAR: MESSTAB[].
ENDFORM.

*---------------------------------------------------------------------*
*       FORM BD_OKCODE                                                *
*---------------------------------------------------------------------*
*       Add record for okcode to BDC table                            *
*---------------------------------------------------------------------*
*  --> BD                                                             *
*  --> OKCODE                                                         *
*---------------------------------------------------------------------*
FORM BDC_OKCODE TABLES BD STRUCTURE BDCDATA
                USING  OKCODE LIKE BDCDATA-FVAL.

  CLEAR BD.
  BD-FNAM      = 'BDC_OKCODE'.
  BD-FVAL      = OKCODE.
  APPEND BD.
```

```
ENDFORM.

*-----------------------------------------.*
*       FORM BDC_FIELD                                *
*-----------------------------------------.*
*       Add record for a new field to BDC table      *
*-----------------------------------------.*
*  —>  BD                                             *
*  —>  FIELD                                          *
*  —>  VALUE                                          *
*-----------------------------------------.*
FORM BDC_FIELD TABLES BD STRUCTURE BDCDATA
                USING  FIELD LIKE BDCDATA-FNAM
                       VALUE LIKE BDCDATA-FVAL.

  CLEAR BD.
  BD-FNAM      = FIELD.
  BD-FVAL      = VALUE.
  APPEND BD.

ENDFORM.

*-----------------------------------------.*
*       FORM BDC_SCREEN                               *
*-----------------------------------------.*
*       Add record for a new screen to BDC table     *
*-----------------------------------------.*
*  —>  BD                                             *
*  —>  PROGRAM                                        *
*  —>  SCREEN                                         *
*-----------------------------------------.*
FORM BDC_SCREEN TABLES BD STRUCTURE BDCDATA
                USING  PROGRAM LIKE BDCDATA-PROGRAM
                       SCREEN LIKE BDCDATA-DYNPRO.
```

```
    CLEAR BD.
    BD-PROGRAM  = PROGRAM.
    BD-DYNPRO   = SCREEN.
    BD-DYNBEGIN = 'X'.
    APPEND BD.

ENDFORM.
```

You can use this example with any transaction. Simply replace the Build BDC form with the BDC table you want to test. Then you can compare the different ways to process a transaction.

A BDC Program to Create Project Planning Data

This final example creates planning data for a project in SAP. In SAP, a *project* is an object against which you can charge costs. A project is broken down into one or more elements in the *work breakdown structure* (WBS). A WBS element describes either a concrete task or a partial one that can be further subdivided. A WBS element can have a planned budget for use in forecasting future expenses. A typical project might be opening a new manufacturing plant. This project has many tasks, each of which is assigned to a WBS element. One such element is purchasing the land for the plant; this element has a planned budget of $1 million dollars. It's this type of planned budget data that this program will be creating in SAP via a BDC session.

Once again the Help system is used to identify the field name for each field, producing the list shown in Table 16-6.

Table 16-6 Field Names for the Change Transaction

Field	Contents
	Field Names for Screen 1
Project Number	PROJ-PSID
WBS Element	PRPS-POSID
	Field Names for Screen 2
Amount	BPDY-WERT1

Figures 16-8 and 16-9 show the first and second screens for the transaction. Notice that the second screen uses multiple lines. In this case, the current year, 1996, is the third line; in order to populate it, the field would be `BPDY-WER1(3)`.

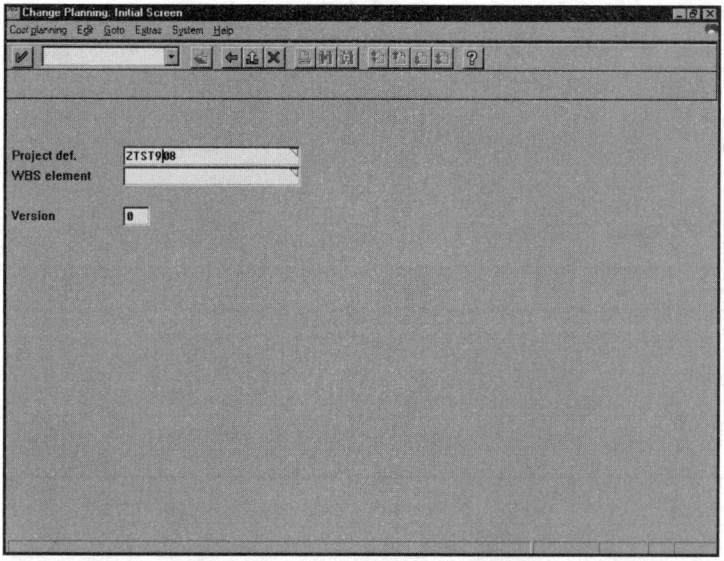

FIGURE 16-8

The first screen of the Change Planning Data transaction

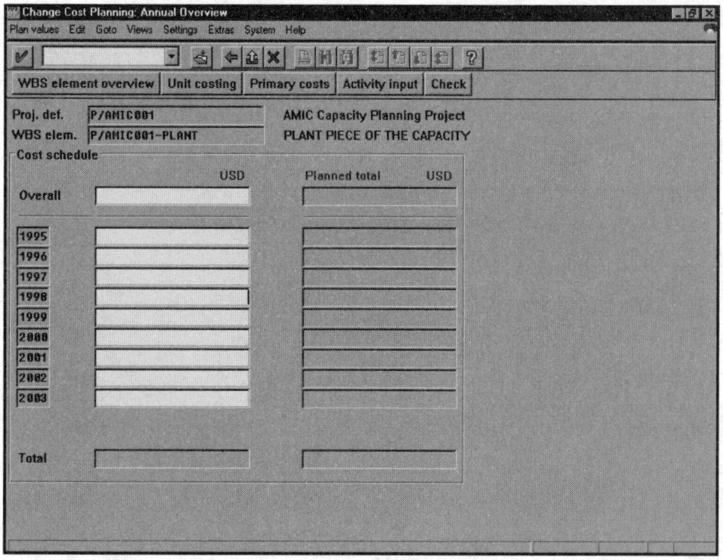

FIGURE 16-9

The second screen of the Change Planning Data transaction

The program should read a data file and use the information to execute the transaction as many times as needed.

This program demonstrates a technique to use both `CALL TRANSACTION` and `BDC_INSERT` to process the transactions. By using both, you get the speed of `CALL TRANSACTION` and the error handling of `BDC_INSERT`. The `CALL TRANSACTION` command should be used to submit each transaction for processing, but if an error is detected, the transaction should be resubmitted with `BDC_INSERT`. Thus, transactions without errors are processed quickly; those with errors get to use SAP's built-in error handling.

The program will read a text file with the file format shown in Table 16-7.

Table 16-7 Input File Format

Field Name	Position	Data Type	Length
Project Number	1	C	24
WBS Element	25	C	24
Project Plan Value	49	C	13
Project Plan Fiscal Year	62	C	4

Here's the code for the Change Costs transaction:

```
*-----------------------------------------*
* Program Name: Project Plan Costs          Date   : 10/01/96 *
* SAP Name    : ZPROJCO                                        *
*                                                             *
* Programmer  : Robert Lyfareff                               *
*-----------------------------------------*
REPORT ZPROJCO  NO STANDARD PAGE HEADING
                LINE-SIZE 132
                LINE-COUNT 65
                MESSAGE-ID ZZ.

*-----------------------------------------*
* Variables                                                   *
*-----------------------------------------*
**** Work fields used during BDC Processing
DATA:WS_INDEX(2)  TYPE N, "Index for Fields
        WS_BDC_CREATEDVALUE 'N',        "Flag For Errors
        WS_YEAR(4)    TYPE N, "Temp year
        WS_WERT1(14)  TYPE C   "Plan Value
             VALUE 'BPDY-WERT1(  )'.
```

```
*-----------------------------------------------------------------------*
* Internal Tables                                                       *
*-----------------------------------------------------------------------*
**** BDC Processing
DATA: BEGIN OF INT_BDC  OCCURS 0.
        INCLUDE STRUCTURE BDCDATA.
DATA: END OF INT_BDC.

**** Project Plan Value
DATA: BEGIN OF REC_PROJ,
         PSPID       LIKE PROJ-PSPID,     "Project Number
         POSID       LIKE PRPS-POSID,     "WBS Element
         WERT1(21)   TYPE C,              "Plan Value
         GJAHR(4)    TYPE C,              "Plan Year
      END OF REC_PROJ.

*-----------------------------------------------------------------------*
* Select Options/Parameters                                             *
*-----------------------------------------------------------------------*
PARAMETERS  P_INF(80)  TYPE C LOWER CASE.   "Input file name and path

*-----------------------------------------------------------------------*
*     Main Processing                                                   *
*-----------------------------------------------------------------------*
START-OF-SELECTION.
  PERFORM INITIALIZATION.
  PERFORM PROCESS_FILE.
END-OF-SELECTION.
  PERFORM CLEAN_UP.

* ----------------------------------------------------------------------.*
*-      Form INITIALIZATION                                             *
*-----------------------------------------------------------------------*
*      This form will open the input file.                              *
* ----------------------------------------------------------------------.*
```

```
FORM INITIALIZATION.

  OPEN DATASET P_INF FOR INPUT IN TEXT MODE.

*** Show Error Message
   IF SY-SUBRC <> 0.
     MESSAGE E999 WITH 'Error Opening' P_INF.
   ENDIF.

ENDFORM.                        " F1000_INITIALIZATION

*---------------------------------------------------------------------*
*       Form  PROCESS_FILE                                            *
*---------------------------------------------------------------------*
*       This form will read the vendor file and build the BDC table  *
*       For each record.  It will then submit each transaction and   *
*       save any errors recorded.                                     *
*---------------------------------------------------------------------*
FORM PROCESS_FILE.

   DO.
      READ DATASET P_INF INTO REC_PROJ.
      IF SY-SUBRC <> 0.
         EXIT.
      ENDIF.

      PERFORM BUILD_BDC.
      PERFORM SUBMIT_BDC.

   ENDDO.

ENDFORM.                        "PROCESS_FILE

*---------------------------------------------------------------------*
*       Form  BUILD_BDC                                               *
```

```
*-----------------------------------------------------------------.*
*      This form will build the BDC table for each transaction.   *
*                                                                  *
*-----------------------------------------------------------------.*
FORM BUILD_BDC.

*** Build First Screen
  PERFORM BDC_SCREEN TABLES INT_BDC
                  USING 'SAPMKBUD' '200'.

  PERFORM BDC_FIELD TABLES INT_BDC:
                   USING 'PROJ-PSPID'   REC_PROJ-PSPID,
                   USING 'PRPS-POSID'   REC_PROJ-POSID,
                   USING 'BDC_OKCODE'   '/0'.

*** Build Second Screen

*** Calculate Index
  WRITE SY-DATUM(4) TO WS_YEAR.
*** Current Year is always Line 3
  WS_INDEX = 3 + REC_PROJ-GJAHR - WS_YEAR.

*** Build Amount using index
  WS_WERT1 = ' BPDY-WERT1(  )'.
  MOVE WS_INDEX TO WS_WERT1+11(2).

  PERFORM BDC_SCREEN TABLES INT_BDC
                  USING 'SAPLKBPP' '200'.

  PERFORM BDC_FIELD TABLES INT_BDC:
        USING WS_WERT1 REC_PROJ-WERT1,
        USING 'BDC_OKCODE'   '/11'.

ENDFORM.                        "Build BDC
```

```
*-----------------------------------------------------------------.*
*       Form  SUBMIT_BDC                                           *
*-----------------------------------------------------------------.*
*       This form will submit the BDC table using CALL TRANSACTION.   *
*       If an error occurs a BDC session is created and the transaction*
*       is resubmitted to make use of SAP's built in error handling   *
*-----------------------------------------------------------------.*
FORM SUBMIT_BDC.

CALL TRANSACTION 'CJ40' USING INT_BDC
                 MODE 'N'
                 UPDATE 'S'.
  IF SY-SUBRC <> 0.
    PERFORM PROCESS_ERROR.
  ENDIF.

*** Clear the BDC Table
  REFRESH INT_BDC.

ENDFORM.       "End Form Submit BDC

*-----------------------------------------------------------------.*
*       Form  PROCESS_ERROR                                        *
*-----------------------------------------------------------------.*
*       For an error a BDC session is created and the transaction    *
*       is resubmitted to make use of SAP's built in error handling  *
*-----------------------------------------------------------------.*
FORM PROCESS_ERROR.

*** Open BDC Session Once Only
  IF WS_BDC_CREATED = 'N'.
    CALL FUNCTION 'BDC_OPEN_GROUP'
         EXPORTING
              CLIENT = SY-MANDT
              GROUP  = 'PLANERR'
```

```
                  KEEP    = 'X'
                  USER    = SY-UNAME.
     WS_BDC_CREATED = 'Y'.
   ENDIF.

*** Insert Error Transaction
   CALL FUNCTION 'BDC_INSERT'
        EXPORTING
             TCODE      = 'CJ40'
        TABLES
             DYNPROTAB = INT_BDC.
   IF SY-SUBRC <> 0.
     MESSAGE E999 WITH 'BDC Error'.
   ENDIF.

*** Clear the BDC Table
       REFRESH INT_BDC.
ENDFORM.                     "End Form Process Error

* ---------------------------------------------------------------.*
*        Form  CLEAN_UP
* ---------------------------------------------------------------.*
*        This is for Closing the Inbound file of Project Plan Values  *
* ---------------------------------------------------------------.*
FORM CLEAN_UP.

*** Close Inbound file
   CLOSE DATASET P_INF.
   IF SY-SUBRC <> 0.
     MESSAGE E999 WITH 'Error Closing' P_INF.
   ENDIF.

*** Close the BDC Session if Needed
   IF WS_BDC_CREATED = 'Y'.
     CALL FUNCTION 'BDC_CLOSE_GROUP'.
```

```
    IF SY-SUBRC <> 0.
      MESSAGE E999 WITH 'Error Closing BDC Session'.
    ENDIF.
  ENDIF.

ENDFORM.     "End Clean_Up

*-----------------------------------------------------------*
*       Form BDC_SCREEN
*-----------------------------------------------------------*
*       This form takes two parameters and makes an entry into a BDC *
*       table specified for a new screen.                         *
*-----------------------------------------------------------*
FORM BDC_SCREEN TABLES P_BDC STRUCTURE BDCDATA
                USING P_PROGRAM P_SCREEN.
  CLEAR P_BDC.                          "Clears table work area

  P_BDC-PROGRAM = P_PROGRAM.
  P_BDC-DYNPRO = P_SCREEN.
  P_BDC-DYNBEGIN = 'X'.
  APPEND P_BDC.

ENDFORM.

*-----------------------------------------------------------*
*       Form BDC_FIELD
*-----------------------------------------------------------*
*       This form takes two parameters and makes an entry into a BDC *
*       table specified for a new field.                          *
*-----------------------------------------------------------*
FORM BDC_FIELD TABLES P_BDC STRUCTURE BDCDATA
               USING P_NAME P_VALUE.

  CASE P_VALUE.
    WHEN ' '.                           "Don't move if value is blank
    WHEN OTHERS.                        "Move value
```

```
        MOVE P_NAME TO P_BDC-FNAM.
        MOVE P_VALUE TO P_BDC-FVAL.
        APPEND P_BDC.
    ENDCASE.

ENDFORM.
```

This is an excellent example of using both `BDC_INSERT` and `CALL TRANSACTION` to get the best of both techniques. The only drawback to this example is that transactions that are successfully processed aren't logged by SAP. Logging takes place only when using `BDC_INSERT`, and only errors are submitted this way. Of course, there's often no need to log successful transactions, only transactions with errors need to be logged.

Summary

Interfaces that use BDC sessions to load data into SAP are some of the most critical. At many SAP sites, the majority of programming done during an SAP installation is interface work. BDCs are a unique aspect of ABAP/4 and are very difficult to explain. They really do require hands-on experience to be done well. One thing to look out for is a transaction, which behaves differently in a BDC session than it does when a user enters the data by hand. Transactions aren't supposed to act differently, but sometimes it happens. If unexpected errors are encountered when processing a BDC session, the best way to examine what's happening is by using `MODE A` of `CALL TRANSACTION`, which displays all screens. If unexpected screens pop up during the processing of the BDC, they'll be displayed, and the program that builds the BDC table can be modified to compensate for them.

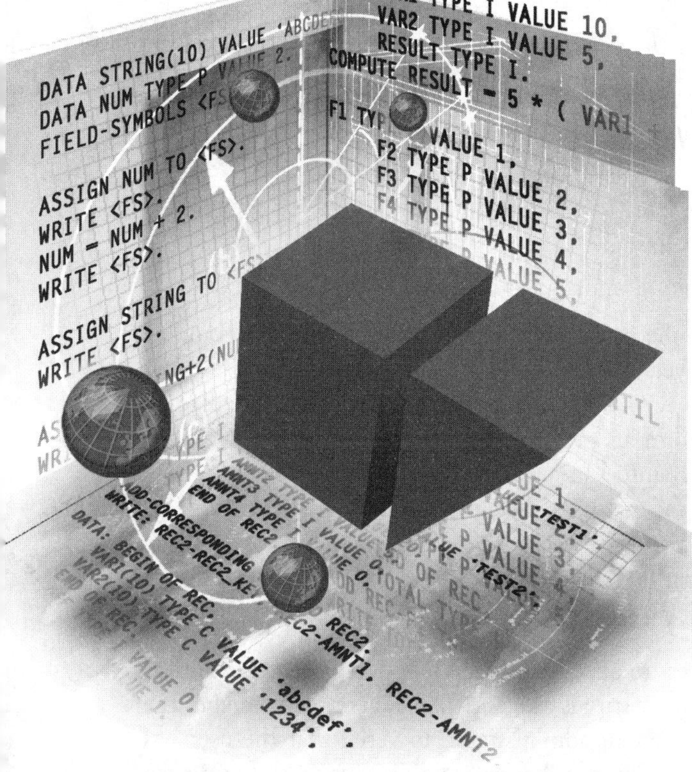

Chapter 17

Working with SAP Security and Authorizations

In This Chapter

- The SAP Security Model
- Creating Authorization Objects
- Using the `Authority-Check` Command to Enforce Security

This chapter introduces some of the basics of SAP R/3 security. Like any complex system, SAP R/3 has multiple layers of security. This chapter covers the making of security checks from within ABAP/4 programs. In R/3, security is referred to as *authorizations*. The ability to perform an operation in the system is referred to as an *authorization object*. When the programmer makes an authority check against an authority object, the system ensures that the user has the ability to perform that operation.

The SAP Security Model

Authorization checks control access to operations in SAP. A developer places authorization checks in programs when security is an issue. The system then searches the user's profile, maintained by the system administrator, to verify that the user has access to the object being checked. These authorization objects consist of up to ten fields, which may contain specific values to be checked. You can contact the administrator of your system for more information.

The Authorization Object

The authorization object grants the ability to perform some operation in the system. For example, the authorization object could be a requirement that only some people be allowed to view or maintain a list of suppliers with quality problems. This would be mapped to an authorization object with the name `Z:SUPPPRB`. When a program displays or changes data on the supplier list, a check should be made against the `Z:SUPPPRB`.

Authorization Fields

An authorization object can have up to ten authorization fields. Each field is the equivalent of an SAP data element. (See Chapter 7, "Working with the Data Dictionary," for information about data elements.) For example, the supplier authorization just described, `Z:SUPPPRB`, might have two fields—one called `REGIO` and another called `ACTVT`. The `REGIO` field holds a region value and all suppliers are assigned to a region. The `ACTVT` field is used in many objects and holds activity values. In general, when ACTVT has the value 01, it indicates the ability to create data. An ACTVT of 02 indicates the ability to change data and a value of 03 indicates the ability to display data.

The User Master Record

Each user in a SAP R/3 system has a master record that contains all authorizations that the user may perform. For example, a user might have the object Z:SUPPRB and fields REGIO with the value USA and ACTVT with a value of 03. This indicates that the user could display suppliers for the USA region, but if this user attempts to execute a program that changes data in the USA region, the user would fail any authority checks. This is not an automatic process—to enforce this security, the programmer must perform the authority check correctly in the program.

Creating Authorization Objects

When creating a custom authorization object, the first step is to create any custom authorization fields needed. Most of the time you will not need to create custom fields and will simply use fields created by SAP. Most major SAP data elements have corresponding authorization fields including plant (WERKS), sales office (VKBUR), and activity (ACTVT). Be sure to check for an existing field before creating new ones. To view or create authorization fields, select Tools|ABAP/4 Workbench|Development|Other tools|Authorization objs|Fields (see Figure 17-1).

Next choose "customer" to create custom fields (see Figure 17-2).

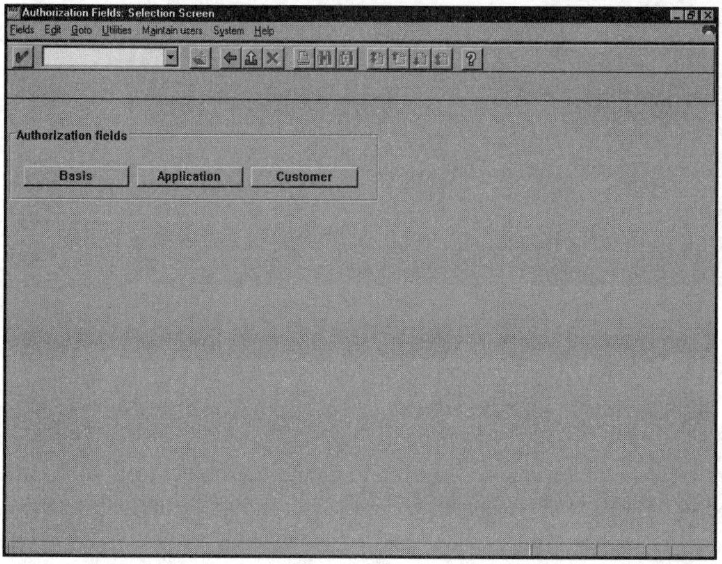

FIGURE 17-1

Creating an authorization Step 1

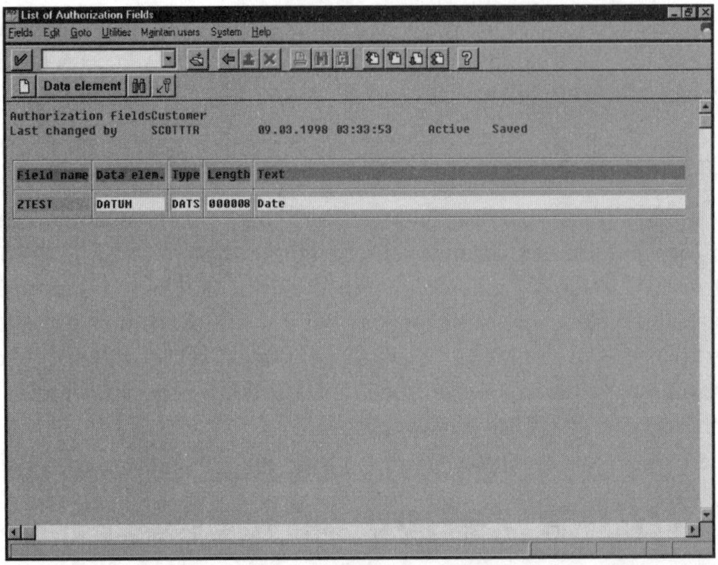

FIGURE 17-2

Customer created authorization fields

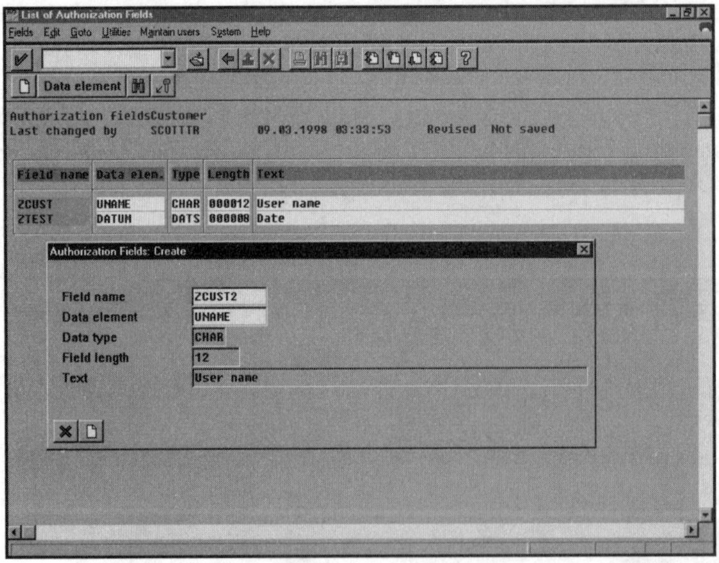

FIGURE 17-3

Create a new authorization field

From this screen choose Field|Create to create a new field. Enter a name and data element. Like all custom objects, the name should start with "Z", as shown in Figure 17-3.

After you create custom fields, it is time to create the object to hold them. Because SAP groups authorization objects into classes, you should create a custom class before you create a custom object. To create an authorization object class, select

Tools|ABAP/4 Workbench|Development|Other tools|Authorization objs|Objects. From this screen, choose Class|Create to create a custom class and get a pop up menu to enter the new class (see Figure 17-4).

Once the class has been created, double-click on it to access the object list for that class. Because it is new, it is empty (see Figure 17-5).

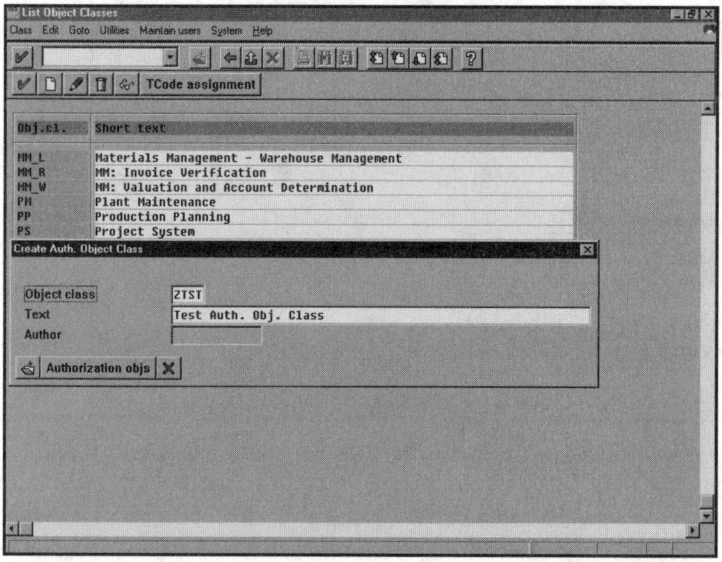

FIGURE 17-4

Creating a new object class

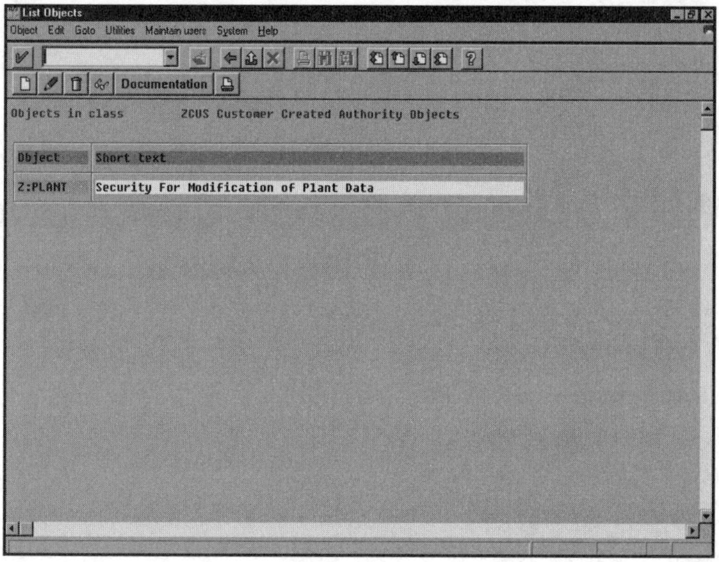

FIGURE 17-5

Customer created authorization objects

From this screen, choose Object|Create to create your custom object. This brings up the screen seen in Figure 17-6.

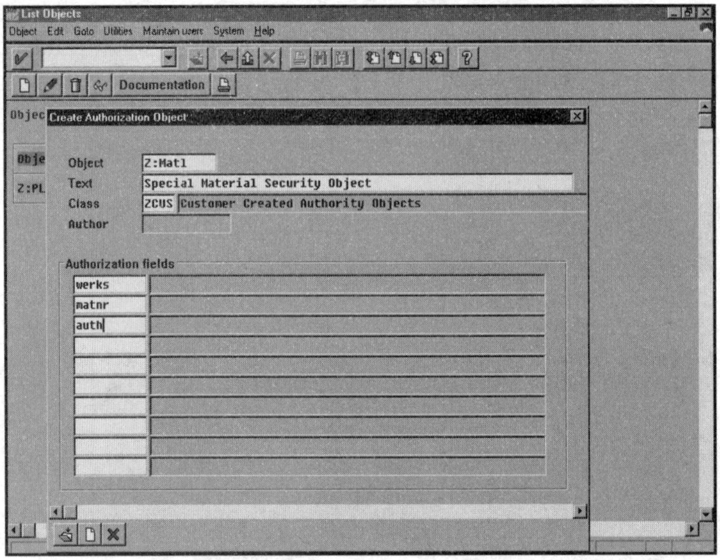

FIGURE 17-6

Create a new authorization object

As shown in Figure 17-6, when creating an authorization object, it is required that you enter a name, descriptive text, the class, and the list of authorization fields which will be contained in the object. In the example shown in Figure 17-6, an object called Z:PLANT is being created. This will contain the names of people who have authorization for a plant.

Once you create your authorization object, you are ready to add the checks to your programs.

Using the Authority-Check Command

You are now ready to use custom authorization objects in your programs. The AUTHORITY-CHECK command checks authorizations in ABAP/4 programs. The syntax of the command is:

```
AUTHORITY-CHECK OBJECT obj
    ID name1  FIELD val¦DUMMY
    ID name2  FIELD val¦DUMMY
    ...
    ID name10 FIELD val¦DUMMY
```

You will be checking the `val` value against the user master record. If you do not want to check a field, you can substitute the keyword `DUMMY` for the `FIELD val` option. This causes the system to ignore the value of the field when performing the authorization check. When this command is performed, you can tell if the check is successful by a return code of the command. Any value other than zero indicates a failure of the check. Table 17-1 contains a list of possible return codes.

Table 17-1 AUTHORIZATION-CHECK Return Codes

Return	Description
0	Check is successful
4	Check failed because user is not authorized
8	Number of fields submitted for check exceeds 10
12	Object does not exist
24	Field names listed in the check do not match the fields of the object.
28, 32, 36	System Error

Here are some simple examples of the use of the `AUTHORITY-CHECK` command:

```
AUTHORITY-CHECK OBJECT 'Z:CUST'
    ID 'ACTVT' FIELD '01'.
IF SY-SUBRC NE 0.
   MESSAGE E999 WITH 'You are not authorized to use this program!'.
ENDIF.


AUTHORITY-CHECK OBJECT 'Z:PLANT'
    ID 'WERKS' FIELD 'P100'
    ID 'MATNR' DUMMY
    ID 'ACTVT' FIELD '02'.
IF SY-SUBRC NE 0.
   MESSAGE E999 WITH 'You are not authorized to change data in Plant P100'.
ENDIF.
```

The following is a program featuring several of the concepts previously presented including authority checks, function modules, forms, and a BDC session. The purpose of this program is to change the delivery dates of items on a sales order. When a sales order is created in SAP, it is broken up into two pieces—the header and a list of items. The sales order header holds a default delivery date that records when the customer wants the item delivered. In addition, each item on the order has its own delivery date. The delivery dates of each may vary in an order.

This program reads a file containing sales order numbers and dates. For each order, the system checks the user's authority for running the program to change the order. If the user has authority, a BDC session builds and then processes via the `CALL TRANSACTION` command. The results of each transaction is saved and reported back to the user at the end. Note that the authority check is made before the processing of the sales order takes place. SAP has its own security on changing documents like sales orders; but in this case, a custom authority object is checked.

```
REPORT ZCVDATE1 LINE-SIZE 132 LINE-COUNT 65 MESSAGE-ID ZZ.
*-----------------------------------------------------------------*
* Report name: ZCVDATE1
* Author: Bob Lyfareff
* Date:   May 27,1998
* Type: Program - Alter delivery date in sales items
*-----------------------------------------------------------------*
* Description of function:
* This program will take a list of items and change the delivery date
* of all items on a sales order.  It will change the delivery
* date in the sales order header back to the original date.
* The user's authorization will be checked by the system for
* each order to ensure the user has change authorization
* for the sales group (VBAK-VKBUR).
* The data will be changed using transaction VA02.
*-----------------------------------------------------------------*

TABLES: T100,           "Message Texts Table
        VBAK.           "Sales Order Header Table

DATA: BEGIN OF INT_ORDER OCCURS 100,     "Input file with orders
        LINE(120),
      END OF INT_ORDER.
```

```
DATA: BEGIN OF INT_DATA OCCURS 100,       "Data to be processed
        VBELN LIKE VBAP-VBELN,
        DELDATE(8),
      END OF INT_DATA.


DATA: BEGIN OF INT_RES OCCURS 200,          "Results Table
        VBELN LIKE VBAP-VBELN,
        POSNR LIKE VBAP-POSNR,
        MSGID LIKE BDCMSGCOLL-MSGID,
        MSGNR LIKE BDCMSGCOLL-MSGNR,
        MSGNUM LIKE SY-TABIX,
        SUBRC  LIKE SY-SUBRC,
        SAV_TEXT(275),
       END OF INT_RES.

DATA: BEGIN OF BD OCCURS 10.            "BDC Table
        INCLUDE STRUCTURE BDCDATA.
DATA: END OF BD.

DATA: BEGIN OF XBDCMSGCOLL OCCURS 10.  "Transaction Messages
        INCLUDE STRUCTURE BDCMSGCOLL.
DATA: END OF XBDCMSGCOLL.

DATA: WS_TOTAL TYPE I,
      WS_VBELN LIKE VBAP-VBELN,
      FLG_ERR,
      WS_SUBRC(10),
      WS_TOP,
      WS_MODE VALUE 'N'.

PARAMETERS: P_FILE LIKE RLGRAP-FILENAME DEFAULT 'C:\PULLIN.TXT'.
```

```
* Start Main Program
START-OF-SELECTION.
* Open file and read records
  PERFORM INIT_DAT.

  LOOP AT INT_DATA.
    CHECK INT_DATA-VBELN NE SPACE.     "check order is not blank
    WS_TOTAL = SY-TABIX.                "Keep track of total
*   Build BDC table to change data
    CLEAR BD[].
    PERFORM BUILD_BDC.
*   Call transaction VA02 and record result
    PERFORM PROCESS_ITEM.
  ENDLOOP.
WRITE: /, WS_TOTAL, 'Total Items Processed'(023).
* Print Results Report
  PERFORM PRINT_RESULTS.


*eject
*Begin forms
*---------------------------------------------------------------------*
*        FORM INIT_DAT                                                *
*---------------------------------------------------------------------*
*        Read file and get orders and dates                           *
*---------------------------------------------------------------------*
FORM INIT_DAT.

* Use data file to get item list, read local PC file
  CALL FUNCTION 'WS_UPLOAD'
       EXPORTING
            FILENAME            = P_FILE
            FILETYPE            = 'ASC'
       TABLES
            DATA_TAB            = INT_ORDER
```

```
     EXCEPTIONS
          CONVERSION_ERROR    = 1
          FILE_OPEN_ERROR     = 2
          FILE_READ_ERROR     = 3
          INVALID_TABLE_WIDTH = 4
          INVALID_TYPE        = 5
          NO_BATCH            = 6
          UNKNOWN_ERROR       = 7
          OTHERS              = 8.
  IF SY-SUBRC NE 0.
    MESSAGE E999 WITH 'Error opening PC file!'(109) SY-SUBRC.
  ENDIF.

  LOOP AT INT_ORDER.
    CHECK INT_ORDER-LINE NE SPACE.
    CLEAR INT_DATA.
*   Set Delivery Date
    INT_DATA-DELDATE = INT_ORDER-LINE+10(8).
*   Set Sales Order
    INT_DATA-VBELN = INT_ORDER-LINE(10).
*   Pad Sales order with leading zeros if needed
    SHIFT INT_DATA-VBELN RIGHT DELETING TRAILING SPACE.
    DO.
      REPLACE SPACE WITH '0' INTO INT_DATA-VBELN.
      IF SY-SUBRC NE 0. EXIT. ENDIF.
    ENDDO.

*   Check that Order exists and get sales office
    SELECT SINGLE * FROM VBAK WHERE VBELN =  INT_DATA-VBELN.
    IF SY-SUBRC NE 0.
      WRITE: / 'SAP Order#'(110), INT_ORDER-LINE(10), 'Not Found'(111).
    ELSE.
*     Check authorization to see if user has change authority
*     for the Sales Office of this order
      AUTHORITY-CHECK OBJECT 'Z:SOOFF'
```

```
                        ID 'VKBUR' FIELD VBAK-VKBUR
                        ID 'ACTVT' FIELD '02'.
      IF SY-SUBRC EQ 0.
        APPEND INT_DATA.
      ELSE.
        WRITE: /, 'Failed to change order'(111), VBAK-VBELN,
          / 'You do not have authorization to change Sales Office'(112),
          VBAK-VKBUR.
      ENDIF.
    ENDIF.
  ENDLOOP.
ENDFORM.

*---------------------------------------------------------------------*
*       FORM BUILD_BDC                                                *
*---------------------------------------------------------------------*
*       Build BDC table for current order                             *
*---------------------------------------------------------------------*
FORM BUILD_BDC.

  DATA: WS_VDAT LIKE VBAK-VDATU,
        WS_TEMP(10).

* Get Current delivery date
  SELECT SINGLE VDATU INTO (WS_VDAT)
           FROM VBAK WHERE VBELN = INT_DATA-VBELN.

* Screen start.
  PERFORM SCREEN TABLES BD USING 'SAPMV45A' '0102'.

* Fill sales document number
  PERFORM FIELD TABLES BD
          USING 'VBAK-VBELN' INT_DATA-VBELN.

* Move to first sales order screen
  PERFORM OKCODE TABLES BD USING 'UER2'.
```

```
* Screen start.
  PERFORM SCREEN TABLES BD USING 'SAPMV45A' '0400'.

* Select all sales items to be changed
  PERFORM OKCODE TABLES BD USING 'MKAL'.

* Screen start.
  PERFORM SCREEN TABLES BD USING 'SAPMV45A' '0400'.

* Function change delivery date in selected items
  PERFORM OKCODE TABLES BD USING 'SWLD'.

* Screen Start
  PERFORM SCREEN TABLES BD USING 'SAPMV45A' '0255'.

* Change delivery date to date found in input file
  PERFORM FIELD TABLES BD USING 'RV45A-S_ETDAT' INT_DATA-DELDATE.

* Move old delivery date to a text field to ensure proper format
  WRITE WS_VDAT TO WS_TEMP.

* Screen Start
  PERFORM SCREEN TABLES BD USING 'SAPMV45A' '0255'.

* Continue to next screen
  PERFORM OKCODE TABLES BD USING 'SUEB'.

* Screen Start
  PERFORM SCREEN TABLES BD USING 'SAPMV45A' '0400'.

* Restore original req date to header
  PERFORM FIELD TABLES BD USING 'RV45A-KETDAT' WS_TEMP.

* Screen Start
  PERFORM SCREEN TABLES BD USING 'SAPMV45A' '0400'.
```

```
* Save changes to sales order
  PERFORM OKCODE TABLES BD USING 'SAVE'.
ENDFORM.

*----------------------------------------------------------------*
*       FORM PROCESS_ITEM                                         *
*----------------------------------------------------------------*
*       Call transaction VA02 to change the sales order using the *
*       BDC table created earlier.  Any success or error messages *
*       will be capture in a table for later use.
*----------------------------------------------------------------*
FORM PROCESS_ITEM.

  CALL TRANSACTION 'VA02' USING BD
                           MODE  WS_MODE
                           UPDATE 'S'
                           MESSAGES INTO XBDCMSGCOLL.
* Save return code
  WS_SUBRC = SY-SUBRC.
  IF WS_SUBRC EQ 0.
*   This will appear in the system log
    MESSAGE S999 WITH INT_DATA-VBELN 'Processed Successfully!'(124).
  ELSE.
*   This will appear in the system log
    MESSAGE S999 WITH INT_DATA-VBELN 'Failed_due_to_Error!'(125).
  ENDIF.

* Loop at transaction messages table to record any errors
  LOOP AT XBDCMSGCOLL.
*   Clear header of results table
    CLEAR INT_RES.

    MOVE: INT_DATA-VBELN     TO INT_RES-VBELN,   "Sales Order
          XBDCMSGCOLL-MSGID TO INT_RES-MSGID,   "Message ID
          XBDCMSGCOLL-MSGNR TO INT_RES-MSGNR,   "Message Number
          WS_SUBRC TO INT_RES-SUBRC,   "Return Code
```

```
        SY-TABIX TO INT_RES-MSGNUM.  "For later sorting

*   Table T100 holds the texts for error messages
    SELECT SINGLE * FROM T100 WHERE SPRSL = SY-LANGU
                                AND ARBGB = XBDCMSGCOLL-MSGID
                                AND MSGNR = XBDCMSGCOLL-MSGNR.
    INT_RES-SAV_TEXT = T100-TEXT.
*   Replace & with the results stored in the MSGV# fields
    REPLACE '&' WITH XBDCMSGCOLL-MSGV1 INTO INT_RES-SAV_TEXT.
    REPLACE '&' WITH XBDCMSGCOLL-MSGV2 INTO INT_RES-SAV_TEXT.
    REPLACE '&' WITH XBDCMSGCOLL-MSGV3 INTO INT_RES-SAV_TEXT.
    REPLACE '&' WITH XBDCMSGCOLL-MSGV4 INTO INT_RES-SAV_TEXT.
    CONDENSE INT_RES-SAV_TEXT.
*   Save messages for later reporting to results table
    APPEND INT_RES.
  ENDLOOP.

* Clear tables
  CLEAR: BD[], XBDCMSGCOLL[].
ENDFORM.

*---------------------------------------------------------------------*
*       FORM PRINT_RESULTS                                             *
*---------------------------------------------------------------------*
*       Print results for all orders processed                        *
*---------------------------------------------------------------------*
FORM PRINT_RESULTS.
* Sort by return code so successful transactions (subrc=0) come last
  SORT INT_RES BY SUBRC DESCENDING VBELN POSNR MSGNUM.

  WRITE /.
  ULINE.
  WRITE: / '******* Results of Processing *******'(100).
  ULINE.

  WRITE: /, 'Transactions With Errors:'(101).
```

```
  LOOP AT INT_RES.
    IF INT_RES-SUBRC EQ 0 AND WS_TOP = SPACE.
*     When subrc = 0 successful transactions begin
      WRITE: /, 'Transactions Not Raising Errors:'(103).
      WS_TOP = 'X'.
    ENDIF.
    WRITE: / ' '.
    IF INT_RES-MSGNUM = 1.
*     Print the order number for on the first message
      WRITE: /, 'SO'(104), INT_RES-VBELN.
    ENDIF.
    WRITE: / INT_RES-MSGID,
             INT_RES-MSGNR,
             INT_RES-SAV_TEXT(100).
  ENDLOOP.
ENDFORM.

*---------------------------------------------------------------------*
*       FORM SCREEN                                                   *
*---------------------------------------------------------------------*
*       Add BD entry for screen start.                                *
*---------------------------------------------------------------------*
*  --> PROGRAM   application program                                  *
*      SCREEN    screen number                                        *
*  <-> BD        batch input data table                               *
*---------------------------------------------------------------------*
FORM SCREEN TABLES BD STRUCTURE BDCDATA
                USING  PROGRAM SCREEN.

  CLEAR BD.
  BD-PROGRAM  = PROGRAM.
  BD-DYNPRO   = SCREEN.
  BD-DYNBEGIN = 'X'.
  APPEND BD.

ENDFORM.
```

```
*-------------------------------------------------------------*
*       FORM FIELD                                                *
*-------------------------------------------------------------*
*       Create BD entry for a field value                         *
*-------------------------------------------------------------*
*   -->  FIELD     screen field                                   *
*        VALUE     field value                                    *
*   <->  BD        batch input data table                         *
*-------------------------------------------------------------*
FORM FIELD TABLES BD STRUCTURE BDCDATA
                 USING  FIELD VALUE.

  CLEAR BD.
  BD-FNAM      = FIELD.
  BD-FVAL      = VALUE.
  APPEND BD.

ENDFORM.
*-------------------------------------------------------------*
*       FORM OKCODE                                               *
*-------------------------------------------------------------*
*       Create BD entry for a transaction code                    *
*-------------------------------------------------------------*
*   -->  OKCODE    trasnaction code                               *
*   <->  BD        batch input data table                         *
*-------------------------------------------------------------*
FORM OKCODE TABLES BD STRUCTURE BDCDATA
                  USING  OKCODE.

  CLEAR BD.
  BD-FNAM      = 'BDC_OKCODE'.
  BD-FVAL      = OKCODE.
  APPEND BD.

ENDFORM.
*End Program
```

FORM INIT_DAT

This first form initializes the data to be processed by the program. First it reads the PC file which holds the data to be processed into an internal table. Then it loops through that table and extracts the sales order number and the new delivery date. It compares the sales order number against the sales order table, `VBAK`, to make sure the order really exists in the system. Once it confirms the order number, it checks to see if the user has the authority to change sales orders based on the sales office (`VBAK-VKBUR`).

FORM BUILD_BDC

This is where the BDC session is built that will change the delivery date of items on the sales order. Also the original delivery date is saved in the sales order header.

FORM PROCESS_ITEM

In this form, submitting the BDC via the `Call Transaction` command changes the date. Messages encountered during the transaction are saved in the `XBDCMSGCOLL` table. This table captures both success and failure messages. The data form is then transferred to the results table which is later reported to the user.

FORM PRINT_RESULTS

Here both success and failure messages are reported to the user out of the results table.

Summary

This is simply one aspect of the SAP security model. To learn more about security and authorizations in SAP R/3, consult your system administrator or books on SAP System Administration.

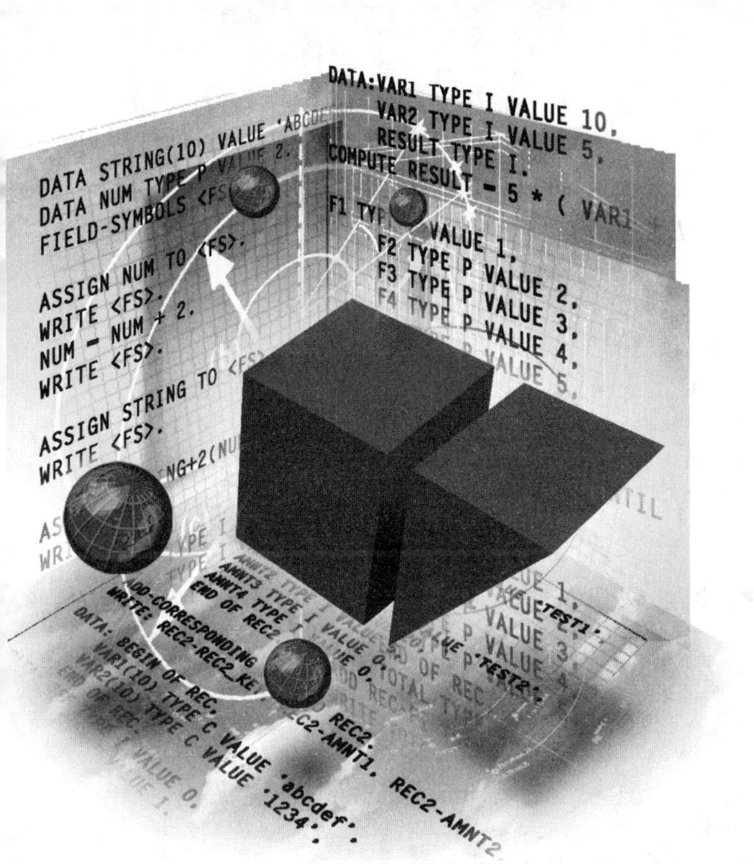

Chapter 18

ABAP/4 Workbench (Debugger)

In This Chapter

- The ABAP/4 Debugger
- Debugging Techniques

This chapter introduces the ABAP/4 debugger and some techniques used to analyze programs. It also covers the methods used to enter "debug mode;" setting breakpoints, both manually and dynamically; a tour around the debug screen; and techniques to effectively debug your code.

The ABAP/4 Debugger

The ABAP/4 debugger is probably the most important development tool you'll utilize aside from the workbench. The use of the debugger allows for line-by-line execution, along with supervision over the contents of certain variables and internal tables in real time. The debugger gives you a different perspective on coding. It can be used to see what is happening in SAP transactions that are running, or to analyze your programs that you are coding. In either case, what you view is ABAP/4 code, and you are able to control its execution to a line-by-line process.

Entering "Debug Mode"

The first step to debugging code is to enter debug mode. There are three methods for accomplishing this task. The first method is formally entering debug mode from the editor. Another is the "slash h" method. The final method is setting breakpoints inside the code.

The first method is reached from the ABAP/4 editor, either in the initial screen or in editor mode. Both paths are demonstrated in Figures 18-1 and 18-2.

Let's use some sample code to debug:

```
REPORT ZTEST.


WRITE:/ 'This is my debugging test program.'.
```

Via both of these methods, you would enter a screen that looks like Figure 18-3. Essentially, this figure introduces you to what the debugger looks like. This screen and all of its components are completely explained in the second section of this chapter, which covers the debugger's functionality. The debugger allows you process your ABAP/4 code line by line.

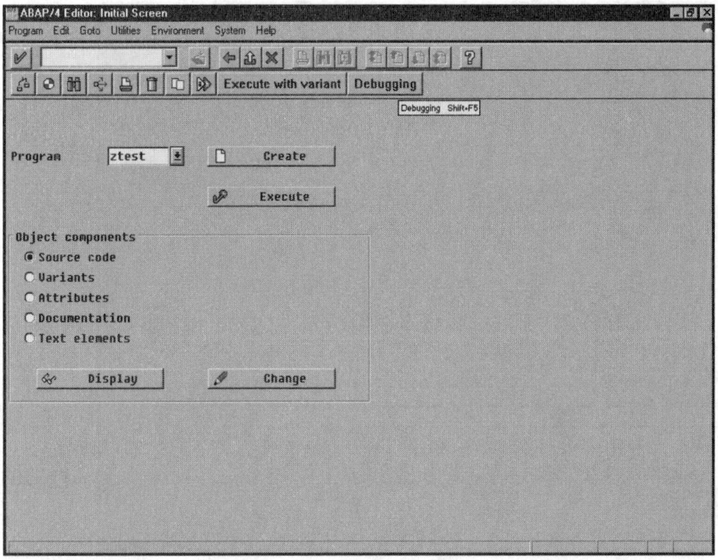

FIGURE 18-1

Click the Debugging button to execute a program in debug mode.

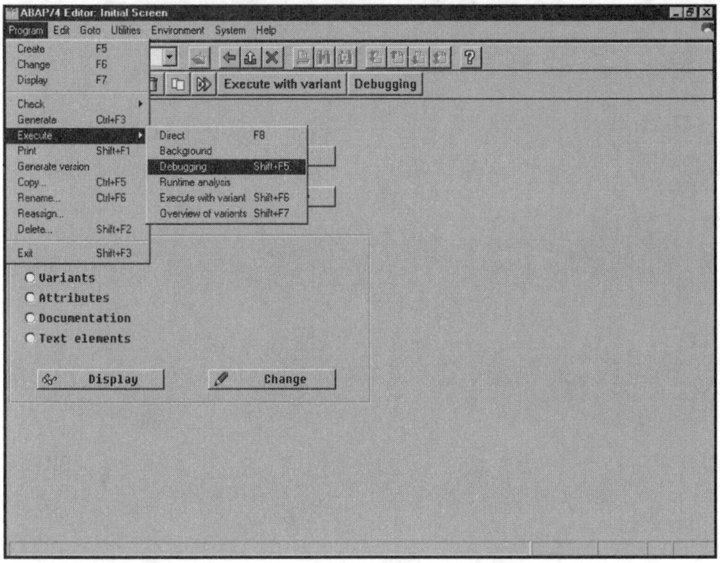

FIGURE 18-2

Follow the menu path to execute a program in debug mode from the editor mode screen.

This method does have some limitations. For example, you can only debug reports or programs which you can execute from the se38 screen. If you wish to debug a transaction, you must use the "slash h" method. To enter debug mode anywhere in SAP, just type **/h** in the command box in the top-left corner of the screen (see Figure 18-4).

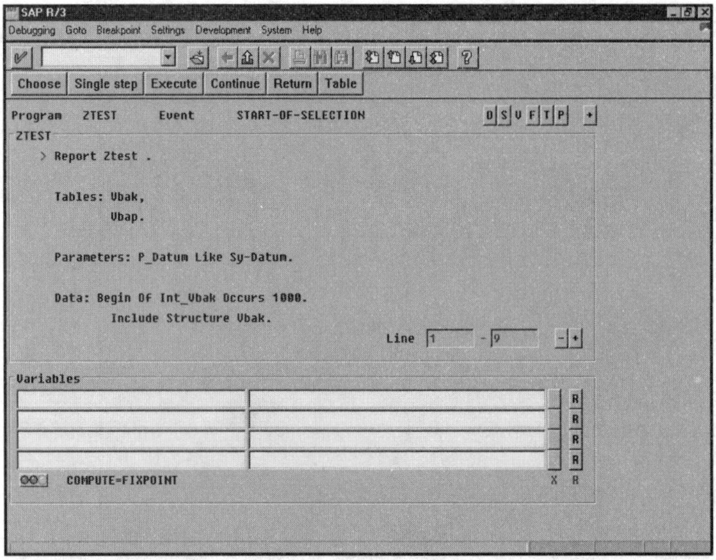

FIGURE 18-3

The initial debugging screen

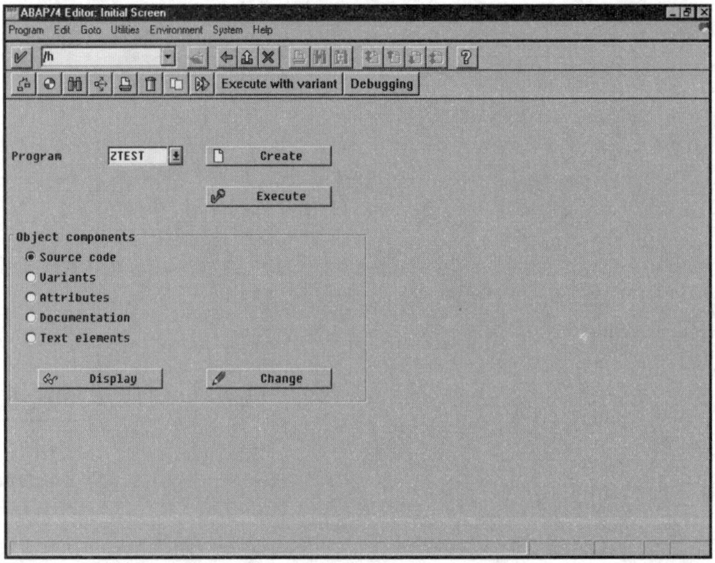

FIGURE 18-4

Type /h in the command box.

After pressing Enter on the keyboard, a message at the bottom-left portion of the screen says, "Debugging mode is on" (see Figure 18-5).

At this point, proceed with pressing the buttons you usually would to continue in the transaction, and immediately you will enter the code behind the transaction. Because this book's scope deals only with programs executable from the se38 screen, it does

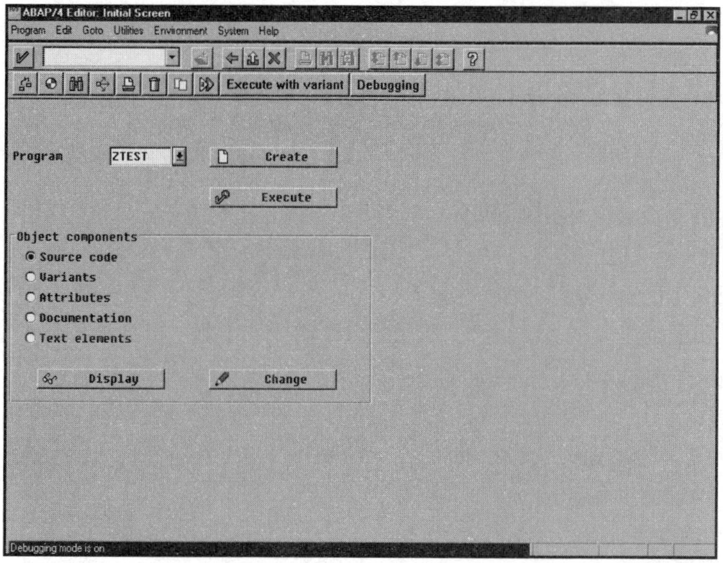

FIGURE 18-5

"debugging mode is on"

not cover specific techniques used to debug transactions. Many of the methods can be used, however for a deeper understanding of debugging transactions, read our next book to be released in a couple months which will cover transactions and online programming. All of the techniques and examples covered here can be used to debug online transactions. Of course, if you have any specific questions, please feel free to e-mail the authors. We will be happy to field your questions.

Gareth M. de Bruyn	debcor@bigfoot.com
Robert W. Lyfareff	rlyf@bigfoot.com

Defining the Debugger's Screen

Now that you are in debug mode, what does this new screen mean to you? Debug mode is almost like a brand new transaction within the program you are running. This section gives you a tour of the screen and the most useful commands. Once you know your way around the debugging screens, you can move on to the debugging techniques section of this chapter which covers a more strategic approach to tackling the debugging of your programs.

For consistency, please type in the following program into your system, and then debug it. If you follow these instructions, your screen should look exactly like the ones here.

```
REPORT ZTEST .

TABLES: VBAK,
        VBAP.

PARAMETERS: P_DATUM LIKE SY-DATUM.

DATA: BEGIN OF INT_VBAK OCCURS 1000.
        INCLUDE STRUCTURE VBAK.
DATA: END OF INT_VBAK.

DATA: BEGIN OF INT_VBAP OCCURS 1000.
        INCLUDE STRUCTURE VBAP.
DATA: END OF INT_VBAP.


SELECT * FROM VBAK INTO TABLE INT_VBAK WHERE
                                            ERDAT = P_DATUM.

LOOP AT INT_VBAK.

  IF INT_VBAK-ERNAM = 'BATCHUSER'.
    PERFORM VBAP_DISPLAY.
  ELSE.
    WRITE:/                 INT_VBAK-VBELN,
                      15    'Not Relevant'.
  ENDIF.

ENDLOOP.
*&---------------------------------------------------------------------*
*&      Form  VBAP_DISPLAY
*&---------------------------------------------------------------------*
*       text                                                           *
*----------------------------------------------------------------------*
```

```
*   —>  p1        text
*   <—  p2        text
*----------------------------------------------------------*
FORM VBAP_DISPLAY.
  REFRESH INT_VBAP.
  SELECT * FROM VBAP INTO TABLE INT_VBAP WHERE
                                     VBELN = INT_VBAK-VBELN.
  LOOP AT INT_VBAP.
    WRITE:/                      INT_VBAP-VBELN,
                            11   INT_VBAP-POSNR,
                            20   INT_VBAP-ARKTX.
  ENDLOOP.

ENDFORM.                                  " VBAP_DISPLAY
```

Use the Debugging button to execute this program from the ABAP/4 editor (or se38 screen) and enter a date for your selection criteria. You should have a screen that looks like Figure 18-6. In some 3.1h systems, the 'V' button is replaced by a 'W' button. They are the same in function. This chapter refers to the 'V' button. Replace it in your mind with a 'W' if you are on one of those systems.

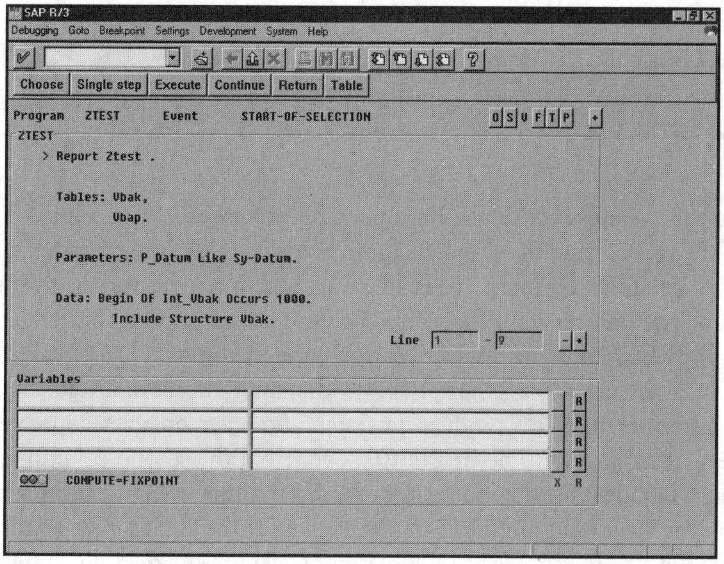

FIGURE 18-6

The initial debugging screen

General Commands

The most useful and most frequently used functions of the debugging screen have been defined as buttons. The Choose, Single step, Execute, Continue, Return, Table, and various view buttons help you in your quest to dissect and analyze your new application.

The first view button is the V view. The initial screen is the V view, or Variables view.

Each command is explained and demonstrated in the next section. First define some of the screen areas.

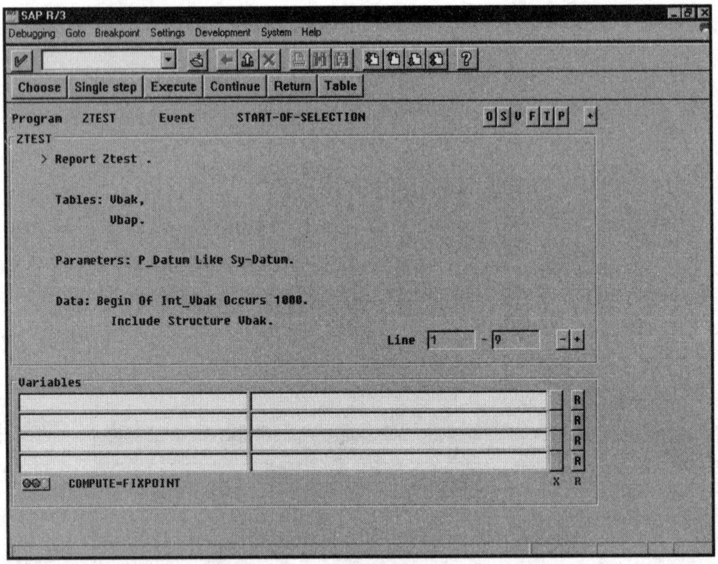

FIGURE 18-7

The initial debugging screen. Use this to reference the default buttons and areas of the debugging screen.

Focus on the Variables box at the bottom of the screen. The first column holds the name of the variable and the second column holds its value. You can track up to four variables at one time. Of course, you can always add or remove variables at any time. The second button over from the second column is a very special button. It enables you (if your system administrator gives you enough authority) to replace the contents of what is currently in the variable with something new. Of course this is a very dangerous feature on a production system; however, on a development system it is a very useful feature. The first button over from the second column is to view variables in hexadecimal notation. I have not found this useful at all in my debugging, but you have that ability if you wish. Under the fourth row of the second column, if the system variable SY-SUBRC is not equal to zero, the value displays along with the variable name.

Choose

There are several ways to insert a variable into the first column (refer to Figure 18-6). A variable is a regular data field, a parameter, a select option, a field in the header of a database table, or a field inside of an internal table. One way to insert a variable is to manually type the name of the variable. But, who wants to do things the long way! The second method is to double-click on the variable in the code. The variable will appear in the next available blank row in the first column. If all four rows are filled, the last row is replaced with the new variable. The value stored in the variable displays in the second column. The third method is to select the variable in the code, and click on the Choose button. Even though this button is convenient, you will probably find that double-clicking is the best method. See Figure 18-8.

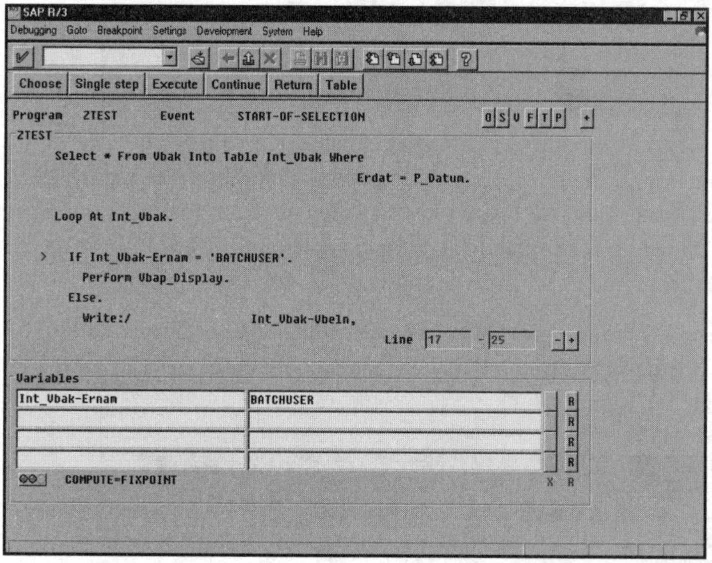

FIGURE 18-8

If you enter a variable in the first column, the value held in that variable is displayed in the second column.

To add a new dimension to the variable display, you can click on the Choose button without selecting any variable. You are transferred to a new screen, which looks like Figure 18-9.

This screen can also be reached by clicking on the F button in the top-right corner of the debugging screen. Now, once in this screen, type in the name of the variable. In addition to the variable's contents, administrative data regarding the variable also displays (for example, length, type, and so on). Of course, there is a faster way to reach this screen and populate the field box. Starting at the screen shown in Figure 18-7, double-click on any of the variables shown in any of the first columns from any one

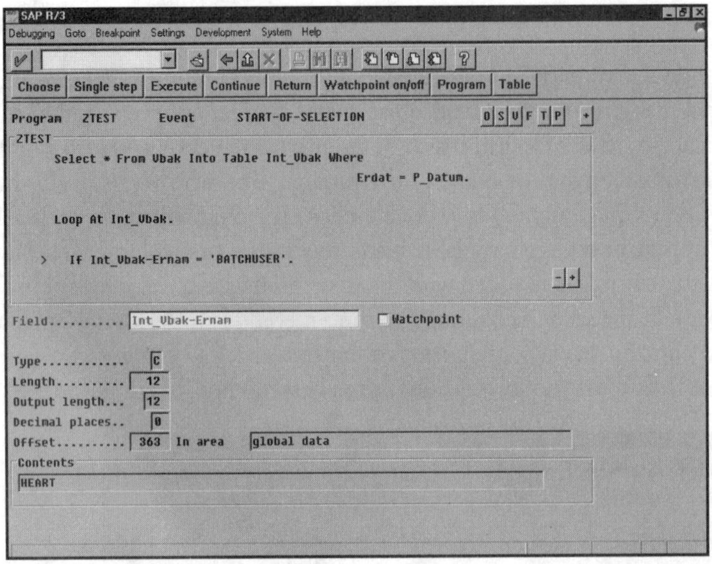

FIGURE 18-9

The 'F' view showing detail about a variable

of the four rows. The screen immediately transfers to one like Figure 18-9, and the variable is already entered. If you type the name of an internal table in one of the four columns shown in the initial debugging screen (Figure 18-7), the header displays in the second column. This display is shown in Figure 18-10.

By clicking on the internal table name and pressing the Choose button, or double-clicking, one navigates to the field view screen once more, except that it has changed somewhat. See Figure 18-11.

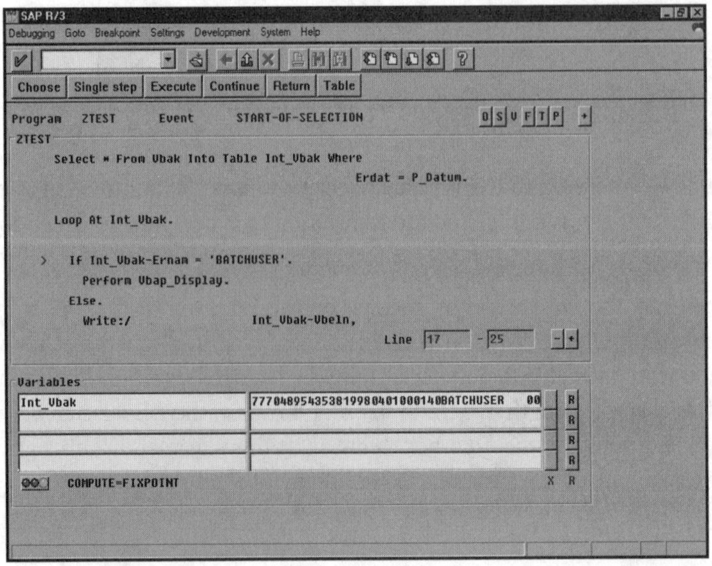

FIGURE 18-10

Internal table name with header displayed

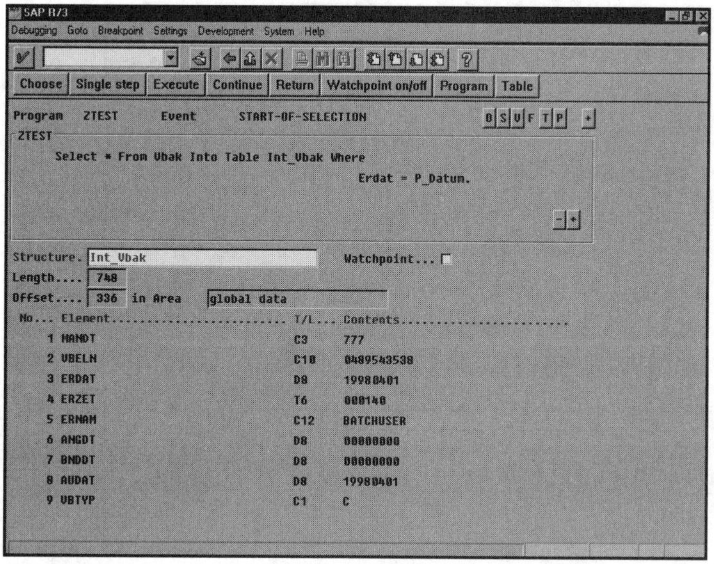

FIGURE 18-11

The 'F' or field view for an internal table

The screen displays the structure view. Each field is named, and the contents of the header display in the far-right column. The type and length of each field displays in the second column.

This view is a very useful one for fields or internal tables. Despite only displaying one variable, it does have one big advantage over other screens. This advantage is the watchpoint check box to the right of the structure or field. If the watchpoint box is checked, the program stops in debug mode at the point at which that variable has changed in any way. The use of the watchpoint command is explained in detail in the "Tips and Techniques" section of this chapter.

Single Step

Right now, you are probably double-clicking like mad, but no values are in your variables. So, the challenge is how to execute commands in the program to populate the variables with data. One of the solutions to this challenge is the Single step command. Enter debug mode and navigate to Figure 18-7 (your initial screen). Notice where the blue > marker is on the left side and press the Single step button. Initially the marker resides next to the `REPORT` statement.

The marker resides next to the first `SELECT` statement, but what happened to all those `DATA` commands? The program declares those and passes you to the first executable command (in this case, the `SELECT` command). By pressing the Single step button once more, the `SELECT` command executes and the table `INT_VBAK` is populated with

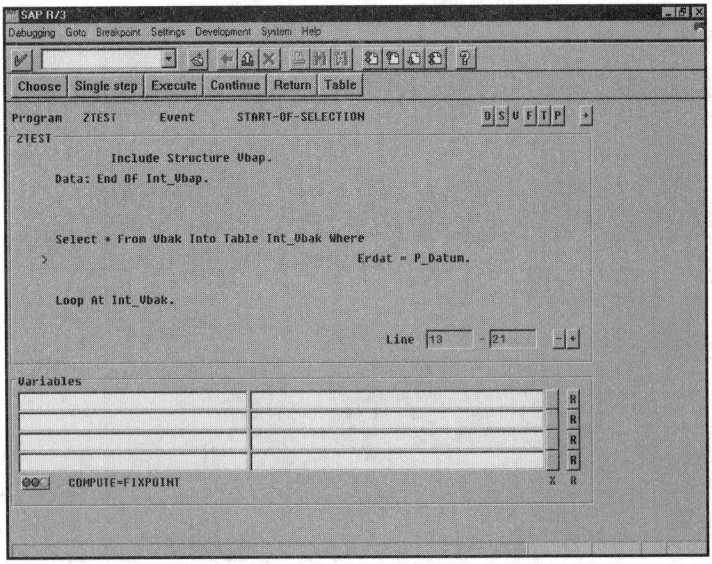

FIGURE 18-12

Figure 18-7, but after pressing the Single step button

X number of records. You can type in one of the INT_VBAK fields into the variable column, or double-click on one of them to display the contents of that field.

Continue single stepping until you reach the IF statement. The BATCHUSER value is hard coded into the program. Feel free to change this value. Or, put some debugging knowledge to work. You should be looking at a screen like Figure 18-13.

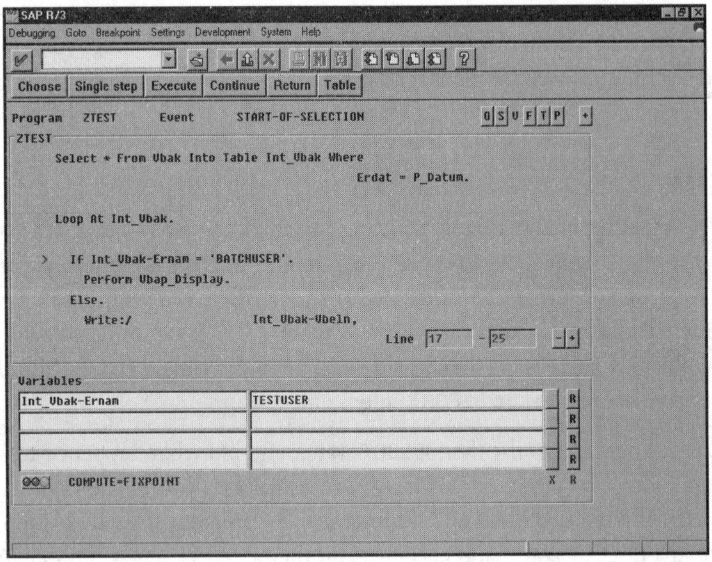

FIGURE 18-13

Screen showing the value of INT_VBAK-ERNAM *as* 'TESTUSER'

The INT_VBAK-ERNAM field displays in the first column, and the TESTUSER value displays in the second column. You want to have this logical statement be true, so delete TESTUSER, and type in **BATCHUSER**. Click on the R button to the right of the second column. You should see a screen like Figure 18-14.

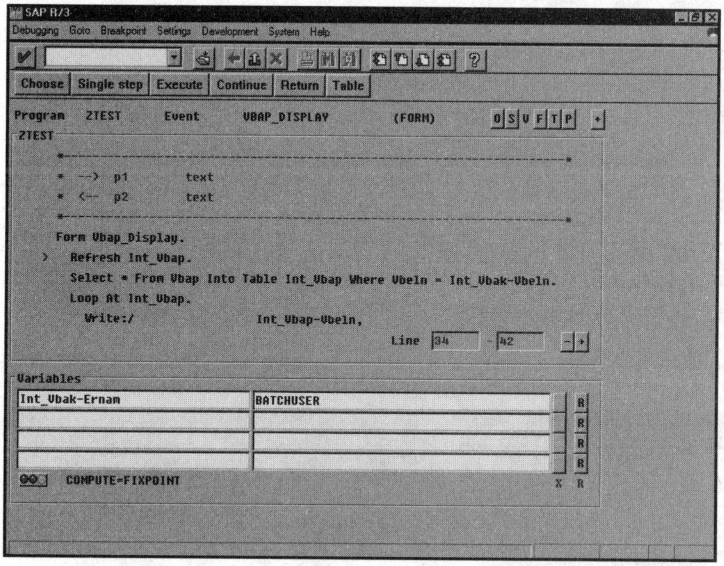

FIGURE 18-14

INT_VBAK-ERNAM's *value has now been replaced with the value of* 'BATCHUSER'.

You have effectively replaced the value of the internal table field with another one. By single stepping, you can navigate to the line, which will execute a subroutine. Because you are single stepping through the code, by clicking the Single step button once more, you will find that you have navigated deeper into the code and down into the subroutine code itself. See Figure 18-15.

This rule holds true when executing outside programs, function calls, screens, or subroutines. Single stepping always takes you into the next piece of code. This fact differentiates the SINGLE STEP command from the EXECUTE command in that the EXECUTE command performs the call as one command.

Execute

The Execute command is very similar to the Single step command, but there is one big difference. If you navigate down in the code where the subroutine is called with the PERFORM command, and then click the Execute button, you see the difference in results. Whereas Single Step took us into the subroutine code, the Execute button treats the entire subroutine as one command and the > marker moves from the PERFORM line directly to the next one, the ELSE line. See Figure 18-16.

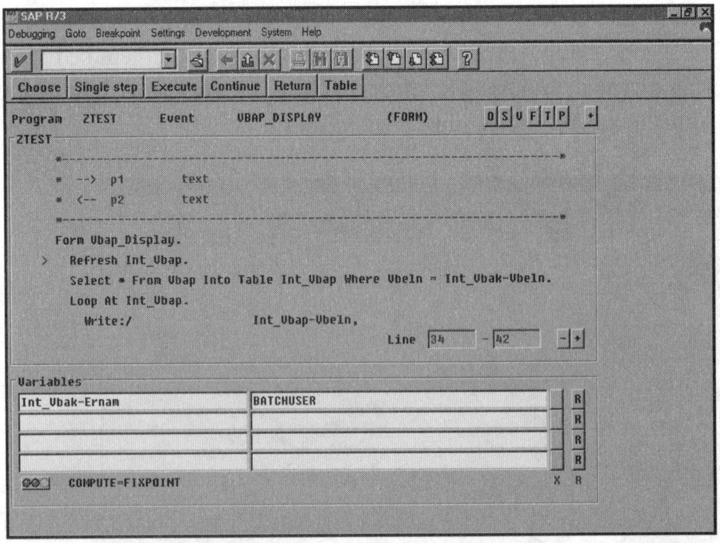

FIGURE 18-15

The debugger has navigated from the PERFORM *statement into the actual subroutine itself.*

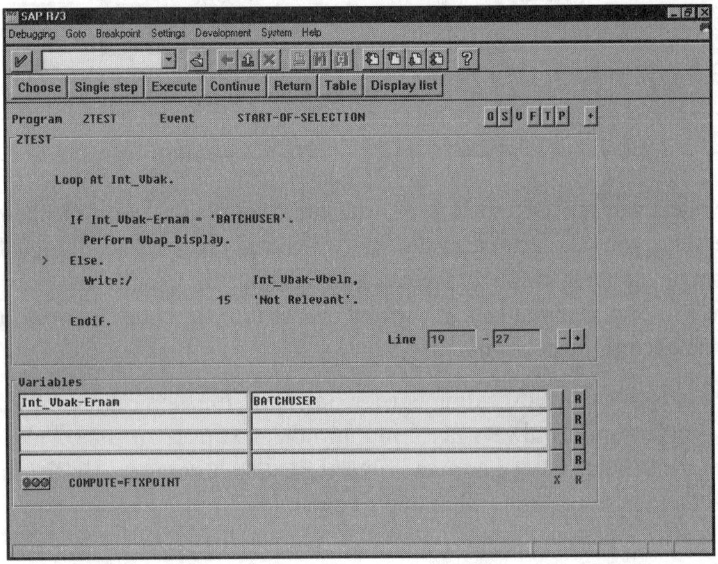

FIGURE 18-16

Using the EXECUTE *button, you do not navigate into the subroutine, but rather proceed to the next step, in this case the '*ELSE*' statement.*

This functionality is very desirable. For example, if you are ten layers deep inside SAP code, there is no need for you to single step through this function module, especially if it is in a loop and is repeated several hundred or thousand times. The Execute command is very useful in situations like this.

Continue

The next button is the Continue button. This button releases the program from running step by step to running freely through the code. The benefit is that the program stops if it reaches a manually set breakpoint, or a hard-coded breakpoint in the code. To set a manual breakpoint in the code, you have two choices. Either double-click to the left of the line of code, and a stop sign icon appears to left of the code (See Figure 18-17), or click on the line of code at which you wish to place a breakpoint, and follow the menu path Breakpoint | Set/delete (See Figure 18-18).

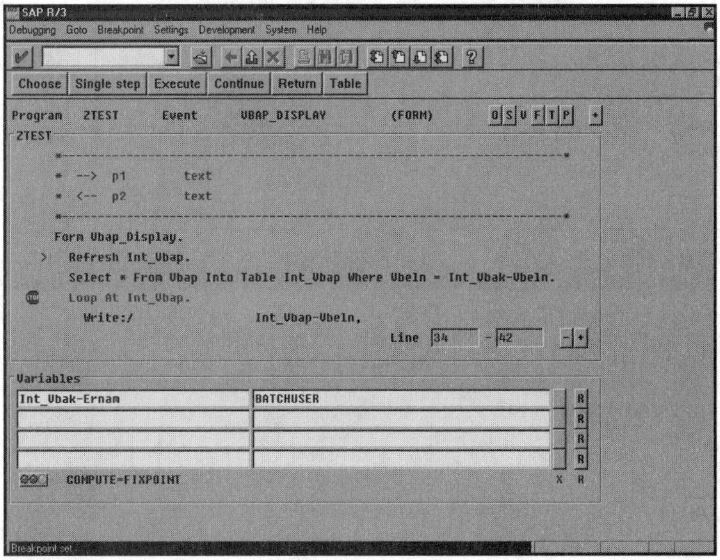

FIGURE 18-17

If you double-click to the left of a line of code, a stop sign appears, which represents a break point.

Another method is to code a breakpoint into your code. The two commands are:

```
Break-Point.
```

or

```
Break <username>.
```

The more desirable of the two choices is the second one. If you are debugging code that is being used by other developers, you do not want them kicked into debug mode while they are running their programs. The second coding method is better because the breakpoint is only triggered if you are the one running the code (assuming the username you enter is your own). So, for example, put a breakpoint inside your code. BREAK <USERNAME> executes a global macro that has a break point command in it which is only triggered if the user, <USERNAME> is running the code. Creating and

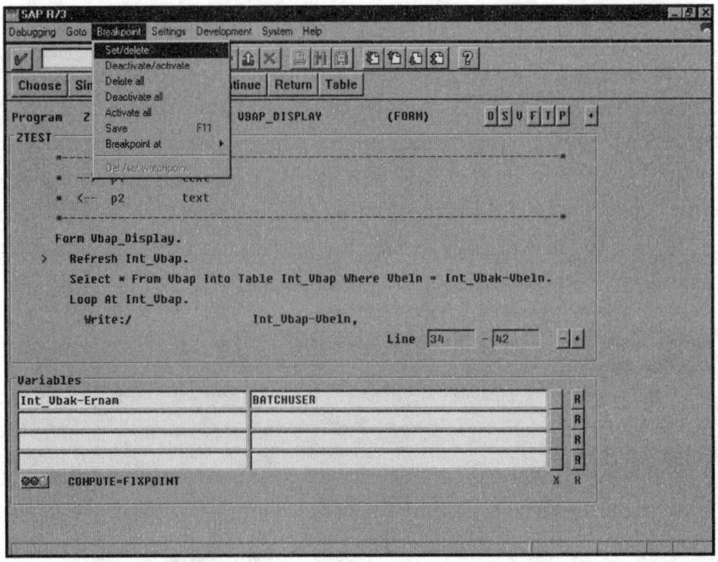

FIGURE 18-18

Another way to set a break point is by following the menu path Breakpoint|Set/delete.

defining macros will be covered in the soon-to-be-released ABAP/4 book covering advanced topics in programming R/3.

```
REPORT ZTEST .


TABLES: VBAK,
        VBAP.


PARAMETERS: P_DATUM LIKE SY-DATUM.


DATA: BEGIN OF INT_VBAK OCCURS 1000.
        INCLUDE STRUCTURE VBAK.
DATA: END OF INT_VBAK.


DATA: BEGIN OF INT_VBAP OCCURS 1000.
        INCLUDE STRUCTURE VBAP.
DATA: END OF INT_VBAP.



SELECT * FROM VBAK INTO TABLE INT_VBAK WHERE
                                             ERDAT = P_DATUM.
```

```
LOOP AT INT_VBAK.

  IF INT_VBAK-ERNAM = 'BATCHUSER'.
    BREAK GARETHD.
    PERFORM VBAP_DISPLAY.
  ELSE.
    WRITE:/                    INT_VBAK-VBELN,
                         15    'Not Relevant'.
  ENDIF.

ENDLOOP.
*&---------------------------------------------------------------------*
*&      Form  VBAP_DISPLAY
*&---------------------------------------------------------------------*
*       text                                                           *
*----------------------------------------------------------------------*
*  -->  p1        text
*  <--  p2        text
*----------------------------------------------------------------------*
FORM VBAP_DISPLAY.
  REFRESH INT_VBAP.
  SELECT * FROM VBAP INTO TABLE INT_VBAP WHERE
                                       VBELN = INT_VBAK-VBELN.
  LOOP AT INT_VBAP.
    WRITE:/                    INT_VBAP-VBELN,
                         11    INT_VBAP-POSNR,
                         20    INT_VBAP-ARKTX.
  ENDLOOP.

ENDFORM.                                  " VBAP_DISPLAY
```

The breakpoint is put into your code after the line:

```
IF INT_VBAK-ERNAM = 'BATCHUSER'
```

This way, the program can execute in a normal fashion, and the debugging screen appears when breakpoint is encountered. Also, one can enter debug mode, and click on the Continue button. If a breakpoint is encountered, either manually set or coded, the program halts at that point. The Continue button allows you to skip parts of code which you do not suspect of having problems. The Continue feature improves your efficiency in debugging programs.

Return

Return is a fairly simple command. Imagine that you are debugging a program and the program calls a subroutine which in turn calls a function module. You single step through the code and find yourself inside the function module code. By pressing the return button, the debugger returns you and the marker > to the next higher level (in this case to the point in the subroutine where the function module is called). If you press Return again, the debugger navigates you to the next higher level which is the main program, and leaves you at the point just after the subroutine is called. This command is especially helpful when debugging SAP code or transactional code because sometimes you can find yourself many layers deep inside code.

Display List

One additional command which may or may not display is the Display List button. This button displays if a report is being run or a transaction and a `WRITE` command is executed. By pressing it, you see the existing output in regular report format. See Figure 18-19.

Press the Program button to return to the regular debugging screen (V view). The Program button always displays when you are in a view other than the V view. Press the V or the Program button to return to your default view.

Watchpoints

Watchpoints are used to dynamically set breakpoints in your code. If a variable (either the header of an internal table, or any field) is marked as a watchpoint, the program halts in debug mode every time the value inside that field changes. For example, your program loops through a series of sales orders, printing the line items for each one. If you want to look for one particular sales order, or perhaps in another program see where a variable changes (on which line), you would put `INT_VBAK-VBELN` in the first column of the initial debugging screen. See Figure 18-20.

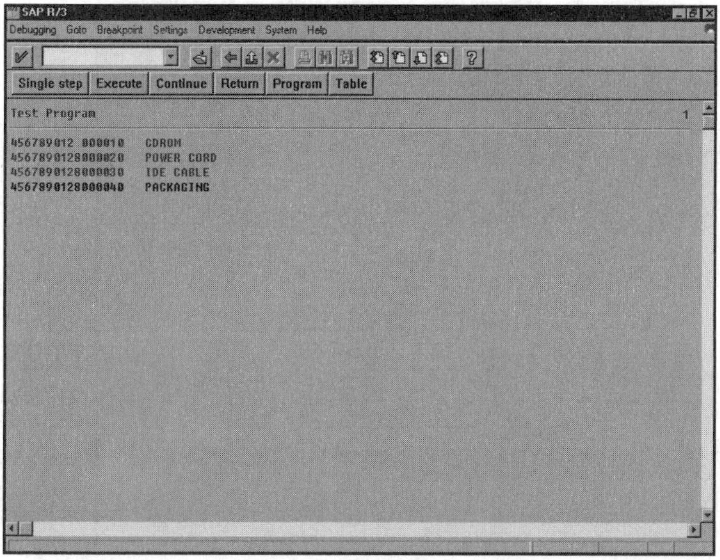

FIGURE 18-19

List Display shown in debugging.

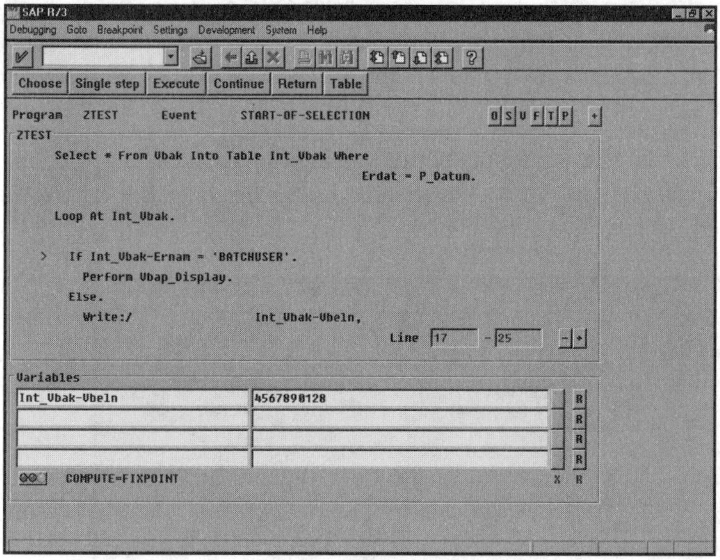

FIGURE 18-20

The initial debugging screen with the field, INT_VBAK-VBELN *shown in one of the variable columns*

Double-click on the field, select the field, and click on the Choose button, or just click the F view button. Place a check mark in the Watchpoint box next to the field and press Return, or click on the Watchpoint on/off button. See Figure 18-21 for illustration.

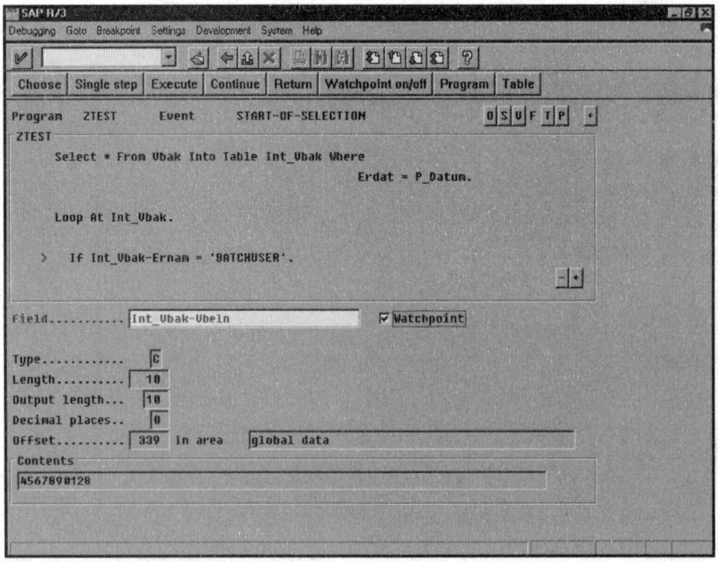

FIGURE 18-21

The Field or "F" view of the variable INT_VBAK-VBELN. *This view shows the watchpoint checkbox.*

Click on the Program button to return back to the main screen. Click on the Continue button. The program immediately stops at the line after the LOOP AT INT_VBAK. A message at the bottom of the screen reads "Watchpoint triggered." See Figure 18-22.

If you click on the Continue button again, the program stops again at this line; however, the INT_VBAK-VBELN value has changed to the next value in the internal table.

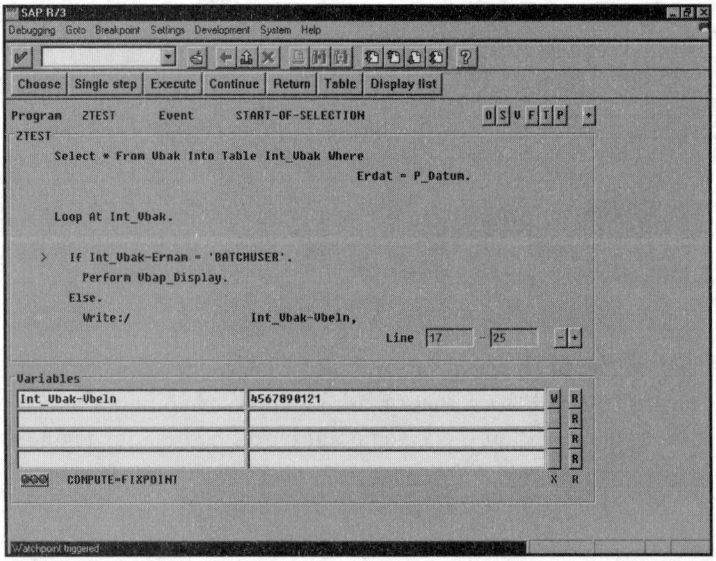

FIGURE 18-22

When a watchpoint is triggered, the program stops at the line where the variable has changed.

Internal Tables

The most important view is the Internal Table view. The contents of internal tables can display in this view. To display database table values, you must use the General Table Display. Run your test program once again. This time, set a breakpoint just after the `SELECT` statement from the database table `VBAK`. See Figure 18-23.

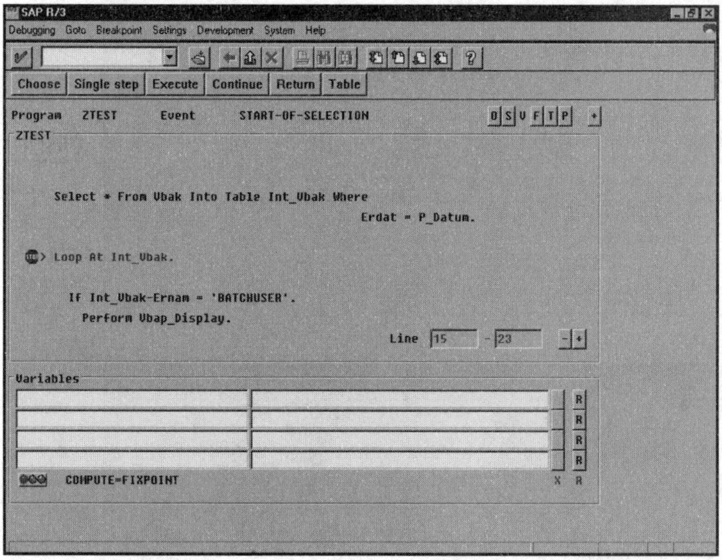

FIGURE 18-23

A breakpoint has been set just after the `SELECT` *statement in your program.*

With the marker right after the SQL statement, you hope that an internal table is populated. If `SY-SUBRC` displays below the four rows with a value other than zero, there will be no records in your internal table. Try using a different date until you retrieve data. Now that you have data in your internal table, it is time to look at its contents. Click on the Table button or the T view button. Type in `INT_VBAK` for the name of the internal table and press Return to display its contents.

If you press Shift+F12, or press the Last Page button in the command bar, you will see the last records in the internal table, as well as the number of entries in the internal table.

Take a look at a few other buttons and entry boxes on this screen. To the right of the box where you entered the name of the internal table is the Index box. Enter a number in this box (500 was used for Figure 18-25), and that record number is the top line in the display, with its proceeding records displayed after it.

The Format box is next to the Index box. You may view the internal table in one of three formats. E is to display the columns with formatting. X is to display the lines in hexadecimal format. C is to display the line in type C format. E is the most intuitive

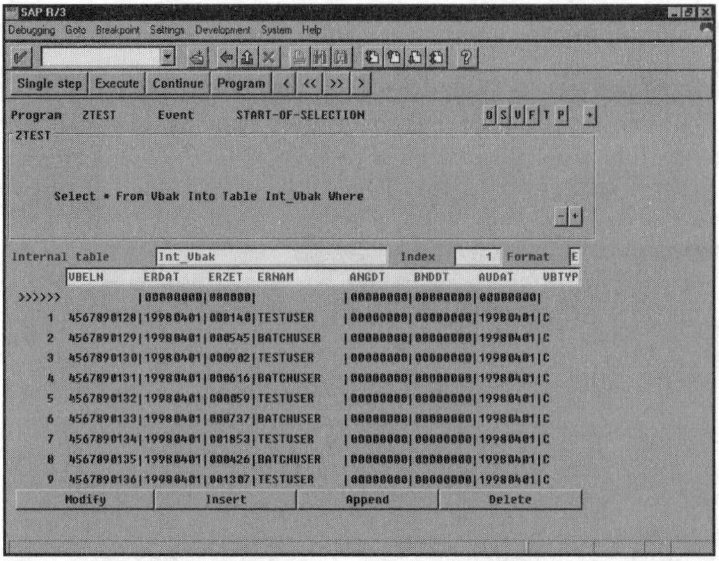

FIGURE 18-24

The internal table view of the internal table `INT_VBAK`, *showing what data it contains*

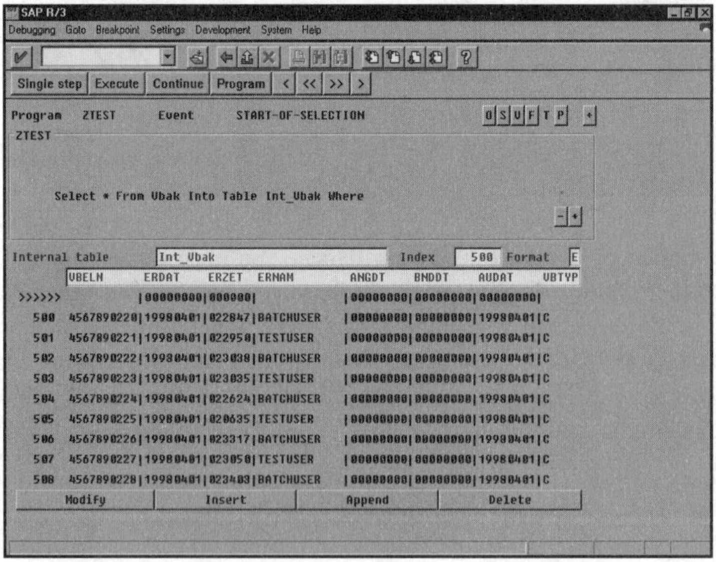

FIGURE 18-25

By entering a record number in the index box, you can navigate through the data stored in the internal table.

way to look at the table, so try not to use X. C displays the internal table as if you were to look at the contents in ASCII format. All of the column headings are removed and so are the separators between fields.

There are a few new buttons to click on the screen. Click << to move left one field at a time. Click >> to move right one field at a time. Click < to move to the first field in the table. Click > to move to the last field in the table.

The last four buttons on the bottom row allow you to modify, insert, append, and delete the internal table.

The Modify button is used by selecting a row again and then depressing Modify. That row is now editable. Be sure to edit the correct field though. Change any values, and then press Enter on the keyboard. The change is made.

The Insert button is similar except that you are allowed to fill a row with data. Select a row and click the Insert button. The row that occupied the position before moves to the next higher position. You can enter information in that row. See Figure 18-26.

The Append button is exactly the same as the Insert button, except that you are adding a record at the very end of the internal table.

To delete a row, select a row and click the Delete button. The row is deleted.

Press Enter on your keyboard after you finish entering the appropriate data. The record is an official record of the internal table.

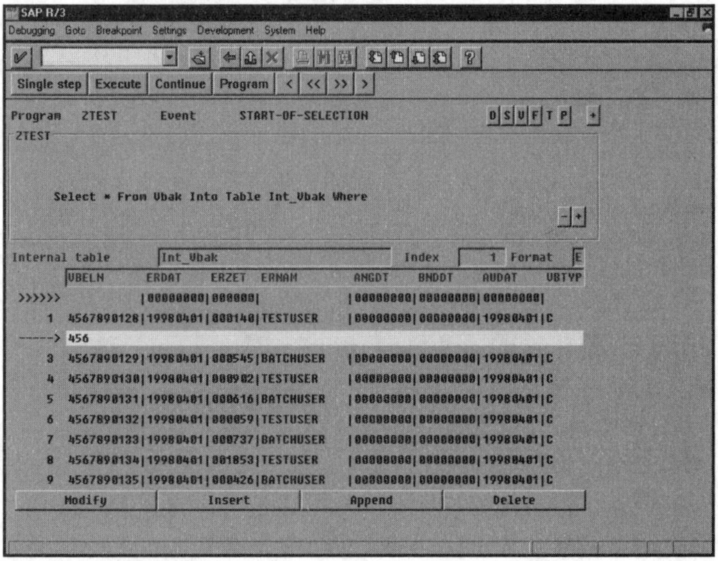

FIGURE 18-26

By clicking on the INSERT *button, you can enter your own data into a record in the internal table.*

Breakpoints

You already know how to set breakpoints by double-clicking on lines, setting watchpoints, and coding breaks in the code. However, there are a few other methods worth mentioning.

The breakpoints that are very useful to you are shown in the expanded drop-down menu in Figure 18-27. A breakpoint is set at the beginning of each of these entities. If the program reaches one of these breakpoints, the program stops at that line. The three choices are:

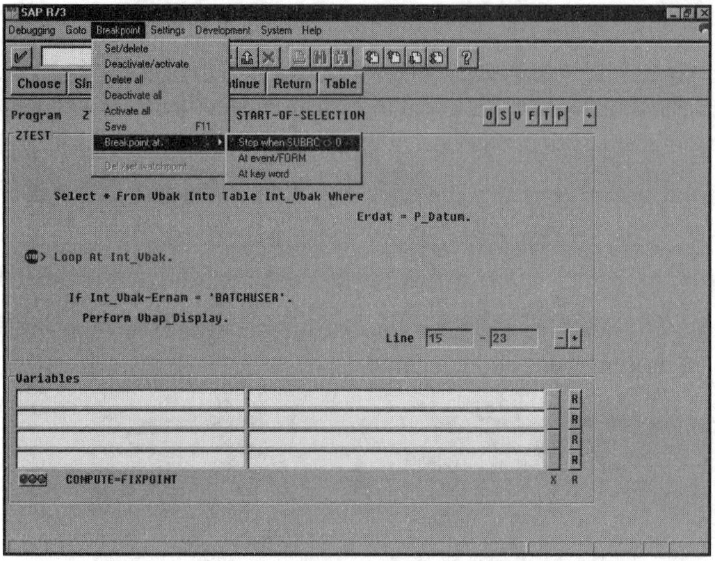

FIGURE 18-27

Drop-down menu of Breakpoints

- Stop when SY-SUBRC <> 0—When there is an error, or for some reason the system field, SY-SUBRC, is set to a value other than zero, the program stops in debug mode at the next line in the code.
- At event/FORM — pick either a form, a function module, or an event that is inside the program. See Figure 18-28.
- At key word — set a breakpoint at a key word. A key word is any ABAP/4 command. See Figure 18-29.

If you enter any ABAP/4 command, a breakpoint is set at that command inside your program or in any subsequent programs your program calls. When the program encounters the breakpoint, it stops in debug mode at that line.

Tips and Techniques

Just as with anything you do in life, learning the parts does not always make you an expert on the whole. You must learn how to easily navigate through programs and quickly find the source of errors. There is no secret in this section to tell you how to do this except the old adage, "Practice makes perfect." Keep debugging and you will get more and more efficient at the process. Some helpful tips are:

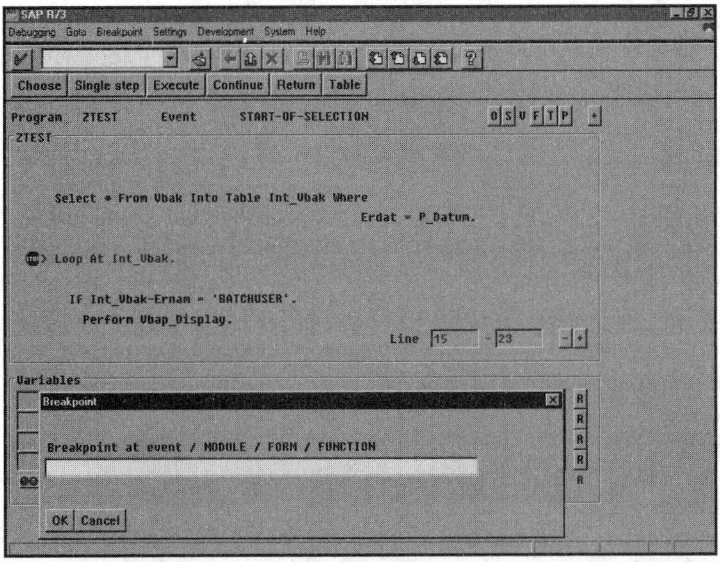

FIGURE 18-28

Popup box to enter form/function module/event

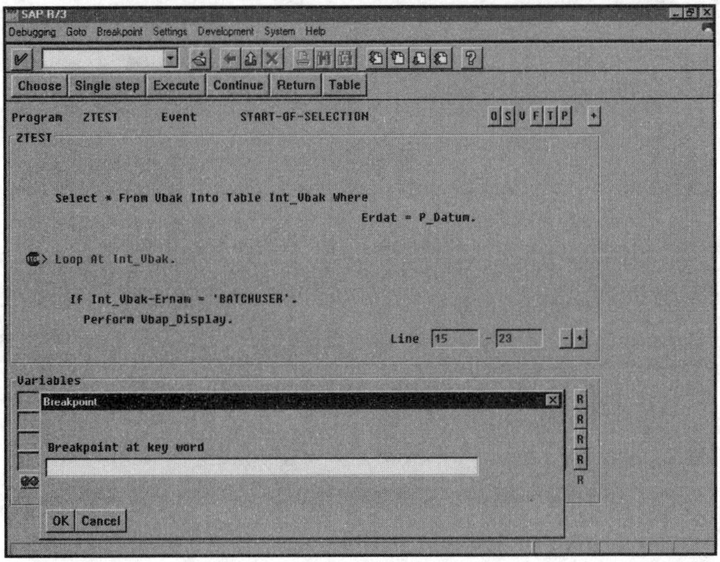

FIGURE 18-29

Breakpoint at key word

Do not debug inside an open SELECT statement because you will get an ABAP/4 short dump. While the database cursor is open (a SELECT statement has not retrieved all of its records from the database), debugging will not be permitted. Instead, set a breakpoint after the ENDSELECT statement and let the program run its course until it arrives at the breakpoint.

Set breakpoints at certain safety points: for example, in case you happen to click the Continue button instead of the Single step button, and don't want your program to finish. Try to set breakpoints at strategic points in your code where they will stop you just before crucial steps in your code. Especially use this technique if you are updating the database in any way.

If you have worked with SAP for a while, you probably noticed that certain programs run differently in background mode than in foreground mode. Foreground is typically defined as executing the program from the ABAP/4 editor. Background mode can also be triggered from the editor, or it can be started from the job monitoring screen. If you execute a program in background mode, you can still debug the program from the job monitoring screen (see Figure 18-30).

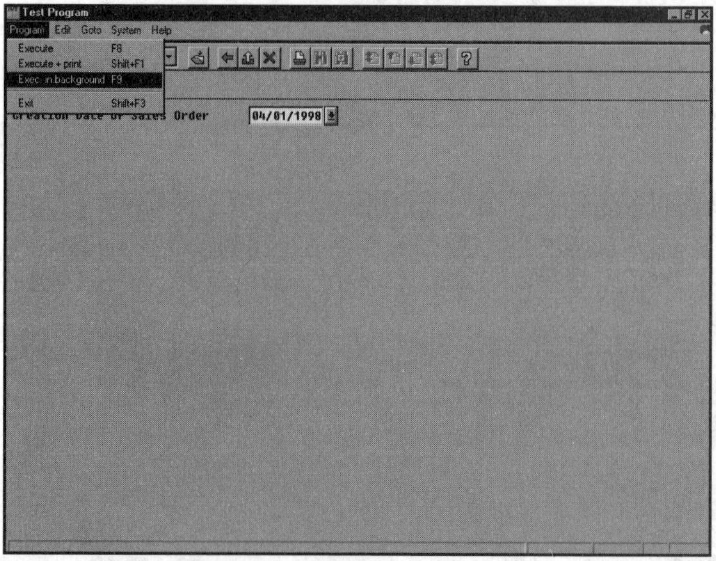

FIGURE 18-30

Path to execute in background mode

Navigate to the job monitoring screen, which displays all background programs that are running. Follow the menu path from any SAP screen, System | Services | Jobs | Job Overview. You will reach the initial job overview screen. See Figure 18-31.

Enter the name of your program in the Job Name text box, replacing the *. Press Return. You reach a screen showing your program and its status. See Figure 18-32.

If the program is still active, click on it once, and then follow the menu path Job | Capture. See Figure 18-33.

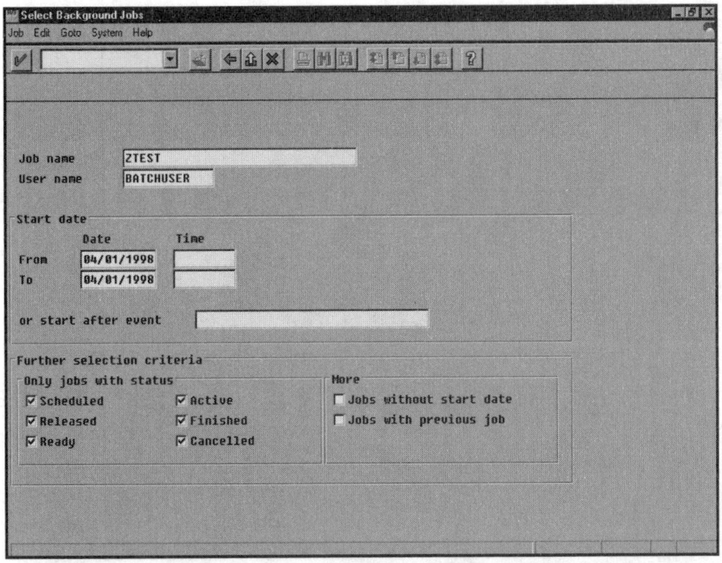

FIGURE 18-31

Initial job overview screen

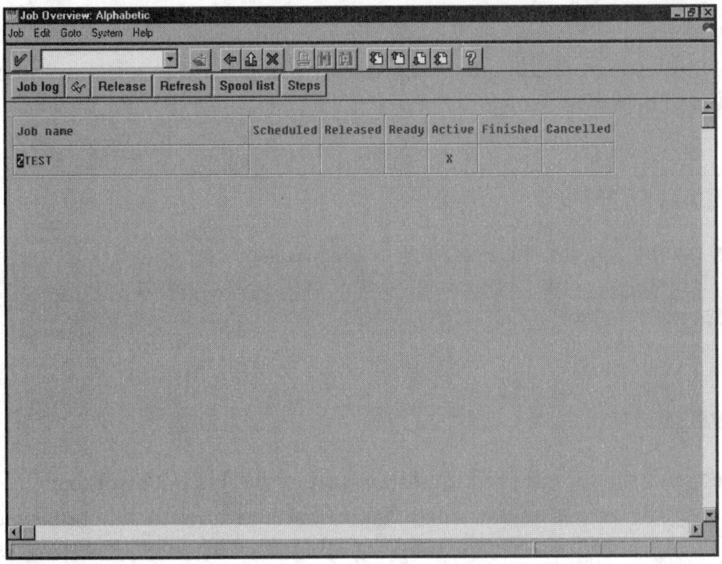

FIGURE 18-32

Screen showing your program as "Active" in background mode

Be patient and wait a few seconds and a new screen appears, which looks exactly like the debugging screen you were working with. From then on, use all the techniques that were mentioned to debug the program as usual. To make the screen disappear and to get the program to continue, clear all breakpoints and click on Continue.

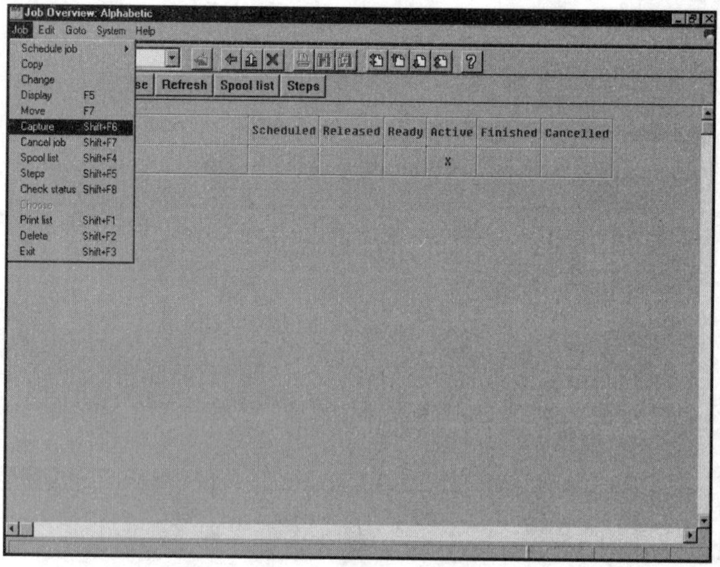

FIGURE 18-33

To debug a program running in background mode, follow the menu path and select "Capture".

For fast and efficient debugging, you can use a combination of setting watchpoints on variables and setting breakpoints at key words. Using these two features in conjunction proves to be very effective.

CAUTION

Be very careful about debugging in a production environment. If you debug a transaction and stop the debug halfway through, some records may be updated and some may not.

Summary

The debugger is the second most important tool in the ABAP/4 workbench. The first is, of course, the actual editor. This chapter covered how to navigate around the debugger tool, as well as the functionality of each of its parts. Knowing your way around the debugger and the functionality of each view and button is very important. The debugging tool in SAP is a very simple one, and if you work through it step by step, it will not intimidate you. Try to use each part, one at a time, before you tackle a complex debugging project.

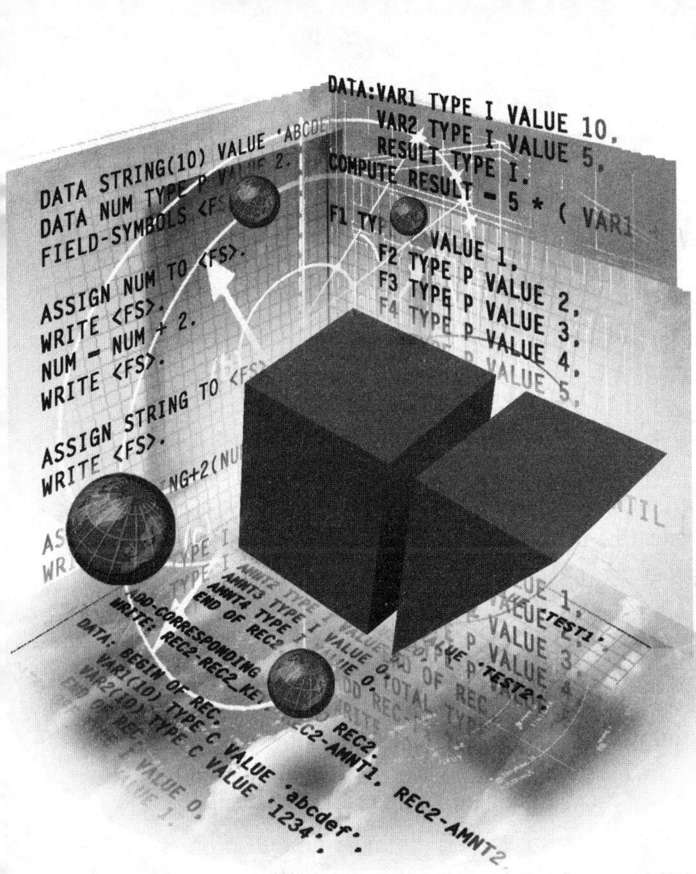

Chapter 19

Performance Analysis

In This Chapter

- The ABAP/4 Runtime Analysis Tool
- SQL Trace

This chapter introduces some of the basics of SAP R/3 performance analysis. Like any complex system, SAP R/3 has multiple variables which affect performance. The area you will focus on is the performance of ABAP/4 programs. R/3 provides several tools to assist programmers in evaluating the performance of programs. These tools can monitor the performance of programs and record the steps the program takes.

The ABAP/4 Runtime Analysis Tool

The Runtime Analysis Tool captures information about a program as it's being run. After the program completes this information, it can be displayed for the programmer to get a better understanding of what occurred during the execution. Examples of information would be: which database tables are being accessed, how long it took to retrieve the information, and which subroutines took the most time to process. The programmer can then use this information to focus on the parts of the program which most affect the runtime. Another good use for the tool is to capture data about SAP programs and transactions. For example, if you are asked to write a report about customers but you are unsure of which database tables contain customer information. You could use the tool to trace SAP transactions such as VD03 and view the tables accessed by the transaction. This would give you a starting point for your report.

The Runtime Analysis Tool is accessed via transaction `SE30`. From this first screen (Figure 19-1) the analysis is started. The first step is to enter the program name or transaction code to be analyzed.

There are several optional check boxes that control how the analysis is done:

- With Subroutines

This records the usage of a perform command. If this is not checked, the activity within that form is still recorded but it is not grouped into a discrete block. You should always leave this checked.

- With Internal Tables

Records all internal table activity such as append, insert, and sort. Check this if you are interested in this sort of activity.

- With Technical DB Info

This setting is for SAP use only and should not be checked.

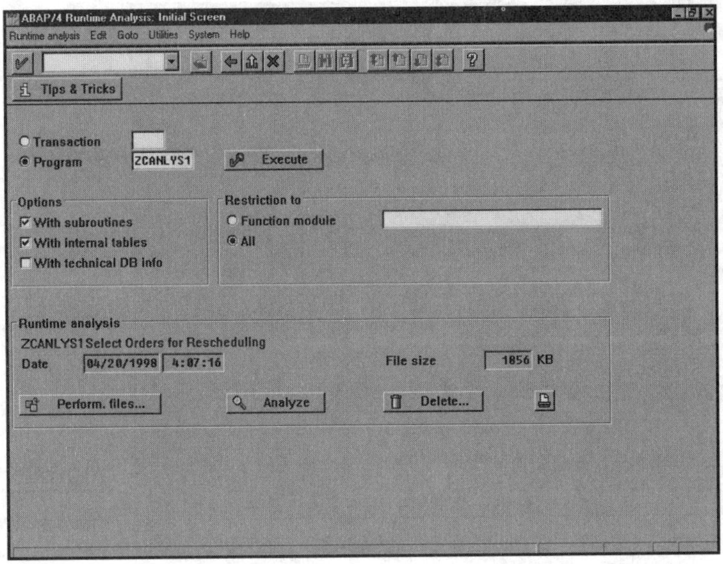

FIGURE 19-1

Runtime Analysis Tool screen one

Once the options are set, the program may be executed by clicking the Execute button. The program then fully executes, enters any parameters or screen data, and then when the program or transaction comes to an end, returns you to the first screen. All system activity is captured in a log file.

When you return to the first screen, a new set of buttons appears if you had never completed a runtime analysis before. The last log file created by the tool is displayed. Click the analyze button to display the results. The next screen displayed is shown in Figure 19-2. This is the overview screen. As the name implies, it presents an overview of the activity recorded during the execution of the program. The bar graph seen at the top of the screen breaks down the total execution time into ABAP/4, Database, and R/3 System. ABAP/4 refers to the processing of ABAP/4 commands on the application server. Database refers to the time spent accessing the database server. R/3 System refers to the overhead of R/3 system activity, which coordinates all programs being executed.

In the lower portion of the screen, you will see information regarding memory usage and conversions. In general, a lower value for both these figures is best. Conversions refer to converting one data type to another. Conversions involving packed decimals, type P, are very costly and should be avoided when possible. You can click on any of the statistics to display the source code where the conversion is being done.

From the overview, you can reach any of the detailed screens. The four buttons across the top take you to the four detail screens. They are:

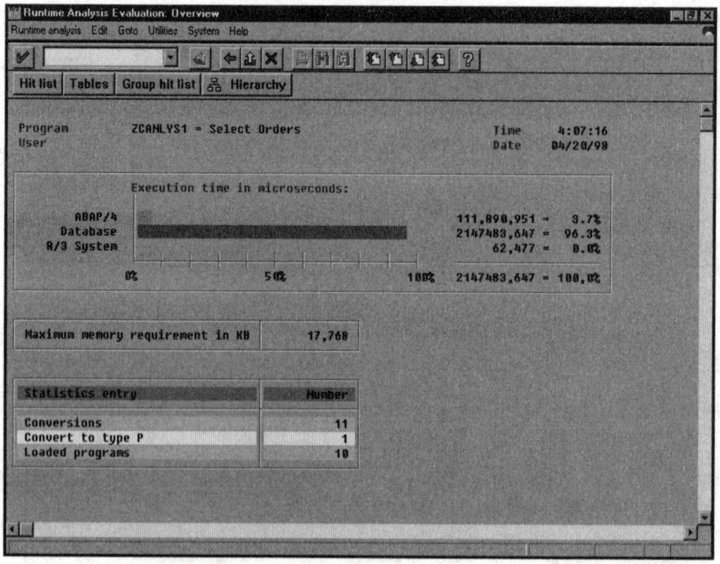

FIGURE 19-2

Runtime Analysis overview screen

- Hit List

  Displays the execution time of each statement in the program.
- Tables

  Displays the database tables accessed during the executing.
- Group Hit List

  Displays the execution time of all statements while grouping them based on type of command, such as performs, SQL, and internal tables.
- Hierarchy

  Displays the execution time of each statement in the actual order in which they were executed. Uses indentation to indicate the level of nesting of statements within subroutines.

In Figure 19-3, the Hit List screen is displayed. It lists the execution time of all statements in descending order. Totals are listed for each type of statement, so if you have the same command executed twice in the program, it appears only once in this list and the time listed is the total time for both.

The Absolute<->% button switches between the execution time of a statement in microseconds and the percentage of execution time spent on the statement. In general, percentage is the most usable setting because it allows you to easily judge between the impact of two statements.

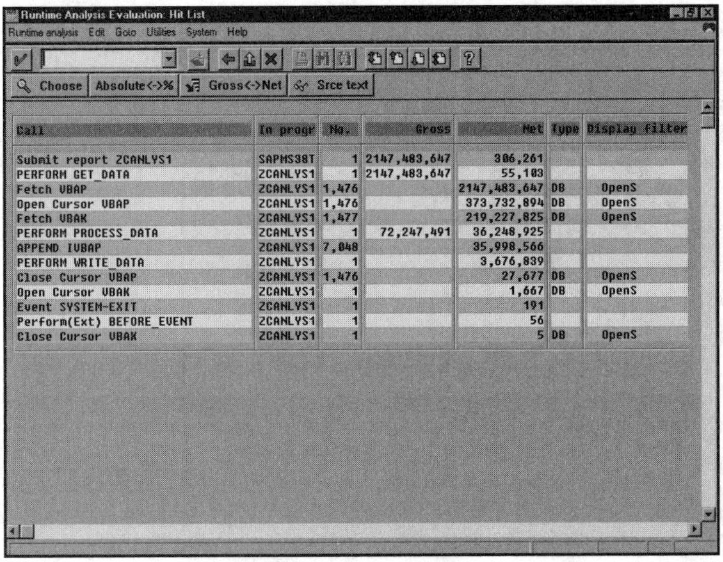

FIGURE 19-3

Hit List screen

The Gross<->Net button sorts the list by gross time and by net time. Gross Time is only displayed for commands which call subroutines such as perform, submit, and call function. Gross time is the total time taken by the subroutine call. Net time for these commands is equal to the gross time of the command minus the net time of all commands within the subroutine. Basically, net time is the overhead associated with making the subroutine call. Selecting a statement and clicking the Choose button brings up a list of each time that command is called in the program. Double-clicking on a statement has the same effect.

The final button is Srce Text. If you select a statement and click Srce Text, it takes you directly to the source code from which that statement is called. If the statement is called multiple times, it brings up a list of all times it is called. You can select one of them and click Srce Text again to go to the source code.

The next screen is the Tables screen as seen in Figure 19-4. This is a list of all database tables and information such as the number of accesses, the total time, and so on. By double-clicking on a table name, it brings up a list of all statements which access that table.

This screen is very useful if you need to find out which tables hold a certain type of data. Simply use the tool on a program or transaction that accesses the data you are interested in and go to the Tables screen. The data should be in one of the tables listed. The description of each table should help you find the right one. From the statement list, you can get to the location in the source code where the `SELECT` statement is. This gives you all the information you need to access this data yourself.

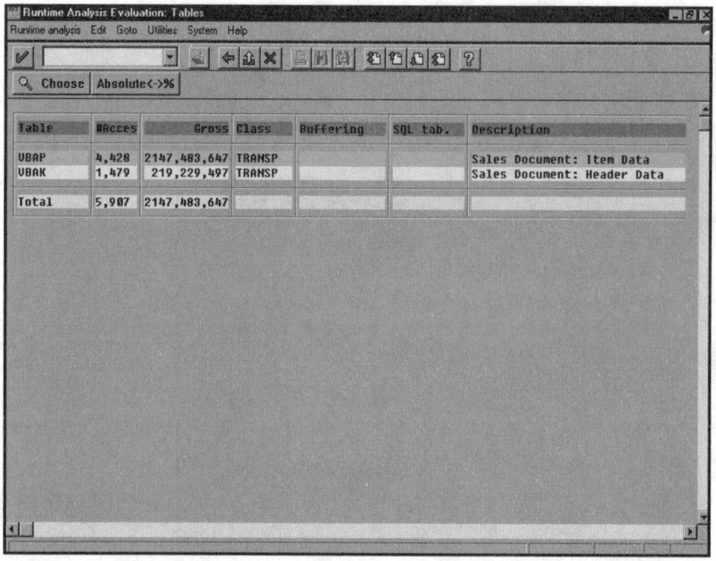

FIGURE 19-4

Database Tables screen

The next screen is the Group Hit List and can be seen in Figure 19-5. The functionality is similar to the Hit list except the statements are grouped by type of command.

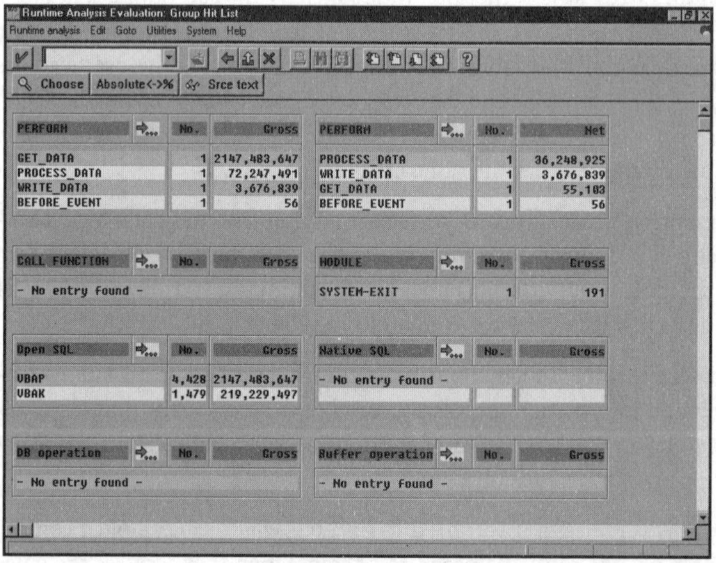

FIGURE 19-5

Group Hit List screen

The final screen is the Hierarchy and can be seen in Figure 19-6. In this screen, all statements are listed in the exact order in which they were executed. Statements, which are part of a subroutine, are indented. If you are coding your programs properly and using subroutines to break down tasks into small pieces, it's very easy to

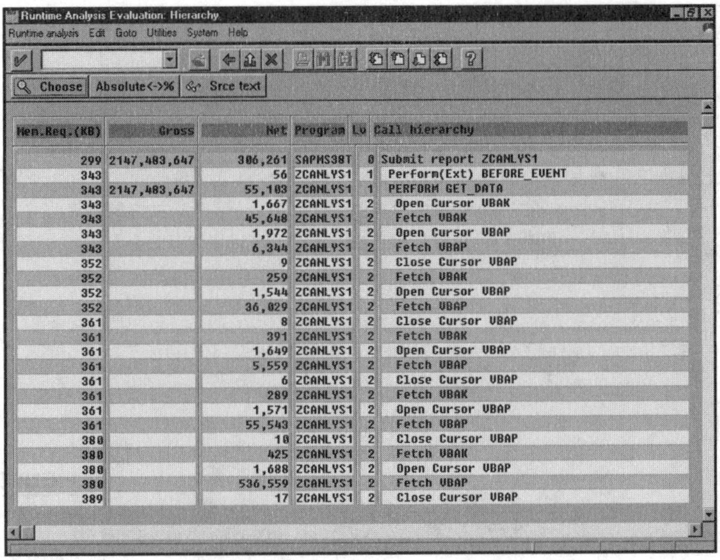

FIGURE 19-6

The Hierarchy screen

understand how each piece affects the total performance of your program. Double-clicking on a statement brings you to a version of the overview screen. But in this case, it will be an overview of that statement only. For statements that call subroutines, this works very nicely. For example, you can get an overview of the activity in a Function Module by double-clicking on the Call Function Statement.

The Runtime Analysis tool is extremely important to writing ABAP/4 programs that perform efficiently. But, since it focuses on a single program and not on overall system performance, it only presents part of the picture. It is important to do testing in a larger context and understand how your programs impact the overall system. But for fine-tuning of a single program, the tool provides a wealth of features to aid you.

The SQL Trace

Another tool which helps you understand how your programs affect system performance is the SQL Trace. SQL Trace captures information about database access made on the system. Unlike the Runtime Analysis, SQL Trace is not limited to a single program. It can be turned on for a single user and all activity by that user is logged. After the logging is complete, SQL trace provides tools to analyze the logs.

The SQL Trace is accessed through transaction `ST05`. The first screen is seen in Figure 19-7. It is here that the trace is turned on. Once it is turned on, you can run transactions and programs as you normally would. When you have completed the activities you are interested in tracing, return to transaction `ST05` and click the trace off button. You can then begin the analysis of the trace log by clicking list trace.

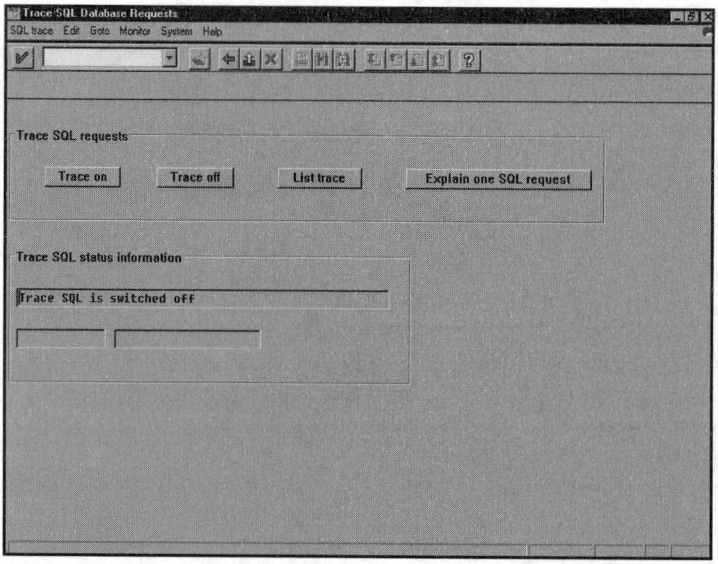

FIGURE 19-7

The SQL Trace control screen

The first screen of the trace is seen in Figure 19-8. This is simply the raw trace log showing every database access made by the user for the duration of the trace. Included is information such as the program making the request, the table being accessed, and the text of the database access.

By clicking on a line and clicking the Details button, the raw text of the database request can be seen. See Figure 19-9 for an example of details on a `SELECT` statement. In general, this is of little use.

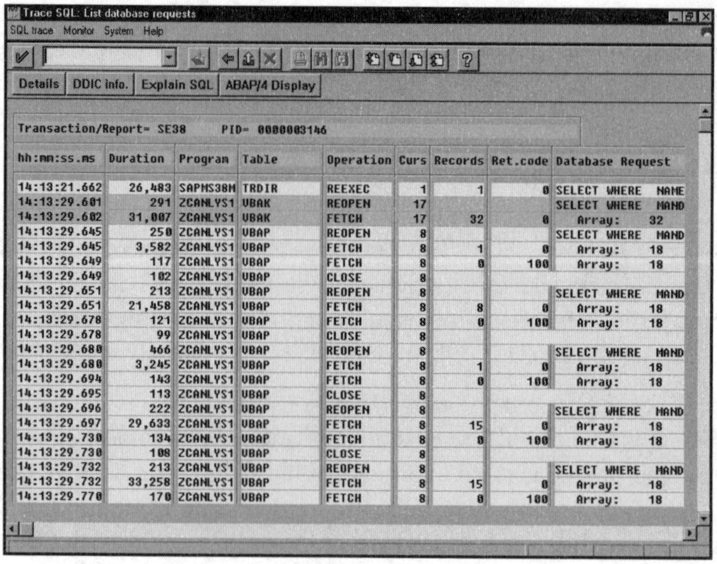

FIGURE 19-8

SQL Trace Log screen

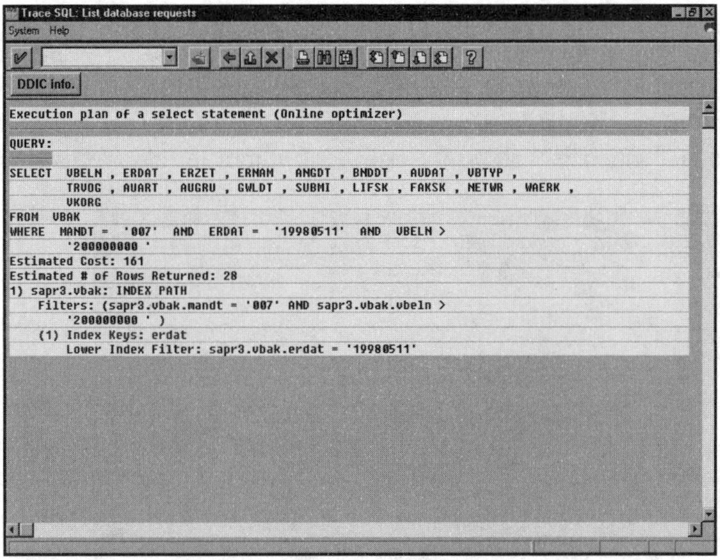

FIGURE 19-9

Details of the database request

Another option from the SQL Trace Log screen (Figure 19-8) is available by selecting a line and clicking the DDIC info button; you can get detailed information on the database table. As seen in Figure 19-10, information such as a description, type, and indices are listed. This saves you the time of looking up the information in the data dictionary manually.

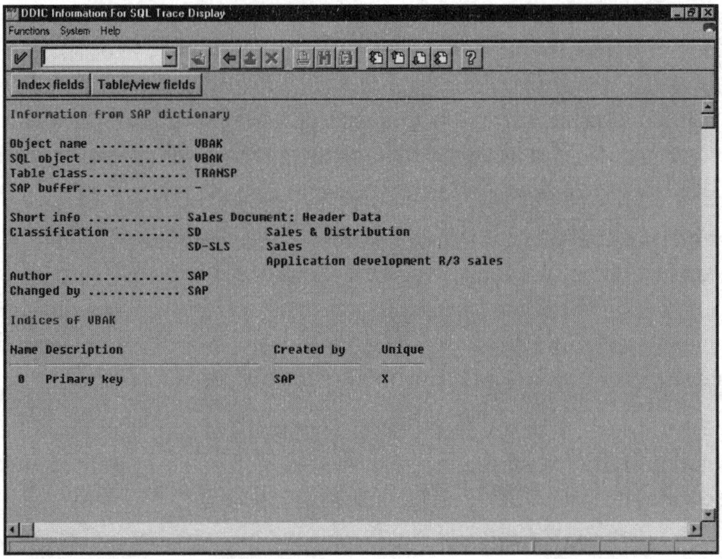

FIGURE 19-10

Data dictionary information

The most useful button available from the SQL Trace Log screen (Figure 19-8) is the Explain SQL button. By clicking on an Open or Prepare select record, an explain plan can be displayed for the statement. The exact syntax of the explain plan will vary based on the type of database you are using, but in general they will have similar information. Figure 19-11 shows the explain plan from an Informix database.

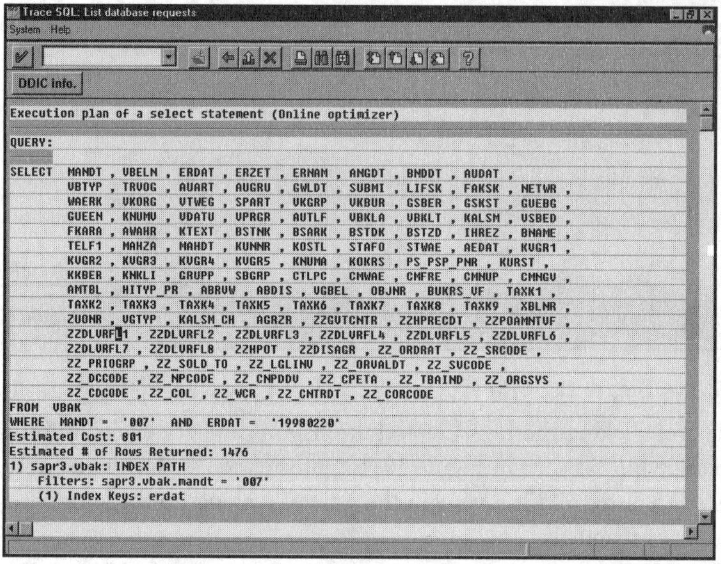

FIGURE 19-11

The explain plan from an Informix database

The most important piece of information on the screen is the estimated cost at the bottom. Here the database attempts to rate how expensive the SELECT statement will be to perform. The lower the number the better. What you can do is experiment with specifying different criteria in the WHERE clause to get the best result with the estimated cost. In general, if you can use the primary key fields as criteria or any fields in the secondary indices, you will get better results.

The index information found at the very bottom is also important. If an index is being used to access the table, it will be found here. You should try modifying your SELECT statement if you know that an index exists for a table but it did not show up in the explain plan. Often times it is useful for developers to work with their database administrator to tune select statements to get the best possible results.

SQL trace is very useful, so it is important to get familiar with it. If you do not have a background in relational databases, make sure to get some help from your administrator when attempting to analyze the results of the trace. The basics of database theory are very easy to pick up. You will be surprised at how fast you learn to recognize the differences between a well written SQL statement and a poor one.

Summary

These SQL Trace and Runtime Anaylsis tools are extremely important when developing software in ABAP/4. They should be used as part of a complete program of performance tuning. See Chapter 20, "Performance Tuning" for detailed tips on writing code for optimal performance.

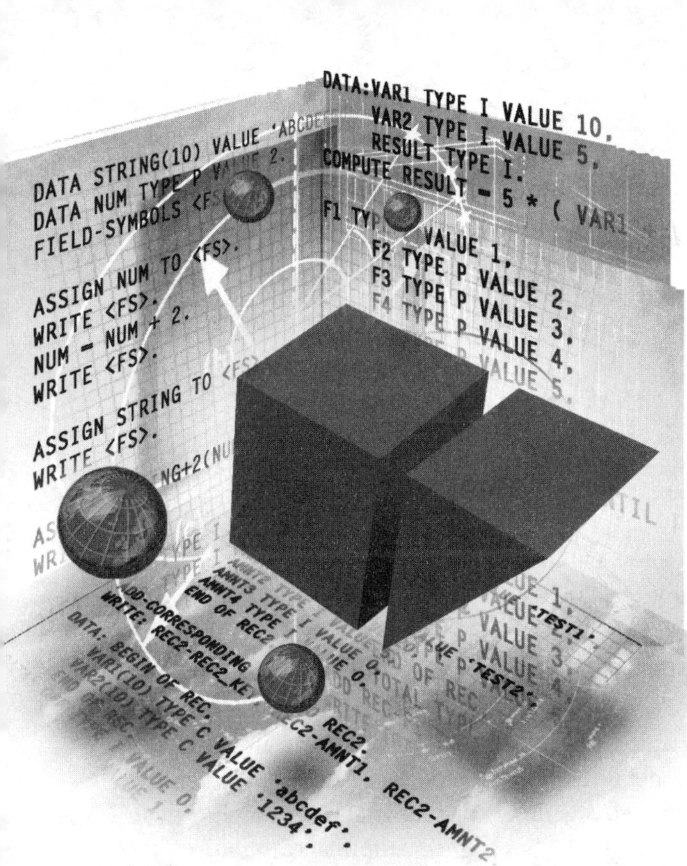

Chapter 20

Performance Tuning

In This Chapter

- Using `SELECT *`
- Using the Primary Key
- Using `CHECK` Statements
- Using Tables
- Using the `MOVE` Statement
- Looping
- Choosing Internal Tables Versus Field Groups
- Working with Logical Databases
- Using Batching Versus Online Programs

Performance tuning is the task to which most of the senior ABAP programmers will be assigned. Essentially, this task is defined as *making current code faster*. This chapter highlights some methods by which you, as a new programmer, can accomplish this task in your own code. Whereas you might not be assigned performance-tuning tasks for some time, by following a few tips from this chapter you can gain a reputation for having clean efficient code that doesn't need to be performance-tuned.

SAP has graciously provided a list of performance tips for the programmer. Besides the tips listed in this chapter, it is an excellent resource from which to learn good programming skills. Follow the menu path System|Utilities|Runtime Analysis from any screen in SAP. A new screen will appear, which looks like Figure 20-1.

Click on any of the green hands and you will be hyperlinked with the supporting documentation explaining each tip.

Using SELECT *

The most notorious problem in most ABAP/4 programs exists with the use of the `SELECT *` statement, which extracts data from database tables. If the search is done improperly, the program can take hours upon hours to finish; however, if the same program is written efficiently, it can take just minutes.

If you refer to Chapter 8, which covers SAP and SQL, you will find new ABAP/4 functionality on how to write a join statement in ABAP/4. If you are reading from multiple tables, learn how to use this statement effectively.

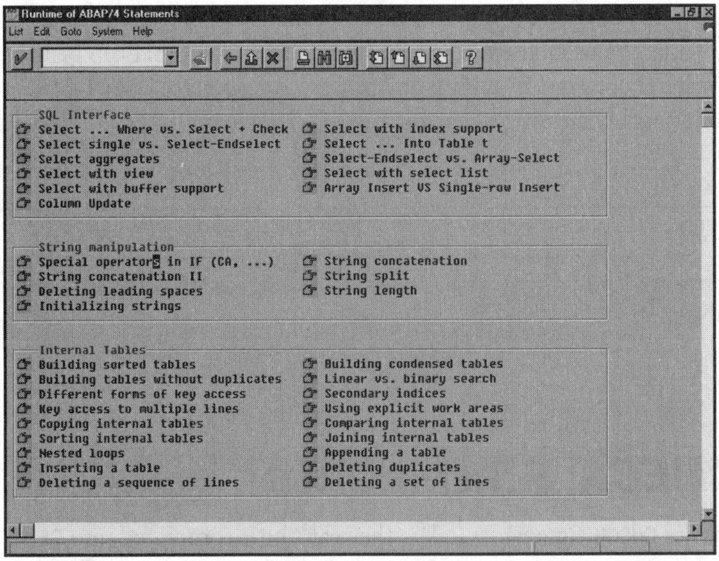

FIGURE 20-1

The "tips and tricks" screen in SAP—helpful tips to make you a better programmer

The first tip to you as a programmer is to choose the proper order by which you read the tables. Some tables exist in partnership with each other. There are header tables that contain the summary data for a particular part, while another table contains the line-item-level detail for that part.

TIP

Read the header table first, and then read the line-item table. If you need to read a certain table several times in a program, try to incorporate all those reads into one read so that you "hit" the database table only once, or a minimal number of times.

Using the Primary Key

If you can fill in the primary key of the database table that you're searching, the read on the table will be faster. If you fill in the entire key, a `SELECT SINGLE *` statement is possible, which is a direct read on the database. The more of the primary key you use, the faster the read is on that table. If you use fields other than the keyed fields, or very few of the keyed fields, the read is a sequential read, which is very slow. The primary key is described in Chapter 7, "Working with the Data Dictionary." You will want to go to the data dictionary and view the characteristics of the table. If the primary key cannot be used, there are multiple secondary keys that can be used. If your selection criteria does not fit within any of the keys, speak to your BASIS administrator about possibly creating a key for you!

TIP

Use as much of the primary key as possible when making your reads on database tables.

Using CHECK Statements

Try not to use `CHECK` statements unless they can't be incorporated into `SELECT` statements. By incorporating the restriction into the `SELECT` statement, fewer records are retrieved from the database, and fewer loops are processed through the `SELECT` and `ENDSELECT` statements.

TIP

Avoid using CHECK statements.

Using Tables

If you receive specifications from your functional analyst detailing which tables you must read in order to obtain the appropriate data, don't take this information at face value. Check to see whether any of the tables referenced are long tables, cluster tables, or problematic tables that you prefer to avoid. Then use the information system in the data dictionary to try to find a table with the same data that doesn't present a performance problem to your program.

The following sections provide specific suggestions on when to use which kind of table.

Cluster Tables Versus Transparent Tables

Reads on cluster tables, in my experience, must be done via the primary key. If any fields outside the primary key are used, the program will take *forever* to finish. A big culprit of many time-consuming programs in pre-3.1 SAP is the table VBFA (Document Flow), used primarily with the SD (Sales and Distribution) module of SAP. Access to this table, using a SELECT * command, requires the use of the primary key in order to access it. Preferably, use as much of the primary key as possible to utilize the primary index for a faster read. Before 3.1, the document flow table was a cluster table. Now in 3.1 the table has been converted to a transparent one. The primary key must be used with cluster tables. This is a rule when dealing with cluster tables.

Transparent tables are relatively easy to access. The read can utilize any fields to extract the data from the database. The primary key is preferable, but other fields can be used as well. If the table is relatively large (many records), talk to your BASIS administrator about setting up an index for this table if you are using fields outside of the primary key.

A general rule of thumb with SAP is that data doesn't exist in one place only. If the table you want to read is a problematic one that might tie up system resources, use the information system of the data dictionary to find other tables that are smaller or transparent and have the same data fields populated.

Avoiding Tables with Many Records

Searching through tables with a great number of records is a burden to the system, both at the database and application server level. The one rule of the SAP R/3 environment is that data exists on multiple tables. This rule must be acknowledged, especially by seasoned mainframe programmers who are used to finding data in only one place.

The reason behind this emphatic tirade is that many programs which run slowly do so because they access the main tables with the greatest number of records. Typical tables include BSEG (accounting detail), MSEG (material master detail), text tables, and history logging tables. Most of the relevant data found in BSEG is also found in the table BSIS. Most of the data found in MSEG can be found in the views MARC and MARD. Ask your BASIS (system) consultant which tables are currently the largest, or if any of the tables you plan to use are lengthy. Then use the information system to search for the same data elements from the lengthy table in other, smaller tables. As you gain more experience with SAP and your system, you'll learn which are the problem or large tables, just from dealing with them on a regular basis.

Selecting into Tables

The fastest possible read from a database table and copy procedure into an internal table is the version of `SELECT *` that reads the data it finds directly into the internal table:

```
SELECT * FROM dbtab INTO TABLE internal table
                                                  WHERE condition clauses.
```

The database copies the records that match the `WHERE` clause into the internal table and adds them to the internal table directly. The entire process is one step, rather than the several steps required if you used the regular `SELECT *` statement along with some `APPEND` and `CLEAR` commands. If you compare the `SELECT * ... INTO TABLE` code with the following code, you'll see that the first set of code only takes one step, whereas the second set has five steps:

```
SELECT * FROM dbtab WHERE condition clauses.
     MOVE dbtab TO internal table.
     APPEND internal table.
     CLEAR internal table.
ENDSELECT.
```

So the time you save in terms of steps is obvious.

Using the MOVE Statement

Every time you make the application server "think," you burn extra CPU time. The `MOVE-CORRESPONDING` command makes the application server think about where it needs to put the data that you're moving. `MOVE-CORRESPONDING` is a very convenient command, but a faster method of moving data to fields is by using multiple `MOVE` statements. For example, if your program used the `MOVE-CORRESPONDING` statement in the following manner, it could be optimized by replacing it with individual `MOVE` statements:

```
TABLES: BKPF, MSEG, KNA1.

PARAMETERS:        P_YEAR    LIKE BKPF-GJAHR,
                   P_MATNR   LIKE MSEG-MATNR,
                   P_COMPANY LIKE BKPF-BUKRS.
```

```
DATA:       BEGIN OF DEMO_TABLE OCCURS 1000,
                      YEAR    LIKE BKPF-GJAHR,
                      MATNR   LIKE MSEG-MATNR,
                      COMPANY LIKE BKPF-BUKRS,
                      CITY    LIKE KNA1-ORT01.
DATA:       END OF DEMO_TABLE.

SELECT * FROM BKPF WHERE GJAHR = P_YEAR AND
                         BUKRS = P_COMPANY.
MOVE-CORRESPONDING BKPF TO DEMO_TABLE.

SELECT * FROM MSEG UP TO 1 ROWS
                               WHERE MATNR = P_MATNR.
MOVE-CORRESPONDING MSEG INTO DEMO_TABLE.
ENDSELECT.
SELECT * FROM KNA1 UP TO 1 ROWS
                               WHERE KUNNR = mseg-KUNNR.
     MOVE-CORRESPONDING KNA1 TO DEMO_TABLE.
ENDSELECT.
APPEND DEMO_TABLE.
CLEAR DEMO_TABLE.
ENDSELECT.
```

All of these `MOVE-CORRESPONDING` statements can be replaced by individual `MOVE` statements. The code change would be as follows:

```
PARAMETERS:         P_YEAR    LIKE BKPF-GJAHR,
                    P_MATNR   LIKE MSEG-MATNR,
                    P_COMPANY LIKE BKPF-BUKRS.

DATA:       BEGIN OF DEMO_TABLE OCCURS 1000,
                      YEAR    LIKE BKPF-GJAHR,
                      MATNR   LIKE MSEG-MATNR,
                      COMPANY LIKE BKPF-BUKRS,
                      CITY    LIKE KNA1-ORT1.
DATA:       END OF DEMO_TABLE.
```

```
SELECT * FROM BKPF WHERE GJAHR = P_YEAR AND
                         BUKRS = P_COMPANY.

MOVE BKPF-GJAHR INTO DEMO_TABLE-YEAR.
MOVE BKPF-BUKRS INTO DEMO_TABLE-COMPANY.

SELECT * FROM MSEG UP TO 1 ROWS
                         WHERE MATNR = P_MATNR.
MOVE MSEG-MATNR INTO DEMO_TABLE-MATNR.
ENDSELECT.
SELECT * FROM KNA1 UP TO 1 ROWS
                         WHERE KUNNR = BKPF-KUNNR.
     MOVE KNA1-ORT1 TO DEMO_TABLE-ORT1.
ENDSELECT.
APPEND DEMO_TABLE.
CLEAR DEMO_TABLE.
ENDSELECT.
```

The new code moves the data from the database table fields directly into the internal table fields, rather than comparing every field of the database table against every field of the internal table. Keep in mind that, despite the fact that typing the extra code is tedious, the performance enhancement to your program is important enough to do it.

TIP

Avoid using `MOVE-CORRESPONDING`.

Looping

In SAP, many records are read and processed, which implies that much data must be looped through in order to process the data. The commands to loop through this data must be used correctly; otherwise, valuable processor time can be wasted.

If your program is reading through only one or two tables, try to incorporate the processing inside the nested `SELECT *` commands. If three or more tables are accessed, move the data to an internal table that will be processed after all the data is read from the database tables.

If the internal table method is used, you must use the correct commands to loop through the internal table or process any other set of data that must be looped through. The `WHILE`, `DO`, and `LOOP` commands are used in this case. The following three sections review the positives and negatives of each. It's essential that the programmer understand the subtle differences between these commands and when to use one rather than the other.

Using WHILE

The `WHILE` loop contains a logical expression along with the `WHILE` command. All commands included between `WHILE` and `ENDWHILE` are executed as long as that logical expression remains true. It's also possible to put an `EXIT` command inside a `WHILE` loop, but it's preferable to make the `EXIT` part of the logical expression.

If you can define a logical expression to process your data, use the `WHILE` command. The `WHILE` command exits at the first line of the loop, whereas a `DO` or `LOOP` command processes several lines further before "realizing" that the time to end the loop has come.

TIP

If you can define a logical expression to process your data, use `WHILE` instead of `DO` or `LOOP`.

Using DO

The `DO` loop is used when the number of loop passes is known, or when an `EXIT` or `STOP` command is part of the commands in order to prevent an endless loop. `DO` loops are used most of all when reading flat files from the application server. Flat files contain an unknown number of records most of the time, so the `DO` loop continues endlessly. To exit at an appropriate time, an `IF` statement is incorporated after the `READ DATASET` statement to check the status of `SY-SUBRC`. If the value is not `0`, the program exits the loop and assumes that the file has been completely read into the internal table.

Using LOOP

The `LOOP` command is used to loop through internal tables to read the data line by line automatically. The `LOOP` command can also be used in the context of `LOOP AT` *`internal table`* `WHERE` *`logical expression`*. By utilizing the `LOOP` command in this context, you can loop through only certain records of *internal table*—those in which your selection criteria are met.

For a review on looping, see Chapter 5, "Using the Looping Commands." As you code more and more programs, you'll learn by experience which is the best `LOOP` command to use in which situations.

Choosing Internal Tables Versus Field Groups

The number of records allocated to an internal table is a number that at minimum is zero and at maximum is a parameter set by your system administrators. A general rule is that in your entire program you shouldn't have more than 100,000 records allocated to internal tables. This number defines how much memory will be allocated from the system to your application. Don't just pick a random number out of the air and give that number to your internal table.

If the amount of memory you allocate is too large, the program will fail to initiate and won't run. If the number you pick is too small, each record appended to the table after that number is stored in the paging area of memory. This memory area is slower to respond than the allotted memory claimed by your program. So the consequences of underestimating the number of records is a performance issue with your program. However, it's better to choose a number that's too small than a number that's too large. If the number is too small, the program runs a little slower. If the number is too large, the program doesn't run, and it impedes the performance of other applications running on the system.

TIP

It's worth repeating: It's better to pick a record number size that's too small than a number that's too big. The program with the smaller number will run, but the program with too much memory allocated will fail. The extra records will be stored in the paging area, rather than in the memory allocated to the internal table.

A good way to estimate the number of records that will be stored in the internal table is to ask the functional analyst who is working with you in developing the specifications for the program. Remember, programming in SAP is a team effort. Utilize the resources you have at hand, which most importantly is composed of human talent all around you.

Another way to estimate is to write the program and find out how many records are generally extracted from the database. Then go back into the code and adjust the number of records to reflect an accurate number. This last suggestion is tough to do, as most development environments don't have a good data copy of the current production system. Talk to your system administrator to find out the current status of the system.

If you define an internal table as having `0` records, all of the records appended to it will be stored in the paging area of memory. As mentioned in Chapter 10, "Advanced Data Output," the field groups are all written to the paging area as well. The difference in access time between an internal table with an `OCCURS` statement of `0` and field groups should be zero. However, field groups are much more efficient in their storage handling. The data is compressed and can be stored much more efficiently than internal table records.

TIP

If the number of records you will extract from the database is a large number, try to use field groups instead of internal tables. By avoiding internal tables, you free memory for other applications running at the same time.

Working with Logical Databases

Logical databases are a good idea if you utilize them to view which tables you should read and in what order. If you actually want to use a logical database and use the `GET` command, make sure that the user knows to fill in as much data as possible in the selection screen provided with that database. If only one field is filled in (or only a few), the program takes a long time to retrieve the data the user wants to view or analyze. If all the fields are filled in (of course, this is very rare), the data return is very fast and the hit on the system is very low.

Reading Specific Tables

At the logical database screen (review Chapter 13, "Working with Logical Databases"), click the option button for the structure of the logical database, and display it. SAP has set up the database to read the data from the top level down. Rather than hitting all the tables that SAP will hit automatically if you use the logical database, type code directly into your ABAP editor. Specify that you read from only the tables you want, and then read them in the same order as SAP suggests from the viewed structure.

Optimizing with Obligatory Fields

One way to make sure that the users fill in a required number of fields is to do a check at the beginning of the program to see whether any of the fields are still initial. If certain fields are initial, give the user an error message, saying that he must enter data in those fields before the program will execute.

Using Batching Versus Online Programs

If your online program will run for more than 15 minutes, run it in background mode instead. It will have to be a scheduled program that your administrator sets up, but at least it won't time out after 15 minutes of run time. Fifteen minutes is the limit for an online program to run without the system automatically canceling it.

If you feel that one of your programs will hinder the system if it's run in online mode, do a check at the beginning of the program to make sure that batch mode is turned on (the program is being run in the background). Otherwise, send an error message saying that this program can be run only in background mode:

```
REPORT ZABAP.


IF SY-BATCH <> ' '.
     MESSAGE E999 WITH 'PROGRAM ONLY TO BE RUN IN BACKGROUND MODE'.
ENDIF.
```

Summary

This chapter highlighted some useful tricks of the trade for speeding up your code. After reviewing this chapter, you should have a pretty good idea of how to improve the performance of your current code and how to write better code in the future.

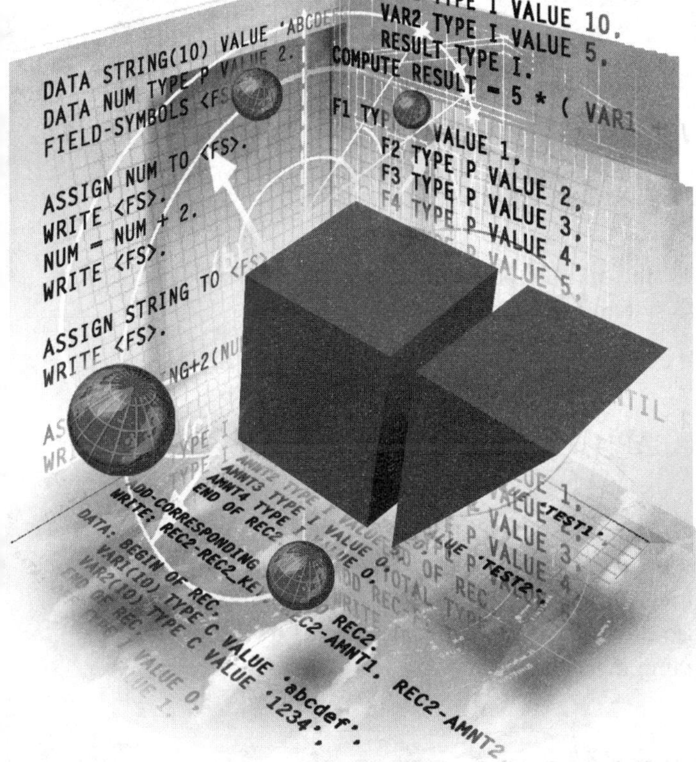

Chapter 21

Integrating the Web with R/3

In This Chapter

- Introducing the Internet Transaction Server and its role in an SAP R/3 system.
- Going on a detailed tour of the SAP@Web Studio and learning how to configure it to your R/3 system and Web server.
- Creating a Web page that executes an ABAP/4 report and displays the output on a Web page.
- Adding all your existing ABAP/4 reports directly to the Web using the reporting tree.

You should have a very good grasp of the information found in Chapter 14, "Writing a Report." The new Internet toolset introduced with release 3.1 also includes BAPIs (Business Application Programming Interfaces) and coding online transactions. Coding online transactions are also discussed in the upcoming sequel to this book covering advanced ABAP/4 programming skills.

ITS (Internet Transaction Server)

ITS (Internet Transaction Server) is a software package provided by SAP America. The software is installed on a separate NT Server which has Web server software installed.

TIP

One can find a copy for download of the latest version of the Internet Transaction Server on SAP's Web site. The current URL is:

http://www.sap.com/bfw/interf/bapis/resource/software/software.htm

If that URL has expired, try doing a site search for the software from the home page.

ITS and its intracacies are of concern mainly to your BASIS administrator, as he will have to configure the server. This introduction gives an overview from a need-to-know basis for the beginning developer. The ITS server acts independently from the main SAP application servers. A Web page initiates a call to SAP. The call goes directly to ITS which then communicates with one of the application servers. The transaction is processed, and the SAP server communicates back to the ITS, which then funnels the information back to the Web server where it is published. There are advantages to routing these reports over the Web. One advantage is that the user does not need an SAP logon to access the reports, depending on how one sets up security. A simple Web page made accessible to only key personnel (persons cleared to view the contents of those reports) can obtain the links to the pertinent reports. Otherwise, certain logons can be made available, but that is an advanced topic to be covered in a future ABAP/4 advanced book.

The most important piece of information that you need from the BASIS team is the location of the `wgate.dll` file on the ITS server. You need this piece of information to be able to configure your development studio. This directory is where your Web page accesses SAP. This information is found in the section, "SAP@Web Studio (Web Development Tool)."

A good test to see if your ITS is working properly is to put its Web address in your Web browser. If the server is configured properly, you should see a screen like the one shown in Figure 21-1. Click on your respective language (for the example English), and the browser navigates to a screen like the one in Figure 21-2.

This book does not cover all the functionality that comes with the ITS. Instead, advanced ABAP/4 functionality will be covered in a later book. This chapter is meant to introduce the Web to and familiarize the reader with the new development environment.

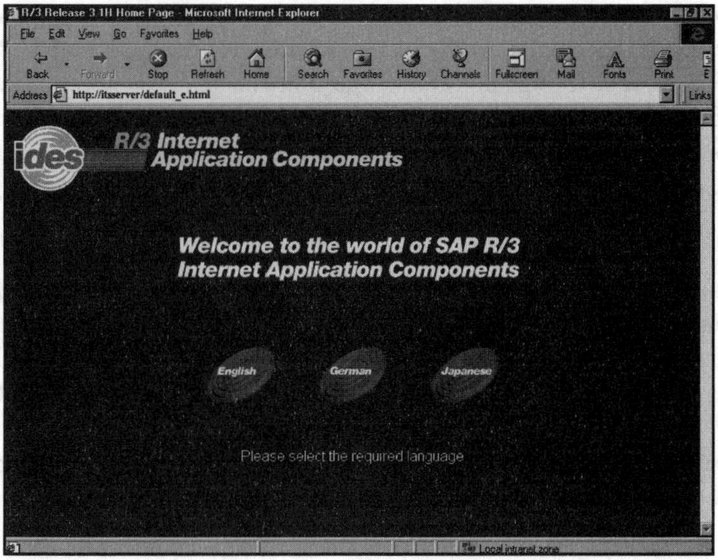

FIGURE 21-1

The home page of the ITS (Internet Transaction Server)

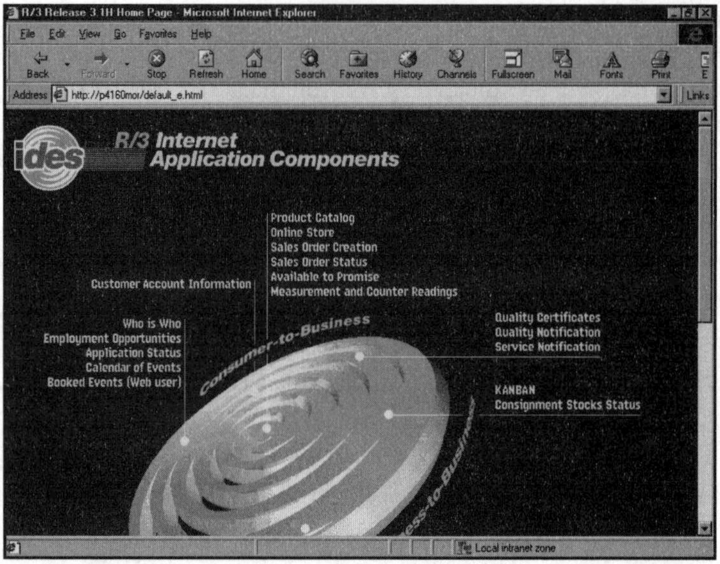

FIGURE 21-2

Once you click on your respective language, your Web browser brings up a screen showing all the built-in functionality that comes with ITS.

SAP@Web Studio (Web Development Tool)

The *SAP@Web Studio* is a separate application that runs on your Windows environment. This tool allows you to develop Web pages that interface with SAP. This section covers how to install and configure the SAP@Web Studio.

Your first step should be to download and install the SAP@Web Studio, version 2.0. The software can be found using the same URL found at the beginning of the chapter. Speak to your BASIS administrator who is in charge of the ITS to obtain permission for your computer to access the Web as well as the ITS. Now that you have all the preparatory steps done, it is time to start and configure the application. Execute SAP@Web Studio. You should see a screen like the one in Figure 21-3.

Follow the Menu path Project|Site Definition. A screen should appear as in Figure 21-4.

First, click on the NEW button in the bottom-left corner. Create a unique definition. For naming conventions, perhaps use your SAP logon as this unique definition. It is very essential that you do this step. Click on your new site definition and fill in the fields appropriately. You need the location of the root directory for the Web directory on your Web server. This is a different directory than the root directory for the ITS server. Click on your new site definition and enter the name of the Web server, the Web root directory, and the location of the `wgate.dll` file in the appropriate boxes.

Click on the Its Host tab. A screen appears which looks like Figure 21-5.

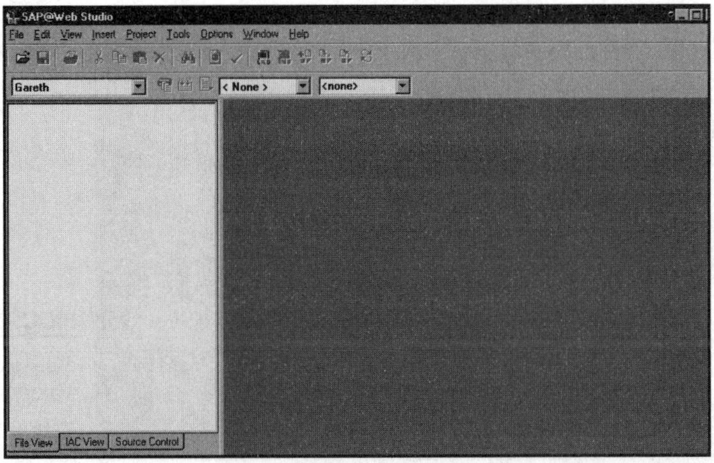

FIGURE 21-3

Once SAP@Web is initially executed, you should see a screen very similar to this one.

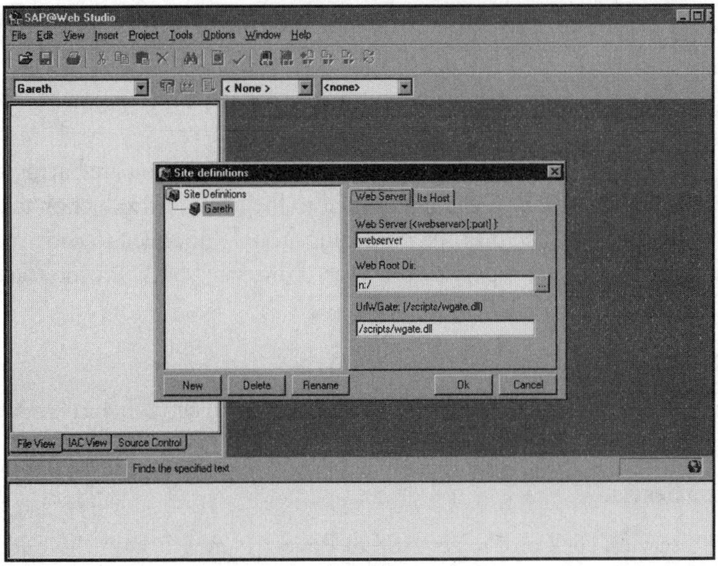

FIGURE 21-4

The first step in configuring your new development tool is to create a unique site definition. After this step is complete, you can specify the addresses of your Web server as well as where the `wgate.dll` *file is stored.*

Enter the server's name where ITS is installed as the host. Enter **`<its host>/itsmnt/`** in the `Its Data Directory` field. Click on OK. Your SAP@Web Studio is now configured. Congratulations!!

SAP Web Reporting

Currently, the easiest and most efficient way to link an SAP Report to the Web is to add it to the Reporting Tree. Because this functionality is already built into the ITS Server.

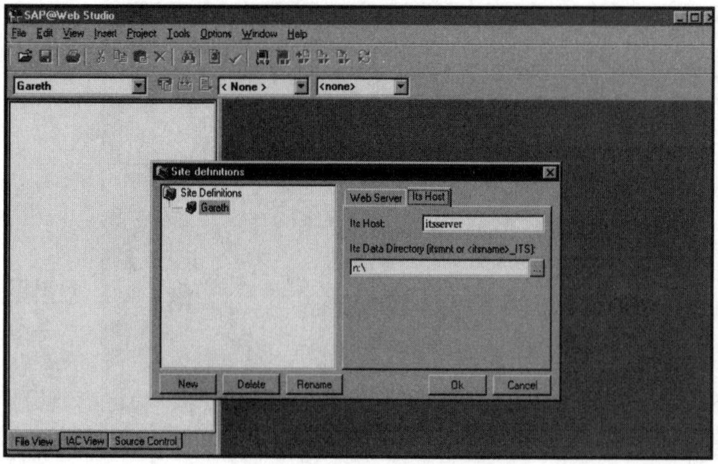

FIGURE 21-5

The name and location of the ITS on the network must be specified.

The next steps show how to create an ABAP/4 report and programatically link it to the Web.

1. **Create your ABAP/4 Report**

Create your report on SAP just as you would normally do. If you are having any trouble programming in ABAP/4, you might refer to the book, "Introduction to ABAP/4 Programming for SAP," 1996 PrimaPublishing. You do not need to code your report any differently to link the report to the Web. However, you will code transactional code differently for the Web.

2. **Create a Project**

To create a project, click on File|New. Click on the Project Tab and enter a unique name for your project (see Figure 21-6).

3. **Create a Service**

To create a service, click on Project|Add to Project|New. Click on the File Wizards Tab as shown in Figure 21-7.

Select Service Wizard and click on OK. Give your Service a name. This can be anything, but have "Z" as the first letter. Click on NEXT. Specify your SAP HOST NAME as your logon for that service. Click on NEXT. Click on NEXT again, accepting the global service logon. Set the timeout parameter to 15 minutes. Click on NEXT. For reporting, select RFC IO-Channel. For transactions, select Diag-Channel. Enter **SAP HOST NAME** as the destination. Click on NEXT, and then FINISH. Congratulations, your first Service has been built.

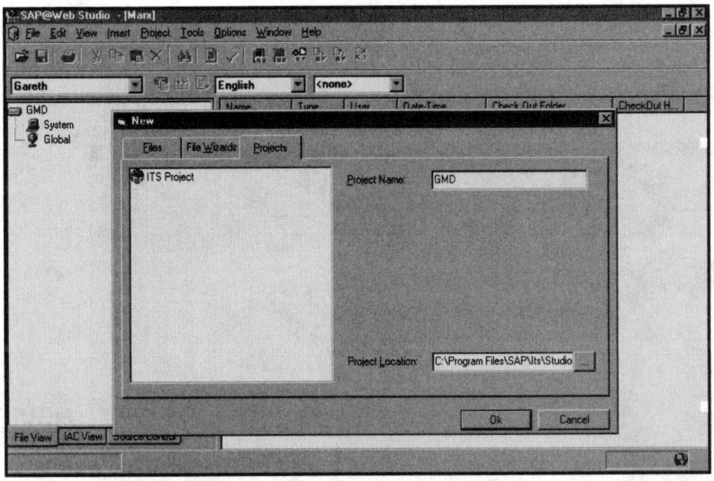

FIGURE 21-6

Enter your logon ID as a unique name for your project. This practice keeps your work separate from other developers.

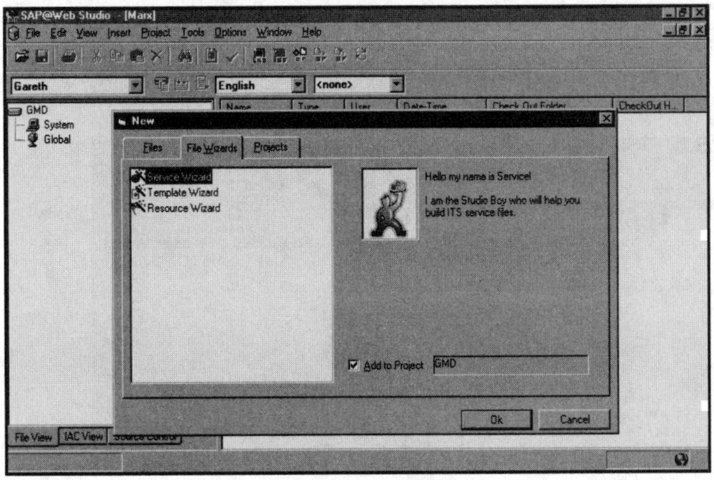

FIGURE 21-7

Using the file wizard, you can create a service to associate all your Web reports.

4. **Create a Theme**

Right-click on your new Service. Click on Insert|Theme. A new folder appears under your service. Label it **99**. See the example in Figure 21-8.

5. **Importing HTML Templates**

Once again, follow the menu path Project|Add to Project|New. Click on File Wizards. Select Template Wizard and click on OK. Select your development system as your R/3 system. Click on NEXT. Enter your client number, userid, password, and logon language. Click on NEXT. On the next screen, enter **SAPMS38M** for program. Enter **100** as the screen number. Select your new service from the drop-down menu. Enter **99** as your theme and select your language. Click on NEXT|Finish. The program connects to the R/3 system you specified and import the program as an HTML template under your service. You should see the example as in Figure 21-9.

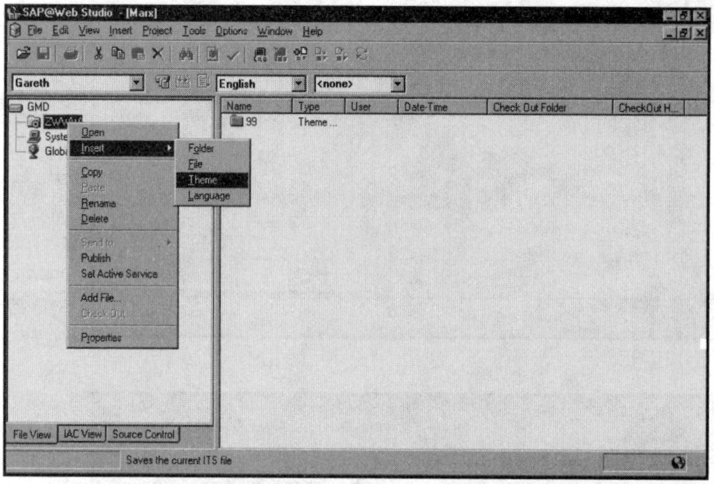

FIGURE 21-8

For every service, at least one theme must be created under which you can publish all your reports.

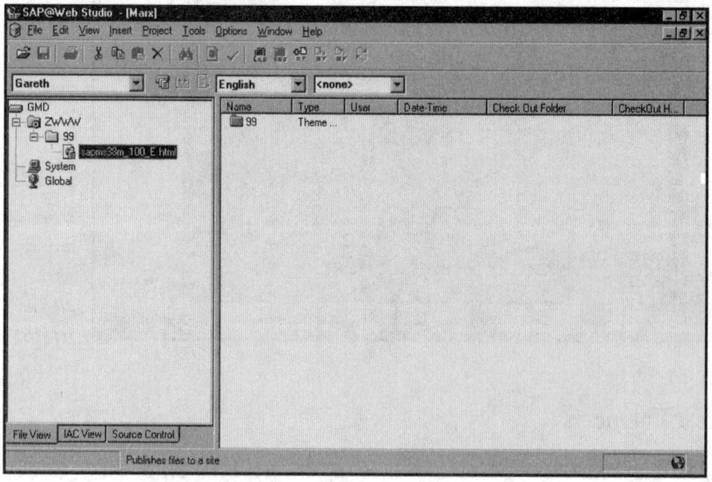

FIGURE 21-9

SAP automatically creates an HTML template from the existing ABAP/4 program you specify.

6. **Modifying the HTML Template**

Double-click on your new template. The HTML code appears. Delete the following lines:

```
'RS38M-PROGRAMM.label'
<INPUT TYPE="text" name="RS38M-PROGRAMM" VALUE="'RS38M-PROGRAMM'" maxlength=" 8"
size=" 8" >
```

Add the following new line:

```
<a HREF="/scripts/wgate.dll?~service=<your new
service>&_FUNCTION=WWW_SEL_SCREEN&_REPORT=<your abap report name>">Execute
Report</a>
```

Make sure to replace `<your new service>` with your new service, and `<your abap report name>` with your new SAP ABAP/4 report.

Congratulations. You have created your first Web Report which is linked to SAP. To publish and build your new files to the Web, press F7. Go to your Web browser and enter the following URL:

http://webserver/scripts/wgate.dll?~service=<your new service>.

A Web page appears with an Execute Report link. Click on it and your report should execute.

Web-Enabling Your Reporting Tree

Another method by which to publish ABAP/4 reports on the Web is to Web-enable your reporting tree. A simple way to do this is to add an entry to the `W3TREE` table. The entry you must add is found by doing a matchcode search on the tree ID from the Serp transaction. You can make regular SAP trees available or any custom ones. From the ITS screen, click on your preferred language (English in this case). On the second screen, (refer to Figure 21-2) scroll down to the bottom and click on the Reporting Tree selection. The screen should look like Figure 21-10.

Click on the Report Selections hyperlink to navigate to a list of report topics as shown in Figure 21-11.

Select a topic and navigate down the branches until you find a specific report. Click on the report name. A selection screen appears on a Web page, as shown in Figure 21-12. Once you enter your parameters, click on Execute report and the output displays on a Web page.

Adding HTML Tags to your SAP Web Application

Think of your final SAP HTML Template as any other Web page in this respect. At this point, you can add regular HTML commands to the page to specify font color, to specify background color, or to insert images. The syntax for these three commands follows, however other HTML commands should work.

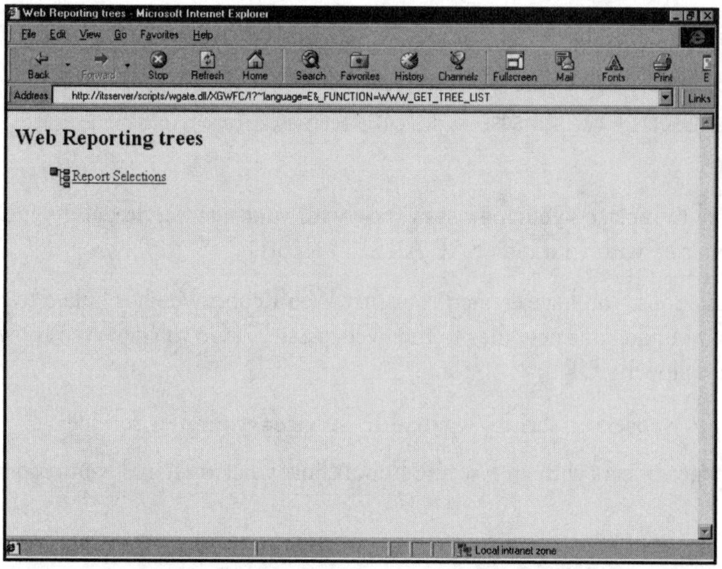

FIGURE 21-10

The first screen of the Web reporting tree.

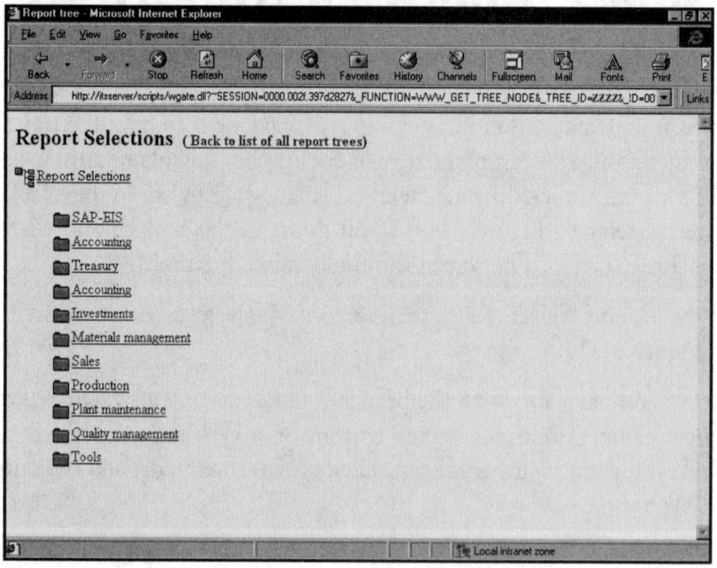

FIGURE 21-11

The first branch of the Web reporting tree

```
Specifying Font Color
        <font color = [color]>
                                                    (color is a literal such
as 'red', 'blue', etc.)
    Specifying Background Color
        <body bgcolor = [color.background]>
```

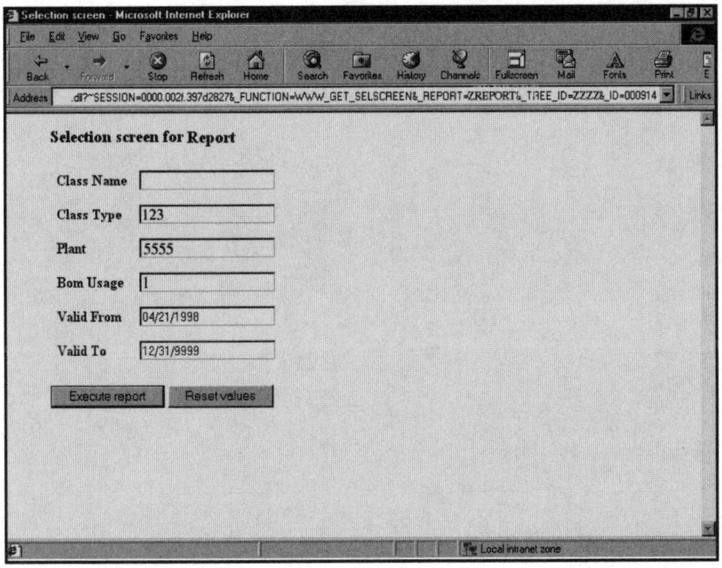

FIGURE 21-12

Once you select a report, the same selection screen seen on R/3 displays on a Web page.

```
                                          (color.background is a
coded color such as #dddddd for gray)
Inserting an Image
    <img src = "[<path> / <file>]"
                                          (<path> is the pathname to the
<file> which is the image file)
```

Summary

This chapter touched on the new Web functionality that is available with SAP R/3 version 3.1h. With the advent of the Web interface with R/3, two new components were introduced, the ITS (Internet Transaction Server) and SAP@Web Studio, the new Web development tool.

How to put a report on the Web is covered in this chapter. R/3 is also capable of putting full online transactions on the Web. We thank you for buying and reading our book. It is our hope that you have learned a great deal from this text and have found the examples and explanations applicable to your day-to-day experience with SAP. Our further hope is that you master the information in this text and progress to the upcoming book which will cover advanced ABAP/4 topics, including online transactions.

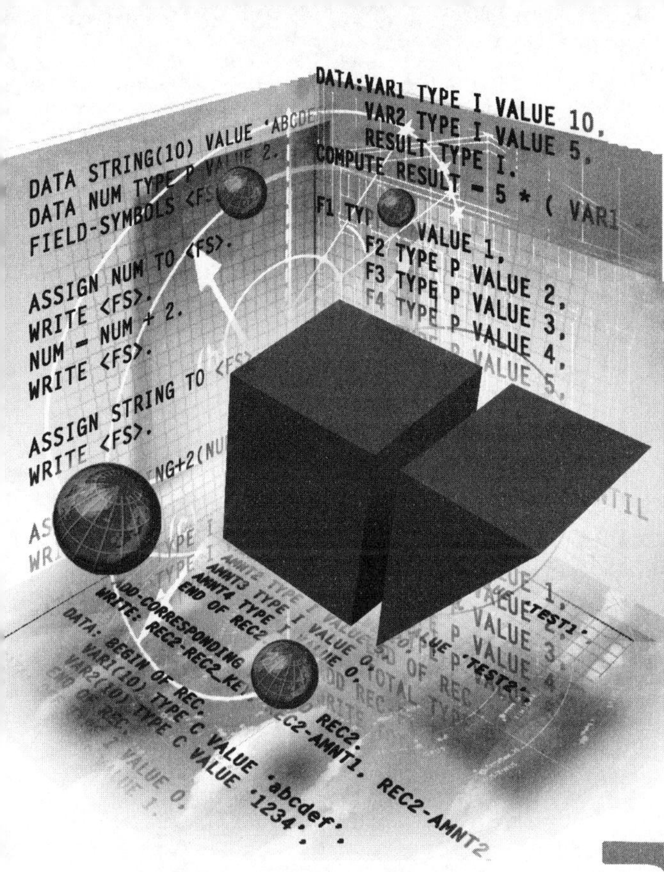

PART IV

Appendixes

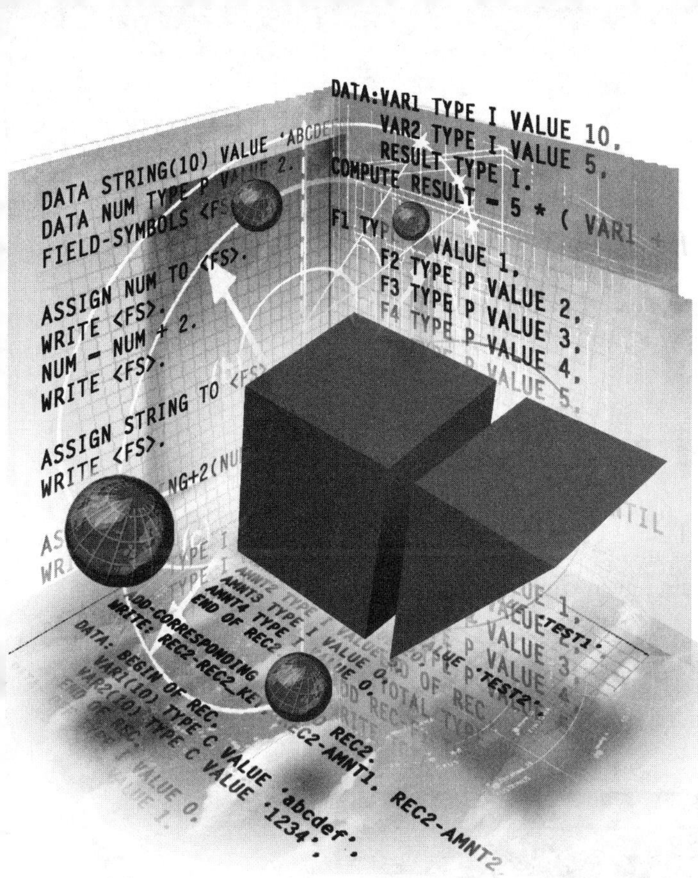

Appendix A

Using the ABAP/4 Editor

SAP includes an editor that you can use to write and manage ABAP/4 programs. This appendix reviews the basic features and commands of the ABAP/4 editor, discussing creating, copying, renaming, deleting, and executing programs, as well as the basic editor commands you use to write ABAP/4 programs.

Managing ABAP/4 Programs

- The ABAP/4 editor is transaction `se38`, which you reach via the menu path Tools | Development Workbench | ABAP/4 Editor. Figure A-1 shows the main screen. You manage programs with this screen.

The main screen includes several useful features:

- To create a new program, type the name of the program in the

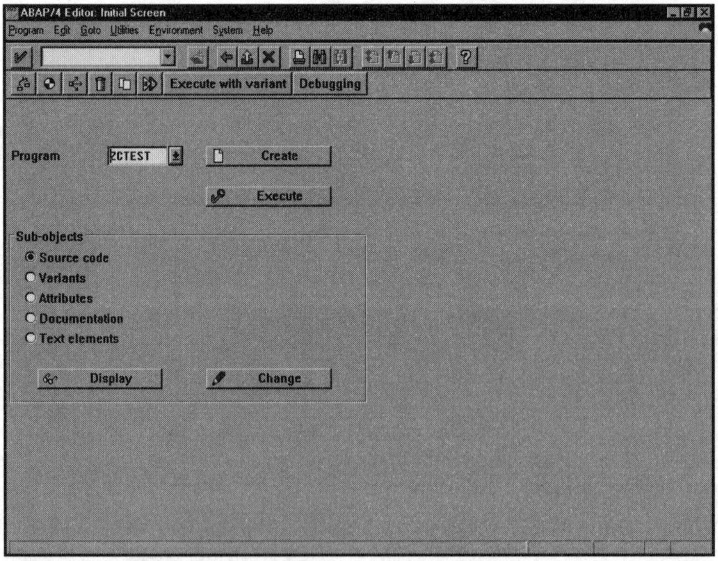

FIGURE A-1

The ABAP/4 Program Maintenance screen

NOTE

All user-created ABAP/4 programs must start with the letter Z or Y. The name can be a mix of up to eight letters and numbers.

Program text box and click the Create button.

- Execute runs the program specified in the Program text box. If you don't know the name of the program with which you want to work, type an asterisk in the Program field; then press Enter to display a special screen you can use to search for the desired program (see Figure A-2). In this screen, enter any known data—such as the creator name or perhaps part of the program name—using an asterisk as the wildcard into the appropriate fields.
- Display opens the source code in read-only mode.
- Change enables the source code to be changed with the editor (see the next section for details).
- In addition to the buttons, the Utilities menu holds commands to copy, rename, find, and delete programs. Simply choose the appropriate command and enter the name of the program.

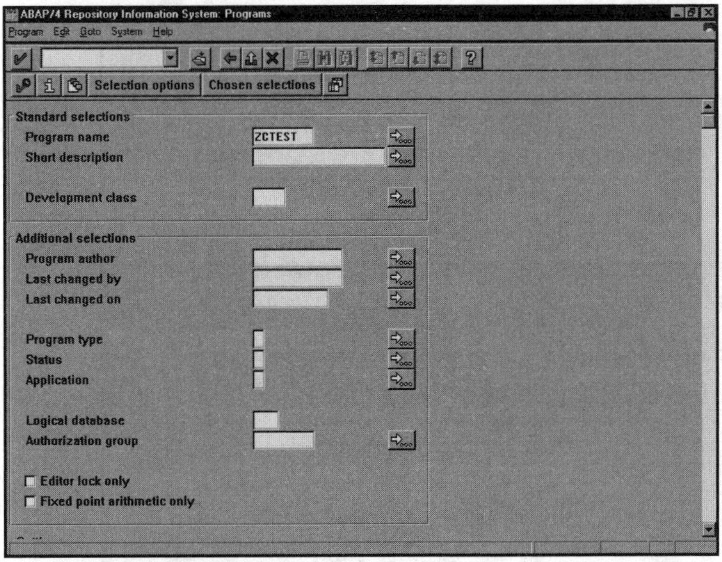

FIGURE A-2

Use this screen to search for programs.

Using the Editor to Edit Programs

Clicking the Change button opens a screen where you can edit the specified program (see Figure A-3). The line above the program code is the *command line*, which you can use to enter several commands.

There's no line wrap in this editor; each line is separate. The first column holds the line number. Commands that affect a line are entered here. For example, the command CC copies a block of lines. The first time you enter CC, it defines the start of the block; the second time CC is entered, it defines the end of the block, as shown in Figure A-4.

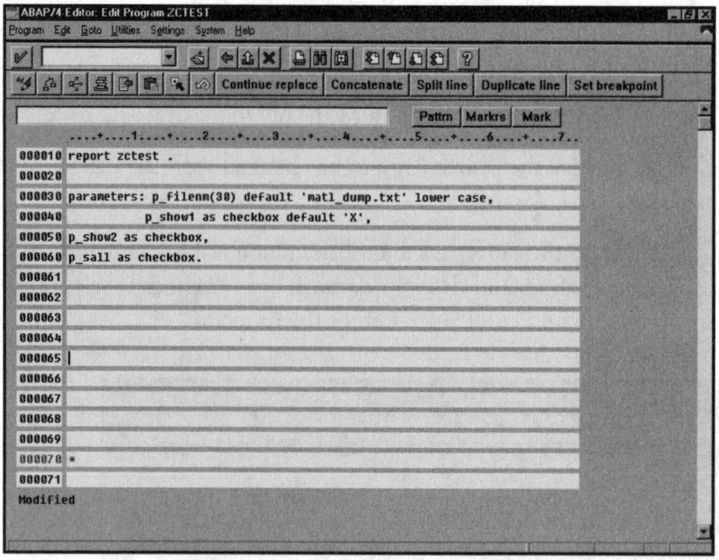

FIGURE A-3

Defining the start of a block

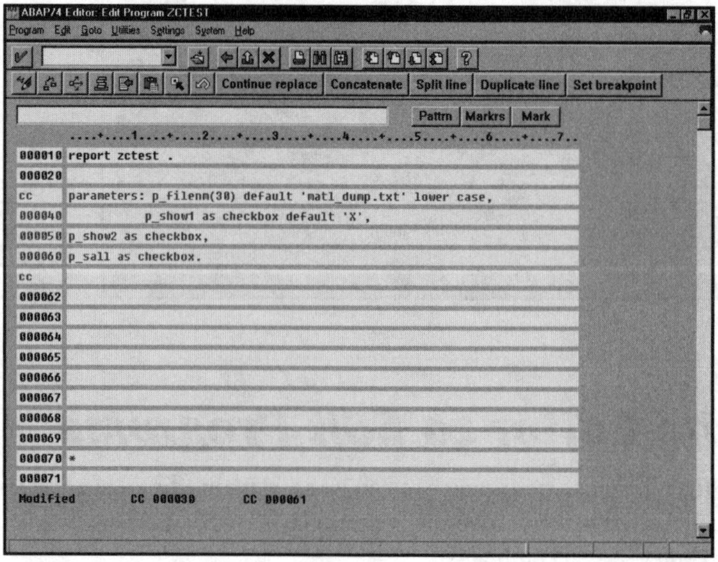

FIGURE A-4

Defining the end of a block

Line Commands

Line commands can affect a single line or a block of lines. If you want to apply a single-line command, simply overwrite the numbers in the line number column. To select a block of lines, overwrite the numbers of the line number column in the first line of the block; then repeat the command on the last line of the block. Table A-1 shows the single-line commands.

NOTE

Commands aren't case-sensitive in ABAP/4.

Table A-1 Single-Line Commands

Command	Description
I#	Inserts a line below the current line. To insert more than one line, enter a digit from 1 to 9 to replace # in the command.
D#	Deletes the current line. To delete the current line and additional lines below it, enter a digit from 1 to 9 to replace # in the command.
C	Copies the current line. Use the B or A command to paste the line.
M	Moves the current line. Use the B or A command to paste the line to the new location.
A	Pastes a previously copied or pasted line after the current line.
B	Pastes a previously copied or pasted line before the current line.
R	Duplicates the current line.
J	Join current line and next.
X, Y, Z	Pastes the contents of the X, Y, or Z buffer below the current line. See the XX command in the next table for more information.

The next set of commands are *line block commands*, which can be used to affect a block of lines. Enter the command in the number column of the first line of the block and again at the final line. Table A-2 describes the commands.

Table A-2 Line Block Commands

Command	Description
CC	Copies a block of lines. Use the B or A command to paste the block.
DD	Deletes a block of lines from the program.
MM	Moves a block of lines. Use the B or A command to paste the block.
PR	Prints a block of lines.
WW, XX, YY, ZZ	Copies a block of lines much like the CC command. In this case, however, three buffers—W, X, Y, and Z—save the text even if you exit the editor. Using these three buffers, you can copy blocks of text from one program to another. If a block of text is copied with XX, you can exit the current program and bring up a second program and then paste the block of text. If you have multiple windows open, you can paste the text from one editor session to another. To paste the text from a buffer, use the X, Y, or Z command.

Using the Command Line

Commands entered in the command line tend to affect the entire program. Many of them can be accessed from the editor menu, but it can be easier to type some of them on the command line. Table A-3 describes the commands.

Table A-3 Commands Used on the Command Line

Command	Description
I	Inserts a line at the end of the program.
Find string	Finds the first occurrence of *string* in the program.
N	Finds the next occurrence of the *string* previously entered.
PP (Pretty Printer)	Indents the lines in program blocks such as IF [el] ENDIF or LOOP [el] ENDLOOP.
PC	Downloads the program to a local directory on your personal computer. This command brings up a dialog box into which you enter the path and file type (see Figure A-5).

(continued)

Table A-3 Commands Used on the Command Line (continued)

Command	Description
`FC`	Uploads a file from a local directory to the ABAP/4 editor. The current ABAP/4 program being edited is overwritten by the contents of the file, so be careful using this command. If you make a mistake, you can exit the editor without saving to restore the original program. The file must be a standard ASCII text file. Any text exceeding 80 characters will be truncated.
`Show <table>`	Shows the list of fields for the table.
`Help <command>`	Shows the online help for the command.
`Reset`	Undoes the last line command entered—such as inserting, deleting, or pasting.
`Save`	Saves changes made to the program.

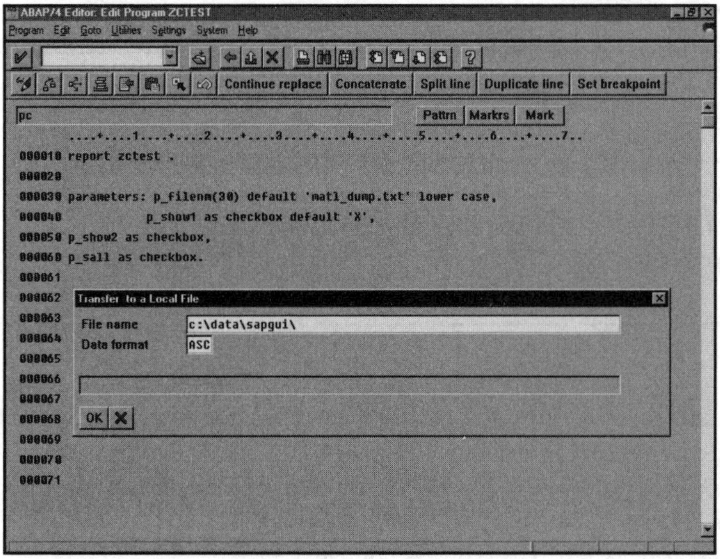

FIGURE A-5

Downloading a fileart of a block

Using the Buttons

Above the command line are several buttons, as shown in Figure A-6. (The exact number depends on your screen resolution.) These buttons activate common commands that you will use often. Table A-4 describes how to use the buttons.

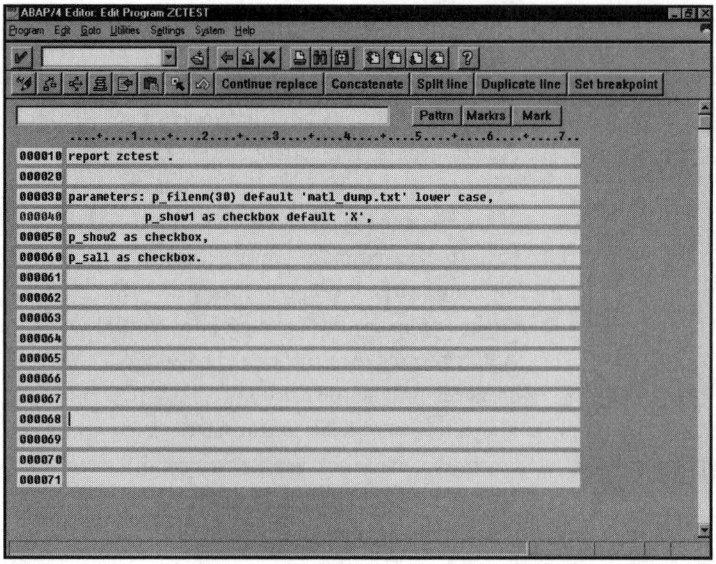

FIGURE A-6

The ABAP/4 editor with function buttons

Table A-4 Command Buttons

Command	*Description*
Continue Replace	Enables the programmer to do a global search-and-replace of any word or phrase in the current program.
Concatenate	Concatenate the current line and the next.
Split Line	Splits the current line at the point of the cursor.
Duplicate Line	Duplicate the current line.
Set Breakpoint	Set a breakpoint at the current line to stop execution of the program when it is reached.

If you are running the SAP GUI on a Windows machine, you can use standard cut and paste functionality in the editor. Highlight a single line of text and use Ctrl-C to copy and then place your cursor and press Ctrl-V to paste. If you wish to copy multiple lines, you must first press Ctrl-Y and then you will be allowed to highlight multiple lines. Then use Ctrl-C to copy as normal.

The ABAP/4 editor isn't exactly impressive. If you have trouble with it you can use the download command to pull the program out of SAP, work in your favorite editor, and then use the upload command to return it to the ABAP/4 editor.

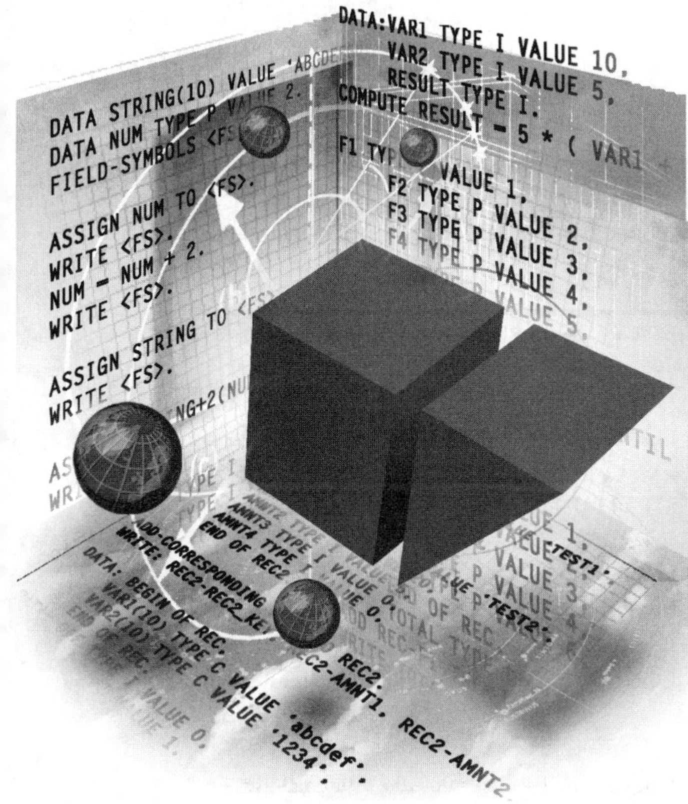

Appendix B

System Fields

This appendix is the full listing of the system fields utilized by the SAP software. Throughout this text, this table is referenced by the sample code. In code, the fields are referenced by the prefix SY, a hyphen, and the field name listed in the table (for example, SY SUBRC).

Field name	***Data element***	***Domain***	***Type***	***Length***	***Short text:*** *SYST*
_INDEX	SYINDEX	SYST_LONG	INT4	000010	Number of loop passes
_PAGNO	SYPAGNO	SYST_SHORT	INT4	000010	Runtime: Current page in list
_TABIX	SYTABIX	SYST_LONG	INT4	000010	Runtime: Current line of an internal table
_TFILL	SYTFILL	SYST_LONG	INT4	000010	Current number of entries in internal table
_TLOPC	YTLOPC	SYST_LONG	INT4	000010	Internal use
_TMAXL	SYTMAXL	SYST_LONG	INT4	000010	Maximum number of entries in internal table
_TOCCU	SYTOCCU	SYST_LONG	INT4	000010	OCCURS parameter with internal tables
_TTABC	SYTTABC	SYST_LONG	INT4	000010	Number of line last read in an internal table
_TSTIS	SYTSTIS	SYST_LONG	INT4	000010	Internal use
_TTABI	SYTTABI	SYST_LONG	INT4	000010	Offset of internal table in roll area
_DBCNT	SYDBCNT	SYST_LONG	INT4	000010	Number of elements in edited dataset with DB operations
_FDPOS	SYFDPOS	SYST_SHORT	INT4	000010	Location of a string
_COLNO	SYCOLNO	SYST_SHORT	INT4	000010	Current column during list creation
_LINCT	SYLINCT	SYST_SHORT	INT4	000010	Number of list lines
_LINNO	SYLINNO	SYST_SHORT	INT4	000010	Current line for list creation

(continued)

Field name	Data element	Domain	Type	Length	Short text: SYST
_LINSZ	SYLINSZ	SYST_SHORT	INT4	000010	Line size of list
_PAGCT	SYPAGCT	SYST_SHORT	INT4	000010	Page size of list from REPORT statement
_MACOL	SYMACOL	SYST_SHORT	INT4	000010	Number of columns from SET MARGIN
_MAROW	SYMAROW	SYST_SHORT	INT4	000010	No. of lines from SET MARGIN statement
_TLENG	SYTLENG	SYST_SHORT	INT4	000010	Line width of an internal table
_SFOFF	SYSFOFF	SYST_SHORT	INT4	000010	Internal use
_WILLI	SYWILLI	SYST_SHORT	INT4	000010	Number of current window line
_LILLI	SYLILLI	SYST_SHORT	INT4	000010	Number of current list line
_SUBRC	SYSUBRC	SYST_SHORT	INT4	000010	Return value after specific ABAP/4 statements
_FLENG	SYFLENG	SYST_SHORT	INT4	000010	Internal use (field length)
_CUCOL	SYCUCOL	SYST_SHORT	INT4	000010	Cursor position (column)
_CUROW	SYCUROW	SYST_SHORT	INT4	000010	Cursor position (line)
_LSIND	SYLSIND	SYST_BYTE	INT4	000010	Number of secondary list
_LISTI	SYLISTI	SYST_SHORT	INT4	000010	Number of current list line
_STEPL	SYSTEPL	SYST_BYTE	INT4	000010	Number of LOOP line at screen step
_TPAGI	SYTPAGI	SYST_BYTE	INT4	000010	Flag indicating roll-out of internal table to paging area
_WINX1	SYWINX1	SYST_SHORT	INT4	000010	Window coordinate (column left)

(continued)

Field name	Data element	Domain	Type	Length	Short text: SYST
_WINY1	SYWINY1	SYST_SHORT	INT4	000010	Window coordinate (line left)
_WINX2	SYWINX2	SYST_SHORT	INT4	000010	Window coordinate (column right)
_WINY2	SYWINY2	SYST_SHORT	INT4	000010	Window coordinate (line right)
_WINCO	SYWINCO	SYST_SHORT	INT4	000010	Cursor position in window (column)
_WINRO	SYWINRO	SYST_SHORT	INT4	000010	Cursor position in window (line)
_WINDI	SYWINDI	SYST_SHORT	INT4	000010	Index of current window line
_SROWS	SYSROWS	SYST_BYTE	INT4	000010	Lines on screen
_SCOLS	SYSCOLS	SYST_BYTE	INT4	000010	Columns on screen
_LOOPC	SYLOOPC	SYST_BYTE	INT4	000010	Number of LOOP lines at screen step loop
_FOLEN	SYFOLEN	SYST_BYTE	INT4	000010	Internal use (field output length)
_FODEC	SYFODEC	SYST_BYTE	INT4	000010	Internal use (field decimal places)
_TZONE	SYTZONE	SYST_SHORT	INT4	000010	Time difference from 'Greenwich Mean Time' (UTC) in seconds
_DAYST	SYDAYST	SYST_FLAG	CHAR	000001	Summertime active ? ('daylight saving time')
_FTYPE	SYFTYPE	SYCHAR01	CHAR	000001	Internal use (field type)
_APPLI	SYAPPLI	SYHEX02	RAW	000002	SAP applications
_FDAYW	SYFDAYW	SYBIN1	INT1	000003	Factory calendar weekday

(continued)

Field name	Data element	Domain	Type	Length	Short text: SYST
_CCURS	SYCCURS	SYPACK05	DEC	000009	Rate specification/ result field (CURRENCY CONVERT)
_CCURT	SYCCURT	SYPACK05	DEC	000009	Table rate from currency conversion
_DEBUG	SYDEBUG	SYCHAR01	CHAR	000001	Internal use
_CTYPE	SYCTYPE	SYCHAR01	CHAR	000001	Exchange rate type 'M','B','G' from CURRENCY CONVERSION
_INPUT	SYINPUT	SYCHAR01	CHAR	000001	Internal use
_LANGU	SYLANGU	SYLANGU	LANG	000001	SAP logon language key
_MODNO	SYMODNO	SYCHAR01	CHAR	000001	Number of alternative modi
_BATCH	SYBATCH	SYCHAR01	CHAR	000001	Background active (X)
_BINPT	SYBINPT	SYCHAR01	CHAR	000001	Batch input active (X)
_CALLD	SYCALLD	SYCHAR01	CHAR	000001	CALL mode active (X)
_DYNNR	SYDYNNR	SYCHAR04	CHAR	000004	Number of current screen
_DYNGR	SYDYNGR	SYCHAR04	CHAR	000004	Screen group of current screen
_NEWPA	SYNEWPA	SYCHAR01	CHAR	000001	Internal use
_PRI40	SYPRI40	SYCHAR01	CHAR	000001	Internal use
_RSTRT	SYRSTRT	SYCHAR01	CHAR	000001	Internal use
_WTITL	SYWTITL	SYCHAR01	CHAR	000001	Standard page header indicator
_CPAGE	SYCPAGE	SYST_LONG	INT4	000010	Current page number
_DBNAM	SYDBNAM	SYCHAR02	CHAR	000002	Logical database for ABAP/4 program
_MANDT	SYMANDT	MANDT	CLNT	000003	Client number from SAP logon

(continued)

Field name	**Data element**	**Domain**	**Type**	**Length**	**Short text:** *SYST*
_PREFX	SYPREFX	SYCHAR03	CHAR	000003	ABAP/4 prefix for background jobs
_FMKEY	SYFMKEY	SYCHAR03	CHAR	000003	Current function code menu
_PEXPI	SYPEXPI	SYNUM01	NUMC	000001	Print: Spool retention period
_PRINI	SYPRINI	SYNUM01	NUMC	000001	Internal use
_PRIMM	SYPRIMM	SYCHAR01	CHAR	000001	Print: Print immediately
_PRREL	SYPRREL	SYCHAR01	CHAR	000001	Print: Delete after printing
_PLAYO	SYPLAYO	SYCHAR05	CHAR	000005	Internal use
_PRBIG	SYPRBIG	SYCHAR01	CHAR	000001	Print: Selection cover sheet
_PLAYP	SYPLAYP	SYCHAR01	CHAR	000001	Internal use
_PRNEW	SYPRNEW	SYCHAR01	CHAR	000001	Print: New spool request (list)
_PRLOG	SYPRLOG	SYCHAR01	CHAR	000001	Internal use
_PDEST	SYPDEST	SYCHAR04	CHAR	000004	Print: Output device
_PLIST	SYPLIST	SYCHAR12	CHAR	000012	Print: Name of spool request (list name)
_PAUTH	SYPAUTH	SYNUM02	NUMC	000002	Internal use
_PRDSN	SYPRDSN	SYCHAR06	CHAR	000006	Print: Name of spool dataset
_PNWPA	SYPNWPA	SYCHAR01	CHAR	000001	Internal use
_CALLR	SYCALLR	SYCHAR08	CHAR	000008	Print: ID for print dialog function
_REPI2	SYREPI2	SYCHAR08	CHAR	000008	Internal use
_RTITL	SYRTITL	SYCHAR70	CHAR	000070	Print: Report title of program to be printed
_PRREC	SYPRREC	SYCHAR12	CHAR	000012	Print: Recipient
_PRTXT	SYPRTXT	SYCHAR68K	CHAR	000068	Print: Text for cover sheet

(continued)

Field name	Data element	Domain	Type	Length	Short text: SYST
_PRABT	SYPRABT	SYCHAR12K	CHAR	000012	Print: Department on cover sheet
_LPASS	SYLPASS	SYCHAR04	CHAR	000004	Internal use
_NRPAG	SYNRPAG	SYCHAR01	CHAR	000001	Internal use
_PAART	SYPAART	RSPOPAPER	CHAR	000016	Print: Format
_PRCOP	SYPRCOP	SYNUM03	NUMC	000003	Print: Number of copies
_BATZS	SYBATZS	SYCHAR01	CHAR	000001	Background SUBMIT: Immediately
_BSPLD	SYBSPLD	SYCHAR01	CHAR	000001	Background SUBMIT: List output to spool
_BREP4	SYBREP4	SYCHAR04	CHAR	000004	Background SUBMIT: Root name of request report
_BATZO	SYBATZO	SYCHAR01	CHAR	000001	Background SUBMIT: Once
_BATZD	SYBATZD	SYCHAR01	CHAR	000001	Background SUBMIT: Daily
_BATZW	SYBATZW	SYCHAR01	CHAR	000001	Background SUBMIT: Weekly
_BATZM	SYBATZM	SYCHAR01	CHAR	000001	Background SUBMIT: Monthly
_CTABL	SYCTABL	SYCHAR04	CHAR	000004	Exchange rate table from currency conversion
_DBSYS	SYDBSYS	SYCHAR10	CHAR	000010	System: Database system
_DCSYS	SYDCSYS	SYCHAR04	CHAR	000004	System: Dialog system
_MACDB	SYMACDB	SYCHAR04	CHAR	000004	Program: Name of file for matchcode access

(continued)

Field name	Data element	Domain	Type	Length	Short text: SYST
_SYSID	SYSYSID	SYCHAR08	CHAR	000008	System: SAP System ID
_OPSYS	SYOPSYS	SYCHAR10	CHAR	000010	System: Operating system
_PFKEY	SYPFKEY	SYCHAR08	CHAR	000008	Runtime: Current F key status
_SAPRL	SYSAPRL	SYCHAR04	CHAR	000004	System: SAP Release
_TCODE	SYTCODE	SYCHAR04	CHAR	000004	Session: Current transaction code
_UCOMM	SYUCOMM	SYCHAR70	CHAR	000070	Interact.: Command field function entry
_CFWAE	SYCFWAE	SYCUKY	CUKY	000005	Internal use
_CHWAE	SYCHWAE	SYCUKY	CUKY	000005	Internal use
_SPONO	SYSPONO	SYNUM05	NUMC	000005	Runtime: Spool number for list output
_SPONR	SYSPONR	SYNUM05	NUMC	000005	Runtime: Spool number from TRANSFER statement
_WAERS	SYWAERS	SYCUKY	CUKY	000005	T001: Company code currency after reading B segment
_CDATE	SYCDATE	SYDATS	DATS	000008	Date of rate from currency conversion
_DATUM	SYDATUM	SYDATS	DATS	000008	System: Date
_SLSET	SYSLSET	SYCHAR14	CHAR	000014	Name of selection set
_SUBTY	SYSUBTY	SYHEX01	RAW	000001	ABAP/4: Call type for SUBMIT
_SUBCS	SYSUBCS	SYCHAR01	CHAR	000001	Internal: CALL status of program
_GROUP	SYGROUP	SYCHAR01	CHAR	000001	Internal: Bundling

(continued)

Field name	Data element	Domain	Type	Length	Short text: SYST
_FFILE	SYFFILE	SYCHAR08	CHAR	000008	Internal: Flat file (USING/ GENERATING DATASET)
_UZEIT	SYUZEIT	SYTIME	TIMS	000006	System: Time
_DSNAM	SYDSNAM	SYCHAR08	CHAR	000008	Runtime: Name of dataset for spool output
_REPID	SYREPID	SYCHAR08	CHAR	000008	Program: Name of ABAP/4 program
_TABID	SYTABID	SYCHAR08	CHAR	000008	Internal use
_TFDSN	SYTFDSN	SYCHAR08	CHAR	000008	Runtime: Dataset for data extracts
_UNAME	SYUNAME	SYCHAR12	CHAR	000012	Session: SAP user from SAP logon
_LSTAT	SYLSTAT	SYCHAR16	CHAR	000016	Interact.: Status information for each list level
_ABCDE	SYABCDE	SYCHAR26	CHAR	000026	Constant: Alphabet (A,B,C,...)
_MARKY	SYMARKY	SYCHAR01	CHAR	000001	Current line character for MARK
_SFNAM	SYSFNAM	SYCHAR30	CHAR	000030	No longer used
_TNAME	SYTNAME	SYCHAR30	CHAR	000030	Name of internal table after an access
_MSGLI	SYMSGLI	SYCHAR60	CHAR	000060	Interact.: Message line (line 23)
_TITLE	SYTITLE	SYCHAR70	CHAR	000070	Title of ABAP/4 program
_ENTRY	SYENTRY	SYCHAR72	CHAR	000072	Internal use
_LISEL	SYLISEL	SYCHAR255	CHAR	000255	Interact.: Selected line
_ULINE	SYULINE	SYCHAR255	CHAR	000255	Constant: Underline (...)
_XCODE	SYXCODE	SYCHAR70	CHAR	000070	Extended command field

(continued)

Field name	Data element	Domain	Type	Length	Short text: SYST
_CPROG	SYCPROG	SYCHAR08	CHAR	000008	Runtime: Main program
_XPROG	SYXPROG	SYCHAR08	CHAR	000008	Internal use (SYSTEM-EXIT program)
_XFORM	SYXFORM	SYCHAR30	CHAR	000030	Internal use (SYSTEM-EXIT form)
_LDBPG	SYLDBPG	SYCHAR08	CHAR	000008	Program: ABAP/4 database program for SY-DBNAM
_TVAR0	SYTVAR	SYCHAR20	CHAR	000020	Runtime: Text variable for ABAP/4 text elements
_TVAR1	SYTVAR	SYCHAR20	CHAR	000020	Runtime: Text variable for ABAP/4 text elements
_TVAR2	SYTVAR	SYCHAR20	CHAR	000020	Runtime: Text variable for ABAP/4 text elements
_TVAR3	SYTVAR	SYCHAR20	CHAR	000020	Runtime: Text variable for ABAP/4 text elements
_TVAR4	SYTVAR	SYCHAR20	CHAR	000020	Runtime: Text variable for ABAP/4 text elements
_TVAR5	SYTVAR	SYCHAR20	CHAR	000020	Runtime: Text variable for ABAP/4 text elements
_TVAR6	SYTVAR	SYCHAR20	CHAR	000020	Runtime: Text variable for ABAP/4 text elements
_TVAR7	SYTVAR	SYCHAR20	CHAR	000020	Runtime: Text variable for ABAP/4 text elements

(continued)

Field name	Data element	Domain	Type	Length	Short text: SYST
_TVAR8	SYTVAR	SYCHAR20	CHAR	000020	Runtime: Text variable for ABAP/4 text elements
_TVAR9	SYTVAR	SYCHAR20	CHAR	000020	Runtime: Text variable for ABAP/4 text elements
_MSGID	SYMSGID	SYCHAR02	CHAR	000002	Message ID
_MSGTY	SYMSGTY	SYCHAR01	CHAR	000001	Message type (E,I.W,...)
_MSGNO	SYMSGNO	SYMSGNO	NUMC	000003	Message number
_MSGV1	SYMSGV	SYCHAR50	CHAR	000050	Message variable
_MSGV2	SYMSGV	SYCHAR50	CHAR	000050	Message variable
_MSGV3	SYMSGV	SYCHAR50	CHAR	000050	Message variable
_MSGV4	SYMSGV	SYCHAR50	CHAR	000050	Message variable
_ONCOM	SYONCOM	SYCHAR01	CHAR	000001	Internal: ON COMMIT flag
_VLINE	SYVLINE	SYCHAR01	CHAR	000001	Constant: Vertical bar
_WINSL	SYWINSL	SYCHAR79	CHAR	000079	Interact.: Selected window line
_STACO	SYSTACO	SYST_LONG	INT4	000010	Interact.: List displayed from column
_STARO	SYSTARO	SYST_LONG	INT4	000010	Interact.: Page displayd from line
_DATAR	SYDATAR	SYST_FLAG	CHAR	000001	Flag: Data received
_HOST	SYHOST	HOST_ID	CHAR	000008	Host
_LOCDB	SYSTLOCDB	SYST_FLAG	CHAR	000001	Local database exists
_LOCOP	SYSTLOCOP	SYST_FLAG	CHAR	000001	Local database operation
_DATLO	SYSTDATLO	SYDATS	DATS	000008	Local date for user
_TIMLO	SYSTTIMLO	SYTIME	TIMS	000006	Local time for user
_TSTLO	SYSTTSTLO	SYTSTP	NUMC	000014	Timestamp (date and time) for user
_ZONLO	SYSTZONLO	SYCHAR06	CHAR	000006	Time zone of user
_DATUT	SYSTDATUT	SYDATS	DATS	000008	Global date related to UTC (GMT)

(continued)

Field name	**Data element**	**Domain**	**Type**	**Length**	**Short text:** SYST
_TIMUT	SYSTTIMUT	SYTIME	TIMS	000006	Global time related to UTC (GMT)
_TSTUT	SYSTTSTUT	SYTSTP	NUMC	000014	Timestamp (date and time) related to UTC (GMT)

Index

A

B

C

D

E

G

H

I

J

K

L

M

N

O

S

T

W

Z

Introduction to ABAP/4 Programming for SAP, Revised Edition:

Send Us YOUR COMMENTS

Dear Reader:

Thank you for buying this book. In order to offer you more quality books on the topics ***you*** would like to see, we need your input. At Prima Publishing, we pride ourselves on timely responsiveness to our readers needs. If you'll complete and return this brief questionnaire, ***we will listen!***

Name: (first) ______ (M.I.) ______ (last) ______

Company: ______ Type of business: ______

Address: ______ City: ______ State: ______ Zip: ______

Phone: ______ Fax: ______ E-mail address: ______

May we contact you for research purposes? ❑ Yes ❑ No

(If you participate in a research project, we will supply you with your choice of a book from Prima Tech)

❶ How would you rate this book, overall?

- ❑ Excellent
- ❑ Very Good
- ❑ Good
- ❑ Fair
- ❑ Below Average
- ❑ Poor

❷ Why did you buy this book?

- ❑ Price of book
- ❑ Content
- ❑ Author's reputation
- ❑ Prima's reputation
- ❑ CD-ROM/disk included with book
- ❑ Information highlighted on cover
- ❑ Other (Please specify): ______

❸ How did you discover this book?

- ❑ Found it on bookstore shelf
- ❑ Saw it in Prima Publishing catalog
- ❑ Recommended by store personnel
- ❑ Recommended by friend or colleague
- ❑ Saw an advertisement in: ______
- ❑ Read book review in: ______
- ❑ Saw it on Web site: ______
- ❑ Other (Please specify): ______

❹ Where did you buy this book?

- ❑ Bookstore (name) ______
- ❑ Computer Store (name) ______
- ❑ Electronics Store (name) ______
- ❑ Wholesale Club (name) ______
- ❑ Mail Order (name) ______
- ❑ Direct from Prima Publishing
- ❑ Other (please specify): ______

❺ Which computer periodicals do you read regularly? ______

❻ Would you like to see your name in print?

May we use your name and quote you in future Prima Publishing books or promotional materials?

❑ Yes ❑ No

❼ Comments & Suggestions: ______

PLEASE
PLACE
STAMP
HERE

PRIMA PUBLISHING
Prima Tech
3875 Atherton Rd.
Rocklin, CA 95765

8 Where do you use your computer?

Work	❑ 100%	❑ 75%	❑ 50%	❑ 25%
Home	❑ 100%	❑ 75%	❑ 50%	❑ 25%
School	❑ 100%	❑ 75%	❑ 50%	❑ 25%

Other ______________________

9 How do you rate your level of computer skills?

❑ Beginner
❑ Advanced
❑ Intermediate

10 What is your age?

❑ Under 18
❑ 18-24 ❑ 40-49
❑ 25-29 ❑ 50-59
❑ 30-39 ❑ 60-over

11 I would be interested in computer books on these topics

❑ Word Processing ❑ Database:
❑ Networking ❑ Spreadsheets
❑ Desktop Publishing ❑ Web site design
Other ______________________

SAVE A STAMP

Visit our Web Site at: **www.primapublishing.com/comments**
and simply fill in one of our online Response Forms

Other Books from Prima Tech
A Division of Prima Publishing

ISBN	Title	Price
0-7615-1046-X	Hands On Visual Basic 5	$40.00
0-7615-1047-8	Hands On JavaBeans	$40.00
0-7615-1339-6	Hands On Access 97	$40.00
0-7615-0955-0	Hands On Visual Basic 5 for Web Development	$40.00
0-7615-0751-5	Windows NT Server 4 Administrator's Guide	$50.00
0-7615-1005-2	Internet Information Server 3 Administrator's Guide	$40.00
0-7615-1387-6	Internet Information Server 4 Administrator's Guide	$50.00

Coming Soon:

ISBN	Title	Price
0-7615-1647-6	Hands On Visual Basic 6 for Web Development	$40.00
0-7615-1635-2	Hands On Visual Basic 6	$40.00
0-7615-1394-9	Hands On Visual C++ 6 for Web Development	$40.00
0-7615-1678-6	Hands On Visual InterDev 6	$40.00
0-7615-1514-3	Hands On Cold Fusion 4.0	$40.00
0-7615-1535-6	Hands On XML	$40.00
0-7615-1386-8	Hands on SQL Server 7 with Access	$40.00
0-7615-1385-X	Hands On SQL Server 7 with Visual Basic 6	$40.00
0-7615-1381-7	Visual FoxPro 6 Enterprise Development	$55.00
0-7615-1533-X	Windows 98 Complete Reference	$50.00
0-7615-1389-2	Microsoft SQL Server 7 Administrator's Guide	$50.00
0-7615-1390-6	Exchange Server 6 Administrator's Guide	$50.00
0-7615-1395-7	Windows NT Server 5 Administrator's Guide	$50.00
0-7615-1750-2	Supporting SAP R/3	$50.00

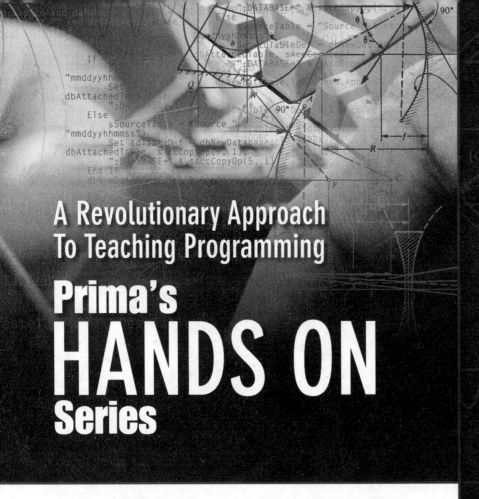